INVITATION TO THE TALMUD

INVITATION
TO THE
TALMUD

A Teaching Book

REVISED AND EXPANDED EDITION

JACOB NEUSNER

1817

Harper & Row, Publishers, San Francisco

Cambridge, Hagerstown, New York, Philadelphia
London, Mexico City, São Paulo, Sydney

Designer: Jim Mennick

Compositor: Bet Sha'ar Press, Inc.

Library of Congress Cataloging in Publication Data

Neusner, Jacob, 1932–
    INVITATION TO THE TALMUD.

    Bibliography: p.
    Includes indexes.
    1. Talmud—Introductions. I. Title.
BM503.5.N48 1984   296.1'2061   83–48422
ISBN 0-06-066099-6

---

84 85 86 87 88 10 9 8 7 6 5 4 3 2 1

In Memory of
MAX RICHTER
1896–1973

—my wife's father,
our children's grandfather
and loyal, beloved friend to us all

Contents

Preface

My thanks go to my friends and colleagues, undergraduate and graduate students at Brown University, who share in exploring the place of Talmudic learning within the curriculum of the humanities, in general, and of the study of religions, in particular. It is my happy privilege to participate in the academic community formed by these teachers and friends. The following read the manuscript in various stages of its preparation and gave valuable criticism, though none of course bears the onus of errors or other failures: Professors Ernest S. Frerichs, Horst R. Moehring, and Wendell S. Dietrich, Brown University, Baruch A. Levine, New York University, David Goodblatt, Haifa University, Gary G. Porton, University of Illinois, William Scott Green, University of Rochester, Wayne A. Meeks and Brevard S. Childs, Yale University, Paul Ritterband, City University of New York, Jonathan Z. Smith, University of Chicago, Jakob J. Petuchowski, Hebrew Union College–Jewish Institute of Religion, Cincinnati, Rabbi Baruch M. Bokser, Rabbi Joel Zaiman, Mr. Joel Gereboff, Mr. Stuart Himmelfarb, Mr. Tom Tisch, and Mr. Charles Primus.

J.N.

Brown University

Preface to the Second Edition

When I wrote this book, ten years ago, I was concerned to avoid what people call sexist usages, referring to "man" when I meant not only males but also females. But there was, and remains, a problem that cannot be satisfactorily worked out. The documents under study take for granted they speak for, and about, a world of men. Women play no active role in their system or their world. Now when I speak for the texts and attempt to express their viewpoint, it would not only prove anachronistic to avoid sexist usages; it would misrepresent the real state of affairs. On the other hand, when I speak for myself and present my own judgments, I have as a matter of conviction and conscience to speak about all of humanity, both halves. I was a feminist before the present prominence of the feminist movement; I left a college I otherwise liked, in some part because it excluded women. I am proud of the fact that, from Brown University, on the average of one woman a year has gone to rabbinical school from the time that women were first accepted. So I am pained by the sexism of some of the passages that follow. But, as I said, if God here occurs as a he, and if the collectivity is assumed to be male, it is because I am attempting to replicate the language and viewpoint of the texts I here represent.

The long life of this book, reaching a second edition thoroughly revised and augmented ten years after the first, gives a good bit of satisfaction. When the book first appeared, it had a fair number of competing volumes, some of which circulated far more widely. It also suffered savage, if irrational, reviews. But the competition is out of print, while my book continues to find new readers, year after year. And no one but me remembers the original abuse. That does not mean I do not see ways in which to improve the book. In addition to correcting a number of minor matters, I have, in fact, reorganized the book completely. The order of the chapters in the original edition conformed to the conventions of understanding of that time. In this edition, I have moved the Yerushalmi ahead of the Bavli, since the document reached closure a century or two before. I also moved the introductory discussion for "the Talmud," meaning the Babylonian Talmud, out of its position as Chapter Two of the first edition and into its logical place as an introductory unit of the chapter on the Babylonian Talmud. I have also added far more ample descriptions and explanations for the principal texts, the Mishnah, the Tosefta, and the Palestinian Talmud. I could not have written these paragraphs ten years ago. They emerge from a very protracted period of study. I have added the Hebrew and Aramaic texts throughout, as well as giving them as a group at the end. This makes the book useful for a large audience of classroom students.

I have deleted some sentences from the first edition, which seem to me to speak from a viewpoint not authentic to me. So passes the bathetic influence of an unmissed editor, who wanted to be the book's writer.

Mr. Paul Flesher, a doctoral student of mine at Brown University, served as research assistant for this project. He looked up all the Hebrew and Aramaic texts and saw to it that each found its proper place alongside the English. He did much more work in helping to prepare the manuscript for publication and shares in the credit that may accrue to this book. Because he came to me for doctoral studies after his baccalaureate work with Professor William Scott Green, who worked on the original text, there is a continuity I find heartening and rewarding. May the third or fourth edition have as its research assistant Paul Flesher's student of some age to come.

Professor Steven A. Kaufman, Hebrew Union College–Jewish Institute of Religion, took full charge of providing the vowels for the Hebrew and Aramaic texts and also proofread them. I turned to him, because I have always regarded him as the foremost Aramaist of our time and place. From the days, in 1968–1969, when we studied Syriac together in the classroom of Professor Franz Rosenthal at Yale, I have looked upon Steven Kaufman as not only a young friend but also a mature and masterful guide to matters of linguistics. He was the best student of the class in those days, and, in my book, he will always remain the best at what he does. I am grateful for his help with this book.

Professor Richard S. Sarason, Hebrew Union College–Jewish Institute of Religion, Cincinnati, supplied many corrections of detail, all of which I have made.

The idea of a second edition and of including in it the Hebrew and Aramaic texts came from Seymour Rossel, my dear friend and publisher.

I finished this book just after the tragic death, in a drowning accident in Jerusalem on the eve of the New Year 5733 (1973), of my father-in-law, Max Richter. I dedicated it to his memory. They say time heals. But he has been dead for ten years, and my sense of loss is as keen as if it were only yesterday. Apart from my wife, his daughter, and our children, his grandchildren, he was the best friend I ever had, and I miss him every day.

J.N.

Brown University

Foreword

This book invites the reader to try to get into the Talmud. Nowadays, people are scarcely able to try. They do not know how to begin or where—or why. Getting into the Talmud is no easy matter, even for those Jews who are ardent to recover for themselves what their ancestors once knew. This invitation is to join a community of learning men and women, for Talmudic learning is collective. You do not "read" the Talmud, you "learn" it, preferably with a *haver*, or a fellow student, and always with a rabbi. Here I shall be your rabbi. In the traditional *yeshivah*, the Talmud is not "learned" in a monotone. The Talmud is the music for a choir of voices; it is sung, and the music conveys the thrust and parry, the give and take of argument, which is what is truly Talmudic about the Talmud. So let us sing together.

The Talmud is a compendium of religious laws, wise sayings, and stories. These, obviously, preserve a particular idiom and present a unique viewpoint, that of the rabbinical sages of Babylonia and the Land of Israel in late antiquity, from the first through the seventh centuries A.D. But the Talmud's laws, sayings, and stories are, as individual units of literature, not strikingly different from those produced within other religious communities. They are, however, put together differently, in a literary form quite without parallel in world literature. They are so related to one another that they constitute a whole which is more than the sum of its parts. That "whole" not only relates the parts in theme but uncovers their underlying principles and harmonies, and shows how remote elements relate to one another. The Talmudic method consists in rigorous, abstract argument about fundamentally practical, mostly trivial matters, an argument thoroughly articulated and tested against all possible objections. The purpose of the argument is to discover the principles that make sense of things. The power of the argument is to subject all things to rigorous reason. The reward for the effort is knowledge that things can and do make sense, that reality is orderly. The Talmud promises a way beyond chaos and past unreason and mere habit.

The Talmudic inquiry is phrased as a singing conversation among open and rational minds, united by a devotion to reason and commitment to unobstructed criticism, and dedicated in common to the cause of applying reason to the mundane issues of the workaday world. So the Talmud represents a sustained effort to apply to secular, mostly trivial and ordinary affairs the disciplines of thoughtful analysis and order. Its fundamental building block is the self-contained analysis of a law and all materials pertinent to that law. But "building block" is a false metaphor, for it obscures the Talmud's vigorous movement, the dialectic of its argument, the suppleness of its analytical capacities—its melodic line.

But you must not think that the Talmud is simply another document of law, not much different, except in detail, from Roman or Canon law. You must not suppose your rabbi's apologetic for the Talmud consists in the claim that the Talmud is an interesting document in the history of practical and applied reason. The Talmud is a document of faith, passionate and vivid. Its faith, which I shall spell out in the first and last chapters, is in the revealed will of God.

What makes that faith interesting is the capacity of rabbis to discover, in both ordinary and extraordinary conduct, matters of interest to God and the divinely revealed Torah. The rabbi's logical and rational inquiry is not mere logic-chopping. It is a most serious and substantive effort to locate in trivialities the fundamental principles of the revealed will of God to guide and to sanctify the most specific and concrete actions in the workaday world. Reason and logic therefore serve as the vehicle, so to speak, to carry Torah—revealed teaching—from heaven down to earth, and, conversely, to make the profane sacred. They are modes of religious expression. In other religions of the Talmud's day, the pious served God, achieved holiness or sainthood, through prayer, or sacrifice, or celibacy, or martyrdom. Just as the last-named, martyrdom, is essential to the understanding of the early Christian and his imitation of Christ, so reason and logic are essential to the understanding of the rabbi and his imitation of Moses "our rabbi"—that is to say, of classical, Talmudic Judaism. What God does in heaven, as we shall see, is to study Torah in accord with those very rules of reason that rabbis follow. He taught the Torah to Moses, just as a rabbi teaches Torah to his disciple. In this setting, the mode of piety, the imitation of God, and the focus of sanctity— these are therefore the use of your mind. In context we are not talking about wonder-working philosophers, but about fully revealed religious men, within their setting, saints—but whose sainthood consisted in critical intelligence!

The importance of Talmudic faith therefore is not that it is rational. The contemporary interest of Talmudic Judaism is hardly that it is another form of reasonable, amiable, liberal intellectualism. The rabbis are not represented here as forerunners of good-natured, professorial *illuminés*, able to speak to contemporary men and women because all that they have to say is what we already hear, in any case, from reasonable people. If that were so, we should not need to hear from the rabbis at all. I should not ask you to accept me as your rabbi.

To be sure, a well-established apologetic argument, deriving from nineteenth-century Reform Judaism, stresses the ways in which "Judaism" of biblical or Talmudic times was already saying what we now want to hear, whether what we want to hear is about democracy in politics, or equity in economic life, or an open and just society. "Judaism" is a good thing, this argument holds, because it conforms more or less to the good hopes of our own age. The prophetic tradition taught the primacy of justice and morality over "ritual," and, living in an age incapable of entering into and being transformed by rite, people were glad to learn they had good precedent for their spiritual incapacities as much as for their social aspirations.

But if all to be heard from the prophets or the rabbis were what we already learn from the politics, economics, and social philosophy of our own day and of our own sector, generally on the leftward wing, of modern life, why listen at all to prophets or rabbis of old? What need do we have to make over into our own image the saints of ancient times? What moral authority is left to them if their message is supplied to them by us, and if in doing so, we distort, misinterpret, or simply obscure their particular meanings? Is this not a peculiarly sophisticated kind of fetishism, something that, for us, is a dishonest ritual? It is false because, if honest, we know we have made the prophets and the rabbis over into what we want them to be, rather than making ourselves over so as to be able to perceive what they were and mean even now. Like the carpenter described by II Isaiah (44:9–17), who plants a cedar and raises it, then chops it down and uses part for fuel, and part for a graven image, who roasts meat over part and turns the rest into a god, his idol, then prays to it and says, "Deliver me, for thou art my god," so are those who turn the prophets into liberal democrats and say, "These are our authorities." "*We* were right all the time." They make the rabbis into paragons of rational and liberal intellectuality and say, "These are our precedent. Nothing mysterious here, only sweet reason, 'justice' and 'mercy,' made over for our own solace."

At the same time, others approach the study of the Talmud from a quite opposite perspective. They rightly see the Talmud as Torah, God's revelation to Israel, the Jewish people, and they study it because it is Torah. Well and good—so long as the study then does not turn into mere ritual. But when the Talmud is studied in some circles of the pious, the document ceases to lay claim upon the disciples because it is a monument to reason and the genius of the human mind. The content of the text proves far less important to these disciples than the mere repetition of the words in it. Accordingly, the procedure is to read a few lines, translate, then proceed to free-associate about this and that, then to read a few more lines, translate them, and to invent some more homiletics. This other reading of the Talmud advocates the document as God's revelation but then ignores what the document says, except episodically and unsystematically. And that is not reading the Talmud, or learning, or studying it either. It is an approach as essentially disdainful of the document as that of the Reform Jews of an earlier age who made the document over into their own image. To be mindless and indifferent to the text's own points of insistence, to study as an act of ritual and not as an act of mind—these do not constitute acts of respect, and they betray and disgrace the document that supposedly is honored in the rite. Ritual-learning is not learning. Swaying, singing, jabbering, mumbling, shaking, dancing, fist-shaking, yelling, screaming, and all the other rites meant to convey intensity of learning do not necessarily bear relationship to mind so long as the things the Talmud says do not stand at the center of things. So when, in the yeshiva-world today, newcomers attempt to enter into the Talmud, they come for the wrong reasons, and so never reach the threshold of the mansion of the mind at hand. I shall repeatedly insist that the rabbis of the Talmud are not third- and fourth-century college professors or social reformers or liberal, rational philosophers of a mildly religious, benign spirit. Nor were they engaged in cultic mumbling about nothing anyone can grasp. They were holy men—saints in an age which took sanctity seriously. But, as I just said, they were not like other saints of their day, whose holiness was expressed through ascetic, flesh-suppressing disciplines—through sitting on pillars or dwelling in caves, through eating only wormwood and dressing only in rags. Their sainthood consisted in the analysis of trivial and commonplace things through practical and penetrating logic and criticism. Their chief rite was *argument*. To be sure, they prayed like other people, but to them, learning in Torah was peculiarly "ours," praying was "theirs"—that of ordinary folk. Their heroes were men of learning, and they turned their biblical heroes, beginning with Moses, into men of learning. When we read their writings closely, we shall see exactly what that learning consisted of, and how they carried on their religious life and sought sanctity through arguments.

What we shall find out is a curious thing. We can, on the whole, follow and even participate in those arguments. They are not spun out within a private or esoteric logic. They center upon arcane matters, but are wholly public and remarkably open to our involvement. The modes of thought turn out to be not much different from those which shape our own intellects. The importance of this fact is not to be missed. It is not, as I have stressed, that the rabbis' mode of thought is worthwhile because it is like our own. The point is that, since ours is like theirs, we may talk with them about *their* ultimate convictions.

What I find strange and awesome is that the rabbis, unlike us, were able to conceive of practical and critical thinking as holy. They were able to claim sainthood in behalf of learned men, to see as religiously significant, indeed as sanctified, what the modern intellectual perceives as the very instrument of secularity: the capacity to think critically and to reason. Here is the mystery of Talmudic Judaism: the alien and remote conviction that the intellect is an instrument not of unbelief and desacralization but of sanctification. That conviction is the most difficult aspect of the Talmud to comprehend, because it is so easy to misunderstand and misrepresent. The external form of the belief—our ability to think clearly, to be mindful— is readily accessible to us. But the meaning of the belief, its substance, its place in the shaping of the religious imagination and the formation of the religious and traditional culture of the Jewish people—these are not so obvious. For when people believe that when they use their minds in the proper way, they are like God, they make a statement not of philosophy but of theology. They carry out a judgment of anthropology: "Who is man, that you are mindful of him?" We men and women are like God because we think like God, and when we think like God, we are what God made us to be: in God's image, in God's likeness. These statements in no way fit neatly into some merely humanistic, merely secular philosophy. They ring out in sounds our ears scarcely recognize. They glimmer like strange lights over a far horizon, illumination from a light not of our own making at all. So the Talmud constitutes a religious document, therefore something alien, out of another world from the one we know every day and here and now. The Talmud defines, stands for everything authentic in Judaism and, given the state of matters, we have to recognize, therefore, that we deal with something unfamiliar, scarcely part of our world at all. True, the Talmud speaks in logic we can follow and take up. But if you therefore think you treat something familiar, you do not understand matters at all, and if what I have said strikes you as conventional and clichéd, then the true character of the argument has not yet penetrated. Explaining these things will, I contend, account also for the whole of the history and character of Judaism from the first century A.D. onward. It will provide the key for everything else, make sense, too, of much that has happened to the Jews in the nearly two centuries since so many of them parted company with the classical modes of Judaic spirituality: intellectual and otherworldly at the same time.

What has happened is that the secular Jews, continuing in the momentum of the tradition behind them, remained within the conviction that the intellectual life was the most important expressive mode of humanity. But they lost touch with the mythic and religious sources which relate that conviction to the fundamental structure of reality and impart to it cosmic meaning and metaphysical grandeur. The mind remained holy, but without the faith which made holiness matter, distinguishing the sacred from the common. This persistence, within secularity, of the effects of sanctity accounts for the former apolo-

getic in behalf of Talmudism or biblical prophecy or anything
that might plausibly be represented as "Judaism." The appeal
from within the borders of the religious camp—though from
people on its fringes, for above all apologists seek and need to
persuade themselves—was that, on our side of the line of religious sensibility also may be found the virtues you, on your
side of the line, prize so dearly. Those outside the camp did
not, for a long time, heed this invitation, or, if they did,
declined it for the obvious reason: We already have, without
myth, rite, faith, and mystery, what you offer us along with
that unclaimed baggage.

Yet Jewish intellectualism without Judaic faith proves want-
ing. How so? Divorced from the soul of Talmudic being, secular reason among Jewish intellectuals remained formless and
formal, producing, on the one side, the grotesque and the
absurd and, on the other, an empty formalism. The Jewish
intellectual without roots in Judaic intellectualism was seen
(by enemies) to be a creature of mere clever words, a polished,
glistening surface covering nothing. But if the enemies said so,
some among the intellectuals told themselves something strikingly similar. For they went in search of "faith" or "roots"
wherever these might be found, except in the one sure place,
the very ground on which they had all the time been standing.
But that ground seemed hard and intractable, not to say infer-
tile. And it was and would remain so, as long as the secret of its
cultivation was not perceived. In its stead would come the lush
growths of mysticism, in place of substantive conviction, and
faddism, in place of steady, enduring commitment. That
accounts for the return to the classical Judaic way of life of
people lacking all sustained interest in the classical Judaic way
of thought. Coming with excessive belief, the renewed Jew—the
reversioner—takes for granted that the mind's critical capacities
somehow endanger the faith. So, the reversioners think, if they
continue to use their minds rigorously, they will end up once
more outside the framework of the faith. If they think clearly,

they also will eat pork, so to speak. That pathetic perception may bear true witness to the condition within the beleaguered camp of faith, but it bears false witness to the faith.

I do not see how matters could have been otherwise, so long as Talmudic intellectualism was represented either by its enemies as desiccated logic-chopping, or by its friends as nothing other than the tired academicism everyone knew about and no one found sufficient. But wherein lay the soul which had been lost and now was so much missed? Where, if not in the very texts which to begin with had given it permanence? But these too seemed closed, for those able to open them could not then give an account of what was to be found. They reported, chiefly in addressing other scholars, about the meanings of words and the variations in manuscript readings, perhaps—in a primitive way—about history and sociology. But they seldom spoke about the religion—the life of piety and spirituality—expressed within the very study of the ancient books. For the books had once been holy books; the words sacred words, spoken as prayers were spoken; the sentences had expressed a craving for sanctity and a thirst after God. And now they were reduced to their syntax alone, to the examination of logic or philology. Or, as I said, they were presented as peculiarly modern and therefore "relevant," as though people seeking a way beyond the modern, who already knew the emptiness of relevance without a criterion for importance and meaning, should be impressed. People rich in reason were told the Talmud was rich too, and indeed it is so.

But the rationally rich lived in the poverty created by the deprivation of meaning, of purposeful living. The Talmud's wealth for such people remained a hidden treasure. They might perceive in the lives of classical Jews of their own day resources of the spirit, of trust, confidence, meaning, which they did not perceive within themselves. They might even lavish nostalgia upon a lost, blessed life within the tradition. But, never confronted by the specific, uncompromising claims of Talmudic

Judaism—claims about what is important in life, what is sacred in humanity—they took for granted that for modern Jews, the holy tradition had come to an end.

And they were surely right, for the Talmud divorced from its mythic context, its larger meanings for the construction of reality and the interpretation of life, was nothing else than a mere tradition. And a tradition perceived as traditional is also conceived as passed. But the Talmud understood as a document of religion, as the expression of the soul and of the inner world of saints, becomes a vivid alternative. For ultimate meanings are not bound to a particular place or time, and a way to the sacred, once discovered, remains forever open. What is sought, and I think what is acutely required, is not what we already have, but what we realize we do not have: a mythic context for our being, a larger world of meanings for our private and individual existence. These have been found by seekers of mystic experience in the suppression of the intellect and the willful suspension of unbelief. Within the Talmud we are able to seek them by the cultivation of the intellect and the criticism even of belief.

The mystery of the Talmud is its capacity to sanctify the one thing I do not propose to abandon, which is my capacity to doubt, my commitment to criticize, and above all, the beautiful, reasoned, open-ended discourse created among contentious learning men and women. The wonder of the Talmud is its tough-minded claims in behalf of the intellect, not in search, but in the service, of God. I wrote this book to try to unravel that tangled knot, composed of strands of rationality, religiosity, and mythic perception alike: How is it possible to serve God through the life of the mind? Why is "study" the holy act within the Judaic way of life? How did the religious culture of the Jewish people come to express itself through arguments and debates, more than through prayers or asceticism? Why does the Judaic tradition find God in the thrust and parry of argument, as it does when it claims God himself studies Torah?

How is the exercise of the mind, and not the suspension of its function, a sacred act?

The answers to these questions are found only within the direct encounter with the Talmudic text. The purpose of this book, therefore, is twofold. First, it offers the concrete experience of Talmudic study. Second, it proposes to explain, not its relevance to today, but the judgment of Talmudic modes of thought upon contemporary culture.

Just how are we going to get inside of the Talmud? The answer is simple. The Talmud is a complex text. So we are going to take up each of the simplest components of the text, one by one. That is how we see how the Talmud works—that is to say, what the authors of the text have done to create the document they have given us. What they did, specifically, is not complicated. They created a commentary to a text and then amplified and augmented that commentary. The basic text on which the Talmud is constructed is the Mishnah, a philosophical law code brought to closure at about A.D. 200. The Talmud then draws together the Mishnah and yet another, augmentative text to the Mishnah, which is called the Tosefta, meaning "supplements." The passage we shall study consists of a long abstract from the Mishnah, joined together with important additional materials from the Tosefta, and which are then unpacked, analyzed, and amplified by the Talmud itself—those three things.

In fact, the Talmud is really two Talmuds, for there was one systematic commentary for the Mishnah composed by rabbis in the Land of Israel ("Palestine," hence "Palestinian Talmud" or "Talmud of the Land of Israel" or "Yerushalmi" for "Talmud of Jerusalem"), and another one composed by the rabbis of Babylonia. The Yerushalmi reached its conclusion at about A.D. 400, and the Bavli, or Babylonian Talmud, another century or two later. These dates are rough guesses.

So this book works its way through the Mishnah and the Tosefta, then the first of the two Talmuds, the Talmud of the

Land of Israel and finally, the second of them, the Babylonian Talmud. What we do, specifically, is follow a single chapter as it wends its way from document to document, from the Mishnah, through the Tosefta, then, as is clear, onward and upward into the two great Talmuds themselves.

I lead you through the text by pointing to the smallest whole units of meaning—we would call them "sentences"—and analyzing those, and then showing how these smallest whole units of meaning combine to make up larger exercises of analysis. For what the Talmud contributes is not statements of fact but an ongoing and moving argument, from point to point, in which the effect of the whole—the argument as it is fully exposed—makes up the Talmud's principal contribution. I divide the abstract taken from the Mishnah into its smallest possible units, each marked for ready reference with a letter, *A, B,* and so on. Then we shall see how these small units were put together and composed into larger statements, first of fact, then of meaning, as the editors over the centuries did their work of reconstruction. The Mishnah passage, then the two Talmuds, reaches us through a process by which some scholars framed facts and ideas, then others undertook to put together those facts and ideas into larger constructions, and, at the end, still others proposed to harmonize the results into a single coherent picture.

What it means, in my view, to get inside of a book is to see how it works. That requires us to take it apart and put it back together. When I was a boy, I remember, I liked that most of all: to see how things worked. True, it was always easier to take things apart than to put them back together and make them work again. But the main thing always was, and remains, the intense curiosity. I think we have before us one of the great intellectual accomplishments of humankind, a document so dense, so rich, so subtle that it has kept superb minds busy for more than a millenium and a half. True, many of the things it treats are not everyday concerns anymore. But the mode of thought, the rigor of argument, the power to sustain an inquiry

of pure logic and applied, practical reason alike—these represent remarkable achievements of mind.

So the reason you should want to follow this strange and
alien text is not merely to learn about ancient writings, or even
to study about "Judaism." That is really beside the point. The
reason to study this document is that it exemplifies how reason
works, how great minds produced—in their world, for their
purposes—an exercise in finding order in chaos and in classify-
ing and so making sense of things. Just as zoologists have
found that the Linnaean principles of classification may be
replicated even in Papuan-New Guinea cultures untutored in
zoology and biology and unfamiliar with Darwin, so we shall
now see a glimpse at the ubiquity of the power of mind to
control the world by explaining it in accord with the rules of
the human mind itself. So let the Talmud stand in judgment
before the tribunal of wit and wisdom, intelligence and insight,
rationality and reason. In the age in which we live, few documents can confidently stand before those judges. But this one
can. And from it flows whatever truth Jews have to offer to the
world as Judaism.

To summarize the method of this book, the invitation is in
two parts: first, a protracted and close reading of texts, and
second, an effort to generalize not upon the contents of the text
but upon the methods and modes of thought and argument
exemplified by them. As I said, I shall set forth the first part of
the invitation by presenting a single chapter of Talmudic law.
That chapter of law occurs in four closely interrelated documents: first, the *Mishnah,* the law code of Judah, Patriarch of
the Jewish Community of Palestine in the last quarter of the
second century A.D.; second, the *Tosefta,* a corpus of supplementary traditions associated with the Mishnah; third, the
Babylonian Talmud, a commentary on the Mishnah and
Tosefta, produced in Babylonian rabbinical circles between the
third and the seventh centuries A.D.; and fourth, the *Palestinian
Talmud,* the equivalent, produced in Palestinian rabbinical
circles from the third through the fifth centuries A.D. Laws on

the same themes, in some instances identical in intent and even in language, thus produce a weave of rigorous literary and legal analyses. We shall first study the elements of the chapters of the four documents, then, in the case of the Mishnah and the Babylonian Talmud, we shall ask how these elements have been put together into a coherent corpus of legal literature.

The second part of this invitation to get into the Talmud is concentrated mostly in the concluding chapter, though in expounding the text much is suggested. I give a sustained theological statement, reasoned out of the texts at hand—a theological statement of the Talmudic mode of thought. Thus I deal with the issue: What does the Talmudic mode of critical thought and persistent, skeptical argumentation mean for contemporaries? My answer cannot be exhaustive, but it may at least propose both how those who will may appropriate part of the Talmud's achievements, and how Talmudic values of inquiry may even alter contemporary sensibility. The answer really is found in the chapters devoted to a close reading, line by line, of a significant specimen of Talmudic literature and thought. All I have done at the end is to bring to the surface what I believe is contained and hinted at within the antecedent pages. For me, concreteness, the actual texts, the specific details of complex arguments—these are more important than generalizations about the theology of modernity and culture, for they contain whatever is worthwhile in the consequent abstractions. Readers may well compose their own answers to the question of relevance, long before they reach mine. To do so, they owe the text a measure of patience with arcane details and alien laws, restraint at the superficially petty problems raised and solved by the masters of the Talmud. All that is of ultimate, enduring importance lies in the details.

I have not repeated the information conveniently available in Hermann L. Strack, *Introduction to the Talmud and Midrash*.* Strack seems to me to say almost everything worth

---

* New York: Harper & Row, 1965.

knowing *about* the Talmud. He defines technical terms, tells
about the several components of the Talmud and describes
their contents, supplies the facts about Talmudic hermeneutics
and the more important teachers. He gives exceptionally
thorough, critical bibliographies (to 1925) on all aspects of
Talmudic studies. Then he does the same for the biblical-
exegetical literature, known as Midrash, produced by the
Talmudic rabbis. His book has full notes, indices, appendices.
Nothing is lacking except one thing, which my teacher,
Abraham Heschel, of blessed memory, called "the spirit of the
Talmud." And that spirit can be found, quite naturally, only
within the Talmud's pages. Since the English reader will need
some guidance in opening and studying those pages (nothing
remotely Talmudic can be merely "read"), I took upon myself
the tasks just now outlined. But this book may be read without
reference to any other, though, if it succeeds in engaging the
reader's interest in its subject, later on one will make reference
to many further works on Talmudic literature, religion, and
history.

This invitation is traditional. It must take its humble place
at the end of a very long line, beginning over a thousand years
ago, of works introducing the Talmud. Clearly, the character
of these efforts depends upon the nature of the reader to whom
the Talmud is to be introduced. None of them took for its
reader the ordinary educated person, whether Jewish or otherwise, who wants to know what, if anything, the Talmud has to
do with the life of the mind and its current concerns. Before
modern America, it is difficult to find a situation in which
gentiles took an interest in Judaism, in particular in the
Judaism which flourished after the first century A.D. On the
other hand, before modern times it also is difficult to find a
Jewish community so remote from the classical sources of the
faith of Israel as that found in this country. Curiously, one may
address Jew and gentile in the same language, with the same
expectations about what is and is not known in advance,
because nowadays there is not much difference between them.

That ignorant and indifferent sameness, Jewish and gentile, seems to me to present advantages which outweigh the obvious disadvantages. The rabbis who produced the Talmud exhibit little "ethnic self-consciousness"—these words would have no meaning for them—for they legislated for a community of ordinary folk living commonplace lives, not much different in the fundamental ways from other groups. The Talmud is not an ethnic document. When it raises an ethical question, it speaks of "the good way in which a *person* should walk," not "in which a *Jew* should walk." When it treats dilemmas of social conflict, all parties to the conflict normally are assumed to be plain men and women—Jewish men and women, to be sure—whose claims to a cow or a palm tree are adjudicated by principles of justice everywhere pertinent and invariably right. While, admittedly, questions of mercy and of how God is to be served are referred to, and answered within, the disciplines of the Torah, the revealed will of God given to the people of Israel, and while the rabbis are well aware that some people are Jews and many are not, the Talmud is essentially interested in ordinary folk, not exclusively in Jews.

The reason is that its issues are not ethnic at all. Its modes of thought and argument invariably are rational and logical, therefore useful to anyone and any group, not limited to a single community, however distinguished by possession of divine revelation. The Talmud contains no special language, no esoteric or capricious logic, no private, uniquely "Jewish" forms of reasoning. If, therefore, the Talmud has to be introduced to a society exhibiting remarkably little substantive cultural and ethnic differentiation, that is appropriate and advantageous, because it is to the generality of man and woman in society that the Talmud, in the first place, is addressed.

Earlier invitations, or introductions, to the Talmud, described by Jacob Schachter,* fall into three periods of development,

---

* *The Student's Guide through the Talmud by the Eminent Teacher, Z. H. Chajes, Translated from the Hebrew, Edited, and Critically Annotated* (N.Y., 1960: Philipp Feldheim, Inc.), pp. xv ff.

the ninth through the twelfth centuries, the thirteenth through
the eighteenth, and the nineteenth. Naturally, all introductions
focused upon the discovery of general principles of Talmudic
inquiry. The earliest tended to stress historical and biographical questions, the classification of the masters by generations
and the assignment to them of approximate dates. In the
twelfth century Maimonides offered guidance on how to study
the Talmud systematically, not merely episodically. The second
period continued the earlier historical and biographical work
and added an interest in the analysis of Talmudic method and
modes of interpretation and argument. The "modern period,"
which began in the nineteenth century, was marked by a wholly
new range of questions, derived from modern philology, text
criticism and the recovery of manuscript evidences as to the
exact reading of the document, a critical approach to historical
questions, and the illumination of specific passages by com-
parative studies of Greek and other cultures cognate to Jewish
culture.

Before now no one recognized the necessity to introduce the
literary and logical traits of the text itself. Anyone interested in
an introduction to the Talmud already knew considerable parts
of the Talmud. Anyone who had not already studied the
Talmud was not likely to want to be introduced to it. As I said,
we face a different situation. That is why I have tried to do
what aforetime was either unnecessary or unwanted.

INVITATION TO THE TALMUD

CHAPTER 1

The Talmud in Context

The Talmud is the single most influential document in the history of Judaism. It therefore must be read not as a historical source or a law code, though it is both, but as fundamentally and deeply religious literature. And we must come to it, if we are to learn anything about its meaning, in the spirit of anthropologists, with questions not of faith but of understanding.

We cannot today pay a visit to a distant community or tribe to study the classical Judaic religious tradition. All forms of contemporary Judaism, though deriving from Talmudic teachings and values, stand at too great a distance to testify to the religious world of the rabbis who created the Talmud. Too much has happened between the seventh and the twentieth centuries for any movement in contemporary Judaism to claim today exactly to represent and replicate the classical, formative tradition of the first seven centuries A.D. To pay our visit to the Talmud and through that visit to come to an understanding of the modes of faith and understanding characteristic of the men who created it, we have, therefore, to stand back. We must set aside, for the moment, the question of what the Talmud means to us, though at the end I shall argue it can mean a great deal.

Since I have alleged the Talmud is a document of religion, I owe at the outset a definition of religion. It comes from Clifford

Geertz:* "What a given religion is—its specific content—is
embodied in the images and metaphors its adherents use to
characterize reality. . . . But such a religion's career—its historical course—rests upon the institutions which render these
images and metaphors available to those who thus employ
them."

First of all we shall survey the central images of Talmudic
Judaism. At the same time we shall attend to the organized
movement of rabbis which produced the Talmud. That movement constitutes the institutionalization of Talmudic images,
is responsible for making available to the Jews of its times—as
of ages afterward—the Talmud's beliefs, ideals, and metaphors.
Here we shall describe the context of the Talmud, and afterward
shall proceed to the literature itself.

The Talmud is the product of a small group of Jewish sages,
men who lived in the land of Israel, which they called "the
holy land," and in Babylonia, from the first to the seventh
centuries A.D. What is important about them, however, is not
the historical events of their day. What we want to describe is
their context, their situation as men.**

Four facts about them emerge even in this simple opening
sentence.

First, they saw themselves as sages—men of wisdom. That
means they stressed the importance of two things, learning
what already is known and understanding the new in terms of

---

* *Islam Observed: Religious Development in Morocco* (New Haven, 1968:
Yale University Press; Chicago, 1971: University of Chicago Press), pp. 2–3.

** I speak of men, not women, because the rabbinic movement after the second
century was exclusively male, remaining so until the last quarter of the twentieth
century. It is self-evident that the document, therefore the system it generated,
defines from a male viewpoint both the world at large and also the status and role
of women. Precisely what that meant for women in the system of the Talmud
remains to be investigated. Just how we shall overcome a legacy of subordination
of women also is not entirely clear. But the first step surely is the inauguration
of courses and institutions of Talmud-study for women, and that has been done
by Orthodox Judaism, as well as the ordination of women as rabbis, by
Reconstructionist, Conservative, and Reform Judaisms. Accordingly, we have
passed the beginning stages, though the road ahead remains long and rocky.

the old. Right and wrong, folly and sense—these are not things decided moment to moment. To the sage they are determined within the accumulated experience of the ages. Wisdom is the deposit, the residuum of insight refined from the practical experiments of centuries.

Second, I said the sages (among others) perceived that a land could be holy—of which more later.

Third, we notice that they lived in a time of religious ferment in which religions were coming into being and fading away. The "first" century, after all, is *first* because it marks the beginning of one great religion, Christianity. The Talmud took shape, therefore, in a time in which men faced alternatives and made enduring and influential choices. The rabbis of the Talmud made choices which became normative for the Jews and therefore came to constitute "Judaism."

Finally, we refer to "their situation as men," and this accurately reflects the exclusively male composition of the rabbinic movement. That fact should not surprise us. The men of antiquity held a low opinion of women. Paul thought women in the church should shut up and behave themselves. Philo, the Jewish philosopher of first-century Alexandria, thought sexual relations permissible only because they produce children. Eliezer ben Hyrcanus, a first-century rabbi, said one should not teach his daughter "Torah"—that is, rabbinic lore and law. We thus learn that the rabbis were very much men of their own time. What makes them interesting is their capacity to speak to men and women for a long time thereafter.

Let us now abandon the historical mode of discourse. We have to, if we insist that the ancient rabbis *are* interesting. I do not come merely to report that they once lived and therefore should be described as objects of historical curiosity. The rabbis are interesting because they and the literature they produced constitute alternatives for people interested in how societies take shape, how life is to be lived, and, especially, how the issues of human existence may be thoughtfully analyzed and

decided. Therefore, I am going to use the present tense, even
though my sources derive from men dead more than sixteen
centuries.

Furthermore, in contemporary Judaism are many believing
men and women for whom the ancient rabbis live, just as they
live for me. Their vitality for the believers (and I too am one
with them) comes out of the rabbis' faith that their words are
part of the revealed will of God, as we shall see. But for me
their vitality, their intellectual interest, come because I think
they testify in the formation of religion as a cultural system.
They adumbrate ways in which religious belief and rite express
the religious imagination, the perception and interpretation,
of the community as a whole, and so form a rational construction of reality. As I just said, we study the rabbis of the Talmud,
therefore, as an anthropologist would study a community—
literate or otherwise—and not as a historian approaches the
literary evidences of an ancient civilization. Our question is not,
Exactly what happened? Our question is, What *is* happening
within this group, and what does this teach us about ourselves
and our potentialities? That is not a historical question at all.

The first thing we want to know about the rabbis is, What is
their role within the larger community? The negative answer is
of greatest consequence. The rabbis are not the men who ultimately hold power within the community. The Jews live under
two other, coordinated governments.

First is the empire which controls the land in which they
live. The land of Israel is under Rome, part of its considerable
possessions. Babylonia is a province within the Iranian empire,
which extends from the Euphrates eastward into central Asia
and serves as the intermediary, in trade and culture, between
Rome on the west, and China and India on the east.

The two empires, moreover, leave the day-to-day governance
of the Jews in the hands of Jewish authorities. But these are not
rabbis. In Babylonia the state-supported Jewish authority is
called the exilarch, the ruler of the Jewish community "in exile

from the holy land." In the land of Israel he is called the patriarch (*nasi* in Hebrew). He is recognized by the Romans not because of his learning in the Judaic traditions, though the rabbis before the third century conceded it, but because he serves the purpose of Rome. The Romans want to keep the country at peace. The patriarch wants to run the country and claims he can keep the peace and so serve the interests of the empire. It is a fair trade and produces a stable administration from the end of the first century to the beginning of the fifth.

What do the exilarch and the patriarch have in common? Both claim to descend from the biblical king, David. This claim is not a matter of genealogy. It means that the claimant supposes he comes from the family which will produce the king-messiah. Indeed, anyone who wants to govern the Jews is going to claim he either is the messiah or may be the progenitor of the messiah. Everyone knows this genealogy was alleged in behalf of Jesus. But it also was the claim of the Maccabees, who governed the Jews from 160–50 B.C., and even of King Herod, son of an Idumean convert to Judaism in the first century B.C. In other words, the established convention to legitimate and justify your rule of the Jews is that you are, or will father, the Messiah.

Now the rabbis, for their part, form a religious and political movement, a group of men who possess particular beliefs and aim at particular social goals. The one thing they cannot claim to be is—*the* Messiah! For a collectivity may lay claim to keep the messianic promise. But it cannot personify the Messiah, and this is by definition. So it is on an unequal basis that the rabbis have to compete with important and powerful individuals, backed by the force of the great empires, on the one side, and by the inertia of their established bureaucracies, on the other. Not only so, but they will not achieve their goals if they oppose the established authorities. They can hope to accomplish them only by subverting, or taking over for their own purposes, the established authority.

The rabbis do so by serving in the autonomous administrations of exilarch and patriarch, respectively. They regard the former as "ignorant" and accuse him of being "unobservant." This tells us the exilarch is not part of their movement. For what he does not know or observe is not the religion of the ordinary Jews (based on the Hebrew Bible and local traditions) but the mode of living of the rabbi. But institutional control will serve no substantial purpose without something more, a symbolic message—an ideology—as forceful, an image as powerful, as that of the Messiah. What does the Messiah promise? He inaugurates the perfect age, the end of time; he heals the sick, cures the insane, drives out the evil spirits, rids the people of all the things that bother them. He restores the exiles to their land and rebuilds the Temple. If people believe that such wonders come of their ruler, whether he does miracles or not, he is going to have a strong hold upon their imagination and loyalty.

What can the rabbi promise instead? Several things. First, the rabbi teaches that when all the Jews do what he now does, then the Messiah will come. The way to that great day lies not through the court of the exilarch, but within the circle of the sages. So, for example, one of them says, "If all Israel will keep the Sabbath for one time only, the Messiah will come." It should be clear that "all Israel," that is, the Jewish community, do keep the Sabbath, more or less. People do not ordinarily work on that day or violate the other biblical rules which make the day holy. We know this because the rabbis seldom, if ever, complain about outright violation of the biblical commandments respecting the Sabbath as a day of rest. The complaint is, therefore, against people who do not keep the Sabbath the way *the rabbis* say it should be kept.

To take another example, the rabbis, believing they receive communications from the prophet Elijah, say he told one of them, "You ask, Why has not the Messiah come? Now today is the Day of Atonement, and yet how many virgins have been embraced this day in your town!" Modern Judaism knows the

Day of Atonement—Yom Kippur—as a day of fasting and solemn reflection. But before the Temple was destroyed, in A.D. 70, the day called forth a great celebration. After the sin-offering was completed in the Temple, people felt themselves free of sin and guilt. It was a time of tremendous spiritual exultation and excitement. Then young people—we are told—would go out and dance in the fields. Evidently they did more than dance. And the pre-70 spirit of the Day of Atonement continues to prevail among ordinary folk, so the rabbis do not approve. They have another conception of the meaning of the day, of the requirements of atonement, than a mere animal sacrifice.

We observe, therefore, that the rabbis stand apart from the larger community of Israel, but not wholly so. They share the way of living of the ordinary folk, but differ in some important ways. Similarly, some of them serve in the government of the community, though they do not fully accede to the basis on which the head of the government claims to be legitimate. Who, then, are the rabbis, and what are the beliefs and practices which set them apart?

The encompassing myth revealed in the pages of the Babylonian Talmud centers upon the figure of Moses and tells the story of the Moses-piety—spirituality centered on Moses—of the rabbis. That story relates God's disclosure to Moses of a dual revelation, or Torah, at Mount Sinai—one in writing, the other handed orally from master to disciple. The whole Torah—oral and written—contains the design for the universe, the divine architect's plan for reality. It is to be studied, therefore, not merely for information but as an act of piety and reverence for the divine lawgiver. Just as God taught Torah to Moses, so the rabbi, modeling his life after Moses "our rabbi," teaches his own disciple. In "studying Torah," and even more so in effecting it in the lives of Israel, the rabbi thus imitates God. So the study of Torah changes one not in mind alone, but in character and in personality—a transformation that is whole and complete. To be "like God" is a very specific thing. Following the model of the "school" in heaven, the schools for Torah-study bring together masters and disciples and preserve the ancient traditions.

The most striking aspect of these schools is the rabbis' conception that in them live holy men, men who more accurately than anyone else conform to the image of God conveyed by divine revelation through the Torah of Moses "our rabbi." The schools are not holy places only or primarily in the sense that pious people make pilgrimages to them or that miracles are supposed to take place there. The schools are holy because there men achieve sainthood through study of Torah and imitation of the conduct of the masters. In doing so, they conform to the heavenly paradigm, the Torah, believed to have been created by God "in his image," revealed at Sinai, and handed down to their own teachers. Thus obedience to the teachings of the rabbis leads not merely to ethical or moral goodness, but to holiness or sainthood. Discussion of legal traditions, rather than ascetic disciplines or long periods of fasting and prayer, is the rabbis' way to holiness.

If the masters and disciples obey the divine teaching of Moses, "our rabbi," then their society, the school, replicates on earth the heavenly academy, just as the disciple incarnates the heavenly model of Moses, "our rabbi." The rabbis believe that Moses was (and the Messiah will be) a rabbi, God dons phylacteries, and the heavenly court studies Torah precisely as does the earthly one, even arguing about the same questions. These beliefs today may be seen as projections of rabbinical values onto heaven, but the rabbis believe that they themselves are projections of heavenly values onto earth. The rabbis thus conceive that on earth they study Torah just as God, the angels, and Moses, "our rabbi," do in heaven. The heavenly schoolmen are even aware of Babylonian scholastic discussions, so they require a rabbi's information about an aspect of purity taboos.

So the rabbis believe that the man truly made in the divine image is the rabbi; he embodies revelation—both oral and written—and all his actions constitute paradigms that are not merely correct, but holy and heavenly. Rabbis enjoy exceptional grace from heaven. Torah is held to be a source of supernatural power. The rabbis control the power of Torah because of their mastery of its contents. They furthermore use their own mastery of Torah quite independently of heavenly action. They issue blessings and curses, create men and animals, and master witchcraft, incantations, and amulets. They communicate with heaven. Their Torah is sufficiently effective to thwart the action of demons. However much they disapprove of other people's magic, they themselves do the things magicians do.

The rabbis furthermore want to transform the entire Jewish community into an academy where the whole Torah is studied and kept. This belief aids in understanding the rabbis' view that Israel will be redeemed through Torah. Because Israel had sinned, it was punished by being given over into the hands of earthly empires; when it atones, it will be removed from their power. The means of this atonement or reconciliation are study of Torah, practice of commandments, and doing good deeds. These transform each Jew into a rabbi, hence into a saint. When all Jews become rabbis, they then will no longer lie within the power of history. The Messiah will come. So redemption depends upon the "rabbinization" of all Israel, that is, upon the attainment by all Jewry of a full and complete embodiment of revelation or Torah, thus achieving a perfect replica of heaven. When Israel on earth becomes such a replica, it will be able, as a righteous and saintly community, to exercise the supernatural power of Torah, just as some rabbis are already doing. With access to the consequent theurgical capacities, redemption will naturally follow. The issues of Talmudic analysis, while rationally investigated, thus are transcendent and cosmic in significance. In the concluding chapter, I shall try to state in less mythic terms what I conceive to be the contemporary sense for the same anthropology—a theory of what it means to be a human being, "in our image, after our likeness."

Rabbinic theology includes two important elements. First

are secret doctrines pertaining to the being and essence of God, the mysteries of history and redemption, and the like. These doctrines are studied in the schools and rarely, if ever, taught or even alluded to outside of them. Second, the rabbis publicly offer a self-consistent and comprehensive view of man's relationship to God. Man has to submit to God's will, and he demonstrates his submission through observing the commandments. If he sins by not doing so, he will be held responsible. Punishment follows in this world through suffering, but the suffering has to be gladly accepted, for it insures that one has at least begun atonement here, and hence may worry less about the world to come. If people sin and nonetheless prosper, or if they do not sin and yet suffer, an easy explanation is available. The wicked might enjoy this world, but in time to come they pay a terrible penalty. Similarly, the righteous suffer now, but in time to come they enjoy a great reward. This neat account suffices for the orderly conceptions of the schools, although probably not for the disorderly life of the streets.

Other elements of rabbinic theology cannot be ignored. Demons, witchcraft, and incantations; revelations through omens, dreams, and astrology; the efficacy of prayers and magical formulas; rabbinical blessings and curses; the merit acquired through study of the Torah and obedience to both the commandments and the sages—all these constitute important components of the rabbinic world view. A comprehensive account of the rabbis' beliefs about this world and those above and below and about the invisible beings that populate space and carry out divine orders would yield a considerably more complicated theology than that briefly given here. Its main outlines, however, would not be much modified, for magic, angels, demons, and the rest represent the way the rabbis think matters work themselves out—all these elements constitute the *technology* of the rabbis' theological world view.

The spiritual attitude of both rabbis and the masses may be described in the following way: "We are absolutely worthless, and are now deprived even of the former ways of finding favor with You. Once there was a Temple, and we could offer sacrifice there, but now it is no more, so we must give the sacrifice of our flesh and blood. But who are we to propitiate, we who are of no consequence and on our own have no future? We are nothing, except that we are *Israel*, the children of men You loved, and bearers of the revelation You delivered.

"Even in the most private moments of life, therefore, we are not alone, but are surrounded by the merits of the fathers and the presence of memories of the sacred moments of our history. Nor are we hopeless, because we look forward to the fulfillment of the promises made to the prophets in olden times. We are sanctified in all which we do out of love and loyalty to You. In the hour of our greatest private joy, at the marriage canopy, we remember both the public sorrow and the coming joy of Zion, and recall not only its destruction, but what was said by Jeremiah when it was destroyed, that it *will* be rebuilt.

"So if we are sinners, we lie in the hands of a God of great mercy. The passage of the seasons, which we witness regularly month by month, testifies to Your enduring sovereignty. Just as the moon keeps Your laws, so do we, and just as it testifies to the greatness of its Maker, so would we. When we find ourselves in a time of danger, we turn to You and beseech Your blessing."

The ordinary people comprehend and believe in the faith of the rabbis as it is here expressed. The spiritual situation revealed in the rabbis' prayers is precisely congruent to theirs. They too are "Israel," and they revere the Scriptures and remember its lessons. They too long for the coming of the Messiah, and although unable to express their yearnings in the evocative and noble language of the rabbis, they adopt the rabbinical liturgies without difficulty.

The more narrowly academic concerns include the precise and detailed discussions of laws on how and when to pray, the proper blessings to say over one thing or another, the conditions for interrupting prayer, and the like. We shall see how these rules are formulated. It is doubtful that ordinary people are much bothered by liturgical issues posed to the masters or that the instruction imparted to the disciples reaches a broad audience. To learn the proper way of saying grace proves terribly difficult even for many students, and outsiders scarcely comprehend all the rules. Indeed, knowing and keeping these rules is one of the important significations that a person has entered the rabbinical estate. Yet the issues of the common faith are not divorced from the rabbinical discussions. It is precisely *because* they believe in prayer as fervently as do ordinary people that they think one should pray with at least the decorum and respect shown to an earthly king of kings; therefore, they seriously inquire into the proper and improper procedures for praying. In this sense the rabbis' laws represent the continuation of popular faith: If the people believe that prayer matters, then the rabbis—who are, after all, lawyers—set out the rules of conduct and procedure which conform to such a belief.

Prayers composed by rabbis center upon four major themes: (1) the Temple and its cult, (2) the wrath of God, which is revealed in an hour of crisis, (3) the humility and helplessness of man, and (4) the corpus of ideas and symbols embodied in the sacred history of Israel. Above all, however, one is struck by the intensity of rabbinical prayers concerning the Messianic kingdom. In the liturgy for the marriage ceremony the center of attention focuses upon the coming joy of Zion, prefigured by the delight of bridegroom and bride. Just as one loves the other, and rejoices in that love, so in time would God again espouse Israel in Zion, and rejoice in her. The private joy of life is thus seen to be paradigmatic for the public event of coming history. It is the Messianic hope which becomes vivid in times of difficulty. The deep and abiding longing for the Messiah's coming characterizes master, disciple, and outsider alike.

While they might accommodate themselves to the conditions of the current life, the Jews see this world as merely transitory and impoverished. In time to come the advent of the true and permanent age will inaugurate a time of fulfillment and completion. Although the prayers and discussions of the rabbis seem private, personal, and ahistorical, they must be seen against the broader framework of faith in which they find meaning. Within the humble affairs of Israel's life at that time, one discerns, though darkly, the shadowed reflections of the great illumination that is to come.

It therefore would be a gross error to overestimate the differences separating the way of life of the ordinary Jews from that of the rabbinical estate. In general the rabbis' merely conventional social manners or customs are deepened into spiritual conceptions and magnified by their deeply mythic ways of thinking. In the villages the ordinary people regard the rabbi as another holy and therefore exceptional man, but still heart and soul at one in the community with other Jews. The rabbinical ideal is antidualistic; the rabbis believe that all Israel, not just saints, prophets, and sages, stood at Sinai and therefore now bear common responsibilities. No one conceives of two ways of living a holy life—two virtues or two salvations—but of only one Torah to be studied and observed by all. The cutting edge of rabbinical separateness thus is blunted.

The inevitable gap between the holy man and the layman is further reduced by the deep concern felt by rabbis for the conduct of the masses. This concern leads them to involve themselves in the everyday affairs of ordinary people, and it produces considerable impact upon daily life.

Only two really substantial, differentiating characteristics are observable. First is the relationship between master and disciple. The rabbis' social life follows forms wholly alien to those of outsiders. The disciple reveres the master as a living Torah and humbles himself before him as before God. The outsider honors the master as a learned man, fantasizes about his magical powers, submits to his judicial authority, and accepts his communal influence. These reflect basically different attitudes: on the one hand stands a living myth; on the other, the superficial effects of that myth. Furthermore, the disciple of the sages conforms to personality traits and behavior patterns quite unnatural for ordinary folk. He forces himself

into a posture of abject humility with implications far beyond
what outsiders comprehend or accept. We shall see stories
expressing such humility. His reverence for the master is only a
little lower than his fear of the Lord. His imitation of the
master's deeds and his preservation of the memory of those
deeds shape a religious discipline quite alien to the workday
life of common people. The humility shown to God and to the
master is supposed to extend to the disciple's behavior with
everyone else.

The second characteristic separating rabbis from common
Jews is study. Obviously, the reasons are not that ordinary
people do not understand the need for information, that they
are entirely ignorant of the world and its way, or that they
know nothing of traditions. The people know the Scriptures.
They listen to the reading of the Torah in the synagogues.
Prophetic writings and passages of wisdom literature also are
regularly read to them. The masses observe the Sabbath, the
festivals, the holy days, and food and sex taboos. All these
observances require knowledge, and the constant exposure to
Scriptures and to the sages produces a considerable amount of
it. Therefore, the "learning" of the rabbis cannot be spoken of
in total contrast to the "ignorance" of the masses. Unless you
accept the rabbinical belief in the rabbis' sole possession of the
oral Torah, the people cannot be regarded as "ignorant" at all.

What the ordinary Jews do not know and the rabbis always
do know is the one thing that makes a common man into a
rabbi: *"Torah" learned through discipleship.* It begs the question to speak of the ordinary people as "ignorant of Judaism."
One does not have to exaggerate the educational attainments of
the community as a whole to recognize that learning in the
rabbinical traditions does not by itself separate the rabbi from
other people. What is important is the rabbi's attitude toward
his *own* study. Extrinsic qualities deriving from the mythic
context transform the natural actions of learning facts or ideas
or memorizing sayings—which anyone might do—into the
ritual actions unique to the rabbi.

The "Judaism" of the rabbis at this time is in no degree either normal or normative, and speaking descriptively, the schools cannot be called "elite." Whatever their aspirations for the future and pretensions in the present, the rabbis, though powerful and influential, constitute a minority group seeking to exercise authority without much governmental support, to dominate without substantial means of coercion. What they want to accomplish is the formation of the kingdom of priests and holy people demanded at Sinai, and to do so according to the revelation of Sinai as they alone possess it. Admittedly, this description of the rabbinical schools is hardly a portrait of the religious life of Jewry. Yet, in my view, the rabbis do tend more and more to set the standard, the golden measure, the royal way.

Thus far we have viewed the Judaism of the rabbis of the Talmud as a cultural system—a way of viewing the world and organizing and conducting everyday life. That is to say, we have viewed the Talmud as the expression of a system of Judaism, something whole, complete, encompassing, life-enhancing for the participants. We now ask ourselves about how that system comes to concrete expression in detail. For if the description I have given is accurate, then the details should testify to the main points of insistence and concern that characterize the system as a whole. What makes a system, a construction of religion-culture-society, interesting is the capacity of each detail to convey the message of the whole. Now if we ask ourselves what is common to all systems of religion-culture-society, the answer must be, the eating of a meal. That is something everyone must do, though groups may differ on everything else.

Accordingly, we turn to the most general, ordinary, and usual, and want there to find out what is most distinctive, definitive, and unusual. We seek, further, particular texts in which the meal is the subject of concern. For we want to know not only the details of the matter, but the way these details are formulated. We seek not only the conclusions of the system,

but the manner in which these conclusions are reached and
then formulated—the method and mode of thought of the
system, not only its outcome. So if we cannot find definitive
answers when we ask why people do the things they do in
general—for some people may not do those things—we can
and now do ask why people eat the way they eat and not in
some other way.

The Talmudic chapter before us is going to focus upon one
small aspect of the law, and the specific law involves very
minor details of commonplace behavior. Yet within the chapter
are four of the greatest themes of Talmudic Judaism. These
have now to be set forth and explained.

First, the law itself involves eating a meal. Who is supposed
to keep this law? In Talmudic times the laws about conduct at
a meal are observed chiefly by disciples of rabbis, and then
especially when they are in the presence of the master. So we
are about to consider one detail in the larger "ritual of being a
rabbi" we have alluded to. Yet it goes without saying that
nothing in the chapter before us is going to suggest such a
limited focus of law observance. On the contrary, everything is
phrased in terms of what anyone should do. Indeed, subjects
are rarely, if ever, given for predicates, which are simply, "[he]
does . . ." or "[they] do . . ." or "[one] blesses. . . ." Thus while
the law may practically concern only a small group, the formulation of the law conceals that fact and announces a much
wider intention, to speak to everyone and about what all are
supposed to do.

To understand why meals should be subject to rabbinic legislation, we have to turn to the Hebrew Scriptures, the Torah.
There we find numerous laws about food which is cultically or
"ritually" clean, animals which are unclean. One may eat only
the clean, never the unclean. Not only so, but biblical literature
tends to equate the cultically clean with the holy, the unclean
with the profane or unholy. The land of Israel is holy.
Zechariah 14:20-21 holds that in the end of days, the land will

also be clean. The Temple is holy—set apart, sanctified. It therefore has to be kept clean.

But what is this "cleanness" to which we refer? It is not a matter of removing dirt from your hands, of hygienic antisepsis. On the contrary, when we speak of "clean" or "unclean," we are far from a concern with the physical presence of dirt. We are rather confronted with the legacy of concerns left over from pre-Mosaic Israelite culture.

That culture, like many others, regarded some things as taboo, therefore to be kept out of the holy community. Various crucial periods in life—childbirth, or the menstrual period— were regarded as dangerous. Various diseases were particularly feared, regarded as the mark of the presence of an evil spirit or demon. Chief among these was leprosy. Mildew, mysteriously appearing on the wall of a house, was feared.

When we reach the biblical legislation contained in the books of Leviticus and Numbers, we enter a world in which demons, who can do things independent of the will of God, or terrors outside of the divine power, are unknown. The biblical law comes long after the revolution effected by the concept of one, unique, all-powerful God, transcendent over the world, not subject to any of its laws. It cannot take account, therefore, of evil forces, demons, that work their will outside of God's purpose. But the law must and does take account of the archaic remains of those old conceptions—the taboos associated with certain animals, certain periods of life, certain natural phenomena.

These are neutralized, first by being subsumed under the Torah's laws, therefore made to express the will of God. The laws which designate as impure certain animals, excretions, or diseases know nothing of these as malignant enemies operating independent of the divine will. Uncleanness is merely hateful to God and must be avoided by all who have anything to do with the divinity. All biblical views of purity and impurity represent an *interpretation* of taboos which must in their origins have been perceived quite differently. The taboos are not wholly neutralized; they retain the independent, antecedent, autonomous power of evil.

In biblical *literature* what also happens is the transformation of purity and impurity into metaphors for moral and immoral living. "Pure" and "impure" or clean and unclean to begin with connote a condition entirely lacking in ethical or moral traits. They assign to the status of impurity a bodily state, or an animal, or a corpse. But they do not thereby impute a negative ethical or moral valuation. They are the equivalent of the good or morally right, of the evil or immorality.

But the very treatment of purity in the biblical *laws*, made by the priests, accomplishes a correlative purpose. The priestly laws take for granted that whatever its cause, impurity has one constant effect: You cannot go to the Temple. Purity functions solely as the requirement of entering into and participating in the cult. The multiform world of impurities thus is homogenized. While treating purity primarily in the context of the cult may not seem so imaginative as regarding it as a metaphor for moral uprightness, in fact the force of the consequent limitation of the fear of impurity as a cause or mark of evil is enhanced. For if purity and impurity are made relative to the cult, while not emptied of intrinsic power, they are at least limited in the locus of that power's effects. One who is impure is not everywhere a bearer of a malevolent, autonomous power. The menstruating woman or the leper is not dangerous outside of the cult. These people are unclean—which means *only* that they cannot come to the Temple until purified. Focusing the matter upon the Temple therefore begins to convert purity into a matter of relationship or status. It eventually will remove from impurity any sort of independent, material, nonrelative significance. In Talmudic law this process of neutralization is completed. Purity and impurity constitute a set of highly complex relationships, but these have nothing to do with the physical world. All things depend upon intention and purpose, circumstance and time.

The reason we have had to review these facts is that one central issue of the chapter before us is going to concern purity in the ritualistic sense in which we have just treated it. This at the outset is surprising. For the meal of which we shall speak is not in the Temple. The participants—ordinary folk or rabbis—are not priests. But the rabbis believe exactly this: The ordinary meal of an ordinary person in his own home has to be eaten *as if* he were a priest, as if his home were the Temple, and as if he were engaged in the act of sacrifice to God. It is not merely that his food has to conform to the biblical laws of what may or may not be eaten. The man himself, his wife and family and all present also must be in a state of purity in accord with the requirements of the biblical code of the priesthood. The utensils with which he eats, the pots and pans in which the food is prepared, have likewise to conform to those requirements.

For example, a corpse is a source of "uncleanness." For students of nonliterate cultures that is not going to be surprising; in few cultures is a corpse entirely free of taboo. In biblical law the building in which a corpse is lying spreads the "uncleanness of the corpse" to all the objects under its roof. So the pots and pans of our meal must not have been in a building in which a corpse is located. They cannot have been touched by a menstruating woman, or by a leper, or by a man or woman who suffers a genital flux. So we are far from the simple requirement not to eat pork. The range of "purity" and "impurity" is, as I said, drawn from the setting of the Temple cult, on which the Scriptures had focused the application of the purity rules to begin with.

By this point you must surely wonder why I have chosen a chapter centered upon ritual, upon such a remote and arcane matter as the purity and impurity of food and of the setting of a meal. Before I explain, let me introduce the other important themes of the laws before us.

A second major theme is the prayers you say at a meal.

A third is prayers you say at a meal on the Sabbath or on a festival.

This brings in its wake, fourth, concern for the differences between one time and another, between sacred time—a holy day, on which one behaves in accord with various rules—and ordinary days, to which such rules do not apply.

So the interrelated laws before us concern the most commonplace and fundamental concerns of the religious person: eating, praying, awareness of the passage of time, and "ritual." "Ritual" here covers not liturgy, to which it is commonly applied nowadays, but actions or concerns subject to rules extrinsic to their normal, everyday, or "natural" character and explained by reference to a myth, in this case a story about God and his Torah.

Eating is not a ritual. It may be made so if the way in which you eat, or the words you recite before or after eating, or the foods you eat—if any of these is subject to considerations extrinsic to the actual need to prepare and put food into your mouth, eating is set within a ritualistic context. And it would be difficult to find a religious tradition without rituals of eating. Take, for example, the Christian instance, in which are involved specific ritual foods made to represent something quite other than their own substance (wine as the blood of the new covenant).

Anyone familiar with Jewish religious observance will notice that food plays a considerable part throughout. For example, even today particular sorts of food are associated with specific holy days. You have to eat in the *Sukkah*—a frail hut—on Tabernacles. You are supposed to eat a particularly fine meal on the eve and afternoon of the Sabbath. You observe the Atonement rite and commemorate the destruction of the Temple by fasting. A Jewish wedding ceremony must be concluded with special prayers composed as part of the Grace after Meals. Purim is observed by eating a large meal and getting drunk. Passover is laden with food rites and taboos. You must eat unleavened bread and must not eat leavened bread. You eat dairy products on Pentecost (*Shavu'ot*). The list could easily be extended. That this originally religious consideration persists in the secular setting of Jewish culture goes without saying—for instance, the lavish Bar Mitzvah banquet divorced from any religious meaning, or the popularity of *"kosher-*style" delicatessens.

So the Talmud's treatment of food and eating suggests how it will deal with many other important concerns of everyday life. It provides a glimpse into the Talmudic mode of defining, of thinking about, of analyzing the most fundamental actions of ordinary people. At the same time, as I said, the meal will introduce important theological concerns. Because of the importance of praying before, after, and on the occasion of eating and drinking, the meal allows us to review important elements in Talmudic theology as expressed by prayers associated with food. At the same time, the way in which the Talmud deals with such prayers is going to tell us a great deal about its authors' conception of what praying means, how one relates to and addresses God.

Our fourth important theme—the distinctions among various days or hours, the experience of the natural course of time— recurs throughout the laws. The reason is that for the Talmud (as for biblical literature), time is not one and unchanging, but highly differentiated; the setting of the sun on Friday, the sixth day of the week, is a tremendous event. It differentiates the profane from the holy time.

One final question remains: On what basis do the rabbis incorporate the Temple purity laws into the meal? What lies behind the rules, everywhere taken for granted, that you eat your meal like a priest in the Temple—free of contact with a corpse, or with a creeping thing, or with a woman in her menstrual period, careful not to touch unclean objects, thoughtful about what you have done all day long and about what has been done to your food and your dishes? This is a far cry from the biblical priests' interpretation of purity, which limited purity to the Temple. For the rabbinic rule raises purity to a level of consciousness and importance without parallel in the ordinary life of Jewry in pre-Talmudic times, introduces purity and impurity into every aspect of the common life, above all, into the everyday meal.

All Judaisms known to us lay stress on issues of nourishment. Given the notion that God is served, so far as the priestly writers of Leviticus are concerned, by the provision of food to be burned up on an altar, we should hardly be surprised. True, all Judaisms out of antiquity also stress that God wants something other than food, namely, morality. But then the notion of cult and rite automatically invokes the matter of food and eating, rather than, as in other religions-cultures-societies, the matter of sexual action or abstention, holy poverty or wealth, holy war and statecraft, the veneration of the bodies of kings or holy men, or any of the other myriad points of obsession and compulsion selected as God's special object of concern—or revulsion.

How come the Talmudic rabbis took over, in particular, the old Temple and priestly concerns for cultic purity in connection with food? After all, the authors of Leviticus understood that the issues of cultic cleanness in connection with eating pertained principally to the meals eaten by priests in the Temple, or by priests and their families. The conception that ordinary Israelites, eating everyday food and not produce designated as priestly rations, also had to keep the cultic taboos hardly derives from the Torah of Moses. Whence did it reach the rabbis, who, as we shall see, took it so very seriously?

The answer is that the Talmudic rabbis are heirs of the Pharisaic group which flourished one hundred fifty years before the destruction of the Temple in 70. The Pharisees' interest in purity was one significant part of their legacy to the post-70 rabbis, their continuators.

The Pharisees before the destruction were those Jews who believed that one must keep the purity laws outside of the Temple. Other Jews, following the plain sense of Leviticus, supposed that purity laws were to be kept only in the Temple, where the priests had to enter a state of cultic purity in order to carry out the requirements of the cult, such as animal sacrifice.

They also had to eat their Temple food in a state of cultic purity, but lay people did not. To be sure, everyone who went to the Temple had to be cultically pure. But outside of the Temple the laws of cultic purity were not observed, for it was not required that noncultic activities be conducted in a state of Levitical cleanness.

The Pharisees held, to the contrary, that even outside of the Temple, in one's own home, one had to follow the laws of cultic purity in the only circumstance in which they might effectively apply, namely, at the table. They therefore held you must eat secular food, that is, ordinary, everyday meals, in a state of cultic purity *as if you were a Temple priest.* The Pharisees thus arrogated to themselves—and to all Jews equally—the status of the Temple priests and did the things which priests must do on account of that status. The table of every Jew in his home was seen to be like the table of the Lord in the Jerusalem Temple. The commandment, "You shall be a kingdom of priests and a holy people," was taken literally. The whole country was holy. The table of every man possessed the same order of sanctity as the table of the Temple cult. But at this time, before 70, only the Pharisees held such a viewpoint, and eating unconsecrated food as if one were a Temple priest at the Lord's table thus was one of the two significations that a Jew was a Pharisee, a sectarian.

The other was meticulous tithing. The laws of tithing and related agricultural taboos may have been kept primarily by Pharisees. Pharisees clearly regarded keeping the agricultural rules as a chief religious duty. But whether, to what degree, and how other Jews did so is not clear. Both the agricultural laws and purity rules in the end affected table fellowship: *How, with whom, and what you may eat.* That is, they were "dietary laws."

The commonplace setting of Pharisaic table fellowship is striking. The sect ordinarily did not gather as a group at all, but in the home. All meals required cultic purity. Pharisaic table fellowship took place in the same circumstances as did all nonritual table fellowship: common folk eating ordinary meals in an everyday way, among neighbors who were not members of the sect. They were engaged in workaday pursuits like everyone else. The setting for law observance was the field and the kitchen, the bed and the street. The occasion for observance was set every time a person picked up a common nail, which might be unclean, or purchased a bushel of wheat, which had to be tithed—by himself, without priests to bless his deeds or sages to instruct him. Keeping the Pharisaic rule did not require an occasional exceptional rite at, but external to, the meal, as in the Christian sect. Nor did it involve residence in a monastic commune, as in the Dead Sea sect in Judaism. Instead, it imposed the perpetual ritualization of daily life, on the one side, and the constant, inner awareness of the communal order of being, on the other.

The role of purity in the response of the Pharisees to the destruction of the Temple is known to us only from rabbinic materials, which underwent revisions over many centuries. A story about Yohanan b. Zakkai and his disciple, Joshua b. Hananiah, tells us in a few words the main outline of the Pharisaic-rabbinic view of the destruction:

> Once, as Rabban Yohanan b. Zakkai was coming forth from Jerusalem, Rabbi Joshua followed after him and beheld the Temple in ruins.
>
> "Woe unto us," Rabbi Joshua cried, "that this, the place where the iniquities of Israel were atoned for, is laid waste."
>
> "My son," Rabban Yohanan said to him, "be not grieved. We have another atonement as effective as this. And what is it? It is acts of loving-kindness, as it is said, 'For I desire mercy and not sacrifice'" [Hosea 6:6].*

How shall we relate the arcane rules about cultic purity to the public calamity faced by the heirs of the Pharisees at Yavneh,

---

*Avot de Rabbi Natan, Recension A, edited by Solomon Schechter (Reprinted. New York, 1945: Feldheim) p. 11a.

the rabbinic center founded in 70? What connection joins the cultic purity of the "kingdom of priests" to the atonement of sins in the Temple?

To Yohanan b. Zakkai, preserving the Temple was not an end in itself. He taught that there was another means of reconciliation between God and Israel, so that the Temple and its cult were not decisive. What really counted in the life of the Jewish people? Torah, piety. (We should add, Torah as taught by the Pharisees and, later on, by the rabbis, their continuators.) For the zealots and messianists of the day, the answer was power, politics, the right to live under one's own rulers.

What was the will of God? It was doing deeds of loving-kindness; "I desire mercy, not sacrifice" (Hosea 6:6) meant to Yohanan, "We have a means of atonement as effective as the Temple, and it is doing deeds of loving-kindness." Just as willingly as men would contribute bricks and mortar for the rebuilding of a sanctuary, so they ought to contribute renunciation, self-sacrifice, love, for the building of a sacred community. Earlier Pharisaism had held that the Temple should be everywhere, even in the home and the hearth. Now Yohanan went a step further. He taught that sacrifice greater than the Temple's must characterize the life of the community. If one were to do something for God in a time when the Temple was no more, the offering must be the gift of selfless compassion. The holy altar must be the streets and marketplaces of the world as, formerly, the purity of the Temple had to be observed in the streets and marketplaces of Jerusalem. Just as the prophets treated purity as a metaphor just as the Pharisees had done, so now did Yohanan interpret the Temple and its sacrifice. In a sense, therefore, by making the laws of cultic purity incumbent upon the ordinary Jew, the Pharisees already had effectively limited the importance of the Temple cult. The earlier history of the Pharisaic sect had thus laid the groundwork for Yohanan b. Zakkai's response to Joshua b. Hananiah. It was a natural conclusion for one nurtured in a movement based upon the priesthood of all Israel.

The Pharisees determined to concentrate on what they believed was really important, and that was the fulfillment of all the laws of the Torah, even ritual tithing, and the elevation of the life of the people, even at home and in the streets, to what the Torah had commanded: You shall be a kingdom of priests and a holy people. A kingdom in which everyone was a priest, a people all of whom were holy—such a community would live as if it were always in the Temple sanctuary of Jerusalem. Therefore, the purity laws, so complicated and inconvenient, were extended to the life of every Jew in his own home. The Temple altar in Jerusalem would be replicated at the table of all Israel. The biblical limitation of purity is reversed.

We return to our rabbis and to our mythic present tense. We see that in taking over the legacy of Pharisaism as of the much older biblical inheritance, the rabbis face the task of continuing to deal with issues originally raised in quite other circumstances and with the response, now archaic, of much different times. Purity ought not to mean much to them. After all, there now is no Temple to go to. For the Babylonian part of the rabbinic estate, purity is impossible, for one cannot be pure in an unholy land. Yet the rabbis doggedly work out rules based upon the purity laws of olden times. They persist in assigning meaning in terms of those ancient laws to rather humble details of the meal.

It is an extraordinary act of loyalty to the long-ago past and its long-impertinent teachings. But, as we saw, once the purity laws are taken over for ordinary life, the Temple might fall, but the Temple's mode of holiness will endure. The historical event of the destruction of Jerusalem is rendered of little everyday importance for those who keep the Temple's laws wherever they may be, who view their table as the Temple altar, and who see themselves as priests carrying on the ancient cult.

What has happened, therefore, is a curious thing. The rabbis preserve the historical Pharisaic legacy and make it timeless. That legacy consequently frees the rabbis and their followers from the single most important and tragic historical event of their age—thus, from "history." How so? Jewry is a defeated nation and has lost its capital and Temple. But once the Temple may be everywhere and every man may be a priest, the rabbis preserve the Temple's sanctity. The belief that people are close to God and are able to serve him, the certainty that the small and private actions of men and women retain transcendent importance to God and may be holy—these things will go on and on. No longer is the holy life limited to one place, one time, subject to the exigencies of the politics in one state, and disposed of within the affairs of nations. Given the precarious context of the Jews' life on earth, in history, I think this no small achievement.

The reason, I think, that Judaism, as the Talmudic rabbis defined it, functioned so well for so many centuries is simple. Judaism served to explain precisely that situation that Jews endured, and to do so in a way that endowed Israel, the Jewish people, with dignity, self-respect, a sense of value and of worth. The ahistorical and essentially quietistic emphases of the Judaism framed by the Talmud proved congruent to the situation of powerlessness and dispersion. Politics and wars do not matter really—which is just as well, because, in the main, Jews have no politics and fight only in other peoples' wars. What we eat and how we live matter in an ultimate way—which is just as well, because these are the things Jews do sort out and decide. So there was a wonderful fit between necessity and theology.

So much for the context of our particular chapter of the Talmud. Let us now turn to the document itself.

CHAPTER 2

The Mishnah

The Hebrew word *Mishnah* comes from the root *shanah*, to repeat; the word for the ordinal, second, *sheni*, has the same root. As the title of the law code of Judah, the Patriarch of Jewish Palestine in the beginning of the third century A.D., it means "that which is to be learned by repetition," therefore by memory. The further implication is that the Mishnah contains materials which had been memorized and not written down for a very long time. For the Talmudic sages claimed that to Moses had been revealed two Torahs, or revelations, at Mount Sinai. One was contained in the Scriptures—that is, in written books—and the other in oral traditions learned by repetition and handed on in that manner for many centuries. So the Mishnah was represented by the authority behind it as the second essential part of the whole Torah of Moses.

The Mishnah is divided into six large sections, or orders (Hebrew: *Seder*), which deal with, first, agricultural law (called *Zera'im*, seeds); second, Sabbath and festival law (*Mo'ed*, season); third, family law, vows and oaths, marriages, divorces, inheritances (*Nashim*, women); fourth, civil law, torts, damages, criminal law, the structure of the ideal government, penalties and punishments (*Neziqin*, damages); fifth, sacrifices and things devoted to the Temple in Jerusalem, the order and rules of the cult of animal sacrifice (*Qodashim*, holy things); and sixth, rules of cultic purity and impurity, how purity is acquired and how it is removed, sources of impurity and objects which are susceptible to becoming impure (*Toharot*, purities). There are subdivisions in each order of the Mishnah, and these are further divided into chapters; a subdivision is called a tractate (*Massekhet*), of which there are 63 in all. The six orders are divided as follows: *Zeraʿim*, eleven tractates with 74 chapters; *Moʿed*, twelve tractates with 88 chapters; *Nashim*, seven tractates with 71 chapters; *Neziqin*, ten tractates with 73 chapters; *Qodashim*, eleven tractates with 91 chapters; *Toharot*, twelve tractates with 126 chapters.

Our chapter in a general way deals with blessing God for the gift of food at meals. But very rapidly we shall find ourselves in the midst of technicalities, which take for granted a considerable number of further generalities. Indeed, while we shall be told at the outset that the law concerns a meal, it is not a routine meal that is under study at all, but the Sabbath meal in particular. Furthermore, the issues of blessing food before and after a meal are subordinated. More prominent are problems of ritual purity and impurity, on the one hand, and the proper way in which to say the prayers at table for the advent of the Sabbath and for the conclusion of the Sabbath, on the other. We therefore have to begin by describing the general context in which the specific rules are laid forth.

The Mishnah as Literature

Falling into the hands of someone who has never seen this document before, the Mishnah must cause puzzlement. From the first line to the last, discourse takes up questions internal to a system which is never introduced. The Mishnah provides information without establishing context. It presents disputes about facts hardly urgent outside of a circle of faceless disputants. Consequently, we start with the impression that we join a conversation already long under way about topics we can never grasp anyhow. Even though the language is our own, the substance is not. We shall feel as if we are in a transit lounge at a distant airport. We understand the words people say, but are baffled by their meanings and concerns, above all, by the urgency in their voices: What are you telling me? Why must I know it? Who cares if I do not?

No one can take for granted that what is before us makes sense in any context but the Mishnah's own, inaccessible world. Each step in the inquiry into the meaning and importance of the document must be laid forth with ample preparation, taken with adequate care. For before us is a remarkable statement of concerns for matters not only wholly remote from our own world but, in the main, alien to the world of the people who made the Mishnah itself. It is as if people sat down to write letters about things they had never seen, to people they did not know—letters from an unknown city to an undefined and unimagined world: the Mishnah is from no one special in utopia, to whom it may concern.

To state matters more directly: the Mishnah does not identify its authors. It permits only slight variations, if any, in its authorities' patterns of language and speech, so there is no place for individual characteristics of expression. It nowhere tells us when it speaks. It does not address a particular place or time and rarely speaks of events in its own day. It never identifies its prospective audience. There is scarcely a "you" in the entire mass of sayings and rules. The Mishnah begins nowhere. It ends abruptly. There is no predicting where it will commence or explaining why it is done. Where, when, why the document is laid out and set forth are questions not deemed urgent and not answered.

Indeed, the Mishnah contains not a hint about what its authors conceive their work to be. Is it a law code? Is it a schoolbook? Since it makes statements describing what people should and should not do, or rather, do and do not do, we might suppose it is a law code. Since, as we shall see in a moment, it covers topics of both practical and theoretical interest, we might suppose it is a schoolbook. But the Mishnah never expresses a hint about its authors' intent. The reason is that the authors do what they must to efface all traces not only of individuality but even of their own participation in the formation of the document. So it is not only a letter from utopia to whom it may concern. It also is a letter written by no one person—but not by a committee, either. Nor should we fail to notice, even at the outset, that while the Mishnah clearly addresses Israel, the Jewish people, it is remarkably indifferent to the Hebrew Scriptures. The Mishnah makes no effort at imitating the Hebrew of the Hebrew Bible, as do the writers of the Dead Sea Scrolls. The Mishnah does not attribute its sayings to biblical heroes, prophets, or holy men, as do the writings of the pseudepigraphs of the Hebrew Scriptures. The Mishnah does not claim to emerge from a fresh encounter with God through revelation, as is not uncommon in Israelite writings of the preceding four hundred years; the Holy Spirit is not alleged to speak here. So all the devices by which other Israelite writers gain credence for their messages are ignored. Perhaps the authority of the Mishnah was self-evident to its authors. But, self-evident or not, they in no way take the trouble to explain to their document's audience why people should conform to the descriptive statements contained in their holy book.

If then we turn to the contents of the document, we are helped not at all in determining the place of the Mishnah's origination, the purpose of its formation, the reasons for its anonymous and collective plane of discourse and monotonous tone of voice. For the Mishnah covers a carefully defined program of topics, as I shall explain presently. But the Mishnah never tells us why one topic is introduced and another is omitted, or what the agglutination of these particular topics is meant to accomplish in the formation of a system or imaginative construction. Nor is there any predicting how a given topic will be treated, why a given set of issues will be explored in close detail and another set of possible issues ignored. Discourse on a theme begins and ends as if all things are self-evident—including, as I said, the reason for beginning at one point and ending at some other.

In all one might readily imagine, upon first glance at this strange and curious book, that what we have is a rulebook. It appears on the surface to be a book lacking all traces of eloquence and style, revealing no evidence of system and reflection, serving no important purpose. First glance indicates in hand is yet another sherd from remote antiquity—no different from the king-lists inscribed on the ancient sherds, the random catalogue of (to us) useless, meaningless facts: a cookbook, a placard of posted tariffs, detritus of random information, accidentally thrown up on the currents of historical time. Who would want to have made such a thing? Who would now want to refer to it?

The answer to that question is deceptively straightforward: the Mishnah is important because it is a principal component of the canon of Judaism. Indeed, that answer begs the question: Why should some of the ancient Jews of the Holy Land have brought together these particular facts and rules into a book and set them forth for the Israelite people? Why should the Mishnah have been received, as much later on it certainly was received, as a half of the "whole Torah of Moses at Sinai"? The Mishnah was represented, after it was compiled, as the part of the "whole Torah of Moses, our rabbi," that had been formulated and transmitted orally, so it bore the status of divine revelation right alongside the Pentateuch. Yet it is already entirely obvious that little in the actual contents of the document evoked the character or the moral authority of the written Torah of Moses. Indeed, since most of the authorities named in the Mishnah lived in the century and a half prior to the promulgation of the document, the claim that things said by men known to the very framers of the document in fact derived from Moses at Sinai through a long chain of oral tradition contradicted the well-known facts of the matter. So this claim presents a paradox even on the surface: How can the Mishnah be deemed a book of religion, a program for consecration, a mode of sanctification? Why should Jews from the end of the second century to our own day have deemed the study of the Mishnah to be a holy act, a deed of service to God through the study of an important constituent of God's Torah, God's will for Israel, the Jewish people?

In fact, the Mishnah is precisely that, a principal holy book of Judaism. The Mishnah has been and now is memorized in the circle of all those who participate in the religion, Judaism. Of still greater weight, the two great documents formed around the Mishnah and so shaped as to serve, in part, as commentaries to the Mishnah, namely, the Babylonian Talmud and the Palestinian Talmud, form the center of the curriculum of Judaism as a living religion. Consequently, the Mishnah is necessary to the understanding of Judaism. It hardly needs saying that people interested in the study of religions surely will have to reflect upon the same questions I have formulated within the context of Judaism, namely, how such a curious compilation of materials may be deemed a holy book. And, self-evidently, scholars of the formative centuries of Christianity, down to the recognition of Christianity as a legal religion in the fourth century, will be glad to have access to a central document of the kind of Judaism taking shape at precisely the same time as the Christianity studied by them was coming into being. In all, we need not apologize for our interest in this sizable monument to the search for a holy way of life for Israel represented, full and whole, in this massive thing, the Mishnah.

The world addressed by the Mishnah is hardly congruent to the world-view presented within the Mishnah. Let us now consider the time and context in which the document took shape. The Mishnah is made up of sayings bearing the names of authorities who lived, as I just said, in the later first and second centuries. (The book contains very little in the names of people who lived before the destruction of the Temple of Jerusalem in A.D. 70.) These authorities generally fall into two groups, namely, two distinct sets of names, each set of names randomly appearing together, but rarely, if ever, with names of the other set. The former set of names is generally supposed to represent authorities who lived between the destruction of the Temple in 70 and the advent of the second war against Rome, led by

Simeon Bar Kokhba, in 132. The latter set of names belongs to
authorities who flourished between the end of that war, ca. 135,
and the end of the second century. The Mishnah itself is generally supposed to have come to closure at the end of the second
century, and its date, for conventional purposes only, is ca.
A.D. 200. Now, of these two groups—sages from 70–130 and
from 135–200—the latter is represented far more abundantly
than the former. Approximately two-thirds of the named sayings belong to mid-second-century authorities. This is not
surprising, since these are the named authorities whose (mainly
unnamed) students collected, organized, and laid out the document as we now have it. So, in all, the Mishnah represents the
thinking of Jewish sages who flourished in the middle of the
second century. It is that group which took over whatever they
had in hand from the preceding century—and from the whole
legacy of Israelite literature even before that time—and revised
and reshaped the whole into the Mishnah. Let us briefly consider their world.

In the aftermath of the war against Rome in 132–135, the
Temple was declared permanently prohibited to Jews, and
Jerusalem was closed off to them as well. So there was no cult,
no Temple, no holy city to which, at this time, the description
of the Mishnaic laws applied. We observe at the very outset,
therefore, that a sizable proportion of the Mishnah deals with
matters to which the sages had no material access or practical
knowledge at the time of their work. For we have seen that the
Mishnah contains a division on the conduct of the cult, namely,
the fifth, as well as one (the sixth division) on the conduct of
matters so as to preserve the cultic purity of the sacrificial
system along the lines laid out in the book of Leviticus. In fact,
a fair part of the second division, on appointed times, takes up
the conduct of the cult on special days, e.g., the sacrifices offered
on the Day of Atonement, Passover, and the like. Indeed, what
the Mishnah wants to know *about* appointed seasons concerns
the cult far more than it does the synagogue. The fourth
division, on civil law, for its part presents an elaborate account

of a political structure and system of Israelite self-government, in tractates *Sanhedrin* and *Makkot,* not to mention *Shebuot* and *Horayot.* This system speaks of king, priest, Temple, and court. But it was not the Jews, their kings, priests, and judges, but the Romans, who conducted the government of Israel in the Land of Israel in the time in which the second century authorities did their work. So it would appear that well over half of the document before us speaks of cult, Temple, government, priesthood. As we shall see, moreover, the Mishnah takes up a profoundly priestly and Levitical conception of sanctification. When we consider that, in the very time in which the authorities before us did their work, the Temple lay in ruins, the city of Jerusalem was prohibited to all Israelites, and the Jewish government and administration which had centered on the Temple and based its authority on the holy life lived there were in ruins, the fantastic character of the Mishnah's address to its own catastrophic day becomes clear. Much of the Mishnah speaks of matters not in being in the time in which the Mishnah was created, because the Mishnah wishes to make its statement on what really matters.

In the age beyond catastrophe, the problem is to reorder a world off course and adrift, to gain reorientation for an age in which the sun has come out after the night and the fog. The Mishnah is a document of imagination and fantasy, describing how things "are" out of the sherds and remnants of reality, but, in larger measure, building social being out of beams of hope. The Mishnah tells us something about how things were, but everything about how a small group of men wanted things to be. The document is orderly, repetitious, careful in both language and message. It is small-minded, picayune, obvious, dull, routine—everything its age was not. The Mishnah stands in contrast with the world to which it speaks. Its message is one of small achievements and modest hope. It means to defy a world of large disorders and immodest demands. The heirs of heroes build an unheroic folk in the new and ordinary age. The Mishnah's message is that what a person wants matters in

important ways. It states that message to an Israelite world
which can shape affairs in no important ways and speaks to
people who by no means will the way things now are. The
Mishnah therefore lays down a practical judgment upon, and
in favor of, the imagination and will to reshape reality, regain
a system, re-establish that order upon which trustworthy existence is to be built.

If we now ask ourselves why people in our own age should
take an interest in that long-ago time, the answer is not difficult
to find. And it is not a claim for mere antiquarianism, let alone
"knowledge for its own sake"—whatever that might mean.
The sages of the Mishnah addressed Israel at the very end of its
thousand-year life of sanctification through God's service in
the Temple, of anointed kings and holy priests organizing (at
least in theory) time and space of the land in accord with the
model of the sacred Temple and along lines of structure ema-
nating therefrom. The Mishnah, we notice, is the work of men
who had survived the second war against Rome. Now when we
realize that that war was fought roughly three generations after
the destruction of the Temple, we notice yet another point of
importance. When the Temple had been destroyed earlier, in
586 B.C., the prophetic promises of divine forgiveness had been
kept. So the Temple was restored: Israel regained its homeland.
Now, half a millennium later, the Temple had lain in ruins for
another three generations. A great and noble war had been
fought to regain Jerusalem, rebuild the Temple, and restore
the cult. But what had happened was incomprehensible. The
pattern established in the first destruction and restoration now
proved no longer to hold. Indeed, nothing stood firm. This
time around, not only was the Temple not rebuilt, the cult not
restored, Jerusalem itself was declared off-limits to Israelites.
The very center was made inaccessible.

In this context, it is not difficult to look for points of com-
monality between one age of uncertainty and another, also cut
loose from ancient moorings. What the second-century sages of
the Mishnah have to teach the generations of the last decades of

the twentieth century and the first of the twenty-first is how to make use of imagination and fantasy to confront, defy, and overcome chaos and disorder. Behind the Mishnah lay the ruins of half a millennium of continuous, orderly, and systematic Israelite life, which had been centered on the regular and reliable offering of the produce of the field and flock upon the altar of the Temple in Jerusalem, the ordering of society around that Temple, the rhythmic division of time in response to that cult, and the placing of people and things into their proper station in relationship to that center. One disastrous war had ended in the destruction of the Temple. The second, three generations later, had made certain it would not be rebuilt in the foreseeable future—nor, as it now appears, ever. In the aftermath of these two terrible wars the Israelite nation entered upon an existence far more precarious in mind than in material reality. Within a century the social and agricultural effects of the wars had worn off. Galilean synagogues of the third and fourth century testify to an age of material surplus and good comfort. But it would be a very long time before the psychological effects of dislocation and disorientation would pass. In some ways, for the Jewish people, they never have. Our age, which looks back upon the destruction of enduring political and social arrangements in the aftermath of two terrible wars (with numerous skirmishes in-between and since), has the power to confront the second century's world of ancient Judaism, because, it seems, there is a measure of existential congruence between the two ages and their common problems. For both are the kind which challenge the imagination and the will.

The Mishnah As Law Code

First, we have to take most seriously the fact that the ancient rabbis of Israel produced, as their major, enduring documents, collections of law codes, commentaries, rulings of sages about practical affairs. The founders of Talmudic tradition—they

were called "fathers of the world"—who flourished in the first
six centuries A.D. believed that their task was to realize in
everyday life the precepts of the revealed Torah. "To do justice,
love mercy, and walk humbly with God"—to the rabbis these
were not abstractions. They had to be effected in the world, and
nothing is so difficult in secular affairs as to find exactly what
is justice or mercy here and now—and what is to be done that is
just and merciful. Since the Torah contained rules on many
subjects, and since these rules had to be interpreted to apply to
wholly new matters and to issues important only long after
Sinai, we should not be surprised to find the sages' concen-
trating on the minutiae of daily life.

②
"LAW"

   Second, we have to revise our understanding of the word
law, not only because in the Talmud specific laws apply to
matters today not regarded as subject to societal, legal regulation at all, but also because *law* in English is not an accurate
representation of its Hebrew equivalent, *halakhah*. *Halakhah*
derives from the root *halakh*, to go, to walk, and denotes "the
way things are done." In this sense *halakhah* is descriptive as
well as prescriptive. It describes how one normatively does
things. The laws are phrased in present-tense participles: "One
does this, one does not do that." They are not given as commandments, "Do" or "Don't do" or "You *will* do this." They
are not expressed in the form of cases, "If you do this, that will
be the result." The laws (Hebrew plural: *halakhot*) and the
language in which they are phrased therefore should be taken
as something different from what their equivalents mean in
contemporary usage.

   The difference is that through *halakhah* the rabbis described
the way they thought life should be lived, society should be
organized, God should be served. True, they tried to guide
ordinary folk to live life, form society, and serve God in the
ways they thought right. Their description of what was correct
did not depend upon how things were done then. It was meant
to stand as the measure and criterion for reality. *Halakhot* dealt
with many matters over which, in fact, the rabbis had no control. For one instance, the fifth order of the Mishnah concerns

the Temple cult, which by A.D. 200 had been in ruins for more than a century; the sixth deals with purities in the Temple, rules no more relevant to everyday life than the foregoing. For another, the rabbis described, in tractate *Sanhedrin,* the constitution of the government of the Jewish state, although there was no such state. The laws in *Sanhedrin* furthermore had nothing whatever to do with the organization of any Jewish state that had existed even before A.D. 70. The Romans, who ruled the country in the first century, Herod, who reigned in the last half of the first century B.C., and the Maccabees, who governed from ca. 150 to ca. 50 B.C.—none of the antecedent authorities had organized the government as the rabbis responsible for *Sanhedrin* claimed they should, and the rabbis did not say they had. Nor should these historical limitations be taken as exhaustive. The enforcement of many laws lay beyond the power accorded to the Jewish authorities of Palestine and Babylonia by the respective imperial authorities, the Romans and the Iranians; at least some laws had to be enforced in ways different from those prescribed by the rabbis; or they were different from rabbinic law entirely.

What kind of law, therefore, do we approach? It cannot be called utopian, but it also cannot be called entirely practical. It is a kind of "platform" for the future: In the ideal world, this is how things are to be done. Meanwhile, we shall effect as much of the law as we are able. But if this description is accurate, then we must wonder whether *law* is the right word for "teachings" which neither describe nor prescribe, yet do not exhort or threaten. Here is neither prophecy nor history. That is why I warned that we have to revise our understanding of the word *law;* yet the revision is not of one word, but of how we understand the materials before us.

Some Essential Facts

Our chapter consistently refers to the House of Shammai and the House of Hillel. Who were they?

Shammai and Hillel were Pharisaic masters at the beginning

of the Common Era (Christian usage: A.D.). The Houses, or
schools, named after them constituted groups of their followers
within the Pharisaic sect. Their differences concerned minor
matters of detail, within a considerable area of agreement on
basic questions. The Houses flourished in the first century;
eventually, after 70, the Hillelites prevailed over the Shammaites. Specifically, as we saw, the Pharisees believed, first, one
should tithe his food according to the biblical requirements
and otherwise give to the priests all the dues Scripture had
assigned to them; ordinary folk gave some, but not all the
tithes. Second, they believed that Jews should eat ordinary
meals in the state of cultic purity required of priests both in the
Temple and in the time in which they consumed the priestly
gifts, such as Heave-offering of the crops. In other words, the
Pharisees held that everyone at his own table at home was like
a Temple priest at the table of the Lord in the holy sanctuary:
"You shall be a kingdom of priests and a holy people" (Exodus
19:6) was understood by them literally to mean that the people
should act as if they were priests in the Temple. Most though
not all of the differences between the two Houses pertained to
these two fundamental considerations, tithing and purity. Both
considerations affected food. These therefore are dietary laws.
The laws before us exhibit differences about purity rules. These
rules, it should be remembered, fell into disuse during the
second and third centuries. Since, moreover, foreign countries
were impure to begin with, the purity laws never could be kept
outside of the holy land, and so for Babylonian Jews had no
practical meaning. But, as we now understand, that does not
mean the Babylonian sages were indifferent to, or refrained
from studying, these laws and ruling on difficulties pertaining
to them, as if they would be kept.

Three further facts are necessary.

First, we shall hear much about "blessing the day" and
"saying a blessing over the wine." "Blessing the day" refers to
the Prayer of Sanctification of the Sabbath. After the recitation

of Genesis 1:31 and 2:1-3, it begins, in today's liturgy, as
follows:

בָּרוּךְ אַתָּה, יְיָ אֱלֹהֵינוּ, מֶלֶךְ הָעוֹלָם, בּוֹרֵא פְּרִי הַגָּפֶן.
בָּרוּךְ אַתָּה, יְיָ אֱלֹהֵינוּ, מֶלֶךְ הָעוֹלָם, אֲשֶׁר קִדְּשָׁנוּ
בְּמִצְוֹתָיו וְרָצָה בָנוּ, וְשַׁבַּת קָדְשׁוֹ בְּאַהֲבָה וּבְרָצוֹן
הִנְחִילָנוּ, זִכָּרוֹן לְמַעֲשֵׂה בְרֵאשִׁית. כִּי הוּא יוֹם תְּחִלָּה
לְמִקְרָאֵי קֹדֶשׁ, זֵכֶר לִיצִיאַת מִצְרָיִם. כִּי בָנוּ בָחַרְתָּ
וְאוֹתָנוּ קִדַּשְׁתָּ מִכָּל הָעַמִּים, וְשַׁבַּת קָדְשְׁךָ בְּאַהֲבָה
וּבְרָצוֹן הִנְחַלְתָּנוּ. בָּרוּךְ אַתָּה, יְיָ, מְקַדֵּשׁ הַשַּׁבָּת.

Blessed are you, Lord, our God, king of the world, who
has sanctified us by his commandments and taken pleasure in us and in love and good will given us as an
inheritance his holy Sabbath, a memorial to the creation
of the world. For it is the first day of the holy convoca-
tions, a memorial to the exodus from Egypt. For you
have chosen us and sanctified us above all peoples, and
given us as an inheritance, in love and good will, your
holy Sabbath. Blessed are you, Lord, who sanctifies the
Sabbath.

The Sanctification is said with a cup of wine in hand. The
issue is, Which comes first? Does a man say the Sanctification
of the day and then recite the requisite blessing over the wine,
"Blessed are you, Lord our God, king of the world, who creates
the fruit of the vine," or vice versa, the blessing over the wine
and then the Sanctification? What principles set the correct
order?

Second, the laws speak of "light, food, spices, and *Havdalah*." What are these?

At the end of the Sabbath, after the sun has set, you say a
prayer marking the conclusion of the sacred day and the
beginning of the secular week. This prayer, called *Havdalah*,
or division, is as follows in today's liturgy:

בָּרוּךְ אַתָּה, יְיָ אֱלֹהֵינוּ, מֶלֶךְ הָעוֹלָם, הַמַּבְדִּיל בֵּין קֹדֶשׁ
לְחֹל, בֵּין אוֹר לְחֹשֶׁךְ, בֵּין יִשְׂרָאֵל לָעַמִּים, בֵּין יוֹם
הַשְּׁבִיעִי לְשֵׁשֶׁת יְמֵי הַמַּעֲשֶׂה. בָּרוּךְ אַתָּה, יְיָ, הַמַּבְדִּיל
בֵּין קֹדֶשׁ לְחֹל.

Blessed are you, Lord our God, king of the world, who divides between holy and profane, between light and darkness, between Israel and the peoples, between the seventh day and the six days of work. Blessed are you, Lord, who divides between sacred and profane.

Before saying the above prayer, which is recited with a cup of wine in hand, you also recite a blessing over spices or incense and light: "Blessed are you, Lord our God, king of the world, who creates various kinds of spices," and ". . . who creates the lights of fire." Thus we shall have repeated references to (1) light, (2) spices, and (3) *Havdalah*.

Now what do these things mean? Why do they matter to the men who discuss them? The rabbis discuss prayers everyone is expected to say. We cannot suppose they here express a different view of God and the world from that held by other Jews. Everyone believed in the Sabbath. Saying blessings—words of thanks—over food was commonplace. We may take for granted, also, that the prayers at the end of the Sabbath were old and accepted. Why, to be sure, you should say a blessing over light at the end of the Sabbath is not explained here. The Talmud will tell us a story about that. The meal at the end of the Sabbath surely would have to be blessed. The *Havdalah* prayer, marking the distinction between holy time and the ordinary week, expresses a belief of the community as a whole: The people itself is holy, like the land; the course of the natural world is to be interpreted in terms of the historical realities of the life of the holy people. Just as the week consists of the six ordinary days and the holy Sabbath, so humankind consists of the peoples and Israel, made holy by God and divided by him from the rest. So the natural order and the historical life of outsiders and of Israel correspond to each other. Nothing in these prayers speaks only for the rabbinical movement. But the Talmud's concern for them does.

The Talmud wants to know exactly what is the proper way to do things, the right order for prayers. Its creators, first of all, are lawyers. They take very seriously indeed the forms of life, correctly supposing that the form cannot be distinguished from the function and meaning of what a man does. They are, second, religious men, who conceive that the service of God must call forth, is expressed through, man's most thoughtful reflection. As religious men they see themselves like suppliants before a king. They call God the king of kings of kings—for the Roman and Iranian emperors were kings over many kings, but God is king of them all. When the Israelite approaches God in prayer, he comes before the ruler of the universe, the king of the world—and the Talmud will make use of that metaphor many times. Now a man does not approach a king lightheadedly or thoughtlessly, but in accord with the protocol and procedures of the court. This is how you honor the king, express your submission to him. So the careful consideration of the order of prayer expresses through the close analysis of the traditions and reasons of that order an attitude of profound reverence for God and of seriousness in prayer.

To be sure, nowadays people who pray at all tend to show impatience with the concept that there may be rules and regulations in the matter. To pray however one feels, wherever, whenever, and by whatever means—these kinds of spontaneous prayer are more highly valued than the ancient, formal, measured prayers, stately processions, hoary gestures, and dignified music of synagogues or churches. Worship called creative, because someone has made it up on the spot, seems to matter more, is called more sincere, than following the forms of worship created over centuries. The rejection of discipline in favor of perfect spontaneity has not, to be sure, produced more praying or greatly enhanced the liturgical life of synagogues or churches, though enthusiasts think otherwise.

Formlessness of prayer, like the formlessness of music, of art, of education and other things, is something the rabbis before us could not have understood. Their world was orderly, well-regulated, and structured, so too their approach to God. You do not have to enter into their world, but to understand and appreciate their seriousness and interest in detail, in form and movement, in dignity and appropriateness, you have to leave ours.

What about references to "food," which occur throughout our chapter? These allude to reciting a "blessing over food," that is, to the prayers of thanks, or Grace after Meals. The three important elements in the Grace are as follows (in the translation, by Judah Goldin, of the current text):

בָּרוּךְ אַתָּה, יְיָ אֱלֹהֵינוּ, מֶלֶךְ הָעוֹלָם, הַזָּן אֶת הָעוֹלָם כֻּלּוֹ בְּטוּבוֹ, בְּחֵן בְּחֶסֶד וּבְרַחֲמִים. הוּא נוֹתֵן לֶחֶם לְכָל בָּשָׂר, כִּי לְעוֹלָם חַסְדּוֹ. וּבְטוּבוֹ הַגָּדוֹל תָּמִיד לֹא חָסַר לָנוּ, וְאַל יֶחְסַר לָנוּ מָזוֹן לְעוֹלָם וָעֶד בַּעֲבוּר שְׁמוֹ הַגָּדוֹל. כִּי הוּא אֵל זָן וּמְפַרְנֵס לַכֹּל, וּמֵטִיב לַכֹּל, וּמֵכִין מָזוֹן לְכָל בְּרִיּוֹתָיו אֲשֶׁר בָּרָא. בָּרוּךְ אַתָּה, יְיָ, הַזָּן אֶת הַכֹּל.

נוֹדֶה לְךָ, יְיָ אֱלֹהֵינוּ, עַל שֶׁהִנְחַלְתָּ לַאֲבוֹתֵינוּ אֶרֶץ חֶמְדָּה טוֹבָה וּרְחָבָה; וְעַל שֶׁהוֹצֵאתָנוּ, יְיָ אֱלֹהֵינוּ, מֵאֶרֶץ מִצְרַיִם, וּפְדִיתָנוּ מִבֵּית עֲבָדִים; וְעַל בְּרִיתְךָ שֶׁחָתַמְתָּ בִּבְשָׂרֵנוּ; וְעַל תּוֹרָתְךָ שֶׁלִּמַּדְתָּנוּ; וְעַל חֻקֶּיךָ שֶׁהוֹדַעְתָּנוּ; וְעַל חַיִּים, חֵן וָחֶסֶד שֶׁחוֹנַנְתָּנוּ; וְעַל אֲכִילַת מָזוֹן שָׁאַתָּה זָן וּמְפַרְנֵס אוֹתָנוּ תָּמִיד, בְּכָל יוֹם וּבְכָל עֵת וּבְכָל שָׁעָה.

וְעַל הַכֹּל, יְיָ אֱלֹהֵינוּ, אֲנַחְנוּ מוֹדִים לָךְ וּמְבָרְכִים אוֹתָךְ, יִתְבָּרַךְ שִׁמְךָ בְּפִי כָל חַי תָּמִיד לְעוֹלָם וָעֶד, כַּכָּתוּב: וְאָכַלְתָּ וְשָׂבָעְתָּ, וּבֵרַכְתָּ אֶת יְיָ אֱלֹהֶיךָ עַל הָאָרֶץ

הַטּוֹבָה אֲשֶׁר נָתַן לָךְ. בָּרוּךְ אַתָּה, יְיָ, עַל הָאָרֶץ וְעַל
הַמָּזוֹן.

רַחֵם, יְיָ אֱלֹהֵינוּ, עַל יִשְׂרָאֵל עַמֶּךָ, וְעַל יְרוּשָׁלַיִם עִירֶךָ,
וְעַל צִיּוֹן מִשְׁכַּן כְּבוֹדֶךָ, וְעַל מַלְכוּת בֵּית דָּוִד מְשִׁיחֶךָ,
וְעַל הַבַּיִת הַגָּדוֹל וְהַקָּדוֹשׁ שֶׁנִּקְרָא שִׁמְךָ עָלָיו. אֱלֹהֵינוּ
אָבִינוּ, רְעֵנוּ זוּנֵנוּ, פַּרְנְסֵנוּ וְכַלְכְּלֵנוּ וְהַרְוִיחֵנוּ, וְהַרְוַח
לָנוּ, יְיָ אֱלֹהֵינוּ, מְהֵרָה מִכָּל צָרוֹתֵינוּ. וְנָא, אַל תַּצְרִיכֵנוּ,
יְיָ אֱלֹהֵינוּ, לֹא לִידֵי מַתְּנַת בָּשָׂר וָדָם וְלֹא לִידֵי
הַלְוָאָתָם, כִּי אִם לְיָדְךָ הַמְּלֵאָה הַפְּתוּחָה, הַקְּדוֹשָׁה
וְהָרְחָבָה, שֶׁלֹּא נֵבוֹשׁ וְלֹא נִכָּלֵם לְעוֹלָם וָעֶד.
וּבְנֵה יְרוּשָׁלַיִם עִיר הַקֹּדֶשׁ בִּמְהֵרָה בְיָמֵינוּ. בָּרוּךְ אַתָּה,
יְיָ, בּוֹנֵה בְרַחֲמָיו יְרוּשָׁלָיִם, אָמֵן.

1. Blessed art Thou, Lord our God, King of the Universe, who nourishes all the world by His goodness, in
grace, in mercy, and in compassion: "He gives bread to
all flesh, for His mercy is everlasting." And because of
His great goodness we have never lacked, and so may
we never lack, sustenance—for the sake of His great
name. For He nourishes and feeds everyone, is good to
all, and provides food for each one of the creatures He
created.

Blessed art Thou, O Lord, who feeds everyone.

2. We thank Thee, Lord our God, for having given
our fathers as a heritage a pleasant, a good and spacious
land; for having taken us out of the land of Egypt; for
having redeemed us from the house of bondage; for Thy
covenant, which Thou hast set as a seal in our flesh; for
Thy Torah which Thou hast taught us; for Thy statutes
which Thou hast made known to us; for the life of grace
and mercy Thou hast graciously bestowed upon us; and
for the nourishment with which Thou dost nourish us

and feed us always, every day, in every season, and every hour.

For all these things, Lord our God, we thank and praise Thee; may Thy praises continually be in the mouth of every living thing, as it is written, "And thou shalt eat and be satisfied, and bless the Lord thy God for the good land which He hath given thee."

Blessed art Thou, O Lord, for the land and its food.

3. O Lord our God, have pity on Thy people Israel, on Thy city Jerusalem, on Zion the place of Thy glory, on the royal house of David Thy Messiah, and on the great and holy house which is called by Thy name. Our God, our Father, feed us and speed us, nourish us and make us flourish; unstintingly, O Lord our God, speedily free us from all distress.

And let us not, O Lord our God, find ourselves in need of gifts from flesh and blood, or of a loan from anyone save from Thy full, generous, sanctifying, wide-open hand; so we may never be humiliated, or put to shame.

O rebuild Jerusalem, the holy city, speedily in our day. Blessed art Thou, Lord, who in mercy will rebuild Jerusalem. Amen.

This is what is meant by "food," the blessing after a meal.

The Elements of the Chapter

Usually, the Mishnaic parts of a chapter of the Talmud will be quoted discretely, paragraph by paragraph, so that the Talmud's comments follow each element in the Mishnah. Here, however, the entire chapter is given at the outset, and we shall therefore consider it as a unit. This permits us to survey the themes as a whole and to see how carefully they unfold. We also shall observe the formal traits—the way in which the authors have expressed their ideas so as to highlight the important points—of the entire composition. If we read only line by line, as is commonplace in the received tradition of pedagogy of this and other rabbinic texts, we should never grasp the whole or understand how the requirements of a complete composition have dictated the style of the chapter. You will notice, also, that each whole unit of thought is marked with a letter, *A, B,* and so on, as I explained earlier. This allows us to separate one component from the next. Finally, I shall explain below that the authors want their composition to be memorized and so have provided numerous clues to jog our memory and make memorization easy. These are called mnemonic devices. In a little while I shall show you what these are and how they work. But, even at the outset, you will notice a great deal of patterning of language, and that is the principal mnemonic.

I translate following the Kaufmann manuscript of the Mishnah, which is found in the library of the Hungarian Academy of Sciences in Budapest. This is universally regarded as the best manuscript of the Mishnah; it dates from some time before 1500. The best printed text of the Mishnah is that edited by C. Albeck* together with a simple commentary; it does not greatly differ from the readings of the Kaufmann and other manuscripts, though in other parts of the Mishnah the differences are considerable and may be important.

We shall first examine each element of the chapter and afterward consider how the whole has been put together. At the same time we shall not seek on our own the ''reasons'' for the laws. These are supplied in later documents—the Tosefta and the *Gemara*—and in turn will be analyzed and criticized. Our purpose is to consider the Mishnah entirely in its own terms, to point up problems to be dealt with in later strata of the Talmud, thus to participate in the dynamic of the growth of Talmudic literature by replicating in our own study the process of commentary, exegesis, elaboration, and development.

אֵלּוּ דְבָרִים שֶׁבֵּין בֵּית שַׁמַּאי וּבֵית הֹלֵּל בַּסְּעוּדָה. בֵּית
שַׁמַּאי אוֹמְרִים: מְבָרֵךְ עַל הַיּוֹם, וְאַחַר כָּךְ מְבָרֵךְ עַל

---

* *Seder Zera'im* (Jerusalem and Tel Aviv: 1957).

MISHNAH 8:1 ff.

הַיַּיִן. וּבֵית הִלֵּל אוֹמְרִים: מְבָרֵךְ עַל הַיַּיִן, וְאַחַר כָּךְ
מְבָרֵךְ עַל הַיּוֹם.

8:1.A. These are the things which are between the
House of Shammai and the House of Hillel in [regard to]
the meal:

B. The House of Shammai say, "One blesses [says the
blessing for] the day, and afterward one says the blessing
over the wine."**

And the House of Hillel say, "One says the blessing
over the wine, and afterward one blesses the day."

The chapter begins with a superscription, A, which announces the subject and identifies the authorities whose opinions are to be given. No one can suppose that the only laws "in
regard to the meal" derived from the Houses, or that no one
thereafter raised issues or formulated opinions on the same
subject. Nor are these the only points about meals on which
the Houses differed. The *Gemara* lists others. What we have are
elements of a much larger tradition that have been chosen for
redaction and preservation. To some measure omitted materials
are preserved in other compilations of rabbinical traditions, or
occur as singletons, not in collections, in the *Gemara;* they will
be signified as deriving from the authorities of the first and
second centuries, called Tannaim ("repeaters"—the Aramaic
root, TNY, is equivalent to the Hebrew SHNY, thus Mishnah-
teachers), masters whose opinions were formulated and included in the Mishnah or in the stratum of materials from
which the Mishnah was finally selected.

We have already observed that the superscription, A, is misleading. We expect differences in regard to the meal in general,
but then, in B, we have a specific and special meal, that of the
evening of the Sabbath Day, Friday night.

The first difference concerns the order of blessing the wine

**The difference between "blessing wine" and "reciting a blessing over
wine" has important theological implications.

and saying the Sanctification of the Sabbath Day. The House of Shammai say the Sanctification comes first, then the blessing for the wine. The House of Hillel rule contrariwise. The Mishnah explains nothing about these requirements and their meaning. We are supposed to know that "day" means reciting the Sanctification, "wine" means saying a blessing over the wine. So "meal" is not only misleading, but confusing, for it does not hint at the real issue before us at all. That first occurs later on.

בֵּית שַׁמַּאי אוֹמְרִים: נוֹטְלִין לַיָּדַיִם, וְאַחַר כָּךְ מוֹזְגִין אֶת הַכּוֹס. וּבֵית הִלֵּל אוֹמְרִים: מוֹזְגִין אֶת הַכּוֹס, וְאַחַר כָּךְ נוֹטְלִין לַיָּדַיִם.

8:2.A. The House of Shammai say, "They wash the hands and afterward mix the cup."

And the House of Hillel say, "They mix the cup and afterward wash the hands."

With this law we begin the consideration of the details of purity at meals. This is not an abstract concept, but rather a concrete and detailed problem. How do you remove the impurity which will prevent your eating the meal in the cultic purity of a priest in the Temple? That depends upon the normal status accorded to your hands—impure, but in what ways and in what removes? As we shall see, there are several very important considerations. These must now be mastered.

First comes the food itself. Some food is more susceptible to impurity than others. How so? The priests are given various gifts. The most important of these is called "Heave-offering"— that which is "raised up" ("heaved") out of the food for the priesthood's use. Heave-offering is highly susceptible to uncleanness. Ordinary food, never brought to the cult or to the priest, the cultic functionary, is less susceptible. So food in the status of priestly rations is holier, on the upside, but also more susceptible to uncleanness, on the downside, than ordinary food, which has never been designated for consecrated use.

That is how food in one status differs from food in another status.

Second are the removes of uncleanness, which I shall explain in detail later on. Something unclean in the first remove is more capable of rendering food unclean than something unclean in the second remove of uncleanness—and so on, down to the fourth. Now what are these "removes of uncleanness"? The concept is very simple. Something may be an original source of uncleanness, such as a dead creeping thing or (all the more so) a corpse. If you touch a dead creeping thing, you stand in one remove from the original source of uncleanness, hence, "the first remove." If you then touch a piece of wet bread, the bread enters "the second remove," that is, two removes away from the original source of uncleanness. If the bread then is in contact with a piece of altar meat belonging to the priest, that is in the third remove, and so on. That which is unclean in the first remove will, therefore, make more things unclean than something unclean in the second. Something unclean in the first will affect ordinary food as well as the priests' food, the Heave-offering. What is unclean in the second remove will not affect ordinary food, but it will affect the priests' food. Why? Because it is more sensitive.

Again, I remind you, we are in the hands of lawyers, and to them detail is important. They are not interested in a general rule, which might assert that "we are all priests and all holy." To them such an assertion lacks all meaning until it is accompanied by details to give it effect, laws to give it body and substance. If we are all priests, therefore we must *do* such and so. And I think these lawyers are right, for merely asserting you are in the priestly status can carry little weight, until you actually *do* the things priests do, or, at least, pretend to. You are what you do, not merely what you claim to be or say about yourself.

Now we go back to the laws with which we started. They seem out of order. First we spoke of saying a blessing. But now we move back a step, to the preparation for eating at any meal. Two things need to be done before blessing the bread.

First, one has to wash the hands. This is not for hygienic reasons, but for cultic purity. As we observed, the Pharisees and their rabbinic continuators believed that ordinary, noncultic meals had to be eaten in a state of cultic purity, in accord with the laws of Leviticus about the purity of the Temple cult. Washing the hands made them incapable of rendering something else unfit or impure, so was a prophylactic for the cultic purity of the food. (This point will be sharpened later on.)

Mixing the cup of wine with water was necessary, second, because the wine itself, undiluted by water, was too thick to drink. This mixing was done before the meal. This has nothing to do with purity.

The issue is, Which comes first? To understand the reasons we have to know another law about making a vessel unclean. A vessel is not susceptible to being made unclean if it is dry, or if it is touched by clean hands. But if it is wet, and unwashed hands touch it, the hands will make the liquid on the vessel unclean. And the liquid does render the cup unclean. This will be amplified by the Talmuds.

Now we may understand the Shammaites' ruling, which takes this law for granted. The Shammaites first have the hands washed. Why? During the mixing of the wine, liquid may fall on the outer side of the cup. If then the man touches the cup with unwashed hands, he will make the liquid unclean. The liquid then will render the cup unclean. Again: be patient. This will become clear. The House of Hillel differ, for reasons we shall examine later.

בֵּית שַׁמַּאי אוֹמְרִים: מְקַנֵּחַ יָדָיו בַּמַּפָּה, וּמַנִּיחָהּ עַל הַשֻּׁלְחָן. וּבֵית הִלֵּל אוֹמְרִים: עַל הַכֶּסֶת.

8:3.A. The House of Shammai say, "He dries his hands on the cloth and lays it on the table."

And the House of Hillel say, "On the pillow."

After washing the hands, you dry them on a towel, then leave the towel for use as a napkin during the meal. The House of Shammai say you lay it on the table, but not on the cushion on which you are sitting. For the cushion may be unclean and render unclean the liquid in the cloth, which will then make the hands unclean again. This consideration is parallel to the one operative in the foregoing law.

The House of Hillel say you put the napkin on the cushion. Even if the cushion makes the hands unclean, it is not a severe (first remove) uncleanness. Only a first remove uncleanness will affect the food. So this one will not make food unclean. But you should not put it on the table, lest the table be unclean and render the water in the napkin unclean, which in turn will make the food unclean. Why? Wait a moment.

The House of Shammai say that in the first place one cannot make use of a table which is unclean. So the consideration important to the Hillelites does not apply.

The stress on rendering the liquid unclean, rather than the hands themselves, is for the following reason:

Unclean hands are decreed to be in a secondary level, or second remove, of uncleanness. At the second degree of uncleanness one may render Heave-offering *unfit*. That is, if unclean hands touch clean Heave-offering, it suffers contamination. But second remove uncleanness does *not* render food or vessels *unclean*.

On the other hand, liquids made unclean by a second-level source of uncleanness, such as the hands, then forthwith enter the primary level, or first remove, of uncleanness. Something unclean at the first remove indeed *does* render vessels unclean.

So here the napkin will not be made unclean by the cushion. Why not? An unclean vessel cannot render unclean either another vessel or man. But it does render the liquid unclean, and the napkin is assumed to contain some liquid. We shall say more about the cleanness laws later on.

To summarize: We distinguish between liquids and dry substances. The former are always unclean in the first remove. The latter are not. Dry, unclean hands are unclean in the second remove. So they will not make food unclean. Only something unclean in the first remove can do that. If the unclean hands touch (dry) food, the food is not unclean.

But if they touch liquids or something wet, they forthwith make the liquids unclean in the first remove. And if the liquids *then* touch food, they render it unclean. That is the basis of the problem before us. To be sure, in order to make sense of the dispute we have to suppose the Houses are talking about different circumstances, because we take for granted they agree about the principles of the law. So, as we noticed, the House of Shammai take for granted the table has to be insusceptible to uncleanness. The Talmuds are going to have difficulties sorting out the disputes.

Let us stand back and permit ourselves to ask the obvious question: Is this "Judaism"? This is hocus-pocus! Why in the world would people take seriously the nonsense we are now trying to master. And, you must ask me, why of all the noble chapters of the Mishnah have you selected this monumental nonsense?

head-on, as always!

Yes, in that day, in that place, that indeed was "Judaism." And why not, since what these people are trying to do is to take over the laws of the Scripture and live by them. Now when you think of the laws or teachings of the Scripture you would select, you would first of all choose the great ethical and moral doctrines of the Pentateuchal and prophetic writings. But that is because, in the age after Kant, we identify as the important aspect of the religious life the ethical and moral dimensions of our conduct. And it is easy, in both Scripture and the Talmudic canon, to find many passages that say much the same thing.

But I find inspiring something quite different, namely, the spectacle of how people solve their problems. And the people at hand, as I explained just now, confront a spectacular problem: defeat, loss, destruction of the Temple. The Temple had meant the place in which Israel attained oneness with God, atonement for sin, and sanctification. Israel was Israel because

nature met in union with supernature in the cult of Israel, in
Jerusalem, in the Temple. The laws of Leviticus talked about
just those matters. God, people believed, gave those laws,
wanted sacrifice, not only approved, but governed, the conduct
of the cult. True, the prophets and psalmists and priests had
taught God wanted more than animal sacrifice. But in the
moment of calamity, with the Temple gone and the cult no
more, the issue was whether God wanted Israel on any terms.

The rather courageous answer before us is that Israel can
make itself holy outside of the Temple, by keeping the laws
governing the eating of holy, priestly rations at home. With
the Temple gone, the sole remaining focus of holiness was
Israel, the Jewish people, in its homes and villages. So Israel
must be holy and hence pure. The last bastion of sanctification
was the altar of the home, the table, compared because of its
function to the altar of the Temple, the table of the Lord. So let
the table be cultically clean—like the altar. The priesthood had
left and had preserved a corpus of rules about that altar and
how to eat food that had been set aside either for the priests at
the altar or for the rations of the priests and their families. The
people, represented by the Pharisees before 70 and the rabbis at
hand afterward, took over and kept those laws. In this way they
acted out their deepest fantasy, the conviction that they (that is,
Israel) remained holy, and that their food (that is, the ordinary
meals of Israelites) demanded those same conditions of cultic
cleanness that had applied, to begin with, to the holy altar and
the consecrated caste of the priests.

I am not embarrassed by these strange rules, this gibberish,
these meaningless glyphs of the fantasies of long-ago lawyers. I
am astonished at the daring represented by them, at the arroga-
tion to all Jews, all Israel, of that sanctity once imputed only to
the priestly caste, of that consecration once limited to the
priestly rations. In context—and context governs content and
determines meaning—these are heroic affirmations, radical and
revolutionary allegations. True, the meaning rests all in the
details. But God lives in the details. So those are what we must

master and endure. If it all appears unfamiliar and alien, the
context is not: survivors and the things they do to carry on. All
Jews alive in the world today are survivors, and, faced with
memories of our own day, we too carry on against it all and
despite it all—but then, too, in odd, if courageous ways. After
all, who, before our own time, ever heard of a *state* of Israel?

בֵּית שַׁמַּאי אוֹמְרִים: מְכַבְּדִין אֶת הַבַּיִת, וְאַחַר כָּךְ
נוֹטְלִין לַיָּדַיִם. וּבֵית הִלֵּל אוֹמְרִים: נוֹטְלִין לַיָּדַיִם, וְאַחַר
כָּךְ מְכַבְּדִין אֶת הַבַּיִת.

8:4.A. The House of Shammai say, "They clean the
house and afterward wash the hands."
And the House of Hillel say, "They wash the hands
and afterward clean the house."

"Cleaning the house" means sweeping the floor. A second
washing of hands is required after the meal, before the recitation of Grace. The House of Shammai say that first of all the
person sweeps up the crumbs of food, then washes his hands,
so that the remaining crumbs will not be rendered susceptible
to uncleanness through contact with the water. The position of
the House of Hillel remains to be explained.

בֵּית שַׁמַּאי אוֹמְרִים: נֵר, וּמָזוֹן, וּבְשָׂמִים, וְהַבְדָּלָה.
וּבֵית הִלֵּל אוֹמְרִים: נֵר, וּבְשָׂמִים, וּמָזוֹן, וְהַבְדָּלָה. בֵּית
שַׁמַּאי אוֹמְרִים: "שֶׁבָּרָא מְאוֹר הָאֵשׁ"; וּבֵית הִלֵּל
אוֹמְרִים: "בּוֹרֵא מְאוֹרֵי הָאֵשׁ".

8:5.A. The House of Shammai say, "Light, and food,
and spices, and *Havdalah*."
And the House of Hillel say, "Light, and spices, and
food, and *Havdalah*."
B. The House of Shammai say, "'[The blessing of light
is] [Blessed are you, Lord our God] Who *created* the *light*
of the fire.'"

And the House of Hillel say, "'[Blessed are you, Lord our God] Who *creates* the *lights* of the fire.'"

Two further disputes are before us, both concerning *Havdalah.* The first (A) involves the order of the liturgies at a meal which takes place at the end of the Sabbath Day. During the meal, the sun has set and the Sabbath ended. Thus you have to bless light and spices, say *Havdalah,* and also recite the Grace. What is the appropriate order? The Houses agree light comes at the outset, *Havdalah* at the end. The House of Shammai place the Grace before the blessing of spices; the House of Hillel give the opposite order. A cup of wine is blessed for the Grace; here it will also be used for *Havdalah,* and that accounts for the difficulty about which prayer takes priority.

Clearly, the man starts with the light, for it is used as soon as it is kindled, so its blessing is to be said immediately. Afterward one completes Grace, then spices, finally, *Havdalah,* so say the Shammaites. The House of Hillel say the blessing of the light and spices are to be said together; both are brief sentences, as we observed above.

The second dispute (B) concerns the blessing of the light. The issue is whether one refers to the creation of the light of the flame at the creation of the world, or whether one regards the flame as constantly re-created as new lights in the preexistent flame. The larger issue—which is not made explicit here—is the nature of creation: perpetual or one-time only, and of flame: is it a completed substance or constantly renewed? Did God complete his activity of creation at the beginning, or does he continue to exert a creative force in the world perpetually? Is he—by extension—solely transcendent, outside of the created world, or is he immanent and involved daily in the maintenance of creation? So too, is the flame complete? Or is it renewed as it burns? What constitutes the flame *itself,* if it consumes its fuel and so is composed of ever-changing elements? This kind of "philosophical" issue about continuity and change is introduced only and always in concrete terms, never in the abstract.

אֵין מְבָרְכִין לֹא עַל הַנֵּר, וְלֹא עַל הַבְּשָׂמִים שֶׁל גּוֹיִם,
וְלֹא עַל הַנֵּר, וְלֹא עַל הַבְּשָׂמִים שֶׁל מֵתִים, וְלֹא עַל
הַנֵּר, וְלֹא עַל הַבְּשָׂמִים שֶׁלִּפְנֵי עֲבוֹדָה זָרָה. אֵין מְבָרְכִין
עַל הַנֵּר עַד שֶׁיֵּאוֹתוּ לְאוֹרוֹ.

8:6.A. They do not bless over the light or the spices of
gentiles, nor the light or the spices of the dead, nor the
light or the spices which are before an idol.

B. And they do not bless over the light until they
make use of its illumination.

NO
HOUSES

The Houses are dropped. We now have a simple statement of
what all authorities agree is the rule.

Israelites are not allowed to make use of anything, including
spices or light, which has to do with idolatry. The reason one
may not use the light of a gentile is not given; the *Gemara* will
try to supply an explanation.

It is assumed that the spices have also served an idolatrous
purpose—but then the first reference to spices ("of gentiles")
duplicates the third ("before an idol"). And one thing the
Gemara will normally point out is repetitions and duplications
in the Mishnah, not to mention internal contradictions of all
sorts.

Light used for the corpse is not intended for illumination,
but is kindled only for the honor of the corpse. The spices are
used as a deodorant, not for a sweet savor. So in this instance
the light and spices are not serving their normal purpose. They
therefore cannot be used for *Havdalah*.

B gives the rule that one must actually make use of the light.
If he has not made use of an object—drunk the wine, smelled
the spice—he has no right to say a blessing of thanks for that
pleasure. The principles are not different from those of A:
(1) Something must be used for its *normal* purpose, and (2) it
must *actually* be used, before a blessing is to be said. But then
the blessing must be said; one cannot enjoy the benefits of
creation without acknowledging the Creator.

What is the meaning of the law before us? Why do the rabbis
rule that you cannot recite a blessing over the light or the
spices of gentiles in connection with saying the *Havdalah*
prayer? Recall what *Havdalah* alleges: God has made a distinction between Israel and the nations. It would contradict the
meaning of those very words to say them over the light or
spices of the gentiles. But there is a reason: The gentiles are
worshipers of idols. To them the qualities intrinsic to light or
spices, therefore, may not symbolize or represent, but actually
partake of the substance of, the god. Using what may serve the
"false worship of idolatry" to the rabbis is an insult to God.
Israelites may not do so under any circumstances. For instance,
gentiles are supposed always to make an offering of wine before
they drink it. It is done by flicking a drop of wine out of the
bottle or the cup before using the wine.

Gentiles are seen as pious, deeply religious people; they are
strict about making such an offering. Then Israelites may under
no circumstances make use of wine touched by a gentile, for
the pious pagan always will have already devoted it to the god.
And this is abnormal. Similarly, you have to use light and
spices only in the normal way, for the ordinary purpose—not
only not for idolatry, but also not for the honor of the corpse.
The light and incense, therefore, have to be freely available for
the divine worship, which means, as we now see, they are, first,
not contaminated by use in pagan prayer, and second, not
rendered unfit by prior use in some extraordinary way or for
some unusual purpose. What is natural and freely available—
that is to be used in the divine service. These points are important to the Talmud. They will be elaborated, though their
reasons will not be spelled out in greater detail.

מִי שֶׁאָכַל וְשָׁכַח וְלֹא בֵרַךְ — בֵּית שַׁמַּאי אוֹמְרִים:
יַחֲזֹר לִמְקוֹמוֹ וִיבָרֵךְ. וּבֵית הִלֵּל אוֹמְרִים: יְבָרֵךְ בִּמְקוֹם
שֶׁנִּזְכַּר. עַד אֵימָתַי הוּא מְבָרֵךְ? עַד כְּדֵי שֶׁיִּתְעַכֵּל הַמָּזוֹן
שֶׁבְּמֵעָיו.

8:7.A. He who ate and forgot and did not bless [say Grace after meals]—

B. The House of Shammai say, "He should go back to his place and bless."

And the House of Hillel say, "He should bless in the place in which he remembered."

C. Until when does he bless? Until the food has been digested in his bowels.

The Houses have now returned to the text, but in a form very different from before. Instead of extremely abbreviated sayings, lacking a superscription or explanation of the subject matter about which the Houses are supposed to have differed, we have a fully articulated statement of the problem. We further are shifted into an ordinary, everyday circumstance, not only the Sabbath meal, so the frame of reference has changed.

The issue is what a person should do who has eaten a meal and forgotten to say Grace. He is supposed to say a blessing of thanks for every benefit of creation which he enjoys. Obviously, he has to say thank You for the meal. And this should come just as soon as he has eaten it. But he is apt to forget. Should he go back to where he ate? Or may he bless wherever he remembers the blessing? That is the issue before us.

The House of Shammai send the man back where he ate the meal. The House of Hillel rule he may say the blessing wherever he is when he remembers that he forgot it. The *Gemara* will provide theological homilies for both viewpoints.

C is a gloss; once the food is entirely digested, one can no longer make up his failure. But we do not know whence the gloss, or who made it.

בָּא לָהֶם יַיִן לְאַחַר הַמָּזוֹן, וְאֵין שָׁם אֶלָּא אוֹתוֹ הַכּוֹס — בֵּית שַׁמַּאי אוֹמְרִים: מְבָרֵךְ עַל הַיַּיִן, וְאַחַר כָּךְ מְבָרֵךְ עַל הַמָּזוֹן. וּבֵית הִלֵּל אוֹמְרִים: מְבָרֵךְ עַל הַמָּזוֹן, וְאַחַר כָּךְ מְבָרֵךְ עַל הַיַּיִן. עוֹנִין אָמֵן אַחַר

יִשְׂרָאֵל הַמְבָרֵךְ, וְאֵין עוֹנִין אָמֵן אַחַר הַכּוּתִי הַמְבָרֵךְ,
עַד שֶׁיִּשְׁמַע כָּל הַבְּרָכָה.

8:8.A. Wine came to them after the meal, and there is there only that cup—

B. The House of Shammai say, "He blesses over the wine, and afterward he blesses the food."

And the House of Hillel say, "He blesses the food, and afterward he blesses over the wine."

C. They respond *Amen* after an Israelite who blesses, and they do not respond *Amen* after a Samaritan who blesses, until one hears the entire blessing.

Here the answer is clear: Bless the wine, then say Grace, or vice versa. The only problem is, What is the question? The meaning of A is obscure. One explanation of the problem is this: The meal is over. There is only one cup (as stated). You may say a blessing for the wine and drink it and then say Grace without the customary further cup of wine, so the Shammaites. The Hillelites require a blessing of wine before the Grace.

C is a separate law. A person should not respond *Amen*—"so may it be done"—until he knows to what he is responding. A Samaritan is here supposed to be unreliable; you have to hear him out before agreeing with his prayer and seconding it.

Who is this Samaritan?

A Samaritan, so casually introduced into our law, clearly is regarded as someone who says blessings—therefore, he must be a kind of an Israelite. The rabbis here refer to a member of a group which took shape in the aftermath of the destruction of the ten northern tribes of Israel by the Assyrians in 722 B.C. The biblical view, which is very hostile to the Samaritans, reports that the Assyrians brought in a new group of people to repopulate the country, after they had deported the northern Israelites. Those new people, plagued by natural disasters, adopted the cult of the land, the worship of Yahweh, not sincerely, but out of "superstition." So they are called "converts on account of lions," for the story is that wild beasts plagued them, and they supposed it was on account of neglect of the god and cult of the land. That is the hostile view. For their part the Samaritans claimed that they were the true "Israel," the followers of Moses and loyal to the Pentateuch, just as much as were the Judeans, the southern tribes clustered around Jerusalem. They worshiped the one God at their sanctuary, Gerizim, instead of at the Judean one in Jerusalem. So before us are two groups, closely related and sharing a single revealed Torah, but differing as to which of the groups is legitimate. These intergroup tensions produce, among the Jews, considerable hostility toward the Samaritans. Yet the rabbis readily concede that when the Samaritans do keep the law, they do so meticulously and lawfully. Now before us is a Samaritan who is saying a prayer just as does a Jew. But before you may reply and say *Amen*, you have to be sure things are done properly.

In this little law we see how the rabbis coped with the existence, within the Jewish community or on its fringes, of dissenting groups (who, to be sure, would have seen the rabbis and their followers as the dissenting group on their fringes). They were not prepared to write them off entirely and to declare them utterly beyond the pale of "Israel." But the rabbis also could not amiably admit the legitimacy of the other group's religious deeds and ideas. They believed the Samaritans were very wrong in their view and interpretation of Torah. Tolerance is easy when no one really cares about the differences which have to be tolerated, when religion is a matter of indifference. But how do you cope with difference close at hand, when you think the differences important? The rabbis' response to the problem is not bland acceptance of the difference; that would not be possible if you believe God cares about what you say and do. But the rabbis also do not ignore the good deeds rightly done by the other group, the ways in which Samaritans and Jews worship a single God and revere a single Torah. So they are prepared to declare *Amen* to a blessing properly said. But they add, you have to hear the entire blessing. Again, what is decisive is what you actually do, and if you do the right thing, the rabbi adds his *Amen*.

The Chapter As a Whole

Having examined each element in our chapter, we shall now look at the chapter as a whole, so that we may observe its larger units and how they are put together. I discern four units of thought, fully spelled out: the first, a neat construction of the Houses' disagreements, expressed in the most terse possible language; second, a simple statement of a rule; third, a more sophisticated form of a disagreement between the Houses; and fourth, like the second, a rule in quite separate form from that of the Houses' laws. While parts II and IV do not differ in form, they are sufficiently distinct in substance so that we may not suppose they derived originally from a single rulebook which has been split apart by the insertion of the Houses' disputes. And the materials attributed to the Houses are likewise so different from one another both in form and in substance that they cannot be regarded as originally a unity.

I

8:1.A. These are the things which are between the House of Shammai and the House of Hillel in [regard to] the meal:

B. The House of Shammai say, "One blesses over the day, and afterward one blesses over the wine."

And the House of Hillel say, "One blesses over the wine, and afterward one blesses over the day."

8:2.A. The House of Shammai say, "They wash the hands and afterward mix the cup."

And the House of Hillel say, "They mix the cup and afterward wash the hands."

8:3.A. The House of Shammai say, "He dries his hands on the cloth and lays it on the table."

And the House of Hillel say, "On the pillow."

8:4.A. The House of Shammai say, "They clean the house, and afterward they wash the hands."

And the House of Hillel say, "They wash the hands, and afterward they clean the house."

8:5.A. The House of Shammai say, "Light, and food, and spices, and *Havdalah*."

And the House of Hillel say, "'Light, and spices, and food, and *Havdalah*."

B. The House of Shammai say, "'Who created the light of the fire.'"

And the House of Hillel say, "'Who creates the lights of the fire.'"

II

8:6.A. They do not bless over the light or the spices of gentiles, nor the light or the spices of the dead, nor the light or the spices which are before an idol.

B. And they do not bless over the light until they make use of its illumination.

III

8:7.A. He who ate and forgot and did not bless [say Grace]—

B. The House of Shammai say, "He should go back to his place and bless."

And the House of Hillel say, "He should bless in the place in which he remembered."

C. Until when does he bless? Until the food has been digested in his bowels.

8:8.A. Wine came to them after the meal, and there is there only that cup—

B. The House of Shammai say, "He blesses the wine, and afterward he blesses the food."

And the House of Hillel say, "He blesses the food, and afterward he blesses the wine."

IV

C. They respond *Amen* after an Israelite who blesses, and they do not respond *Amen* after a Samaritan who blesses, until hearing the entire blessing.

Let us now analyze the formal traits of our chapter, that is, the patterns of language, the repeated use of the same sort of syntax, and word arrangement. This will tell us about the divisions of the chapter, and what we shall see is that when the subject matter changes, the syntax and other formal traits of language change too. So we begin.

The first unit is introduced by the superscription, 8:1.A, and then continues in the briefest possible language, without further superscriptions, exegeses, debates, or other extraneous materials.

After the superscription serving the whole composite, the first dispute is introduced without an additional superscription to set forth the specific problem. Without it, all we have in effect is *day/wine* vs. *wine/day*, with the same explanatory words in both opinions.

The same form applies in 8:2–5. No general principle, law, or superscription, merely *wash hands, mix cup* vs. *mix cup, wash hands*. There are six Houses' disputes in all.

The Hillelite opinion in 8:3 is not a gloss on the foregoing but rather has been abbreviated. In full form, it would read, *He dries his hands on the napkin and leaves it on the cushion.*

Part II is a separate unit, giving a rule about the light and spices one may not use. It is related to 8:5 in theme, but not in form or expression. The form is a simple statement of fact. The rule is expressed in full detail; no necessary words are omitted, nor does the sense rely upon some foregoing sentence. Complete and fully articulated, the section could have been transmitted all by itself, without reference to any other passage.

Part III introduces a still further dispute about the meal,

unrelated to the foregoing. The form is a superscription followed by the opinions of the Houses; each opinion completes the introductory superscription. Without the contrary view of the opposed House, it would have been a simple sentence, not much different from 8:6, thus: "They do not bless the light. . . . He who ate and forgot and did not bless should go back to his place. . . ." What is curious about the formulation of the Houses' opinions is the assumption that all the Houses' viewpoints were preserved in such an antithetical construction.

But is this how the rulings were originally formulated? It seems unlikely that the House of Shammai deliberating on their own said, "If one forgot to bless, *we say* he should go back, but the House of Hillel say. . . ." More likely, the earliest formulation of an opinion was simple and straightforward, as in 8:6, a plain rule. Only afterward, when an opposed opinion was supplied by another party, could the dispute construction have developed.

And a further requirement for that development must have been a list of items on which the two parties agreed to disagree—and then in diametrically opposite terms: yes or no, but not maybe. So behind the Mishnah before us must lie a considerable corpus of traditions, formulated according to the opinion of an individual authority, or a party, or House. That corpus of opinions only later on was amalgamated with the opinions on the same subject of various other authorities. Then, given the whole range of subjects on which opinions were expressed, a redactional process (which we do not now fully understand) led to the selection, first, of topics for dispute, second, of the particular authorities whose opinions would be allowed to register on those topics, and third, of the actual opinions of the opposed authorities.

We shall review the components of the collection of Houses' opinions:

Shammai			*Hillel*
		I	
8:1	Day/wine	*Blessing*	Wine/day
		II	
8:2	Hands/cup	*Uncleanness*	Cup/hands
8:3	Table	*Uncleanness*	Cushion
8:4	Sweep/wash	*Uncleanness*	Wash/sweep
		III	
8:5A	Food,spices	*Blessing*	Spices, food
8:5B	*Did* create *light*		*Does* create *lights*
8:7	Forgot: Go back	*Blessing*	Forgot: In the place where he recalled he forgot
8:8	Food/wine	*Blessing*	Wine/food

The subject matter (within "matters pertaining to the meal") is
therefore arranged in an orderly and logical way:

Before Sabbath-Festival Meals—Blessing:	8:1
During Meals—Uncleanness:	8:2, 3, 4
After Sabbath-Festival Meals—Blessing:	8:5A, B
After Meals (special case, pertaining to *all* meals):	8:7

And 8:8 is an enigma.

It looks, therefore, as if the collection consists of five separate,
anterior elements or collections: 8:2–4, uncleanness rules for
meals, a neat and simple collection of laws about saying blessings, consisting of a few words attributed to each House: 8:1;
8:5; 8:7; and 8:8.

But 8:8 looks suspiciously like the reverse of 8:1. The capi-
talized consonants stand for Hebrew letters, so you can see that
the Hebrew words produce alliteration. If you want to memorize, you will find such close correspondences very helpful.
Repeating all of the same words but one, or reversing the order

of words, makes memorizing very easy. Then you have to remember only the subject matter, the key words, and the fact that the order for one side is reversed for the other. This will be very clear as we go on.

	8:1	8:8
Shammai:		
	Day/Wine (YWM/YYN)	Wine/Food (YYN/MZWN)
Hillel:		
	Wine/Day (YYN/YWM)	Food/Wine (MZWN/YYN)

The superscription of 8:8 thus brings more difficulties than we might have had in its absence.

Memorizing the Mishnah

Since the authorities behind the Mishnah and related literature claimed their traditions were formulated in final form and handed down orally from Sinai and thereafter memorized but not written down, we should not be surprised to observe that the materials before us have been organized so as to facilitate memorization. Mnemonic devices—that is, aids to memorization—are particularly apparent in the Houses' sections of our chapter. To show how these work, I shall give the Hebrew letters. Since Hebrew has no vowels, the consonants will be represented by their equivalents in English; each stands for a syllable. It will quickly become apparent that nearly the same words are used throughout, though in different arrangements, and, of course, the same number of syllables will be assigned to each House's opinion.

8:1–5 can be readily reduced to brief and alliterative mnemonic elements, as I just explained:

8:1:   YWM/YYN vs. YYN/YWM
8:2:   NTL/MZG vs. MZG/NTL
8:3:   SLHN vs. KST
8:4:   KBD/NTL vs. NTL/KBD

8:5:   NR/MZWN/BSMYM/HBDLH vs.
       NR/BSMYM/MZWN/HBDLH
       Thus: MZWN/BSMYM vs. BSMYM/MZWN

The list is constructed of transitive participles, generally given in third-person plural (8:2, 8:4), though I see no principle that explains why one set should be plural, the next singular. Only 8:3 is significantly glossed; there a simple superscription would have allowed the significant difference to be reduced to two substantives. Like parts 8:1 and 8:8, parts 8:2 and 8:4 look suspiciously alike, and it may be that they began as a single saying, only later on developed into two separate arguments. Parts 8:1, 2, 4, and 5 all depend upon word order, and I see no reason why 8:5 should not have been preserved in fully articulated form right from the outset. In all, it would be difficult to invent a better model of a mnemonic list.

8:7 is another sort of mnemonic apparently built out of the same words and mostly the same letters:

HZR MQWM BRK vs. BRK MQWM ZKR

<u>Here the mnemonic is amazing</u>. How so? Clearly the word order is 1, 2, 3 vs. 3, 2, 1. Only the first word of the Shammaite, and the last word of the Hillelite, sayings are different. The difference, surprisingly, is in a single letter, H vs. K.

On the whole, therefore, we may suppose the mnemonic pattern has been only lightly reworked with the addition of the dative particles, the personal endings, and the relative pronoun (S) demanded by the Hillelite saying.

Even in the fully articulated form before us, we find obvious balances between the Houses' lemmas. They contain the same number of words throughout, e.g.,

8:1:   MBRK 'L HYWM W'HR KK MBRK 'L HYYN
       MBRK 'L HYYN W'HR KK MBRK 'L HYWM

And these words preserve a fixed order and balance from one House-saying to the next, as is obvious above. So the whole collection is now in mnemonic form. You can easily memorize it.

The Mishnah is not the sole primary component of the Talmud. A second, and equally important collection of traditions, also attributed to first- and second-century masters, is the Tosefta, the supplement to the Mishnah. Indeed, as we shall soon see, the *Gemara*, or commentary to the Mishnah, of both the Babylonian and the Palestinian Talmuds centers more on the analysis of the Tosefta than on the Mishnah. While the Mishnah supplies the form and structure for the Talmud as a whole, for our chapter the Tosefta provides the focus of interest. So we move on to it.

CHAPTER 3

The Tosefta

Tosefta means addition or supplement. The Tosefta is a compilation of traditions and sayings closely related to the Mishnah and deriving from many of the same authorities represented in the Mishnah. The Tosefta is organized like the Mishnah, being divided into the same tractates and mostly the same chapters as well. The relationships between the Tosefta and the Mishnah are simple. They are three. First, a passage of the Tosefta will cite a passage of the Mishnah and comment on it. Second, a passage of the Tosefta will amplify, without direct citation or allusion, what is found in the Mishnah. Third, a passage of the Tosefta will frame a rule entirely separate from anything the Mishnah says on the same topic, or deal with a topic not treated in the Mishnah at all. The first and second types of material predominate, and they derive from the time after the Mishnah had reached closure and was subject to commentary and expansion. In most tractates the Tosefta tends to follow and to elaborate the main outlines of the Mishnah, with the same agendum of subjects and legal problems as are discussed in the authoritative code. In a few tractates the Tosefta stands quite separate and independent of the Mishnah.

Our interest in the Tosefta is for two reasons. First, the Tosefta contains important materials pertinent to the Mishnah we have just studied. Second, as we shall soon see, the Tosefta constitutes the first stratum and the most important building block of both the Babylonian and the Palestinian Talmuds (a synonym for Talmud is *Gemara*). We shall therefore be unable to comprehend the components of the *Gemara* if we do not examine the Tosefta in its own terms.

Now it is easy to approach the Tosefta, for it has been edited and elucidated by Saul Lieberman, the great scholar of Talmudic literature. His definitive edition and commentary, which by the time of his death in 1983 had reached the beginning of the fourth order, Damages (*Neziqin*), constitute the authoritative statement both of what is worth knowing about the Tosefta—and that is a great deal—and of what each passage means. In the growth of Talmudic literature, Tosefta forms the connection between the Mishnah, terse, opaque, elliptical, and the *Gemara*, fully articulated, lucid, and elegant. Lieberman's edition and commentary thus permit study of the growth of the Talmudic literature as a whole; he provides the key to the lock of nearly every door.

We shall not be detained by the questions of the date of the Tosefta's compilation and the authorities behind it. It suffices to view the Tosefta before us as a compilation made at about the same time as, or shortly after, the redaction of the Mishnah. For our chapter, the Tosefta certainly comes before the development of the *Gemara*. Why so? The *Gemara* quotes, depends upon, analyzes, and therefore *must* follow, the Tosefta in its present form. We shall examine not the complete corresponding chapter of Tosefta, but only those materials pertinent to the Mishnah already studied. Then we shall compare the Mishnah's and the Tosefta's treatments of the same problems. So, in summary, what we now see are the first stages in the creation of the two Talmuds, that is to say, the Mishnah's first amplification and exegesis, the beginning of the road to the *Gemaras* of the Land of Israel and Babylonia.

The Elements of the Tosefta Pertinent to the Mishnah

גּוֹי הַמְבָרֵךְ בַּשֵּׁם עוֹנִין אַחֲרָיו אָמֵן, אֶת הַשֵּׁם אֵין
עוֹנִין אַחֲרָיו אָמֵן, עַד שֶׁיִּשְׁמַע אֶת כָּל הַבְּרָכָה.

5:21 (Lieberman, p. 28, ls. 41–2). They answer *Amen*
after a gentile who says a blessing with the divine name.
They do not answer *Amen* after a Samaritan who says a
blessing with the divine name until they have heard the
entire blessing.

The Mishnah says you answer *Amen* after an Israelite, but
not after a Samaritan. The distinction now is between a gentile
and a Samaritan. The gentile is not subject to the laws of
Moses; he does not have to say blessings or to mention the
divine name. You may answer each of his blessings with *Amen*,
whether he said the blessing in its proper form or not, for he is
thereby blessing the Lord. But a Samaritan is regarded as subject to the commandments concerning blessings and is supposed not to mention the divine name purposelessly. If he has
changed the accepted pattern of the blessings, one may not
answer *Amen* after him; therefore, a man has to hear the entire
blessing, to be certain he will say it properly. What the Samaritan does matters.

דְּבָרִים שֶׁבֵּין בֵּית שַׁמַּיי לְבֵית הֶלֵּל בַּסְעוּדָה. בֵּית שַׁמַּיי
אוֹמְרִין: מְבָרֵךְ עַל הַיּוֹם וְאַחַר כָּךְ מְבָרֵךְ עַל הַיַּיִן,
שֶׁהַיּוֹם גּוֹרֵם לַיַּיִן שֶׁיָּבֹא, וּכְבָר קָדַשׁ הַיּוֹם וַעֲדַיִין יַיִן
לֹא בָא. וּבֵית הֶלֵּל אוֹמְרִין: מְבָרֵךְ עַל הַיַּיִן וְאַחַר כָּךְ
מְבָרֵךְ עַל הַיּוֹם, שֶׁהַיַּיִן גּוֹרֵם לְקְדוּשַׁת הַיּוֹם שֶׁתֵּאָמֵר.
דָּבָר אַחֵר בִּרְכַּת הַיַּיִן תְּדִירָה וּבִרְכַּת הַיּוֹם אֵינָה
תְּדִירָה. וַהֲלָכָה כְּדִבְרֵי בֵּית הֶלֵּל.

5:25 (Lieberman, p. 29, ls. 53–57). A. [The] things
which are between the House of Shammai and the
House of Hillel in [regard to] the meal:
B. The House of Shammai say, "One blesses over the
day, and afterward he blesses over the wine, for the day
causes the wine to come, and the day is already sanctified, but the wine has not yet come."

C. And the House of Hillel say, "One blesses over the wine, and afterward he blesses over the day, for the wine causes the Sanctification of the day to be said.

"Another explanation: The blessing over the wine is regular [= always required when wine is used], and the blessing over the day is not continual [but is said only on certain days]."

D. And the law is according to the words of the House of Hillel.

A omits *these are*, with which the Mishnah begins, and is therefore curiously abbreviated.

The Tosefta supplies reasons for the rulings of the Mishnah. B explains the opinion of the House of Shammai. You have to have the wine in order to say the Sanctification of the Sabbath. On an ordinary day, not the Sabbath, the man is not required to have wine before the meal. Therefore, the "day," that is, the Sanctification, supplies the occasion for the wine to be brought. The day is already sanctified, for at sunset one no longer works. The Sabbath Day has already begun. The Evening Prayer for the Sabbath has been said before the meal. So the Sanctification is said first. Then comes the recitation of the blessing over the wine.

The House of Hillel, C, argue that what is essential is the blessing of the wine. Without wine you do not say the Sanctification of the Day at all. Therefore, you bless over the wine first, then the day.

The reasons just adduced recall our earlier observation that the rabbis take a keen interest in protocol, especially in relationship to prayer. Two blessings are to be said, one for wine, the other for the Sabbath Day. Which comes first? The answer is not a matter of formalism, despite the interest in forms, but of substance. For saying the Sanctification of the Sabbath Day marks the beginning of the holy time. It is not done lightly, but with all due reverence. The course of nature is turning. As the sun sets, you call to mind the Exodus from Egypt, the creation of the world—a great historical event, corresponding to sunset, a decisive event in nature. The one "creates" Israel's sacred history as the other marks creation, the beginning of nature. So the issues are not inconsiderable.

On the other hand, here is the wine in hand. The wine cannot be drunk without a blessing. Humble, ordinary, mundane—the wine is always here. The turning of time is extraordinary and noteworthy. So which takes precedence? The theological issues inherent in the little legal question—the logic-chopping—are not to be ignored. Where are we to turn our thoughts?

The House of Hillel say the here-and-now comes first. Only then do you turn to the transcendent meaning of the hour. What matters is what is always at hand. Do not neglect the ordinary because of the extraordinary. The profane is always waiting to be sanctified. The House of Shammai take the opposite view. How can you neglect the great moment of sunset at the end of the sixth day of the week and the beginning of the seventh, merely to attend to something which you have in hand only on account of the grand occasion? It stands to reason you cannot and should not. Both Houses have good points. They cannot be resolved. You must in the end choose one over the other.

To return to our text: the House of Hillel are given a second reason for their ruling. The man must always bless wine before he drinks it, on any day of the week. Therefore, the requirement of blessing the wine is continual or perpetual. He first carries out a continuing obligation, then the one which is not continuing, for the former takes precedence under all circumstances.

D then gives the final decision. The law, as is mostly the case, will be observed according to the opinion of the House of Hillel.

בֵּית שַׁמַּיי אוֹמְרִין נוֹטְלִין לַיָּדַיִם וְאַחַר כָּךְ מוֹזְגִין אֶת הַכּוֹס, שֶׁמָּא נִיטְמְאוּ מַשְׁקִין שֶׁבַּאֲחוֹרֵי הַכּוֹס מֵחֲמַת הַיָּדַיִם וְיַחְזְרוּ וִיטַמְּאוּ אֶת הַכּוֹס. בֵּית הַלֵּל אוֹמְרִין:

אֲחוֹרֵי הַכּוֹס לְעוֹלָם טְמֵאִין. דָּבָר אַחֵר אֵין נְטִילַת
יָדַיִם אֶלָּא סָמוּךְ לַסְעוּדָה. מוֹזְגִין אֶת הַכּוֹס וְאַחַר כָּךְ
נוֹטְלִין לַיָּדַיִם.

5:26 (Lieberman, pp. 29–30, ls. 57–61). A. The House
of Shammai say, "They wash the hands and afterward
mix the cup, lest the liquids which are on the outer
surface of the cup be made unclean on account of the
hands, and in turn make the cup unclean."

B. The House of Hillel say, "The outer surfaces of the
cup are always deemed unclean.

"Another explanation: The washing of the hands must
always take place immediately before the meal.

C. "They mix the cup and afterward wash the hands."

As stated above, the hands are presumed to be unclean. But
they are in a second remove of uncleanness. They render
Heave-offering unfit, and cannot make vessels unclean. But
they do make liquids unclean. And the liquids' uncleanness is
in the first remove. So then the liquids will render the cup
unclean.

The contrary procedure—the Shammaites'—would have one
wash the hands first. But then the liquids on the hands may
become unclean on account of the still-unwashed cup. They
will go and make the hands unclean once again. That is the
Hillelites' criticism of the position of the House of Shammai.

The House of Hillel first of all (B) reject the reasoning of the
Shammaites. Their view is that the consideration important to
the House of Shammai is insufficient to require washing the
hands before mixing the cup. No matter what the man does, he
may make use of a cup whose outer sides are unclean, for their
unclean state will *not* affect the insides. So what difference will
it make if one washes his hands before mixing the cup of wine
or afterward? If, furthermore, one is concerned about the drops
of water on the cup, washing the hands first will do no good.
For the liquid dripping on the side of the cup is unclean, and

since it is in the first remove of uncleanness, it certainly will
make the hands unclean.

Then the House of Hillel give their own reason: It is best to
wash the hands right before the beginning of the meal. C then
formulates the Hillelite opinion as a general rule.

בֵּית שַׁמַּאי אוֹמְרִין: מְקַנֵּחַ יָדוֹ בַּמַּפָּה וּמַנִּיחָהּ עַל
הַשֻּׁלְחָן, שֶׁמָּא נִטְמְאוּ מַשְׁקִין שֶׁבַּמַּפָּה מֵחֲמַת הַכֶּסֶת
וְיַחְזְרוּ וִיטַבְּלוּ אֶת הַיָּדַיִם.

5:27 (Lieberman, p. 30, ls. 61–65). A. The House of
Shammai say, "He dries his hand on the napkin and
leaves it on the table, lest the liquids which are in the
napkin be made unclean on account of the cushion, and
then go and make the hands unclean."

The Shammaites' reason for drying hands on the napkin and
then putting the napkin on the table is on account of the
liquid in the napkin. If the napkin is put on the cushion,
which is presumed unclean, then the liquid in the napkin will
be made unclean. It will be touched by the hands, and so make
them unclean.

בֵּית הִלֵּל אוֹמְרִין: סָפֵק מַשְׁקִין לַיָּדַיִם טָהוֹר.

B. And the House of Hillel say, "A doubt in regard to
the condition of liquids so far as the hands are concerned
is resolved as clean."

The answer of the House of Hillel is a good one. We do not
know for sure that the cushion is unclean. It is a matter of
doubt. So far as the hands are concerned, we resolve a matter of
doubt about the cleanness of liquids in favor of assuming they
are clean.

דָּבָר אַחֵר אֵין נְטִילַת יָדַיִם לְחוּלִּין.

C. "Another explanation: Washing the hands does not
pertain to unconsecrated food."

The Hillelites' second reason pulls the rug out from under the Shammaites. They say that if you are eating unconsecrated food, you do not have to wash your hands at all. That is to say, cultically unclean hands do not matter so far as ordinary food is concerned. They will of course make unfit food which derives from the priestly offerings—tithes, Heave-offerings. But they will not affect everyday, nonpriestly food at all. What this means is that the Hillelites have an entirely different picture of the requirements for eating ordinary food in a state of cultic purity.

אֶלָא מְקַנֵחַ יָדָיו בַּמַּפָּה וּמַנִּיחָהּ עַל הַכֶּסֶת, שֶׁמָּא
נִטְמְאוּ מַשְׁקִין שֶׁבַּמַּפָּה מֵחֲמַת הַשֻּׁלְחָן וְיַחְזְרוּ וִיטַמְּאוּ
אֶת הָאוֹכָלִים.

D. "But he dries his hands on the napkin and leaves it on the cushion, lest the liquids which are in the napkin be made unclean on account of the table, and they go and render the food unclean."

The Hillelites now give instructions about why the napkin is a matter of concern at all. The *table* is presumed unclean. The napkin should not be placed on it, for the liquids in the napkin may be made unclean by the table. They will then go and make the food unclean—in the first remove of uncleanness. In fact, this is a complicated "reason."

We have already reviewed the laws that underlie the rulings of the Houses. The Palestinian *Gemara* will explain that the Hillelites speak of a table which is *not* susceptible to uncleanness; therefore, there is no reason to be concerned about putting the napkin on the table. Then the House of Hillel add that one may place the napkin not only on the table but *also* on the cushion.

The further reason (C) of the Hillelites is that washing the hands, which, when unclean, cannot convey uncleanness *except* to Heave-offering, is not required for eating unconsecrated food at all.

Then D gives the Hillelites' rule for the matter. You put the napkin on the pillow—fully spelled out, "he dries . . . and leaves. . . ."

The meaning is that a person does what is comfortable. The custom was to lean on the cushion and to leave the napkin there, not on the table on which the food was laid out, on account of cleanliness. But in point of fact it would be legitimate to put the napkin on the table itself.

בֵּית שַׁמַּאי אוֹמְרִין: מְכַבְּדִין אֶת הַבַּיִת, מִפְּנֵי אוֹבְדָן
שֶׁל אוֹכָלִים, וְאַחַר כָּךְ נוֹטְלִין לַיָּדַיִם. בֵּית הִלֵּל
אוֹמְרִין: אִם הָיָה שַׁמָּשׁ תַּלְמִיד חָכָם מְלַקֵּט פְּרוּרִין
שֶׁיֵּשׁ בָּהֶן כַּזַּיִת. וְנוֹטְלִין לַיָּדַיִם וְאַחַר כָּךְ מְכַבְּדִין אֶת
הַבַּיִת.

5:28 (Lieberman, p. 30, ls. 65–68). A. The House of Shammai say, "They clean the house, on account of the waste of food, and afterward they wash the hands."

B. The House of Hillel say, "If the waiter was a disciple of a sage, he gathers the scraps which contain as much as an olive's bulk.

C. "And they wash the hands and afterward clean the house."

The custom was that, after the meal, but before saying the concluding Grace, the table would be removed and the floor swept. A person does not want to waste the scraps of food. Therefore, you sweep up before washing the hands for the second time, before the Grace after Meals, so that the spilled water will not spoil food which may have dropped to the floor. Then you wash the hands.

The Hillelites say the scraps which are susceptible to uncleanness (they are pieces as large as an olive, the quantity the rabbis consider to be food) will be picked up by the waiter before the washing, if he is a disciple of the sages, for he knows what to do. So one can wash up before sweeping.

Let us stand back and look at the law we have just learned. We are not going to be surprised by the problem of the order in which you sweep up and wash the hands at the end of the meal. We are already used to the query, Which comes first? And why? But who is this "disciple of the sages"? Why does he enter the discussion?

The "disciple of the sages" is a student who has attached himself to a rabbi. He does so because he wants to learn "Torah." But what sort of Torah is involved in serving food? The answer is, it indeed *is* a matter of Torah to learn how to eat a meal. That we know from the substance of the law, the detailed discussions of trivial things. Torah is not learned through the law, but through seeing the law embodied in the gestures and deeds of the living sages. They teach the law by what they do, not alone by what they say. The texts before us do not exhaust the laws they state—they merely hint at them. To apprehend the full weight and meaning of the law, we should need to enter into the household of a master and see just how he does things. We should have to imitate his gestures, not merely reduce them to legal formulae. For studying Torah is through service to the master; through that service one learns to imitate his ways. How, after all, is the master himself supposed within the Torah-myth to have learned what he now teaches if not through service to his master, and his to his, backward to Moses "our rabbi," who received the Torah and learned it from God himself? Imitating the master is imitating Moses' imitation of God.

But this disciple of the sages already knows the law. He is assumed not to be a child, a beginner. He has mastered the rules sufficiently so that he can be relied upon to know what to do with the scraps of food. He is a mature man, worthy of respect and honor. His "service" is not demeaning or degrading; he is not a slave, a major domo. He is an honored man; he brings honor upon himself by his discipleship of the sages. Not everyone is in his place. Only those who are worthy to imitate the master and learn the ways of Moses "our rabbi" may take up the burdens of service.

And, obviously, this Torah is something greater than the histories, laws, and prophecies of Scripture. Scripture says nothing about the conduct of a meal. The revelation of Moses does not include laws about sweeping up the house after a meal. Yet for the rabbis and disciples, how one sweeps the house indeed is a matter of Torah. Nor should Torah be understood only in such a public way, as a matter of communal ritual alone. We have a story about a disciple who hid under the master's bed at night. The disciple heard the master and his wife engaged in sexual intercourse. He was impressed by the enthusiasm of the couple and made a noise. The master looked under the bed and found the disciple. "What are you doing here?" he asked. The disciple answered, "Rabbi, it is a matter of Torah, and I need to learn." This is no exaggeration; rabbinic literature includes stories about how various great authorities engaged in sexual relations, and there are rules about the modesty, the delicacy, but also the vigor and enthusiasm, with which the sexual act is to be performed. People are encouraged to have sexual relations two or three or four times in succession; if they do, they will produce male children, which everyone wants. So "Torah" is not repression, but the liberation of the natural impulses. Law produces freedom, not bondage to the rule. The law gives life and form to the spirit.

Now when I observed that a man is what he does, not what he says, and that "Torah" subsumes all sorts of humble details of life, you probably did not guess the full weight of those words. But now it is clear that "Torah is a way of living" is no abstraction. It is no homily to claim that the rabbis regarded trivialities as part, as the very heart of Torah, God's revealed will. It is not because they were themselves small-minded, or because they had nothing better to do than investigate the reason behind, the logic for, niggling details. It is because to them "life" as an abstraction is nothing, but all the things that, together, add up the way of living—these are everything. Concrete details are not trivial because they are small. They are important because they relate to the whole pattern of conduct and of being, to reason and regulation. If Amos thought that the nation would fall because a shopkeeper cheated a customer, it was not because he claimed the petty thievery led inexorably to the decay of the public interest. He believed God wanted justice, a just society, and he knew these were not abstractions. What do you do to "do justice"? For the rabbis, too, the claims of Torah were important precisely because they extended to the humble things which one actually can control.

I am not going to apologize, therefore, for the "logic-chopping" of the rabbis. That is not what is involved when we wonder, Which comes first, the washing or the sweeping? Nor is it the ultimate issue in what is to follow: In which hand do you hold the cup of wine, in which the sweet oil for the *Havdalah?* If we asked, How do I approach almighty God? What shall I take with me before the throne of his presence?—if we asked such questions, who would call the answers trivial? But who could hear and do those answers, if they were *not* trivial? Tell me to come with clean hands and a pure heart, and I shall not know exactly what I am supposed to do next. But tell me to hold the wine in the right hand, the oil in the left—that is something I can do. And, in doing it, I shall know there are rules for guidance, and these rules stand for reverence and awe, for mindfulness and thoughtfulness, in God's presence. You may ask, What difference do these particular rules make? Why not some other ones? To that there is no ready answer, nor should there be. It is Torah, and I need to learn it. For why should I not learn what Moses "our rabbi" has taught my master? The details—sweep, wash, right hand, left hand— these make sense and become vivid only within the rabbinic Torah-myth, and even there the sense is not spelled out. But the meaning of *having* such details—this I think speaks of something beyond the myth. And the modes of argument about establishing the specifics mean a great deal indeed.

בֵּית שַׁמַּאי אוֹמְרִין: אוֹחֵז כּוֹס יַיִן בִּימִינוֹ וְשֶׁמֶן עָרֵב בִּשְׂמֹאלוֹ, מְבָרֵךְ עַל הַיַּיִן וְאַחַר כָּךְ מְבָרֵךְ עַל הַשֶּׁמֶן.

וּבֵית הַלֵּל אוֹמְרִין: אוֹחֵז שֶׁמֶן עָרֵב בִּימִינוֹ וְכוֹס יַיִן
בִּשְׂמֹאלוֹ, מְבָרֵךְ עַל הַשֶּׁמֶן וְטָחוֹ בְּרֹאשׁ הַשַּׁמָּשׁ. אִם
הָיָה שַׁמָּשׁ תַּלְמִיד חָכָם (מְלַקֵּט פֵּירוּרִין) טָחוֹ בַּכּוֹתֶל,
לְפִי שֶׁאֵין שֶׁבַח תַּלְמִיד חָכָם שֶׁיֵּצֵא מְבוּסָּם.

5:29 (Lieberman, p. 30, ls. 68–72). A. The House of
Shammai say, "He holds the cup of wine in his right
hand and spiced oil in his left hand."

"He blesses over the wine and afterward blesses over
the oil."

B. And the House of Hillel say, "He holds the sweet
oil in his right hand and the cup of wine in his left hand."

C. He blesses over the oil and smears it on the head of
the waiter. If the waiter was a disciple of a sage, he [the
diner] smears it on the wall, because it is not praise-
worthy for a disciple of a sage to go forth perfumed.

We have come to the end of the banquet. One has to recite
the blessing over the wine before saying the final Grace. At the
same time, sweet oil has been served to cleanse the hands and
remove the odor of food. The House of Shammai say the wine
takes precedence—therefore is held in the right hand and
blessed first. The House of Hillel say the sweet oil takes precedence. Then, in C, we are told how one gets rid of the excess of
oil, so that the hands will not continue to smell of it. For this
purpose the waiter serves—or the wall!

But we shall see that the Gemara has things reversed, with
each House holding the opinion here attributed to the opposite
one. And, even more striking, in the Mishnah this is not listed
as one of the disputes between the Houses concerning the meal,
though it is more pertinent to "the meal" than some items in
the Mishnah's list. Lieberman holds that the case before us
concerns wine and oil which are brought after the final washing of hands; the case therefore falls after the meal, not during
it. We therefore have a reference not to the cup of wine to be
blessed before reciting the Grace.

The blessing for the oil is, "Blessed are you, Lord our God, who creates sweet oil," or ". . . who put a good scent into sweet oil."

אָמַר רַבִּי יְהוּדָה: לֹא נֶחְלְקוּ בֵית שַׁמַּיי וּבֵית הִלֵּל עַל בִּרְכַּת הַמָּזוֹן שֶׁהִיא בַתְּחִלָּה וְעַל הַבְדָּלָה שֶׁהִיא בַסּוֹף, עַל מָה נֶחְלְקוּ? עַל הַמָּאוֹר וְעַל הַבְּשָׂמִים, שֶׁבֵּית שַׁמַּיי אוֹמֵר: מָאוֹר וְאַחַר כָּךְ בְּשָׂמִים, וּבֵית הִלֵּל אוֹמֵר: בְּשָׂמִים וְאַחַר כָּךְ מָאוֹר.

5:30 (Lieberman, pp. 30–31, ls. 72–75). A. R. Judah said, "The House of Shammai and the House of Hillel did not dispute concerning the blessing of the food, that it is first, or concerning the *Havdalah,* that it is at the end.

"Concerning what did they dispute?

"Concerning the light and the spices, for—

"The House of Shammai say, 'Light and afterward spices.'

"And the House of Hillel say, 'Spices and afterward light.'"

הַנִּכְנָס לְתוֹךְ בֵּיתוֹ בְּמוֹצָאֵי שַׁבָּת, מְבָרֵךְ עַל הַיַּיִן וְעַל הַמָּאוֹר וְעַל הַבְּשָׂמִים, וְאוֹמֵר הַבְדָּלָה. וְאִם אֵין לוֹ אֶלָּא כּוֹס אֶחָד מַנִּיחוֹ לְאַחַר הַמָּזוֹן וּמְשַׁלְשְׁלָן כּוּלָּן אַחֲרָיו.

5:30 (Lieberman, p. 31, ls. 75–77). B. He who enters his home at the end of the Sabbath blesses the wine, the light, the spices, and then says *Havdalah.*

C. And if he has only one cup [of wine] he leaves it for after the meal and then says all [the liturgies] in order after [reciting the blessing for] it.

A gives us the authority for the Mishnah as we have it: Judah [b. Ilai]. He says the only difference between the Houses is about the middle items, light and spices. Grace comes first,

Havdalah last. Judah's saying occurs in the Palestinian *Gemara* as "spices and light" for the Shammaites, "light and spices" for the Hillelites. The Babylonian *Gemara* gives Judah's saying as we have it. Therefore, the Tosefta may have been corrected in the Babylonian schools to conform to their tradition of Judah's saying.

Note, however, that the next paragraph follows the Shammaite ruling before us: *light, then spices;* so the anonymous rule is phrased against the Hillelites' opinion; the law—which is decided by attribution to the anonymous party—follows the House of Shammai here. Consistent with its own view, the Palestinian *Gemara* states that the Babylonian master, Rav, held the law is that one says the blessing for the spices, then for the light—the Hillelite position before us.

The man says the blessing for spices whenever he smells them, but light is blessed only at the end of the Sabbath. Therefore, "spices are continual," light is not, for it is blessed only in connection with the Sabbath. Accordingly, the reasoning of the Hillelites in 5:25—wine is perpetual—leads to the same conclusion here: spices, then light.

As it stands, C means that if a person has only one cup of wine, he may eat before *Havdalah,* then bless the cup of wine in connection with *Havdalah.* He says the prayers in the order already given: blessing for the wine, then Grace after Meals, spices, light, *Havdalah.* But C certainly recalls Mishnah 8:8's strange superscription, as we shall see when we compare the Mishnaic and Toseftan materials.

Let us return to Judah's saying. Judah b. Ilai was a master in the circle of Tannaitic authorities assembled in the Galilean town of Usha at the end of the Bar Kokhba War, after A.D. 135. How he knew what the Houses had disputed about and what their opinions were is not our problem. What is important for us is that he alleged the Houses did *not* dispute about certain matters. This must mean someone else said they did.

So Judah knew a version of the dispute something like the following:

The House of Shammai say, "(1) *Havdalah,* (2) light, (3) spices, and (4) food." And the House of Hillel say, "(4) food, (3) spices, (2) light, and (1) *Havdalah.*"

That is, Judah knew a version of the dispute which included disagreements on all items, 1 and 4 as well as 2 and 3. He then said the Houses agreed on those broad issues as are represented in 1 and 4, but differed only on the narrow questions presented by 2 and 3.

This revision is a commonplace trait of the post–Bar Kokhba (A.D. 140–170) commentators on traditions of the pre–Bar Kokhba (A.D. 70–135) generations of authorities. They will tend to narrow the range of disagreements between the Houses or other earlier authorities and to claim that the differences were on ever more refined points of law than those suggested in the original traditions. Whether the alternative tradition was prior to Judah's or was simply an alternative brought up in his own generation is difficult to say. But in other instances of the same phenomenon, it is demonstrably earlier, and so it is likely here that Judah's version also is later than the one which has differences on the order of all four items.

The fact that Judah refers to the Houses' tradition suggests a further point. The fixed form in which the Houses' materials are given—Statement of law, House of Shammai say (not, *said*) . . . , House of Hillel say . . . —that fixed form cannot come later than ca. A.D. 140. In fact, it is very well attested by earlier masters as well, backward nearly to the destruction of the Second Temple, shortly after 70, for we have sayings about disputes between the Houses, such as Judah's, attributed to masters who lived between 70 and 100. These sayings stand outside of a dispute between the Houses and comment on that dispute in full knowledge of what is alleged about the Houses' opinions. Such a saying thus attests to the existence of the form and substance of the dispute between the Houses. It is one important way of tracing the history of laws over the one hundred thirty years of development from the beginnings of

the rabbinical movement, after the destruction of the Second
Temple in 70, to the completion of the Mishnah and its
accompanying Tosefta ca. 200.

הָיָה לוֹ נֵר טָמוּן בְּתוֹךְ חֵיקוֹ, אוֹ בְּתוֹךְ הַפָּנָס, רוֹאֶה
אֶת הַשַּׁלְהֶבֶת וְאֵין מִשְׁתַּמֵּשׁ לְאוֹרָה, מִשְׁתַּמֵּשׁ לְאוֹרָה
וְאֵין רוֹאֶה אֶת הַשַּׁלְהֶבֶת, אֵין מְבָרֵךְ עַד שֶׁיִּהְיֶה רוֹאֶה
אֶת הַשַּׁלְהֶבֶת וּמִשְׁתַּמֵּשׁ לְאוֹרָה. עֲשָׂשִׂית אַף עַל פִּי
שֶׁלֹּא כָבְתָה מְבָרֵךְ עָלֶיהָ. נֵר שֶׁל גּוֹיִם אֵין מְבָרְכִין
עָלָיו. יִשְׂרָאֵל שֶׁהִדְלִיק מִגּוֹי, וְגוֹי שֶׁהִדְלִיק מִיִּשְׂרָאֵל,
מְבָרֵךְ עָלָיו.

5:31 (Lieberman, p. 31, ls. 81–85). A. If a person has a
light covered in the folds of his garment or in a lamp,
and sees the flame but does not use its light, or uses its
light but does not see its flame, he does not bless [that
light]. [He says a blessing over the light only] when he
both sees the flame and uses its light.

As to a lantern—even though he had not extinguished
it (that is, it has been burning throughout the Sabbath),
he recites a blessing over it.

B. They do not bless over the light of gentiles. One
may bless over [the flame of] an Israelite kindled from a
gentile, or a gentile who kindled from an Israelite.

The Mishnah requires actual use of the light before one may
say the blessing for it. Now, in A, the Tosefta introduces the
distinction between the illumination of a light and the actual
flame. A person must see both the illumination and the actual
source of the illumination, the flame. A flame covered in a
lantern or seen through a mirror is not available for the blessing. We therefore have three situations: (1) a light in a lantern,
which produces heat but not light; (2) a light you can see but
not make use of, because of distance; and (3) a light the illumination of which you can use, but which you cannot see.

B rules that a man may not bless a light of a gentile, for the
light will not have enjoyed "Sabbath-rest" in the gentile's care.

"Enjoying Sabbath-rest" here means that the light has been used in such a way as to violate the Sabbath. For instance, you are not allowed to kindle a flame on the Sabbath. But this light has been lit on the holy day. So it has not "rested" on the Sabbath. The Sabbath rules must be kept by the Israelite in such a way that, even indirectly, he does not collaborate in their violation. Using the gentile's flame, even though the Israelite did not participate in lighting it, would be a subterfuge to violate the Sabbath.

But you may bless a light kindled by an Israelite from that light. This tradition will be closely examined in the *Gemara*.

בְּבֵית הַמִּדְרָשׁ בֵּית שַׁמַּיי אוֹמֵר: אֶחָד מְבָרֵךְ לְכוּלָן.
וּבֵית הִלֵּל אוֹמֵר: כָּל אֶחָד וְאֶחָד מְבָרֵךְ לְעַצְמוֹ.

5:32 (Lieberman, p. 31, ls. 80–81). In the house of study—

The House of Shammai say, "One [person] blesses for all of them."

And the House of Hillel say, "Each one blesses for himself."

The Babylonian *Gemara*'s version has the opinions reversed. The House of Shammai say each blesses for himself. The House of Hillel say one person does it for all. The bases for the respective positions are given there. The reason each blesses for himself is to avoid a suspension of public study, thus to prevent a waste of time which is to be spent in the study of the Torah. All bless together because it is greater honor to God for a whole congregation to participate in the blessing than for an isolated individual to do so. But we are not told what blessing is being said: in context, it is the *Havdalah* blessing.

The Hebrew reveals a mnemonic pattern:

House of Shammai: 'HD[1] [MBRK] LKWLN[2] (thus: KL)

House of Hillel: KL[2] 'HD[1] (W'HD) [MBRK L'SMW]

The key words therefore are 'HD and KL. In the first saying

the word order is 1, 2, and in the second, 2, 1. So, as earlier, differences in word order will yield the dispute.

The Tosefta and the Mishnah

The relationships between the two compilations of traditions, one produced in the first- and second-century Palestinian rabbinical academies, the other in the third and fourth centuries, are complex. Here we shall see two quite different types of relationship.

In the first, covering the laws dealing with the Houses, the Tosefta seems to be a commentary on, and expansion of, the Mishnah. It gives the reasons for the positions taken by the respective Houses.

In the second, covering the anonymous laws, the Tosefta gives rules which are in substance the same as the Mishnah's, but it gives those rules in very different language, generally greatly expanded and more generalized than the Mishnah's very brief statements. Here it looks as though the Tosefta's lengthy sayings have been summarized by the Mishnah's. Alternatively, we have two autonomous versions, or, third, the authors of the Tosefta amplify and so explain the Mishnah's statements. I incline to the third explanation.

The *Gemara* will combine the two sets of traditions and discuss their contents. But it takes for granted that the whole is a seamless fabric of law. It is not going to perceive that the relationships between the traditions and the ways in which they are formulated pose problems for literary analysis. We shall now review the Mishnah and compare the Tosefta's materials pertinent to it. The Tosefta's additions to the Mishnah's language are given in italics.

MISHNAH	TOSEFTA
M. 8:1.A. These are the things which are between the House of Shammai and the House of Hillel in [regard to] the meal:	Tos. 5:25. [The] things which are between the House of Shammai and the House of Hillel [as regards] the meal:

MISHNAH

TOSEFTA

B. The House of Shammai say, "One blesses the day, and afterward one blesses over the wine."

The House of Shammai say, "One blesses the day, and afterward one blesses over the wine, *for the day causes the wine to come, and the day is already sanctified, but the wine has not yet come.*"

And the House of Hillel say, "One blesses the wine, and afterward one blesses over the day."

And the House of Hillel say, "One blesses over the wine, and afterward one blesses the day, *for the wine causes the Sanctification of the day to be said.*"

"Another matter: The blessing of the wine is continual, and the blessing of the day is not continual."

And the law is according to the words of the House of Hillel.

M. 8:2.A. The House of Shammai say, "They wash the hands and afterward mix the cup."

Tos. 5:26. The House of Shammai say, "They wash the hands and afterward mix the cup, *lest the liquids which are on the outer surfaces of the cup may be made unclean on account of the hands, and they may go back and make the cup unclean.*"

And the House of Hillel say, "They mix the cup and afterward wash the hands."

The House of Hillel say, *"The outer surfaces of the cup are perpetually unclean.*

"Another matter: The washing of the hands is only [done] near [at the outset of] the meal.

"They mix the cup and afterward wash the hands."

8:3.A. The House of Shammai say, "He dries his hands on the napkin and lays it on the table."

5:27. The House of Shammai say, "He dries his hand on the napkin and lays it on the table,

MISHNAH

And the House of Hillel say, "On the cushion."

TOSEFTA

lest the liquids which are in the napkin may be made unclean on account of the pillow, and they may go and make the hands unclean.

The House of Hillel say, "*A doubt in regard to the condition of liquids so far as the hands are concerned is clean.*

"*Another matter: Washing the hands does not pertain to unconsecrated food. But he dries his hands on the napkin and leaves it on the cushion lest the liquids which are in the pillow may be made unclean on account of the table, and they may go and render the food unclean.*"

M. 8:4.A. The House of Shammai say, "They clean the house and afterward wash the hands."

And the House of Hillel say, "They wash the hands and afterward clean the house."

Tos. 5:28. The House of Shammai say, "They clean the house *on account of the waste of food,* and afterward wash the hands."

The House of Hillel say, "*If the waiter was a disciple of a sage, he gathers the scraps which contain as much as an olive's bulk.*

"They wash the hands and afterward clean the house."

8:5.A. The House of Shammai say, "Light, and food, and spices, and *Havdalah.*"

And the House of Hillel say, "Light, and spices, and food, and *Havdalah.*"

5:30. R. Judah said, "*The House of Shammai and the House of Hillel did not dispute concerning the blessing of the food, that it is first, and concerning the* Havdalah *that it is the end. Concerning what did they dispute? Concerning the light and the spices, for* the House of Shammai say,

MISHNAH	TOSEFTA
	'Light and *afterward* spices,' and the House of Hillel say, 'Spices and *afterward* light.' "
B. The House of Shammai say, " 'Who created the light of the fire.' " And the House of Hillel say, " 'Who creates the lights of the fire.' "	[No equivalent.]

The relationships between the Mishnaic and the Toseftan versions of the Houses' disputes are fairly clear. The Tosefta tends to expand the Mishnah's terse laws. These expansions serve to explain and so comment upon the Mishnah. In the first instance, Mishnah 8:1/Tosefta 5:25, the expansion takes the form of an addition to the Mishnah. In the second, Mishnah 8:2/Tosefta 5:26, the Tosefta adds a reason to the Shammaite rule, but then provides the Hillelites with an "introduction" to their opinion, which comes only at the end. This tendency is even more pronounced in the next example, 8:3/5:27, in which the Hillelites have a considerable speech, and the Mishnah's elliptical *on the cushion* is set into a complete sentence, which itself is part of a larger explanation. Here we should be hard put to argue that Tosefta has simply expanded Mishnah's Hillelite saying. It has given them a wholly new saying.

The simpler pattern of 8:2/5:26 recurs in 8:4/5:28, where, before the Hillelites' actual opinion, we are told what to do with the scraps of food. But this is irrelevant to the issue addressed by the House of Shammai, and the Shammaites themselves say only what is already in the Mishnah. So this must be classified as an interpolation of entirely new material, not as a gloss of existing sayings.

There is no close correlation between the ruling of Mishnah 8:5A and Judah's saying in Tosefta 5:30. Rather, we have in the Mishnah what is implied by Judah's saying in Tosefta; but Judah's reformulation, naming only items 2 and 3, is not the language of the Mishnah, which gives all four items. There is no Toseftan equivalent to 8:5B, although some pertinent materials do occur.

The construction of the brief formulaic sayings of Mishnah 8:1-5 is to be credited to Judah the Patriarch. He has stressed the simplest possible formulation. The Tosefta constitutes not another version, but a highly glossed copy of the original, with many interpolations. Thus the Hillelite saying supplies reasons for, and only then gives the equivalent of, the Shammaites' primary formula. In 5:26 the Hillelites do not even have such an equivalent. In 5:27 the Hillelites' view is taken for granted, then explained. In 5:28 the waiter-element has no Shammaite counterpart. So Tosefta presupposes and depends upon knowledge of the Mishnah and looks like a commentary on it, with glosses as needed.

MISHNAH	TOSEFTA
M. 8:8.A. Wine came to them after the meal, and there is there only that cup—	Tos. 5:30 (Lieberman, p. 31, ls. 75-77). A. *He who enters his home at the end of the Sabbath blesses over the wine, the light, the spices, and then says* Havdalah.
B. The House of Shammai say, "He blesses over the wine and afterward he blesses over the food."	
And the House of Hillel say, "He blesses over the food and afterward he blesses over the wine."	B. *And if he has only one cup* [of wine], *he leaves it for after the meal and then says them all in order after* [blessing] *it.*

There is no clear relationship between Mishnah 8:8A and Tosefta 5:30B. But Tosefta 5:30B *may* represent a simple, undisputed statement of the position of the House of Shammai in Mishnah 8:8A:

MISHNAH	TOSEFTA
[If wine came to them after the meal and] there is there only that cup	If he has only one cup [of wine]

Mishnah	Tosefta
House of Shammai say,	[he leaves it for after the meal and
"He blesses the wine and then the	then says them all in order, thus:]
food."	Wine, then food.
(House of Hillel say,	
"He blesses the food and then the	
wine.")	

We see that the net result of the Shammaite position is as is given in Tosefta: The wine is kept for the end of the meal, then blessed in advance of the Grace after Meals, as is normally the case. The Hillelite view then is not pertinent to Tosefta 5:30B.

Mishnah	Tosefta
M. 8:6.A. They do not bless the	Tos. 5:31.B. They do not bless
light or the spices of gentiles, nor	the light of gentiles. *An Israelite*
the light or the spices of the dead,	*who kindled* [a flame] *from a*
nor the light or the spices which	*gentile, or a gentile who kindled*
are before an idol.	*from an Israelite—one may bless*
B. And they do not bless the	[such a flame].
light until they make use of its	Tos. 5:31 (Lieberman, p. 31, ls.
illumination.	81–85). A. *If a person has a light*
	covered in the folds of his gar-
	ment or in a lamp, and he sees
	the flame but does not use its
	light, or uses its light but does
	not see its flame, he does not
	bless. [He blesses only] *when he*
	both sees the flame and uses its
	light.

Now Mishnah and Tosefta represent separate and independent statements of substantially the same law. Mishnah 8:6A speaks of spices, the dead, and idolatry, considerations all absent in Tosefta 5:31A, which speaks only of light and of gentiles. But Tosefta then introduces a new problem, one which will be important in the *Gemara*: What of light transferred from a gentile's flame to one held by an Israelite, or vice versa. The transfer of flame from a gentile to another gentile is not discussed here; it will occur in the *Gemara*. Similarly, Mishnah 8:6B states simply that one has to use the light of the lamp before blessing it. Tosefta 5:31B deals with various problems which that simple rule is going to raise in detailed application. Tosefta cites and glosses Mishnah.

MISHNAH	TOSEFTA
M. 8:8.C. They respond *Amen* after an Israelite who blesses, and they do not respond *Amen* after a Samaritan who blesses, until one hears the entire blessing.	Tos. 5:21 (Lieberman, p. 28, ls. 41–2). *They answer* "Amen" *after a blessing with the divine name recited by a gentile.*
	They do not answer *Amen* after a Samaritan who blesses *with the divine name* until they hear the entire blessing.

Here the correlation is close, but curiously different. Mishnah 8:8C speaks of an Israelite and a Samaritan; the Israelite rule is superfluous. Clearly, if you are going to say *Amen* at all, it is going to be after an Israelite's blessing! Tos. 5:21 introduces the gentile, and that rule is by no means superfluous. Both compilations agree about the Samaritan, but to the Mishnah the problem of the gentile is unknown.

Clearly, both the Mishnah and the Tosefta leave room for elaboration. Simple rules, when applied in practice, raise complicated questions. New conditions of life—for instance, what if you do not have any wine?—will produce still others. Furthermore, as is already obvious, not all of the sayings and rules produced by the authorities in the Mishnah and Tosefta are included in those compilations. Moreover, some rules come down in more than one version. In a few instances the positions of the Houses or other masters are entirely reversed. A still further tendency is pseudepigraphically to create in the names of the early authorities rules and sayings which follow, or might follow, from things they actually did say. These sayings have to be harmonized with those in the Mishnah and the Tosefta; or the position taken by the earlier authorities has to be enlarged to make room for them. This may be done, for instance, by making distinctions among cases so that what seem to be conflicting opinions are shown to refer to differing circumstances. The post-Mishnaic authorities themselves formulated opinions, decided cases to which the former rules did not closely apply, and otherwise participated in the development of pertinent laws. So commentary—the *Gemara*—built in the first instance on the basis of the union of the Mishnah and the Tosefta and the analysis of the correlative traditions of each, is going to proliferate, both as studies continue and as new problems arise.

When people speak of "the Talmud," they normally mean the Babylonian ("Bavli") Talmud, consisting, as we now know, of the Palestinian Mishnah and the *Gemara* produced in the Babylonian rabbinical institutions—courts which served as schools for apprentice lawyers. But we start with the first of the two Talmuds, the Talmud of the Land of Israel. Also called the Palestinian Talmud ("Yerushalmi," or Jerusalemite), it consists of the Palestinian Mishnah and the *Gemara* produced in the rabbinical institutions of Caesarea, Tiberias, and other centers in Palestine.

CHAPTER 4

The Palestinian Talmud

The Palestinian Talmud—composed of the Mishnah and the *Gemara* produced in the third-, fourth-, and early fifth-century Palestinian academies, chiefly at Tiberias, Caesarea, and Sepphoris—in general did not enjoy the benefit of the sophisticated editing and critical development evident in the Babylonian one. It contains full *Gemara* for the first Order, Seeds (*Zera'im*), because the agricultural laws were applied to the Holy Land long after the destruction of the Temple, and for tractate *Sheqalim* (the *Sheqel* offering for the Temple), both of which are absent in the Babylonian Talmud. But it lacks Talmud for the whole fifth and sixth Orders, Holy Things (*Qodashim*) and purities (*Toharot*), and is slight for the fourth, Damages (*Neziqin*). Only the beginning of the tractate, in Purities, on Menstrual Women (*Niddah*), is available. Allusions in medieval commentaries to the Palestinian Talmud suggest that *Gemara* for other tractates then was available. The process of disappearance continued even into early modern times; we have a fourteenth-century reference to a Palestinian *Gemara* for *Avot* (The Fathers), and a sixteenth-century one to *Gemara* for *Makkot*, chapter three, while we now have it only for the first two chapters. In all, we have *Gemara* for thirty-nine tractates, but for each tractate it is considerably briefer than the Babylonian equivalent; in quantity, the Babylonian Talmud, as we shall see in our next chapter, is much larger than the Palestinian one.

What makes the Talmud of the Land of Israel still more challenging is that it has been intensively studied only in our own day. Earlier generations neglected it. The Babylonian Talmud is encyclopedic and serves as the principal source of authoritative law and theology; the Palestinian one was decidedly subordinate. So interest focused upon the larger and more comprehensive document. The Babylonian Talmud attracted the best commentators, the most intelligent and comprehensive interpreters. In many ways, therefore, we deal with a document neglected and ignored, so fresh and novel for our own day's eyes.

The Document

To what shall we compare the labor of opening this difficult and arcane text? And how shall we see ourselves?

Imagine for the moment that a hillside cave in Galilee, carved open to the light for the first time in millennia, yielded a vast library of hitherto unknown writings of ancient Judaism. Pot after pot of documents on blackened leather came forth. Once deciphered and published—a labor of many years—these leather pages turned out to discuss a known document, but to say quite new things about it, to speak in an unfamiliar idiom about already established rules. Consider in your mind's eye the sensation such a discovery would cause, the scholarly lives and energies that would flow to the new find and its explication. Converging interests in not merely philology and history, but also the study of religions and the analysis of the roots of Western culture would contrive to make the new Galilean library a centerpiece of scholarly discourse for many decades. To call the contents of that hillside cave a revolution, to compare them to the finds at Qumran, at the Dead Sea, or at Nag Hammadi, or to any of the other great contemporary discoveries out of ancient times, would hardly be deemed an exaggeration.

The Yerushalmi is such a library. Comprising thirty-nine tractates, it fills many hundreds of pages of barely intelligible writing. Famous for its incomprehensibility, the document has come before the scholarly public in bits and pieces, odd pages snatched from an otherwise inaccessible storage room. A paragraph here, a sentence there—these have been made to serve as representations of this odd and difficult work. The result is that the Yerushalmi as a whole, with its remarkably coherent and systematic statement, has yet to win sustained attention. Its testimony to the world view and way of life of the people who made it up has gone unnoticed. The few Talmudists who took an interest sedulously protected their monopoly of knowledge, declaring all outsiders unclean for entry into the sanctum of learning. Accordingly, with the completion of the first full translation of the Yerushalmi as a whole into a Western language, which I have accomplished, the Yerushalmi comes forth for the first time to the light of day to be viewed whole and complete by the generality of learned people. While, as I said, a handful of Talmudists have long had access to bits and pieces, they mined underground, alone, in deep and barely accessible passages. They traded in a mysterious, closed market whatever nuggets they retrieved. Few in any case spent much time in the depths of the Yerushalmi. With the breaking open of a strip mine, however imperfect for the moment, the whole vein for the first time is open to the light for all to see and plunder in the name of learning.

The Historical Setting

The Judaism to which the Talmud of the Land of Israel gives testimony forms one plank in the bridge that leads from antiquity to the beginning of the Middle Ages, from the Middle East to Europe, from the end of the classical age to the nascent moment of our own time and place. The Mishnah, ca. A.D. 200, describes a neat and orderly world, in which Israelite society is neatly divided among its castes, arranged in priority around the center that is the Temple, systematically engaged in a life of sanctification remote from the disorderly events of the day. The Talmud, ca. A.D. 400, portrays the chaos of Jews living among gentiles, governed by a diversity of authorities, lacking all order and arrangement, awaiting a time of salvation for which, through sanctification, they make themselves ready. The Mishnah's Israel in imagination is governed by an Israelite king, high priest, and sanhedrin. The Talmud's Jews lived both under rabbis near at hand, who settle everyday disputes of streets and households, and also distant archons of a nameless state, to be manipulated and placated on earth as in heaven. The Mishnah's Judaism breathes the pure air of public piazza and stoa, the Talmud's, the ripe stench of private alleyway and courtyard. The image of the Mishnah's Judaism is evoked by the majestic Parthenon, perfect in all its proportions, conceived in a single moment of pure rationality. The Talmud's Judaism is a scarcely choate cathedral in process, the labor of many generations, each of its parts the conception of diverse moments of devotion, all of them the culmination of an ongoing and evolving process of revelation in the here and now.

The Mishnah is Judaism's counterpart to Plato's *Republic* and Aristotle's *Politics,* a noble theory of it all. When we study the Mishnah, we contemplate a fine conception of nowhere in particular, addressed to whom it may concern. When we turn to the Talmud, we see a familiar world, as we have known it from the Talmud's day to our own. We perceive something of our own day as we who study Judaism recognize continuity with those times. So the Mishnah marks the end of the ancient and Near Eastern, the Talmud the beginning of the modern and the Western (as well as the Near Eastern) epoch in the history of Judaism. That is why the Talmud of the Land of Israel deserves attention, in the setting not only of the history of Judaism but also of the formation of the civilization of the West in the period, ca. 200 to 400, to which this Talmud attests.

The period is marked off, at the beginning, by the completion of the Mishnah, ca. A.D. 200, and, at the end, by the closure of the Talmud of the Land of Israel, ca. A.D. 400. These tumultuous centuries witnessed the transition from late antiquity to earlier medieval times. The Roman Empire became two, dividing east from west, turned from pagan to Christian, the mode of being we know as classical to the one we identify as medieval. The birth of this Talmud thus forms a chapter in the history of the movement of the West from its Greek, Roman, and Israelite beginnings to its full expression in Christianity for the generality of Europe; (later on) in Islam, for Africa and Asia; and in Judaism, for the margins of both worlds. True, the birth of Judaism in context fills little more than a paragraph out of the long chapter of the movement from classical to medieval civilization, both east and west. But in the end it may prove a suggestive chapter, exemplifying in its accessibility much that may otherwise lie beyond our capacity for detailed description and explanation. In what is small we may discern large things, in detail, the configuration of the whole.

Let us now come to define what changes, what marks the turning of the way. It is evoked, in literary terms, in the transition from the Mishnah to the Talmud of the Land of Israel. As I said, from the strict and formal classicism of the Mishnah, like Plato's *Republic* describing for no one in particular an ideal society never, in its day, to be seen, the Judaism described by the Talmud of the Land of Israel turned to the disorderly detail of the workaday world, taking the utopian Mishnah along. If Aristotle's *Politics* had been written as a gloss to Plato's *Republic,* amplifying and extending piece by piece the once whole but no longer coherent writing of Plato, we should have a rough analogy to what the Talmud does with the Mishnah of Judah the Patriarch (henceforward: Rabbi). If, further, many philosophers took up the fantastic account of the *Republic* and out of its materials and other writings worked out new *Republics,* bringing diversity to what had been a single conception and book, we should find a possible precedent for what happened from 200 to 400 in the move, in Judaism, from the ancient to the medieval mode: theoretical to practical, monothetic to polythetic, uniform to diverse, coherent to chaotic, and systemic to traditional.

The second century yielded a single document of Judaism,

the Mishnah. The dawn of the fifth century witnessed the beginnings and formation of many and the completion of one, this Talmud. For by that time, the Talmud of the Land of Israel, a vast amplification of the Mishnah, neared closure. Tosefta, a supplement to the Mishnah's materials in the Mishnah's own idiom and structure, was taking shape. Sifra, a compilation of exegeses pertinent to Leviticus, with special interest in the relationship of the Mishnah's laws to those of Leviticus, would soon follow. In the hundred years beyond the closure of the Yerushalmi a quite different mode of collection and organization of sayings, represented by the compilations of exegetical remarks on Genesis and Leviticus called Genesis Rabbah and Leviticus Rabbah, would come to full expression. Nor may we silently pass by the other Talmud, the one created in Babylonia, generally thought to have come to its final condition in the two centuries after the Yerushalmi's closure. Accordingly, the Mishnah, a single document, stands at the head of many paths. Numerous roads lead forward, out of the Mishnah. None lead backward from it, except the leap from the Mishnah to Sinai, accomplished through promiscuous citing of proof-texts of Scripture. Among these paths onward from the Mishnah, the Palestinian and the Babylonian Talmuds mark the principal way forward.

Partial Testimony to a Complete System

The Talmud of the Land of Israel testifies to the existence of a coherent world view and way of life embodied in a distinct and distinctive society, that of the rabbis—masters and disciples—of the third and fourth century in the Land of Israel. Before us in the Yerushalmi is not a complete system of Judaism, contained in a single document. The Yerushalmi is not like the Mishnah, which provides a full and exhaustive account of its system and its viewpoint. Whatever we know about the Mishnah's system is in that book itself. The Judaism to which the Yerushalmi testifies defines the matrix in which, among other documents, the Yerushalmi came into being. But the Yerushalmi does not constitute the sole important corpus of evidence about that kind of Judaism. Nor is there a single document that expresses that whole.

In this regard, as in many other ways, the Yerushalmi and the Mishnah are really not comparable with one another. The Yerushalmi is continuous with the Mishnah. But the character of the document, therefore also the world to which its evidence pertains, presents us with a mirror image of the Mishnah. The first and most important difference, as I said, is simply that the Mishnah, brought to closure ca. 200, constitutes the only document deriving from the period in which it took shape. By contrast, materials of the Yerushalmi often intersect with materials in other documents, such as Tosefta and the Babylonian Talmud. For the Mishnah, the sole point of intersection is with the Tosefta, but that compilation is demonstrably later than the Mishnah and dependent upon it for structure, for organization, for style, and for subject matter. Accordingly, the Judaism in the Talmud of the Land of Israel is not the Judaism *only* of that book, in the same way in which the Judaism to which the Mishnah testifies is, expressed within the Mishnah, whole and complete.

While the Mishnah exhaustively answers any and all questions about its Judaism, the Yerushalmi, answering many questions about its Judaism represented in its pages, is by no means the sole source of answers. Numerous questions dealt with by the Judaism to which Yerushalmi attests are answered— in the same or similar ways—in other documents altogether. The evidence of the Yerushalmi about the Judaism attested in its pages must be described in a way quite different from the way in which we lay out evidence of the Mishnah about the Judaism expressed within the Mishnah. So the one gives evidence of a world beyond itself, a world of which it is an important component. The other gives evidence only about itself and the world view contemplated within its words.

The Text

As it happens, the Palestinian *Gemara* for our chapter is no less interesting than the Babylonian: some of the early discussions, indeed, are better balanced and more elegant than anything we shall see in the next chapter.

The Palestinian Talmud is divided according to the divisions of the Mishnah. The several sections, therefore, are numbered not by page but by Mishnah. The Mishnah is in boldfaced type; Aramaic passages are in italics.

אֵלּוּ דְבָרִים שֶׁבֵּין בֵּית שַׁמַּאי וּבֵית הַלֵּל בַּסְּעוּדָה. בֵּית שַׁמַּאי אוֹמְרִים: מְבָרֵךְ עַל הַיּוֹם וְאַחַר כָּךְ מְבָרֵךְ עַל הַיַּיִן וּבֵית הַלֵּל אוֹמְרִים: מְבָרֵךְ עַל הַיַּיִן וְאַחַר כָּךְ מְבָרֵךְ עַל הַיּוֹם:

גמ' מָה טַעֲמְהוֹן דְּבֵית שַׁמַּאי? שֶׁקְּדוּשַׁת הַיּוֹם גְּרְמָה לַיַּיִן שֶׁיָּבוֹא וּכְבָר נִתְחַיֵּיב בִּקְדוּשַׁת הַיּוֹם עַד שֶׁלֹּא בָא הַיַּיִן. מָה טַעֲמְהוֹן דְּבֵית הַלֵּל? שֶׁהַיַּיִן גּוֹרֵם לִקְדוּשַׁת הַיּוֹם שֶׁתֵּאָמֵר. דָּבָר אַחֵר הַיַּיִן תָּדִיר וּקְדוּשָׁה אֵינָהּ תְּדִירָה.

8:1. . . . **The House of Shammai say, "One blesses the day and afterward one blesses over the wine."**

And the House of Hillel say, "One blesses over the wine and afterward one blesses the day."

A. *What is the reason of the House of Shammai?*

The Sanctification of the day causes the wine to be brought, and the man is already liable for the Sanctification of the day before the wine comes.

What is the reason of the House of Hillel?

The wine causes the Sanctification of the day to be said.

Another matter: Wine is perpetual, and the Sanctifi-

cation is not perpetual. [What is always required takes
precedence over what is required only occasionally.]

The *Gemara* first paraphrases the available Toseftan explanations for the positions of the two Houses. All that is added is
the introduction, "What is the reason . . ."

אָמַר רַבִּי יוֹסֵי: מִדִּבְרֵי שְׁנֵיהֶן יַיִן וְהַבְדָּלָה הַיַּיִן קוֹדֵם.

B. R. Yosé said, "[It follows] from the opinions of them
both that with respect to wine and *Havdalah,* wine comes
first."

Now Yosé begins the analysis of the two opinions. He wants
to prove that both Houses agree the wine takes precedence over
Havdalah. That is, you bless the wine, then you say the
Havdalah prayer.

כְּלוּם טַעֲמְהוֹן דְּבֵית שַׁמַּאי אֶלָּא שֶׁקְּדוּשַׁת הַיּוֹם גָּרְמָה
לַיַּיִן שֶׁיָּבוֹא וְכָאן הוֹאִיל וְלֹא אַבְדָּלָה גָּרְמָה לַיַּיִן שֶׁיָּבוֹא
הַיַּיִן קוֹדֵם?

"Is it not the reason of the House of Shammai that the Sanctification of the day causes the wine to be brought, and
here, since *Havdalah* does not cause wine to be brought,
the wine takes precedence?"

Since the Shammaites hold that the reason wine comes after
the Sanctification is that the Sanctification is the cause, then,
when the prayer is *not* the reason for saying a blessing over
wine, as in the case of *Havdalah,* the wine will normally take
precedence over the prayer.

כְּלוּם טַעֲמְהוֹן דְּבֵית הִלֵּל אֶלָּא שֶׁהַיַּיִן תָּדִיר וּקְדוּשָׁה
אֵינָה תְּדִירָה וְכָן הוֹאִיל וְהַיַּיִן תָּדִיר וְאַבְדָּלָה אֵינָה
תְּדִירָה הַיַּיִן קוֹדֵם?

"Is it not the reason of the House of Hillel that the wine is
perpetual and the Sanctification is not perpetual, and

since the wine is perpetual, and the *Havdalah* is not perpetual, the wine comes first?"

Similarly, since the Hillelites say what is perpetual takes
precedence over what is episodic, they will agree the wine takes
precedence over *Havdalah*. So both Houses will agree on this
point.

אָמַר רַבִּי מָנָא: מִדִּבְרֵי שְׁנֵיהֶן יַיִן וְאַבְדָּלָה, אַבְדָּלָה
קוֹדֶמֶת.

C. R. Mana said, "From the opinions of both of them
[it follows] that with respect to wine and *Havdalah*,
Havdalah comes first."

Now Mana wants to turn things upside down. The opinions
of both Houses are such that they will agree *Havdalah* takes
precedence over wine—the opposite of Yosé's claim!

כְּלוּם טַעֲמְהוֹן דְּבֵית שַׁמַּאי אֶלָּא שֶׁכְּבָר נִתְחַיֵּיב
בְּקִדוּשַׁת הַיּוֹם עַד שֶׁלֹּא בָא הַיַּיִן וְכָאן הוֹאִיל וְנִתְחַיֵּיב
בְּהַבְדָּלָה עַד שֶׁלֹּא בָא הַיַּיִן אַבְדָּלָה קוֹדֶמֶת?

"*Is it not the reason of the House of Shammai that* one is
already obligated [to say] the Sanctification of the day
before the wine comes, and here, since he is already
obligated for *Havdalah* before the wine comes, *Havdalah*
comes first?"

The Shammaites' principle is that a person carries out the
obligation which already applies—the Sanctification—before
the obligation which does not *yet* apply. The reason the Sanctification comes before the wine is that, as soon as the sun sets,
you are obligated to say the Sanctification. But the wine only
comes later.

כְּלוּם טַעֲמְהוֹן דְּבֵית הִלֵּל אֶלָּא שֶׁהַיַּיִן גּוֹרֵם לִקְדוּשַׁת
הַיּוֹם שֶׁתֵּאָמֵר וְכָאן הוֹאִיל וְאֵין הַיַּיִן גּוֹרֵם לָאַבְדָּלָה
שֶׁתֵּאָמֵר, אַבְדָּלָה קוֹדֶמֶת.

"Is it not the reason of the House of Hillel that the wine causes
the Sanctification of the Day to be said, and here, since
the wine does not cause the *Havdalah* to be said, *Havdalah*
comes first?"

The Hillelites are going to agree with Mana's proposition,
for they say wine comes first when it is the pretext for some
other prayer. But the wine is not the pretext for saying
Havdalah.

אָמַר רַבִּי זְעִירָא: מִדִּבְרֵי שְׁנֵיהֶן מַבְדִּילִין בְּלֹא יַיִן וְאֵין
מְקַדְּשִׁין אֶלָּא בְּיַיִן.

D. R. Zeira said, "From the opinions of both of them
[it follows] that they say *Havdalah* without wine, but
they say the Sanctification only with wine."

Zeira draws from the foregoing the necessary consequence:
You may say *Havdalah* without wine. But you may say the
Sanctification only in connection with wine. The House of
Hillel make this point clear: Wine is not the pretext for saying
Havdalah. Therefore, *Havdalah* may be said without wine.
The House of Shammai say that the Sanctification of the day
supplies the pretext for reciting the blessing over the wine. The
Havdalah does not. So they will agree also. Zeira's point seems
well-founded.

הִיא דַעְתֵּיה דְּרַבִּי זְעִירָא דְּרַבִּי זְעִירָא אֲמַר: מַבְדִּילִין
עַל הַשֵּׁכָר וְאָזְלִין מִן אֲתַר לַאֲתַר מִשּׁוּם קְדוּשָׁה.

E. *This is the opinion of R. Zeira, for* R. Zeira said, They
may say *Havdalah* over beer, but *they go from place to place* [in
search of wine] *for the Sanctification.*"

Now Zeira's rule is applied. You must go in search of wine
for Sanctification. But *Havdalah* may be said over beer.
Let us now review the argument as a whole.
Once again, we observe that the Talmud's interest is to find

the reasons for the laws. These will be elucidated, then criticized according to logic, finally tested against the evidence supplied by related rules. Like the Babylonian *Gemara,* the Palestinian one draws heavily upon the Tosefta. Its inquiry into the Tosefta, however, tends to be more thorough and systematic than the one we shall see in the Babylonian version. The opinions of both sides are examined; questions addressed to the one will be brought to the other. Thus a perfect balance is maintained throughout. Then new issues will be raised and worked out.

A sets the stage for what is to follow, rapidly reviewing the reasons given in the Tosefta for the opinions of the respective Houses. Then B, C, and D draw conflicting inferences from the foregoing in respect to *Havdalah.*

Yosé's view, B, is that both Houses agree that the wine comes before the *Havdalah* prayer. The Houses' principles are reviewed. As to the Shammaites: Which one supplies the pretext for the other? *Havdalah* does not require wine, therefore the wine will take precedence. As to the Hillelites: Which is "perpetual"? The wine. The wine therefore is going to precede *Havdalah.* So both Houses will agree that the order is wine, *Havdalah.*

Mana, C, takes the opposite view. If the reason of the House of Shammai is that the obligation to say the Sanctification is already present, then *Havdalah,* the obligation of which *likewise* is already present, will come first. If the reason of the House of Hillel is that wine comes first on the evening of the Sabbath because the Sanctification may not be said without it, then at the end of the Sabbath, *Havdalah* will come first, for it *may* be said without wine. The dispute is made possible, therefore, because both Houses give two reasons for their opinions. Yosé concentrates on one of the reasons of each of the Houses, Mana on the other.

Zeira, D, then concludes that in the opinion of both Houses, *Havdalah* may be said without wine, but Sanctification may not. E then provides an abstract formulation of Zeira's view.

אָמַר רַבִּי יוֹסֵי בְּרַבִּי: נְהִיגִין תַּמָּן בְּמָקוֹם שֶׁאֵין יַיִן
שְׁלִיחַ צִיבּוּר עוֹבֵר לִפְנֵי הַתֵּיבָה וְאוֹמֵר בְּרָכָה אַחַת
מֵעֵין שֶׁבַע וְחוֹתֵם בִּמְקַדֵּשׁ יִשְׂרָאֵל וְאֶת יוֹם הַשַּׁבָּת.

A. R. Yosé b. Rabbi said, "They are accustomed there
[in Babylonia], where there is no wine, for the prayer-
leader to go before the ark and say one blessing which is a
summary of the seven, and complete it with, 'Who sanctifies Israel and the Sabbath Day.'"

The next analysis begins with the simple observation that in
Babylonia the custom is to say the Sanctification as part of the
synagogue prayers on the eve of the Sabbath. But matters are
quickly made complicated, for this is one of the two most
difficult discussions of the whole Palestinian Talmud before
us. (The other is 8:2B.)

וְקַשְׁיָא עַל דְּבֵית שַׁמַּאי: בְּלֵילֵי שַׁבָּת הֵיךְ עֲבִידָה?
הָיָה יוֹשֵׁב וְאוֹכֵל בְּעֶרֶב שַׁבָּת וְחָשְׁכָה לֵילֵי שַׁבָּת וְאֵין
שָׁם אֶלָּא אוֹתוֹ הַכּוֹס.

B. *And thus the following poses a difficulty for the opinion of the
House of Shammai: How should one act on the evenings of the
Sabbath?*
He *who was sitting and eating on the evening of the Sabbath,*
and it grew dark and became Sabbath evening, and there
was there only that one cup—[The House of Shammai
say, "Wine, then food," and the House of Hillel say,
"Food, then wine," so Mishnah 8:8].

Now we review the Mishnah and the Shammaite position in
connection with the Sanctification of the day on the evening of
the Sabbath.

אַתְּ אָמַר מַנִּיחוֹ לְאַחַר הַמָּזוֹן וּמְשַׁלְשֵׁל כּוּלָם עָלָיו?

Do you say he should leave it for the end of the meal
and say all of them [the blessings] on it?

What is the proper order of blessing? We have said "food"
takes precedence over wine, that is, the blessing of food, and so
does Grace over the blessing of the day. We have also agreed the
wine takes precedence over the food. So should the order be
food, then wine, then day? But we also have said the wine takes
precedence over the "food"! So the Talmud points out.

מָה נַפְשָׁךְ? יְבָרֵךְ עַל הַיּוֹם? הַמָּזוֹן קוֹדֶם. יְבָרֵךְ עַל
הַמָּזוֹן? הַיַּיִן קוֹדֶם. יְבָרֵךְ עַל הַיַּיִן? הַיּוֹם קוֹדֶם.

What do you prefer?
Should he [first] bless the day? The food takes prece-
dence.
Should he bless the food? The wine takes precedence.
Should he bless the wine? The day takes precedence.

Now comes the effort at spelling out the answer. We first
allude to Mishnah 8:8, which says wine is blessed, then put
aside, and Grace is said; then the wine is drunk.

נִשְׁמְעִינָה מִן הָדָא: בָּא לָהֶן יַיִן אַחַר הַמָּזוֹן וְאֵין שָׁם
אֶלָּא אוֹתוֹ הַכּוֹס —

C. *We may infer* [the answer] *from this:*
If wine came to them after the meal, and there is there
only that cup—

R. Ba will explain that there is a distinction to be made
between the end of the Sabbath and the beginning. You bless
the wine first, so that you will not forget it. But now, at the end
of the Sabbath, when there are several blessings to be said over
the same cup of wine, you will not likely forget the wine.

אָמַר רַבִּי בָּא עַל יְדֵי שֶׁהוּא בְּרָכָה קְטַנָּה, שֶׁמָּא יִשְׁכַּח
וְיִשְׁתֶּה. בְּרַם הָכָא מִכֵּיוָן שֶׁהוּא מְשַׁלְשֵׁל עַל יְדֵי הַכּוֹס
אֵינוֹ שׁוֹכֵחַ.

R. Ba said, "Because it [the wine's] is a brief blessing,
[he says it first, for] perhaps he may forget and drink

[the wine]. But here, since he says them all over the cup, he will not forget [to say a blessing over the wine in the cup]."

Now we spell out just what the man is to do: food, day, wine.

כֵּיצַד יַעֲשׂוּ עַל דִּבְרֵי בֵית שַׁמַּאי? יְבָרֵךְ עַל הַמָּזוֹן תְּחִילָה וְאַחַר כָּךְ מְבָרֵךְ עַל הַיּוֹם, וְאַחַר כָּךְ עַל הַיַּיִן.

D. What, then, should he do according to the opinion of the House of Shammai?

Let him bless the food first, then bless the day, and then bless the wine.

Now we turn matters around. We pointed out that the problem confronts the House of Shammai on the evening of the Sabbath. But it also faces the House of Hillel at the end of the Sabbath, on Saturday night.

וְקַשְׁיָא עַל דִּבְרֵי בֵּית הִלֵּל: בְּמוֹצָאֵי שַׁבָּת הֵיךְ עֲבִידָה? הָיָה יוֹשֵׁב וְאוֹכֵל בְּשַׁבָּת וְחָשְׁכָה מוֹצָאֵי שַׁבָּת וְאֵין שָׁם אֶלָּא אוֹתוֹ הַכּוֹס —

E. *And this poses difficulty for the opinion of the House of Hillel: How should one act at the end of the Sabbath?*

If he was sitting and eating on the Sabbath and it grew dark and the Sabbath came to an end, and there is there only that cup—

What order should the blessings follow? When should he say a blessing over the cup of wine?

אַתְּ אָמַר מַנִּיחוֹ לְאַחַר הַמָּזוֹן וּמְשַׁלְשֵׁל כּוּלָן עָלָיו? מָה נַפְשָׁךְ? יְבָרֵךְ עַל הַיַּיִן? הַמָּזוֹן קוֹדֵם. יְבָרֵךְ עַל הַמָּזוֹן? הַנֵּר קוֹדֵם. יְבָרֵךְ עַל הַנֵּר? הַבְדָּלָה קוֹדֶמֶת.

Do you say he should leave it [the wine] for after the meal and say them all on it?

What do you prefer?
Should he bless the wine? The food comes first.
Should he bless the food? The light comes first.
Should he bless the light? *Havdalah* comes first.

We have agreed the food comes before the wine. But the light comes before the food. And the Hillelites are supposed to hold that the *Havdalah* comes before the light. The solution derives from Judah's version of the Houses' dispute. All agree the *Havdalah* comes at the end.

נִשְׁמְעִינָה מִן הָדָא: אָמַר רַבִּי יְהוּדָה: לֹא נֶחְלְקוּ בֵּית
שַׁמַּאי וּבֵית הִלֵּל עַל בִּרְכַּת הַמָּזוֹן שֶׁהוּא בַּתְּחִילָה
וְלֹא עַל הַבְדָּלָה שֶׁהִיא בַסּוֹף. עַל מָה נֶחְלְקוּ? עַל הַנֵּר
וְעַל הַבְּשָׂמִים שֶׁבֵּית שַׁמַּאי אוֹמְרִים: בְּשָׂמִים וְאַחַר
כָּךְ נֵר, וּבֵית הִלֵּל אוֹמְרִים: מָאוֹר וְאַחַר כָּךְ בְּשָׂמִים.
ר' בָּא וְרַב יְהוּדָה הֲלָכָה כְּמִי שֶׁהוּא אוֹמֵר בְּשָׂמִים
וְאַחַר כָּךְ נֵר.

F. *We may infer* [the solution to the impasse] *from this:*
R. Judah said, "The House of Shammai and the House of Hillel did not differ concerning the blessing of the food, that it comes first, nor concerning *Havdalah*, that it comes at the end.

"Concerning what did they differ?"

"Concerning the light and the spices, for:

"The House of Shammai say, 'The spices and afterward the light.'

"And the House of Hillel say, 'The light and afterward the spices.'"

[G. R. Ba and R. Judah in the name of Rav (said), "The law is according to him who says, 'Spices and afterward light.'"]

Now we have the instructions: food, then wine, then light.

כֵּיצַד יַעֲשֶׂה עַל דִּבְרֵי בֵית הִלֵּל? יְבָרֵךְ עַל הַמָּזוֹן
תְּחִלָּה וְאַחַר כָּךְ יְבָרֵךְ עַל הַיַּיִן וְאַחַר כָּךְ עַל הַנֵּר.

H. What should he do according to the opinion of the House of Hillel?

Let him bless the food, afterward bless the wine, and afterward bless the light.

Let us review this whole, elegant construction.

Yosé's observation, A, concerns Babylonia, where viticulture was impossible, because the climate was unsatisfactory. Since the Babylonian Jews could not get cheap wine—beer was used instead—the Sanctification of the Sabbath was done publicly, in the synagogue service, thus saving the private person from considerable expense. The Sabbath evening service included a sevenfold blessing, ending, "Blessed are you . . . who sanctifies Israel and the Sabbath Day." This is regarded as adequate substitution for the Sanctification of the day with a cup of wine.

This practice has to be measured against the opinions of the Houses. The Shammaites have to deal with an anomaly posed by the advent of the Sabbath, the Hillelites with one at the end.

The pericope before us presents a neat balance. B, C, and D are exactly paralleled by E, F, and H. G is an interpolation into an otherwise completed structure, but is essential to the structure, as well as to F.

The introductions, the Aramaic parts of B and E, allude to Mishnah 8:8. A man is eating and has only one cup of wine. On the eve of the Sabbath, what should he do? He needs the cup for the Sanctification of the Sabbath, but also for the Grace after Meals. No matter how you arrange matters, there is a problem according to the Shammaites' opinion. Do you tell the man to leave the wine for after the meal and to say all the blessings in order over it? That is what the Mishnah says he should do. Then he is to say the Sanctification and the Grace after Meals. If that is your instruction, then what will be the proper order of the blessings? Should he say the Sanctification?

But the food takes precedence, for he already is obligated, having eaten, to say the Grace after Meals. That is, after all, in accord with the fundamental reasoning of the Shammaites. Then should he bless the food first? The wine takes precedence over the food, as the Mishnah has already ruled in the name of the House of Shammai: "He blesses the wine, then the food." Then do you tell the man to bless the wine first? But this is also impossible, for the House of Shammai say that the Sanctification takes precedence over the wine! We are at an impasse.

C provides the solution. First, Mishnah 8:8 is cited, this time as the source of the solution. Then Ba explains the opinion of the House of Shammai in the afore-cited Mishnah. He removes the difficulty altogether. The reason of the House of Shammai in the situation addressed by Mishnah 8:8 is simply that the blessing of the wine is brief; therefore, it should be said first, lest it be forgotten. But here we are dealing with substantial blessings—Sanctification, Grace after Meals—so it is unlikely the man will forget the wine. Then D provides exact instructions: The Grace after Meals will take precedence, then the Sanctification, then the wine, thus preserving for the last two items the order originally prescribed by the Shammaites.

E addresses the same problem to the House of Hillel. Now the situation concerns the end of the Sabbath, Saturday night, and *Havdalah,* rather than the beginning, Friday evening, and the Sanctification of the Sabbath Day. Mishnah 8:8 poses no problem to the Hillelites. They say one blesses the food, then the wine, then the day—consistent with their ruling in Mishnah 8:1. If a man was sitting and eating toward sunset on the Sabbath, and it grew dark, he now has to say *Havdalah.* But if he has only one cup, what should he do? If he says *Havdalah,* he will have no wine for the Grace after Meals.

Now, if you rule that he should leave the cup for after the meal and say all the blessings in order over it, you do have a problem. Should he first bless the wine? But food takes precedence in the rule of Mishnah 8:8. Should he first bless the food? But the light takes precedence, for the House of Hillel and the

House of Shammai both agree that the order is light at first; they differ on spices and food. Then should he bless the light first? But if he does, the *Havdalah* will come before the Grace after Meals.

F then goes back over the presupposition of this analysis. Judah [b. Ilai, a second-century Tanna] has told us all parties agree food comes first, *Havdalah* at the end; the issue between the Houses is about the blessings which go along with *Havdalah*—light, spices. But these are kept together. If one blesses the light before the food, then the others will follow in sequence, and *Havdalah* will have to come first. But Judah b. Ilai also holds that the food comes first, and *Havdalah* comes at the end. Then what should the man do? He should bless the food, then the wine—as stated in Mishnah 8:8—and only then come the light and the subsequent blessings of *Havdalah*.

What is striking in this construction? First, the careful analysis of the opinions of each party shows a concern for reason, not for politics. We stand, after all, perhaps two or three hundred years after the decision that the law will normally follow the opinion of the House of Hillel in preference to that of the House of Shammai. So it might be natural to dismiss the latter and analyze only the former. The rabbis do no such thing, for they suppose each side has its reason, and under analysis this may produce new insight. The inquiry into theory is no game or puzzle. It is a most serious effort to extend the established rules to new cases, without regard to whether the rules are normative, as with the Hillelites, or merely a matter of discarded theory, as with the Shammaites.

Second, we continue to be confronted with the rabbis' efforts to discover the right order in which to say prayers, the proper way and form. The ideas of the House of Shammai are going to reveal something new in respect to a novel problem on the eve of the Sabbath, those of the House of Hillel to one on the end of the Sabbath. So these ideas are going to be tested against that new problem and worked out. We cannot suppose that for many hundreds of years, this "new" problem had never

occurred in actual fact. It is unlikely that one day in the year
A.D. 349, a man came home and wondered, Now which shall I
bless first in this "new" situation? The contrary is the case.
What probably happened is that for many centuries, no one
wondered at all. Either things were established according to a
rule long taken for granted, or, more likely, people simply did
not give heed to the way they did things at all. The editors who
construct the argument before us also raise to the level of con-
scious analysis what formerly cannot have been given any
mind. That is the larger meaning of this inquiry into the opinions of the first-century authorities—people who themselves
clearly did not pay attention to the issue to begin with. Asking
the question, more than supplying the answer, yields the view
that in an unexamined action is something worth asking
about—so the action may no longer be left out of mind, outside
of rational inquiry. We return to our text.

יוֹם טוֹב שֶׁחָל לִהְיוֹת בְּמוֹצָאֵי שַׁבָּת —

A. As to [the beginning of the] festival day which
coincides with the end of the Sabbath—

The Sabbath comes to an end on Saturday night. But a festival day immediately follows on Saturday night and Sunday.
What is the order of blessings?

רַבִּי יוֹחָנָן אָמַר: יקנ"ה יַיִן קִידוּשׁ נֵר הַבְדָּלָה.

R. Yohanan said, "[The order of prayer is] wine, Sanctification, light, *Havdalah.*"

Yohanan inserts the Sanctification of the festival day after
the blessing over the wine, but before *Havdalah.* Then Hanin
in Rav's name will agree and add two further blessings.

חָנִין בַּר בָּא אָמַר בְּשֵׁם רַב: יַיִן קִידוּשׁ נֵר הַבְדָּלָה
סוּכָּה וּזְמָן. רַבִּי חֲנִינָא אָמַר: ינה"ק. שְׁמוּאֵל לָא אָמַר
כַּהֲדָא דְּרַבִּי חֲנִינָא דַּאֲמַר רַבִּי אָחָא בְּשֵׁם רַבִּי יְהוֹשֻׁעַ

בֶּן לֵוִי: מֶלֶךְ יוֹצֵא וְשִׁלְטוֹן נִכְנָס מַלְוִין אֶת הַמֶּלֶךְ
וְאַחַר כָּךְ מַכְנִיסִין אֶת הַשִּׁלְטוֹן. לֵוִי אָמַר: ינה"ק
מִסְתַּבְרָא דְּלֵוִי אָמַר מֵעֵין שְׁנֵיהֶם.

Hanin bar Ba said in the name of Rav, "Wine, Sanctification, light, *Havdalah, Sukkah,* and season."

R. Hanina said, "Wine, light, *Havdalah,* Sanctification."
And did not Samuel rule according to this teaching of R. Hanina.

B. R. Aha said in the name of R. Joshua b. Levi, "When a king goes out and the governor comes in, they accompany the king and afterward bring in the governor."

C. Levi said, "Wine, *Havdalah,* light, Sanctification."
It stands to reason that Levi gave a summary of both of them.
[That is, *Havdalah* is before Sanctification, as R. Hanina says, and then light and *Havdalah* are kept together, as R. Yohanan says.]

At the end of the Sabbath, as we already know, a person has to bless wine, food, light, spices, and say *Havdalah.* What does he do when a festival day, requiring a prayer of Sanctification as does the Sabbath, begins at the end of the Sabbath? (The several answers omit reference to the Grace after Meals.)

Yohanan says the man blesses the wine first, as the Hillelites say, then come the Sanctification, finally light, and *Havdalah.* To this list Hanin adds the blessings necessary for the festival of Sukkot (Tabernacles). He is in the tabernacle and has to say a blessing as he takes up residence there, ". . . who has sanctified us by his commandments and commanded us to dwell in the *Sukkah.*" Then he says the blessing for the festival season, "Blessed are you, Lord our God, who has kept us in life, sustained us, and brought us to this season."

B then explains the view of those who place *Havdalah* first. You bid farewell to the Sabbath—the king, before bringing in the festival—the governor. The former is more important than the latter.

אָמַר רַבִּי זְעִירָא בְּעָא קוֹמֵי רַבִּי יוֹסֵי: הֵיךְ עוֹבְדִין
עוֹבָדָא? אֲמַר לֵיהּ: כְּרַב וּכְרַבִּי יוֹחָנָן. וְכֵן נְפַק עוֹבָדָא
כְּרַב וּכְרַבִּי יוֹחָנָן וְרַבִּי אַבָּהוּ כַּד הֲוָה אָזֵיל לִדְרוֹמָה
הֲוָה עָבֵיד כְּרַבִּי חֲנִינָא וְכַד הֲוָה נָחֵית לִטְבֶרְיָא הֲוָה
עָבֵיד כְּרַבִּי יוֹחָנָן דְּלָא מִפְלָג עַל בַּר נָשׁ בְּאַתְרֵיהּ. עַל
דַּעְתֵּיהּ דְּרַבִּי חֲנִינָא נִיחָא. וְקַשְׁיָא יוֹחָנָן: עַל דְּרַבִּי
יוֹחָנָן אִילוּ בִּשְׁאָר יְמוֹת הַשָּׁנָה אֵינוּ מְבָרֵךְ עַל הַנֵּר
שֶׁלֹּא יִכְבֶּה וְכָא מְבָרֵךְ עַל הַנֵּר שֶׁלֹּא יִכְבֶּה. מָה עֲבַד
לֵיהּ רַבִּי יוֹחָנָן? מִכֵּיוָן שֶׁיֵּשׁ לוֹ יַיִן אֵין נֵרוֹ כּוֹבֶה. וִיבָרֵךְ
עַל הַנֵּר בַּסּוֹף? שֶׁלֹּא לַעֲקוֹר זְמַן הַשַּׁבָּתוֹת הַבָּאוֹת:

A. R. Zeira asked before R. Yosé, "How shall we do it in practice?"

He said to him, "According to Rav, and according to R. Yohanan."

And so too did the rule come out in practice—according to Rav and according to R. Yohanan.

B. *And when R. Abbahu went south, he would act in accord with R. Hanina, but when he went down to Tiberias, he would act in accord with R. Yohanan, for one does not differ from a man['s ruling] in his own place* [out of courtesy].

C. *According to the opinion of R. Hanina this poses no problem.*

D. *But it poses a problem to the opinion of R. Yohanan:* In the rest of the days of the year does he not bless the light, lest it go out [because of a draft, and he lose the opportunity to say the blessing]? And here too he should bless the light before it goes out!

E. *What did R. Yohanan do in this connection?* [How did he explain this difficulty?]

F. Since he has wine [in hand], his light will not go out [for it is protected].

G. Then let him bless the light at the end?

H. So as not to upset the order [of prayer; lit.: time] of the coming Sabbaths, [he does not do so].

The normative rule for actual practice is given by Yosé: wine, Sanctification, light, *Havdalah*, plus *Sukkah* and the blessing of the festival season. B explains that the great fourth-century authority, Abbahu, who lived in Caesarea, would follow the rule of Hanina when he went to Hanina's locale, and of Yohanan when he went to his. That is, in Tiberias the order was (1) wine, (2) Sanctification, (3) light, and (4) *Havdalah;* in the south, meaning Lydda, it was (1) wine, (3) light, (4) *Havdalah,* and (2) Sanctification. Thus the rabbi paid due respect to his peers.

C continues to analyze the foregoing rulings. The opinion of Hanina poses no problems. After the wine, you bless the light right away; since you already see the light, you are obligated to bless it. And all will agree that the wine comes first.

But Yohanan's view does pose a problem, for he inserts Sanctification (2) between wine (1) and light (3), even though the man sees the light and therefore should bless it right away. On the rest of the days of the year, does he not bless the light right away, so that it not go out and he lose the opportunity to say the blessing? And if now he does not bless the light forthwith, lest it go out and he lose the occasion to say the blessing, he conducts himself contrary to normal usage. So why does Yohanan split up the wine (1) from the light (3)?

Yohanan's solution ("What did . . . do . . .") to the problem is this: Since the man has a cup of wine in his hand and has blessed it but not drunk it, he carefully guards it until he completes the entire order of blessings. He similarly is going to watch out that the light not go out until he says the appropriate blessing. If so, why not leave the light for last? So long as he has not drunk the wine, which he will do only at the end, obviously he likewise will continue to watch out that the light not go out. The answer is, since at the end of all Sabbaths he blesses the light before *Havdalah*, here too he should not change the order on account of all those Sabbaths coming later in the year. C is expressed in extremely apocopated language, but the thrust of the argument is clear. Both opinions have been fully examined and each is shown to be based upon sound reason.

בֵּית שַׁמַּאי אוֹמְרִים נוֹטְלִין לַיָּדַיִם וְאַחַר כָּךְ מוֹזְגִין אֶת הַכּוֹס וּבֵית הַלֵּל אוֹמְרִים מוֹזְגִין הַכּוֹס תְּחִילָה וְאַחַר כָּךְ נוֹטְלִין לַיָּדַיִם:

8:2. **The House of Shammai say, "They wash the hands and afterward mix the cup. And the House of Hillel say, They mix the cup first and afterward wash the hands."**

As before, we shall first go over the reasons given for the Houses' opinions by the Tosefta.

מָן טַעֲמְהוֹן דְּבֵית שַׁמַּאי? שֶׁלֹּא יִטָּמְאוּ מַשְׁקִין שֶׁבַּאֲחוֹרֵי הַכּוֹס מִיָּדָיו וְיַחְזְרוּ וִיטַמְּאוּ אֶת הַכּוֹס. מָה טַעֲמְהוֹן דְּבֵית הַלֵּל? לְעוֹלָם אֲחוֹרֵי הַכּוֹס טְמֵאִין. דָּבָר אַחֵר: אֵין נְטִילַת יָדַיִם אֶלָּא סָמוּךְ לִבְרָכָה.

A. *What is the reason of the House of Shammai?*
So that the liquids which are on the outer side of the cup may not be made unclean by his hands and go and make the cup unclean.
What is the reason of the House of Hillel?
The outer side of the cup is always unclean [so there is no reason to protect it from the hands' uncleanness].
Another matter: One should wash the hands immediately before saying the blessing.

There is nothing new in these citations. But now comes a new problem. We shall try to show that the first-century Houses' opinions are consistent in principle with opinions assigned to later, second-century masters on a different subject entirely. The point is that in both cases the moot principles are the same.

רַבִּי בִּיבָן בְּשֵׁם רַבִּי יוֹחָנָן: אָתְיָא דְבֵית שַׁמַּאי כְּרַבִּי יוֹסֵי וּדְבֵית הִלֵּל כְּרַבִּי מֵאִיר דִּתְנֵינַן תַּמָּן:

B. *R. Biban in the name of R. Yohanan* [said], *"The opinion of the House of Shammai is in accord with R. Yosé and that of the House of Hillel with R. Meir, as we have learned there* [Mishnah Kelim 25:7–8]:

"[In all vessels an outer part and an inner part are distinguished, and also a part by which they are held.]"

The case involves a utensil, which has three elements, an inner part, an outer part, and a handle. These are regarded as separate from one another. If one part is unclean, the others are not necessarily unclean. That is why the inside of the cup is "distinguished" from the outside.

רַבִּי מֵאִיר אוֹמֵר לַיָּדַיִם טְמֵאוֹת וּטְהוֹרוֹת. אָמַר רַבִּי יוֹסֵי: לָא אֲמַרָן אֶלָּא לַיָּדַיִם טְהוֹרוֹת בִּלְבַד.

"R. Meir says, 'For hands which are unclean and clean.'"

"R. Yosé said, 'This applies only to clean hands alone.'"

Meir says that if your hands are unclean and you touch the outer side of the vessel, you do not make the handle unclean. If your hands are clean, and you touch one part which is clean, another part which is unclean has no effect on your hands. The hands still are clean.

Yosé says this distinction among the elements of the cup applies *only* if the hands are clean. How does this have anything to do with the Houses' opinions? I shall give the answer in the extended commentary below.

First let us complete the discussion. The next question is

whether you have to go to a lot of trouble to find water to wash your hands.

רַבִּי יוֹסֵי בְּשֵׁם רַבִּי שַׁבְּתַי וְרַבִּי חִיָּיא בְּשֵׁם רַבִּי שִׁמְעוֹן
בֶּן לָקִישׁ: לְחַלָּה וְלִנְטִילַת יָדַיִם אָדָם מְהַלֵּךְ אַרְבַּע
מִילִין.

C. R. Yosé in the name of R. Shabbetai, and R. Hiyya in the name of R. Simeon b. Laqish [said], "For *Hallah* [Dough-offering] and for washing the hands, a man goes four miles [to find water]."

Abbahu says you do *not* have to go to trouble to find water to clean the hands.

רַבִּי אַבָּהוּ בְּשֵׁם רַבִּי יוֹסֵי בֵּי רַבִּי חֲנִינָא: הָדָא דַאֲמַר:
לְפָנָיו, אֲבָל לְאַחֲרָיו אֵין מַטְרִיחִין עָלָיו.

R. Abbahu in the name of R. Yosé b. R. Hanina said, "This is what he said, '[If the water is] before him [that is, on his way, in his vicinity, or near at hand, he must proceed to it and wash]. But if it is behind him [that is, not on his way], they do not trouble him [to obtain it and wash].'"

Now we ask about people who have the job of guarding a field. We have to take account of their obligation to the employer. They should not be asked to leave their job without good reason. Are they expected to go looking for water to wash the hands so as to preserve the cleanness of both the inside and the outside of a cup?

שׁוֹמְרֵי גַּנּוֹת וּפַרְדֵּיסִים מָה אַתְּ עָבֵד לְהוֹן כִּלְפְנֵיהֶן
כִּלְאַחֲרֵיהֶן?

D. Regarding those who guard gardens and orchards [and who cannot leave their posts], what do you do for them as to the insides and the outer sides [of a cup]? [How do we rule in their case? Do we judge them to be in the status of those for whom the water is] on their way, or in the status of those who would have to backtrack?

The answer derives from a different but related law. A woman is allowed to do her religious duty of separating the Dough-offering even without clothes on. You do not make her go to the trouble of getting a cloak. Yet that is a simple act. Obviously, if you do not bother her to do a very easy thing, you are not going to put a guardian of a field to a great deal more trouble in the same connection.

נִשְׁמִיעֶנָּה מִן הָדָא: הָאִשָּׁה יוֹשֶׁבֶת וְקוֹצָה חַלָּתָהּ
עֲרוּמָה מִפְּנֵי שֶׁהִיא יְכוֹלָה לְכַסּוֹת אֶת עַצְמָהּ אֲבָל לֹא
הָאִישׁ. וְהָדָא אִשָּׁה לֹא בְּתוֹךְ הַבַּיִת הִיא יוֹשֶׁבֶת וְאַתְּ
אָמַר אֵין מַטְרִיחִין עָלֶיהָ. וְכָאן אֵין מַטְרִיחִין עָלָיו.

Let us infer the answer from this [Mishnah Hallah 2:3]:

The woman sits and cuts off her Dough-offering [Hallah] while she is naked, because she can cover herself up, but a man cannot.

Now does not a woman sit in the house, yet you say they do not bother her? So too here they do not bother him.

Let us review the entire construction. We shall want to know, in particular, the relationship between the opinions of Meir and Yosé, on the one hand, and of the Houses of Shammai and Hillel on the other. For it is not yet obvious to us that the two disputes have anything to do with each other.

A is already familiar from the Babylonian Talmud. It is nothing more than the Tosefta's reason.

In B Yohanan tries to show that the position of the first-century Houses is taken up by later masters—mid-second-century authorities—who reason in a similar way on a parallel issue.

Mishnah Kelim 25:7 states that utensils are regarded as divided among an outer part, an inner part, and a handle. If one part becomes unclean, the others do not automatically become unclean. That is the meaning of the "division."

Meir then says this rule applies to unclean and clean hands. That is, if one touched the outer part with unclean hands, he does not make the handle unclean. If, reciprocally, clean hands touched a part, and the other part was unclean, the hands thereby are not made unclean. That is the meaning of "[This ruling applies] to unclean and clean hands." Therefore, according to Meir, the utensil is not regarded as wholly unclean if part of it is unclean.

Yosé says the distinction among parts of the cup is made only in the case of clean hands. The hands will not be made unclean if they touch the outer side, which is clean, even though the handle is unclean. But unclean hands do not follow this rule.

Both Yosé and the House of Shammai therefore hold that the outer part may be clean, even while the inner part is unclean. If the outer part is unclean, the handle may still be clean. So Yosé says the outer side of the cup is *not* always unclean. And this is contrary to the Hillelites' claim. If the hands were clean and liquid was dripping on them, and the outside of the cup was unclean, one may nonetheless hold the cup with the handle and not fear lest his hand be made unclean by the unclean outer part of the cup. We do not suppose, according to the Hillelites, that the liquid on the hands will be made unclean by the outer part of the cup and then go and make the hands unclean.

The House of Hillel therefore do not take account of the possibility important to the House of Shammai. Yosé, by contrast, says this rule applies only to clean hands. That is, if the hands are clean, and the outer part of the cup is unclean, we do not have to worry about uncleanness. But if the hands are unclean, we have to take precautions lest the liquid touch the unclean outer part of the cup and go and make the whole cup unclean.

The parallels therefore are clear. Yosé and the House of Shammai are concerned about unclean hands' not touching the liquid on the outer part of the cup, which then will go and make the cup unclean.

And the House of Hillel and Meir do not take account of that possibility *even* in the case of unclean hands' touching the liquid on the *outside* of the cup and making the whole cup unclean.*

In C we have the rule that in order to prepare the dough for *Hallah*—the Dough-offering—in a state of cleanness, or to wash hands, one has to take trouble to find water. This rule is then qualified: If one has the water in front of him, he has to go to get it, but he is not put to the trouble of walking back.

D asks whether watchmen have to take the trouble to leave their posts and go looking for water—forward or backward. The solution is found in the allusion to Mishnah Hallah 2:3, given in bold-face type. A woman is not required to get up and dress when she prepares the Dough-offering. Then the authorities certainly will not bother the guards to leave their posts to go look for water. That is, if the law is lenient where only a slight inconvenience is involved, it certainly will be lenient where a major inconvenience is at hand.

To this point in the Palestinian Talmud we have seen arguments as intricate and well-constructed as any in the Babylonian one. In the first unit we found a careful analysis of the reasoning of each House, followed by an effort to draw further conclusions based on the respective Houses' principles. The pericope is well-balanced, fair to both sides, characterized by close and careful reasoning. No assertion is allowed to pass without criticism and testing. If the Palestinian Talmud exhibits stylistic differences from the Babylonian one, these are primarily in the mode of expression. The former seems more

---

* The relationship of these materials on dividing cups into their insides and outsides for purposes of cultic cleanness to the famous saying attributed to Jesus, "First cleanse the inside, that the outside too may be clean," is worked out in my *Method and Meaning in Ancient Judaism.* Third Series (Chico, CA: Scholars Press, 1981), pp. 155–164.

terse, less fully spelled out. But there is no qualitative difference in the rational process. The second unit, about the difficulty in finding wine, is certainly the most sophisticated pericope of our chapter in either Talmud. Here we introduce a practical problem and ask for concrete instructions. But the way of defining those instructions leads directly into the theoretical analysis and testing of the fundamental reasoning of each House. The evidence of established law is adduced, then applied in each case. The third and fourth units focus upon the actual procedures of major authorities; but these are more than mere stories or case reports, for each involves reconsideration of basic principles.

The discussion of Mishnah 8:2 brings us into a still more intricate problem: how to establish the continuity of legal opinion from the Houses, in the first century, to the masters of post–Bar Kokhba times ca. A.D. 150? For the Talmud, much is clear in a mere allusion to a law; the commentaries make lucid for us what already was obvious then. C and D introduce a further rule, about not going to a great deal of trouble to find water.

Had the Palestinian *Gemara* ended here, you would reasonably conclude that it in no way is inferior to the Babylonian one in its capacities for logical and sophisticated inquiry into legal principles and cases. And that would have been a quite false conclusion. For the Palestinian Talmud characteristically lacks the sustained, dialectical effort to establish continuities and harmonies, to make sense of simple sayings and cases in terms of larger principles, in all to employ the faculties of rational criticism in the analysis of each and every story and rule.

The exercise of practical reason, such as we have seen in the Palestinian *Gemara* to this point, hereinafter tends not to be consistently carried through and universally applied. We have just seen what *might* have been accomplished. We shall now observe how little was actually achieved in applying reason to practical law. For, from this point onward, our chapter of the

Palestinian Talmud consists of little more than a compendium
of sayings and stories pertinent to the Mishnah. It is solely of
historical and antiquarian interest. But it exhibits few of the
aesthetically satisfying and intellectually engaging traits of the
other Talmud. Had the Babylonian Talmud looked like what
is to follow, it probably would not have earned for itself the
central place in the intellectual life of the Jewish people which
it in fact enjoyed for fifteen centuries and which it will continue
to enjoy wherever people gather to devote intellect to the service
of the religious life. It would have provided only important
information for lawyers in the traditional court system and for
historians and philologians interested in the Near East of late
antiquity. It would, in other words, have functioned not much
differently from the Palestinian Talmud.

תְּנֵי מַיִם שֶׁלִּפְנֵי הַמָּזוֹן רְשׁוּת וְשֶׁלְּאַחַר הַמָּזוֹן חוֹבָה.
אֶלָּא שֶׁבָּרִאשׁוֹנִים נוֹטֵל וּמַפְסִיק, וּבַשְּׁנִיִּים נוֹטֵל וְאֵינוֹ
מַפְסִיק.

A. *It has been taught:*
Washing before the meal is a matter of choice, but
afterward it is a matter of obligation.

But in respect to the first washing, he washes and
interrupts, and in the case of the second washing, he
washes and does not interrupt.

We have two rules. First, a person is obligated to wash the
hands after the meal, before reciting the Grace after Meals.
Beforehand, one may or may not do so. Second, one "washes
and interrupts" in the first washing, not in the second. This
now has to be explained.

מָה הוּא נוֹטֵל וּמַפְסִיק? רַבִּי יַעֲקֹב בַּר אָחָא אָמַר:
נוֹטֵל וְשׁוֹנֶה.

B. What is the meaning of, "He 'washes and interrupts'?"

R. Jacob b. Aha said, "He washes and then repeats the washing."

Jacob b. Aha's reason seems obvious. Washing and interrupting means you have to wash a second time if you have not completed the action in the first place. But this is going to pose a problem. If you are *required* to repeat the washing, then how can you say it is a matter of choice?

רַבִּי שְׁמוּאֵל בַּר יִצְחָק אָמַר בְּעֵי נוֹטֵל וְשׁוֹנֶה וְאַתְּ
אֲמַרְתְּ רְשׁוּת? אָמַר רַבִּי יַעֲקֹב בַּר אִידִי: עַל הָרִאשׁוֹנִים
נֶאֱכַל בְּשַׂר חֲזִיר עַל הַשְּׁנִיִּים יָצְאָה אִשָּׁה מִבֵּיתָהּ וְיֵשׁ
אוֹמְרִים שֶׁנֶּהֶרְגוּ עָלֶיהָ שְׁלֹשָׁה נְפָשׁוֹת.

R. Samuel bar Isaac said, "*If he is required* to repeat the washing, *how do you claim it is a matter of choice?*
["Or if you want, I may point out you require one to go four miles (in search of water), *so how do you claim* it is a matter of choice!"]
C. R. Jacob bar Idi said, "On account of the first [washing of hands], a pig's flesh was eaten; on account of the second [washing of hands], a woman left her house."
"And some say, three souls were killed on her account. [It is not a matter of choice at all.]"

Jacob bar Idi's answer more or less ignores the question. He simply solves the problem by saying the original rule is wrong. You must make both washings. Let us review the whole.

A presents a Tannaitic teaching. B then attempts to explain it. The problem is the meaning of "wash and interrupt." Washing and repeating means that the man does not pour out all the water at once. He washes once, then goes and does it a second time.

If so, doing the act twice can hardly be interpreted as a matter of choice. The man is put to some trouble, and this must mean it is a fixed obligation that the act be done correctly. This seems contrary to the spirit of the rule that one does not have to go to the trouble to find water for washing.

To prove washing is required, Jacob bar Idi then refers to a story of an innkeeper who was selling both properly and improperly slaughtered meat, as well as pork. To whoever washed his hands he gave properly slaughtered (*kosher*) meat. One time a Jew came and did not wash his hands, and the innkeeper thought that he was a gentile and gave him pork.

As to the washing of the hands before Grace after Meals, the allusion is to a story (Babylonian Talmud, Yoma 83b) about Rabbis Judah, Yosé, and Meir who stayed at an inn maintained by a dishonest innkeeper. Judah and Yosé entrusted their purses to him on the Sabbath eve. Meir did not, but put it on the grave of the man's father. Meir retrieved his purse; the others then asked for theirs. The man denied they had deposited money with him. They then took the man to a shop and gave him something to drink. Afterward they saw a residue of lentils on his moustache. They went to his wife and told her that the husband had eaten lentils for lunch—a sign that the innkeeper had confided in them. They then said the husband sent them for the purses. She gave them the money. Outraged, the innkeeper came home and killed the wife: "It is with regard to this that it was taught . . . the 'second washing' killed a person." For had the innkeeper washed his hands after meals and wiped his upper lip, the rabbis would not have known what he had eaten. The man would not have killed his wife.

But Jacob bar Idi's story *should* have the man divorce the wife, for he refers to a woman's leaving home. "Some-say"'s version should have more murders. At any rate this is evidently the main outline of the story to which the vague allusion is made.

שְׁמוּאֵל סָלֵק לְגַבֵּי רַב. חֲמָא יָתֵיה אָכֵל בְּמַפָּה. אֲמַר
לֵיה: מַהוּ כֵן. אֲמַר לֵי: אִיסְתְּנֵיס אֲנִי.

A. *Samuel went up to visit Rav. He saw him eating with* [his hands covered by] *a napkin. He said to him, "How so?* [Did you not wash your hands?]*"*

He said to him, "I am sensitive."

Samuel seems to suppose Rav did not wash his hands.
Rather, he simply covered them with a napkin. That would
serve the same purpose. If he picked up his food in the napkin,
then the uncleanness of the hands would have no effect upon
the food. He is told the reason has nothing to do with washing
the hands. Rav has his private idiosyncrasy.

רַבִּי זְעִירָא כַּד סְלֵיק לְהָכָא חֲמָא כָּהֲנַיָּא אָכְלִין בְּמַפָּה
אֲמַר לְהוֹן: הָא אָזִילָא הַהִיא דְּרַב וּשְׁמוּאֵל. אֲתָא רַבִּי
יוֹסֵי בַּר בַּר כָּהֲנָא בְּשֵׁם שְׁמוּאֵל: נְטִילַת יָדַיִם לְחוּלִין.
אֵין נְטִילַת יָדַיִם לִתְרוּמָה. רַבִּי יוֹסֵי אוֹמֵר: לִתְרוּמָה
וּלְחוּלִין. רַבִּי יוֹסָה בְּשֵׁם רַבִּי חִיָּיא בַּר אַשִׁי וְרַבִּי יוֹנָה
וְרַבִּי חִיָּיא בַּר אַשִׁי בְּשֵׁם רַב: נְטִילַת יָדַיִם לִתְרוּמָה עַד
הַפֶּרֶק וּלְחוּלִין עַד קִשְׁרֵי אֶצְבְּעוֹתָיו. מֵיישָׁא בַּר בְּרֵיהּ
דְּרַבִּי יְהוֹשֻׁעַ בֶּן לֵוִי אֲמַר: מַן דַּהֲוָה אָכֵל עִם סָבִי וְלָא
מְשַׁטֵּף יְדוֹי עַד הַפֶּרֶק לָא הֲוָה אָכֵל עִימֵּיהּ. רַב הוּנָא
אֲמַר: אֵין נְטִילַת יָדַיִם אֶלָּא לְפַת בִּלְבַד. תַּנִי רַבִּי
הוֹשַׁעְיָא: כָּל דָּבָר שֶׁיֵּשׁ בּוֹ לִיכְלוּךְ מַשְׁקֶה. רַבִּי זְעִירָא
אֲמַר: אֲפִילוּ מְקַצֵּץ תּוּרְמוֹסִין הֲוָה נָטֵל יְדֵיהּ.

B. *When R. Zeira came up here* [to Palestine], *he saw the
priests eating with a napkin. He said to them, "Lo, this is in accord
with the story of Rav and Samuel."*

C. R. Yosé bar Kahana came [and said] *in the name of
Samuel,* "One washes the hands for Heave-offering, not
for unconsecrated food."

D. R. Yosé says, "For Heave-offering and for unconsecrated food."

E. R. Yosah in the name of R. Hiyya bar Ashi, and R.
Jonah and R. Hiyya bar Ashi in the name of Rav [said],
"They wash the hands for Heave-offering up to the
wrist, and for unconsecrated food up to the knuckles."

F. *Measha the son of the son of R. Joshua b. Levi said, "If one
was eating with my grandfather and did not wash his hands up to
the wrist, grandfather would not eat with him."*

G. R. Huna said, "Washing the hands applies only for bread."

H. R. Hoshaia taught, "Whatever is unclean on account of liquid [is protected by washing the hands]."

I. R. Zeira said, *"Even for cutting beets, he would wash his hands."*

These stories again illustrate what we observed at the outset, that the deeds of the rabbis, even more than their words, constitute modes of "Torah." You will study Torah not merely by listening to, and memorizing, the masters' words, but also by carefully observing, and preserving the record of, what they actually did.

Samuel (A) thought that since Rav covered his hands with a napkin, he had not washed them. Rav then explained that he had washed them but preferred nonetheless to cover them.

In B Zeira cites this story to account for the behavior of the priests in eating their Heave-offering without washing their hands. So the napkin *is* sufficient protection against the cultic impurity. He concludes that, even in the opinion of both the masters, one still has to wash the hands, for unclean hands render Heave-offering unfit. In C we have the same view; one does have to wash for consecrated food, but not for ordinary food. Yosé bar Kahana differs, presumably an additional "decree" to protect the Heave-offering. Rav then presents the view that one must wash for both, but in the one case more of the hand is to be washed than in the other.

Then in F Measha reports his grandfather, Joshua b. Levi, differed from the ruling of Rav and required washing all the way to the wrist even for unconsecrated food.

In G Huna differs; the washing is only for bread. Hoshaia holds anything which may be mixed with liquid is to be protected by washing the hands. Finally, we have Zeira's view, the most extreme of all. No effort goes into harmonizing these discrete, contradictory opinions. We are left simply with a mere compendium of various rules, but no principles for interpreting, or choosing among them. This is typical of the Palestinian *Gemara.*

רַב אָמַר: נָטַל יָדָיו בַּשַּׁחֲרִית אֵין מַטְרִיחִין עָלָיו בֵּין הָעַרְבַּיִם. רַבִּי אַבִינָא מְפַקֵּיד לְחַמָּרֵיהּ: הֵן דְּאַתּוּן מַשְׁכְּחִין מַיָּא נְסַבּוּן יְדֵיכוֹן וּמִתְּנֵי עַל כָּל יוֹמָא. רַבִּי זְעֵירָא סְלֵיק גַּבֵּיהּ רַבִּי אַבָּהוּ לְקֵיסָרִין אַשְׁכְּחֵיהּ אָמַר: אֲזַל לְמֵיכוֹל, יְהַב לֵיהּ עֲגוּלָה דְּיִקְצֵי. אֲמַר לֵיהּ: סַב בָּרִיךְ. אֲמַר לֵיהּ: בַּעַל הַבַּיִת יוֹדֵעַ כֹּחוֹ שֶׁל כִּכָּרוֹ. מִן דַּאֲכַלוּן אֲמַר לֵיהּ סַב בָּרֵיךְ אֲמַר לֵיהּ חָכֵם רַבִּי לְרַב הוּנָא אֱנָשָׁא רַבָּה וְהוּא הֲוָה אָמַר: הַפּוֹתֵחַ הוּא חוֹתֵם. מַתְנִיתָא פְּלִיגָא עַל רַב הוּנָא דְּתָנֵי: סֵדֶר נְטִילַת יָדַיִם עַד חֲמִשָּׁא מַתְחִילִין מִן הַגָּדוֹל. יוֹתֵר מִיכָּן מַתְחִילִין מִן הַקָּטוֹן בְּאֶמְצַע הַמָּזוֹן מַתְחִילִין מִן הַגָּדוֹל לְאַחַר הַמָּזוֹן מַתְחִילִין מִן הַמְבָרֵךְ. לֹא שֶׁיַּתְקִין עַצְמוֹ לַבְּרָכָה. אֵין תֵּימַר הַפּוֹתֵחַ הוּא חוֹתֵם כְּבָר מוּתְקָן הוּא. אֲמַר רַבִּי יִצְחָק: תִּפְתַּר בְּאִילֵּין דַּהֲווֹ עָלִין קִיטְעִין קִיטְעִין וְלָא יָדְעִין מָה מְבָרְכָה:

A. Rav said, "He who washed his hands in the morning is not required to do so in the afternoon."

B. *R. Abina ordered his wine-steward, "Whenever you find sufficient water, wash your hands and rely on this washing all day long."*

C. *R. Zeira went up to R. Abbahu in Caesarea. He found him saying,* "I shall go to eat."

D. *He gave him a chunk of bread to cut. He* [Abbahu] *said to him* [Zeira], *"Begin, bless."*

E. *He* [Zeira] *said to him* [Abbahu], *"The host knows the value of his loaf."* [You should bless.]

F. *When they had eaten, he* [Abbahu] *said to him* [Zeira], *"Let the elder bless."*

G. *He said to him, "Rabbi, does the rabbi* [you] *know R. Huna, a great man, who would say, 'He who opens* [blesses first] *must* close [and say Grace after Meals]'?"

H. *A Tannaitic teaching differs from. R. Huna, as it has been taught*:

I. The order of washing the hands in this: With up to five people present, they begin with the greatest. [If] more than this [are present], they begin with the least. In the middle of the meal, they begin with the eldest. After the meal they begin with the one who blesses.

J. Is it not [done] so that he may prepare himself for the blessing? [So he did *not* bless at the beginning!]

K. *If you say* the one who opens is the one who closes, he is already prepared [having opened the meal].

L. *R. Isaac said, "Explain it in regard to those who come in one by one and did not know which one had blessed* [at the outset]."

A gives Rav's lenient rule. B has a story indicating Abina supported Rav's position.

The story in C–G concerns the etiquette for saying Grace before and after food. Zeira was invited to bless the bread but advised the host it was proper only for the latter to do so. At the end he cited Huna's view that the man who blessed the bread at the beginning of the meal should also say the Grace at the end.

H–I presents a challenge to Huna's view. As to passing around water for the final washing, if five people are eating together, you begin with the most important; if there are more than five, you start with the least important person and continue until five are left. Then you return to the greatest person who is present.

Finally, we are referred to the mixing of the cup at the end of the meal. You mix first for the one who is going to bless. This is interpreted as a means of designating the person to be assigned the honor of saying Grace after Meals.

But that interpretation is rejected. You begin from the one who is going to bless so that he will prepare himself to bless.

Now if Huna were right that the one who breaks bread at the outset is the one who blesses at the end, why should he be given a sign to prepare himself for the blessing? He already is prepared from the beginning of the meal. So Huna's view seems contradicted. Isaac says the teaching cited in contradiction of Huna deals with a situation in which people came to the table one by one; they did not sit down all at once. Therefore, you cannot be sure who will bless at the end, since not all were present at the outset. So now they are given a sign to that effect. But this interpretation is hardly implied by the tradition cited earlier.

בֵּית שַׁמַּאי אוֹמְרִים מְקַנֵּחַ יָדָיו בַּמַּפָּה וּמַנִּיחָה עַל
הַשֻּׁלְחָן וּבֵית הִלֵּל אוֹמְרִים עַל הַכֶּסֶת:

8:3. The House of Shammai say, "He dries his hands on the napkin and puts it on the table."
And the House of Hillel say, "On the cushion."

We once again are going to look for the reasons behind the Houses' respective rulings. But first, we establish a new definition for the situation.

מַתְנִיתָא בְּשֻׁלְחָן שֶׁל שַׁיִשׁ וְשֶׁל פְּרָקִים שֶׁאֵינוֹ מְקַבֵּל
טוּמְאָה.

A. The Mishnah deals with either a table of marble [which is not susceptible to uncleanness] or a table that can be taken apart and is not susceptible to becoming unclean.

The Houses both agree that we are dealing with a table which is *not* going to receive uncleanness! So the issue important in the Babylonian Talmud's analysis of the law is forthwith excluded. The possibility of leaving the napkin on the table is *not* going to be affected by the table's uncleanness, for our table is *not* susceptible to uncleanness.

מָה טַעֲמוֹן דְּבֵית שַׁמַּאי? שֶׁלֹא יִטָמְאוּ מַשְׁקִין שֶׁבַּמַּפָּה
מִן הַכֶּסֶת וְיַחְזְרוּ וִיטַמְּאוּ אֶת יָדָיו.

B. *What is the reason of the House of Shammai?*
So that the liquids which are on the napkin may not
become unclean from the cushion and go and render his
hands unclean.

The House of Shammai are in the same position as before.
That is, we are concerned about the liquids on the napkin. We
do not want them to be made unclean by the cushion and then
make his hands unclean. The table never was an issue to them.
But the House of Hillel's position is going to change.

וּמָה טַעֲמוֹן דְּבֵית הִלֵּל? לְעוֹלָם סָפֵק מַשְׁקִין לְיָדַיִם
טָהוֹר. דָּבָר אַחֵר: אֵין יָדַיִם לְחוּלִּין.

And what is the reason of the House of Hillel?
The condition of doubt[ful uncleanness] with respect
to the hands is always regarded as clean.
Another reason: The [question of the cleanness of]
hands does not apply to unconsecrated food [which in
any case is not made unclean by unclean hands which
are unclean in the second remove].

The only principle available to the House of Hillel is this:
The hands are *not* going to be made unclean at all! So you may
put the napkin on the cushion. The Shammaite reason is based
upon false premises. Furthermore, even if the hands are
unclean, they will not affect unconsecrated food, but only
Heave-offering—just as we shall notice in the Babylonian
Talmud. But this forthwith raises the question of the Shammaites' opinion on the subject.

וּכְבֵית שַׁמַּאי יֵשׁ יָדַיִם לְחוּלִּין? תִּיפָּתַר אוֹ כְרַבִּי שִׁמְעוֹן
בֶּן אֶלְעָזָר אוֹ כְרַבִּי אֶלְעָזָר בֵּי רַבִּי צָדוֹק.

C. *And according to the House of Shammai,* does [the question of the cleanness of] hands [indeed] apply to unconsecrated food?

D. *You may interpret* [the tradition] either in accord with R. Simeon b. Eleazar or in accord with R. Eleazar b. R. Saddoq.

We now have to find an opinion which will explain the position of the House of Shammai on the cleanness of hands and unconsecrated food (not Heave-offering). The first tells us that the question of cleanness of hands most certainly *does* apply to unconsecrated food. The hands then may make such food unclean.

כְּרַבִּי שִׁמְעוֹן בֶּן אֶלְעָזָר דְּתָנֵי: רַבִּי שִׁמְעוֹן בֶּן אֶלְעָזָר
אוֹמֵר מִשּׁוּם רַבִּי מֵאִיר: הַיָּדַיִם תְּחִילָּה לְחוּלִּין וּשְׁנִיּוֹת
לִתְרוּמָה.

According to R. Simeon b. Eleazar, as it has been taught:

R. Simeon b. Eleazar says in the name of R. Meir, "Hands unclean in the first remove of uncleanness can affect [even] unconsecrated food, and in the second remove of uncleanness can affect [only] Heave-offering."

We may also explain the Shammaites' position in another way. Eleazar b. R. Saddoq says unconsecrated food prepared with consecrated food enters the status of the latter; therefore, it *may* be made unclean by hands, which are unclean in the second remove. So the original question is neatly dealt with according to one of two opinions.

אוֹ כְּרַבִּי אֶלְעָזָר בֵּי רַבִּי צָדוֹק דְּתָנֵינַן תַּמָּן: חוּלִּין
שֶׁנַּעֲשׂוּ עַל גַּבֵּי הַקּוֹדֶשׁ הֲרֵי אִילּוּ כְּחוּלִּין. רַבִּי אֶלְעָזָר
בֵּי רַבִּי צָדוֹק אוֹמֵר: הֲרֵי אִילּוּ כִּתְרוּמָה לְטַמֵּא שְׁנַיִם
וּלְפָסוּל אֶחָד. תַּמָּן תְּנֵינַן: הַסָּךְ שֶׁמֶן טָהוֹר נִטְמָא וְיָרַד
וְטָבַל בֵּית שַׁמַּאי אוֹמְרִים אַף עַל פִּי מְנַטֵּף טָהוֹר וּבֵית

הַלֵּל אוֹמְרִים טָמֵא. וְאִם הָיָה שֶׁמֶן טָמֵא מִתְּחִילָתוֹ
בֵּית שַׁמַּאי אוֹמְרִים כְּדֵי סִיכַת אֵבֶר קָטָן וּבֵית הַלֵּל
אוֹמְרִים מַשְׁקֶה טוֹפֵחַ.

E. Or according to R. Eleazar b. R. Saddoq, *as we have learned there*:

F. Unconsecrated food which has been prepared along with consecrated [food] is like unconsecrated food [and subject to the same, less strict cleanness rules].

G. R. Eleazar b. R. Saddoq says, "Lo, it is like Heave-offering, capable of becoming unclean from [something unclean in the] second remove of uncleanness and being rendered unfit from [something unclean in] still a further remove of uncleanness."

H. *There we have learned*:

I. He who anoints himself with clean oil and is made unclean and goes down and bathes [in a ritual pool]—

J. The House of Shammai say, "Even though he drips [with oil], [the oil] is clean."

K. And the House of Hillel say, "It is unclean [so long as there remains enough to anoint a small member]."

L. And if the oil was unclean in the first place—

M. The House of Shammai say, "[It remains unclean, even after he has immersed himself, so long as there remains] sufficient for anointing a small limb."

N. And the House of Hillel say, "[So long as it remains] a dripping liquid."

The reason this case is cited is not yet clear. But the problem is going to face the Hillelites. If a person who has anointed himself with clean oil becomes unclean and immerses himself, the House of Hillel say that, if the oil is still dripping, it is regarded as unclean. If the oil was unclean to begin with, of course it will remain unclean. So the House of Hillel do pay attention to the uncleanness of the liquid. Yet in the cases we just cited the House of Hillel seem *not* to care that the moist liquid in the napkin may be made unclean by the cushion.

רַבִּי יְהוּדָה אוֹמֵר מְשׁוּם בֵּית הַלֵּל: טוֹפֵחַ וּמַטְפִּיחַ.

O. R. Judah says in the name of the House of Hillel, "So long as it is dripping so as to moisten something else."

The problem will now be pointed out, then solved. The solution is based on a distinction between the two cases, the napkin and the oil. In the case of the napkin, the liquid has been absorbed. Therefore, it is ignored by the Hillelites. In the case of the oil, it is physically present in and of itself. Therefore, it is subject to concern.

מְחַלְפַת שִׁיטַתְהוֹן דְּבֵית הַלֵּל. תַּמָּן אָמְרִין טָמֵא וְהָכָא אָמְרִין טָהוֹר. תַּמָּן בְּעֵינוֹ הוּא. וְהָכָא בָּלוּעַ בַּמַּפָּה הוּא:

P. *The principle of the House of Hillel has been turned around.*

Q. *There* [in the just-cited law] *they say it is* unclean. *And here* [in our Mishnah] *they say it is* clean.

R. *There* it is present. *But here* it is absorbed in the napkin.

How is the foregoing to be put back together? As noted in our discussion of the Tosefta, the Palestinian Talmud takes for granted that the Mishnah deals with a table which is insusceptible to uncleanness. That is why the House of Hillel will allow the man to put the napkin on the table in preference to the cushion. The reason of the House of Shammai is clear: The liquid may be made unclean by the cushion and will go and make the hands unclean.

The House of Hillel are not sure that the cushion really is unclean, or that liquid actually is dripping from the napkin. In matters of doubt concerning the hands, we rule that the doubt is resolved in favor of cleanness. We therefore do not have to take account of the problem of the uncleanness of the cushion *or* of the table. Furthermore, hands will not make unconsecrated food unclean, for they are in the second remove of uncleanness, and something unclean in the second remove makes Heave-offering unfit, but does not make secular, unconsecrated food unclean.

C then raises the necessary query: Do the House of Shammai differ and hold that the unclean hands do make unconsecrated food unclean? If they do *not* hold that position, their opinion here is senseless. The following solution is proposed: The House of Shammai share the opinion of two masters who hold that the hands do indeed render food unclean.

D gives Simeon b. Eleazar's tradition in the name of Meir: the hands are in the *first* remove of uncleanness.

E cites Eleazar b. R. Saddoq, who says that if unconsecrated— nonpriestly—food is prepared in the condition of sanctity appropriate for Holy Things of the Temple, it will be subject to the laws of those Holy Things, which may be made unclean by something unclean in the second remove such as the hands.

H introduces a new problem. The position of the House of Hillel seems inconsistent with their opinion on a related matter concerning unclean liquids. The case concerns a person who anointed himself with clean oil, was made unclean, and then immersed. The House of Hillel hold that, if so much oil remains on him as to be sufficient for anointing a small limb, the oil is regarded as unclean; but less than that amount of oil is clean. Then what if the oil was unclean to begin with? The Shammaites say if the liquid is enough to moisten the hand, the oil remains unclean.

In the first case, the presence of more oil than the specified quantity will mean the oil, made unclean by the man's uncleanness, remains unclean. Oil remaining on his flesh after the ritual bath is unclean. The oil is not made clean in the bath. If the oil to begin with was unclean, then, when at all moist, it remains unclean.

Now, clearly, the two cases take for granted a person is concerned about the unclean liquid. Yet here, by contrast, the House of Hillel are indifferent to the fact that the small amount of liquid in the napkin may be made unclean by the cushion.

The two cases therefore have to be distinguished from each other. In the present one, the liquid is absorbed into the napkin when the man dries his hands. So we are *not* concerned about its cleanness. But in the other case, concerning oil, the oil is apparent on the man's flesh, so remains unclean.

On several occasions we have examined the problem of why you have to wash your hands before eating. Indeed, so many reasons for doing so are before us that we must wonder whether anyone actually knew what originally was in the minds of the Houses. Notice, we worried about the table—clean or unclean, if unclean, in what remove. We asked about the hands—unclean only in the second remove, therefore not able to make the ordinary food unclean at all; or unclean in the first remove. We wondered about liquid which may or may not be on the napkin, or on the cup, or in the cushion. The simplest answer is Meir's: Hands are unclean in the first remove. But no one agrees with Meir. The arguments in both Talmuds take for granted he cannot be right—or they do not know his opinion to begin with. Then there are the Babylonian Talmud's priests, who are, or are not, assumed to be careful about where they eat.

Now what if cleanness plays no role in the original formation of the Houses' opinions? Perhaps their original rulings about washing the hands and mixing the cup, or about where you lay the napkin, have nothing to do with the laws of cleanness at all! Remember, when we came to cleaning the house and washing the hands, no one suggested that the issue was purity. We worried only about not wasting food. Perhaps here too the opinions of the Houses about the order of washing the hands and mixing the cup and about where you place the napkin were nothing more than matters of ordinary etiquette.

Once you ask the question, you are going to get the answer. But if to begin with there is no "question," but merely a procedure without anything more attached to it than "common sense" or customary behavior, what do we need these answers for?

My suspicion is that both the questions and the answers, which have occupied us for a long time, are the creation of the later rabbis, who take for granted some reason lies behind the opinions of the respective Houses and who therefore go in search of appropriate reasons and logical issues. That seems to me expressive of the rabbis' mode of thought. It is not historical. The rabbis do not look in ancient sources for the social or cultural motive behind a ruling. Obviously, if the sources give evidence of such a motive, they take it seriously. But normally the ancient sources in the rabbis' hands are brief and enigmatic. So they leave it up to the rabbis themselves to think up reasons for the opaque laws.

Modern men and women like to find historical reasons, perhaps based upon the economic, or the psychological, or the sociological realities of the day. Let me give one example of a contemporary mode of argument. The House of Shammai wished to give preference to the hands over the cup because their class in society held such-and-such an opinion; the Hillelites, representing a lower class, had the opposite opinion. You put the napkin on the table because you are rich enough to afford to have a napkin. You put it on the cushion because if you show it off, you are going to put to shame the poor man who has no napkin. I do not mean to suggest modern scholars have so interpreted the issues before us, thus reducing them to another set of values or to a different interpretive framework from the one important to the law itself. But this is the sort of reductionist interpretation that gives us a feeling we truly have understood things.

The rabbis too seek satisfying explanations. To begin with, they suppose that such explanations are indeed to be found— the most satisfying conviction of all! Their explanations stress not social realities, economic interests, psychological preferences, even aesthetic concern, but purity laws. The stress on purity is apt to tell us more about the rabbis than it does about the original reasons, if any, of the Houses. And what it tells us we already know. We need to remind ourselves, however, that the fact in *our* hands is what the rabbis have to say about the tradition in *their* hands, not about the original intent of the auhorities behind the tradition. I should not be surprised to learn that, about a hundred years after the Houses' opinions were formed into little mnemonic lists, no one had a clear picture of the reasons, if any, for the arrangements of opinions, let alone for the abstract and general laws reduced to those arrangements. So everyone has a chance to think out his own interpretation.

בֵּית שַׁמַּאי אוֹמְרִים: מְכַבְּדִין אֶת הַבַּיִת וְאַחַר כָּךְ
נוֹטְלִין לַיָּדַיִם. וּבֵית הִלֵּל אוֹמְרִים נוֹטְלִין לַיָּדַיִם וְאַחַר
כָּךְ מְכַבְּדִין אֶת הַבַּיִת: גמ' מָה טַעֲמְהוֹן דְּבֵית שַׁמַּאי?
מִפְּנֵי אוֹבְדַן אוֹכָלִין. וּמָה טַעֲמְהוֹן דְּבֵית הִלֵּל? אִם
הַשַּׁמָּשׁ פִּיקֵּחַ הֲרֵי זֶה מַעֲבִיר פֵּרוּרִין פָּחוֹת מִכְּזַיִת
וְנוֹטְלִין לַיָּדַיִם וְאַחַר כָּךְ מְכַבְּדִין אֶת הַבַּיִת:

8:4. The House of Shammai say, "They clean the house and afterward wash the hands." And the House of Hillel say, "They wash the hands and afterward clean the house."

A. *What is the reason of the House of Shammai?*

B. Because of the waste of food.

C. *And what is the reason of the House of Hillel?*

D. If the servant is clever, he removes the crumbs which are less than an olive's bulk, and they wash their hands and afterward they clean the house.

The discussion does not differ from that in the Babylonian Talmud, as we shall shortly see, except that we should expect the crumbs to be an olive's bulk or *larger*, rather than *less*. So the meaning must be "Crumbs [to a size] less than an olive's bulk are removed."

בֵּית שַׁמַּאי אוֹמְרִים: נֵר מָזוֹן בְּשָׂמִים וְהַבְדָּלָה. וּבֵית
הַלֵּל אוֹמְרִים: נֵר וּבְשָׂמִים וּמָזוֹן וְהַבְדָּלָה. בֵּית שַׁמַּאי
אוֹמְרִים: שֶׁבָּרָא מְאוֹר הָאֵשׁ. וּבֵית הַלֵּל אוֹמְרִים:
בּוֹרֵא מְאוֹרֵי הָאֵשׁ: גמ' תְּנֵי: אָמַר רַבִּי יְהוּדָא לֹא
נֶחְלְקוּ בֵית שַׁמַּאי וּבֵית הַלֵּל עַל הַמָּזוֹן שֶׁהוּא בַּתְּחִילָה
וְעַל הַבְדָּלָה שֶׁהִיא בַסוֹף. וְעַל מָה נֶחְלְקוּ? עַל הַמָּאוֹר
וְעַל הַבְּשָׂמִים שֶׁבֵּית שַׁמַּאי אוֹמְרִים בְּשָׂמִים וּמָאוֹר.
וּבֵית הַלֵּל אוֹמְרִים מָאוֹר וּבְשָׂמִים. רַבִּי בָּא וְרַב יְהוּדָא
בְּשֵׁם רַב: הֲלָכָה כְּדִבְרֵי מִי שֶׁאוֹמֵר בְּשָׂמִים וְאַחַר כָּךְ
מָאוֹר. בֵּית שַׁמַּאי אוֹמְרִים: כּוֹס בִּימִינוֹ וְשֶׁמֶן עָרֵב
בִּשְׂמֹאלוֹ. אוֹמֵר עַל הַכּוֹס וְאַחַר כָּךְ אוֹמֵר עַל שֶׁמֶן
עָרֵב. בֵּית הַלֵּל אוֹמְרִים: שֶׁמֶן עָרֵב בִּימִינוֹ וְכוֹס
בִּשְׂמֹאלוֹ וְאוֹמֵר עַל שֶׁמֶן עָרֵב וְטָחוֹ בְרֹאשׁ הַשַּׁמָּשׁ.
אִם הָיָה שַׁמָּשׁ תַּלְמִיד חָכָם טָחוֹ בַּכּוֹתָל. שֶׁאֵין שְׁבָחוֹ
שֶׁל תַּלְמִיד חָכָם לִהְיוֹת יוֹצֵא מְבוּשָׂם. אַבָּא בַּר בַּר
חַנָּא וְרַב חוּנָא הֲווֹן יָתְבִין אָכְלִין וַהֲוָה רַבִּי זְעֵירָא
קָאִים וּמְשַׁמֵּשׁ קוֹמֵיהוֹן. עָלָה וְטָעֵין תַּרְוֵיהוֹן בַּחֲדָא
יְדֵיה. אָמַר לֵיהּ אַבָּא בַּר בַּר חַנָּא מָה יְדָךְ חוֹרִיתָא
קְטַעוּן? וּכְעַס עִילָוֵי אֲבוּי. אָמַר לֵיהּ לָא מִיסְתָּךְ דְּאַתְּ
רְבִיעַ וְהוּא קָאִים מְשַׁמֵּשׁ. וְעוֹד דְּהוּא כֹהֵן וַאֲמַר
שְׁמוּאֵל הַמִּשְׁתַּמֵּשׁ בַּכְּהוּנָה מָעַל. אַתְּ מֵיקֵל לֵיהּ.
גְּזֵירָה דְּהוּא רָבַע וְאַתְּ קָאִים מְשַׁמֵּשׁ תַּחְתּוֹי.

8:5. **The House of Shammai say, "Light, and food, and spices, and *Havdalah*." And the House of Hillel say, "Light, and spices, and food, and *Havdalah*." The House of Shammai say, "'Who created the light of the fire.'" And the House of Hillel say, "'Who creates the lights of the fire.'"**

A. It was taught:

B. R. Judah said, "The House of Shammai and the House of Hillel did not differ concerning the [blessing for] the meal, that it comes at the beginning, or concerning *Havdalah*, that it comes at the end. And concerning what did they differ? Concerning the light and spices, for the House of Shammai say, 'Spices and light.' And the House of Hillel say, 'Light and spices.'"

C. R. Ba and R. Judah in the name of Rav [said], "The law is in accord with him who says, 'Spices and afterward light.' [That is, Judah's House of Shammai.]"

D. The House of Shammai say, "The cup [should be] in his right hand, and the sweet oil in his left hand. He says [the blessing for] the cup and afterward says the blessing for the sweet oil."

E. The House of Hillel say, "The sweet oil [should be] in his right hand and the cup in his left hand, and he says [the blessing for] the sweet oil and rubs it in the head of the servant. If the servant is a disciple of a sage, he rubs it on the wall, for it is not fitting for a disciple of a sage to go forth scented in public."

F. *Abba bar bar Hanna and R. Huna were sitting and eating, and R. Zeira was standing and serving them. He went and bore both of them [oil and cup] in one hand.*

G. *Abba bar bar Hanna said to him, "Is one of your hands cut off?" And his [Abba's] father was angry at him.*

H. *He [the father] said to him [Abba], "Is it not enough for you that you are sitting and he is standing and serving? And furthermore, he is a priest, and Samuel said,* 'He who makes [secular] use of the priesthood has committed sacrilege.' *You make light of him.*

I. *"I decree for him to sit and you to stand and serve in his place."*

The little story is meant to show several things. First, you should not hold the oil and the cup in the same hand. But, second, you have to show respect for the young man. Now the rule is introduced that you should not make secular use of a priest. That is, just as the Temple is reserved for sacred purposes, so the priests of the Temple cannot be employed for other than sacred tasks.

מִנַּיִן הַמִּשְׁתַּמֵּשׁ בַּכְּהוּנָה מָעַל? רַבִּי אָחָא בְּשֵׁם
שְׁמוּאֵל אָמַר: וָאֹמְרָה לָהֶן אַתֶּם קֹדֶשׁ לה' וְהַכֵּלִים
קֹדֶשׁ מָה כֵּלִים הַמִּשְׁתַּמֵּשׁ בָּהֶן מָעַל אַף הַמִּשְׁתַּמֵּשׁ
בִּכְהֹנִים מָעַל: [פִּיסְקָא ב"ש אומרים שברא וכו'.] עַל
דַּעַתְהוֹן דְּבֵית שַׁמַּאי: אֲשֶׁר בָּרָא פְּרִי הַגָּפֶן.

J. How do we know that he who makes use of the
priesthood has committed sacrilege?

K. R. Aha in the name of Samuel said, "'And I said to
them, You are holy to the Lord and the vessels are holy'
[Ezra 8:28]. Just as one who makes use of the vessels
commits sacrilege, so he who makes use of the priests
commits sacrilege."

L. [**The House of Shammai say, "'Who created . . .'"**]

M. According to the opinion of the House of Shammai,
[one should say as the blessing for wine], "Who created
the fruit of the vine" [instead of "who creates . . . ," as
actually is said].

The criticism of the Shammaite position is a good one. Why
do they take inconsistent positions, on the one hand saying
"who *creates* the fruit of the vine," but on the other, "who
created the light . . ."?

עַל דַּעֲתֵיהוֹן דְּבֵית הִלֵּל: בּוֹרֵי פְּרִי הַגָּפֶן.

N. According to the opinion of the House of Hillel,
[one should say,] "Who creates the fruit of the vine" [as
is indeed the case].

The Shammaites will make a distinction between the two
cases.

יַיִן מִתְחַדֵּשׁ בְּכָל שָׁנָה וְשָׁנָה, הָאֵשׁ אֵינוּ מִתְחַדֵּשׁ בְּכָל
שָׁעָה.

O. [The Shammaite reply:]

P. The wine is newly created every year, but the fire is not newly created every hour.

This is a fair distinction and satisfactorily lays the objection to rest.

The next set of materials is long but poses no problems. It is first asserted that although the fire and the mule were not actually created during the first six days, they were *thought of* during that time. This point will then be proved by reference to various Scriptures. Thus the subject will run on. How do you know the difference between a mule whose sire was an ass, and one whose sire was a horse? Afterward, the story of Zibeon and Anah, which is alluded to at the outset, will be discussed. Finally, the creation of fire, mentioned in the beginning, is going to be described. Fire came at the very end of the first Sabbath, on Saturday night after the first week of creation.

הָאֵשׁ וְהַכִּלְאַיִם אַף עַל פִּי שֶׁלֹּא נִבְרְאוּ מִשֵּׁשֶׁת יְמֵי
בְרֵאשִׁית אֲבָל עָלוּ בַּמַּחֲשָׁבָה מִשֵּׁשֶׁת יְמֵי בְרֵאשִׁית.
הַכִּלְאַיִם וּבְנֵי צִבְעוֹן אַיָּה וַעֲנָה הוּא עֲנָה אֲשֶׁר מָצָא
אֶת הַיֵּמִים בַּמִּדְבָּר. מָהוּ יֵמִים? רַבִּי יְהוּדָה בֶן סִימוֹן
אוֹמֵר: הֶמְיוֹנַס וְרַבָּנָן אֹמְרִין: הַיֵּמִים: חֶצְיוֹ סוּס וְחֶצְיוֹ
חֲמוֹר. וְאֵילוּ הֵן הַסִּימָנִין: אָמַר רַבִּי יְהוּדָה: כֹּל שֶׁאָזְנָיו
קְטַנּוֹת אִמּוֹ סוּס וְאָבִיו חֲמוֹר. גְּדוֹלוֹת אִמּוֹ חֲמוֹרָה
וְאָבִיו סוּס. רַבִּי מָנָא מְפַקֵּד לְאִילֵּין דִּנְשִׂיאָה: אֵין
בָּעֵיתוּן מִיזְבּוֹן מוּלְיוֹן תְּהוֹן זָבְנִין אִילֵּין דְּאוּדְנֵיהוֹן
דְּקִיקִין שֶׁאִמּוֹ סוּסָה וְאָבִיו חֲמוֹר. מֶה עָשָׂה צִבְעוֹן
וַעֲנָה זִמֵּן חֲמוֹרָה וְהֶעֱלָה עָלֶיהָ סוּס זָכָר וְיָצָא מֵהֶן
פִּרְדָה. אָמַר הַקָּדוֹשׁ בָּרוּךְ הוּא לָהֶם: אַתֶּם הֲבֵאתֶם
לָעוֹלָם דָּבָר שֶׁהוּא מַזִּיקָן. אַף אֲנִי מֵבִיא עַל אוֹתוֹ
הָאִישׁ דָּבָר שֶׁהוּא מַזִּיקוֹ. מֶה עָשָׂה הַקָּדוֹשׁ בָּרוּךְ הוּא
זִמֵּן חֲכִינָה וְהֶעֱלָה עָלֶיהָ חַרְדּוֹן וְיָצָא מִמֶּנָּה חַבַּרְבָּר.
מִיָּמָיו לֹא יֹאמַר לְךָ אָדָם שֶׁעֲקָצוֹ חַבַּרְבָּר וְחָיָה, נְשָׁכוֹ

כֶּלֶב שׁוֹטֶה וְהָיָה שֶׁבְּעָטַתוּ פִּרְדָּה וְהָיָה וּבִלְבַד פִּרְדָּה
לְבָנָה. הָאֵשׁ: רַבִּי לֵוִי בְּשֵׁם רַבִּי בְזִירָה: שְׁלֹשִׁים וָשֵׁשׁ
שָׁעוֹת שִׁימְּשָׁה אוֹתָהּ הָאוֹרָה שֶׁנִּבְרֵאת בַּיּוֹם הָרִאשׁוֹן.
שְׁתֵּים עֶשְׂרֵה בְּעֶרֶב שַׁבָּת וּשְׁתֵּים עֶשְׂרֵה בְּלֵיל שַׁבָּת
וּשְׁתֵּים עֶשְׂרֵה בְּשַׁבָּת. וְהָיָה אָדָם הָרִאשׁוֹן מַבִּיט בּוֹ
מִסּוֹף הָעוֹלָם וְעַד סוֹפוֹ כֵּיוָן שֶׁלֹּא פָּסְקָה הָאוֹרָה
הִתְחִיל כָּל הָעוֹלָם כּוּלּוֹ מְשׁוֹרֵר שֶׁנֶּאֱמַר: תַּחַת כָּל
הַשָּׁמַיִם יִשְׁרֵהוּ לְמִי שְׁאוֹרוֹ עַל כַּנְפוֹת הָאָרֶץ. כֵּיוָן
שֶׁיָּצֵאת שַׁבָּת הִתְחִיל מְשַׁמֵּשׁ הַחוֹשֶׁךְ וּבָא וְנִתְיָרֵא
אָדָם וְאָמַר אֵלּוּ הוּא שֶׁכָּתַב בּוֹ: הוּא יְשׁוּפְךָ רֹאשׁ
וְאַתָּה תְּשׁוּפֶנּוּ עָקֵב שְׁמָא בָּא לְנָשְׁכֵנִי וְאָמַר אַךְ חֹשֶׁךְ
יְשׁוּפֵנִי. אָמַר רַבִּי לֵוִי: בְּאוֹתוֹ שָׁעָה זִימֵּן הַקָּדוֹשׁ בָּרוּךְ
הוּא שְׁנֵי רְעָפִין וְהִקִּישָׁן זֶה לָזֶה וְיָצָא מֵהֶן הָאוֹר הָדָא
הוּא דִכְתִיב וְלַיְלָה אוֹר בַּעֲדֵנִי וּבֵירֶךְ עָלֶיהָ: בּוֹרֵא
מְאוֹרֵי הָאֵשׁ.

Q. The fire and the mule, even though they were not created in the six days of creation, were thought of [entered the Creator's mind] in the six days of creation.

R. Proof of the mule: "These are the sons of Zibeon: Aiah and Anah; he is the Anah who found the hot springs (HYYMYM) in the wilderness [as he pastured the asses of Zibeon his father (Genesis 36:24)]."

S. *What is the meaning of* hot springs (HYYMYM)?

T. R. Judah b. Simeon says, "Mule." [Greek: *hemiovos.*]

U. *And the rabbis say,* "Half-a-horse [Greek: *hemi-hippos*], half was a horse, half an ass."

V. And what are the marks [to know whether the father was a horse, the mother an ass, or vice versa]?

W. R. Judah said, "If the ears are small, the mother was a horse and the father an ass. If they are big, the mother was an ass and the father a horse."

X. R. *Mana instructed the members of the Patriarchate, "If you want to buy a mule, buy those whose ears are small,* for the mother was a horse and the father an ass."

Y. What did Zibeon and Anah do? They brought a female ass and mated her with a male horse, and they produced a mule.

Z. The Holy One, blessed be He, said to them, "You have brought into the world something which is destructive. So I too shall bring upon that man [you] something which is destructive."

AA. What did the Holy One, blessed be He, do?

BB. He brought a snake and mated it with a lizard and it produced a *havarbar*-lizard.

CC. A man should never say to you that a *havarbar*-lizard bit him and he lived, or a mad dog nipped him and he lived, or a she-mule butted him and he lived. We speak only of a white she-mule.

DD. As to the fire:

EE. R. Levi in the name of R. Nezira [said], "Thirty-six hours that light which was created on the first day served [the world]. Twelve on the eve of the Sabbath [Friday], twelve on the night of the Sabbath, and twelve on the Sabbath.

FF. "And the First Man [Adam] looked at it from one end of the world to the other. When the light did not cease [from shining], the whole world began to sing, as it is said, 'Under the whole heaven, he lets [his voice] go, and his light to the corners of the earth' [Job 37:3].

GG. "When the Sabbath ended, it began to get dark. Man became frightened, saying, 'This is the one concerning whom it is written, "He will bruise your head, and you shall bruise his heel" [Genesis 3:15].

HH. "'Perhaps this one has come to bite me.' And he said, 'Let only darkness cover me'" [Psalm 139:11].

II. R. Levi said, "At that moment the Holy One,

blessed be He, prepared two flints and struck them against each other, and the light came forth from them. This is the meaning of that which Scripture says, 'And the night around me be light' [Psalm 139:11].

JJ. "And he [man] blessed it, 'Who creates the lights of the fire.'"

Here we have the story of the discovery of fire. Man did not steal it from the god. He was not punished, as was Prometheus, on that account. Fire is a blessing. It was given by God to man to reassure him against the darkness. Fire is a gift of God and so testifies to God's benevolent protection of the fearful man. That is why you thank God for fire and for light—for the darkness is not too dark for God. Samuel will make clear why the blessing for fire comes at *Havdalah*, on the occasion of darkness at the end of the Sabbath.

שְׁמוּאֵל אָמַר: לְפִיכָךְ מְבָרְכִין עַל הָאֵשׁ בְּמוֹצָאֵי שַׁבָּתוֹת שֶׁהִיא תְּחִילַת בְּרִייָתָה. רַב הוּנָא בְּשֵׁם רַבִּי אַבָּהוּ בְּשֵׁם רַבִּי יוֹחָנָן: אַף בְּמוֹצָאֵי יוֹם הַכִּיפּוּרִים מְבָרֵךְ עָלֶיהָ שֶׁכְּבָר שָׁבַת הָאוֹר כָּל אוֹתוֹ הַיּוֹם:

KK. Samuel said, "Therefore they bless the fire at the end of the Sabbath, for that is when it was first created."

LL. R. Huna in the name of R. Abbahu in the name of R. Yohanan [said], "Also at the end of the Day of Atonement one blesses it, for the light has rested that entire day."

The comments on Mishnah 8:5 form a sequence of sayings pertinent to the Mishnah's theme, but none is either closely examined or integrated with any other.

A simply cites Judah [b. Ilai]'s tradition on the difference between the Houses and the opinions assigned to each. Rav's saying tells us the law, but not the House to which that law is attributed according to his version of the Houses' dispute.

D introduces further Toseftan materials, again without examination.

Then F tells us a story, somewhat relevant to the Tosefta's rule about having the cup in one hand, the oil in the other; you should not carry them together in one hand. J–L further augments F–I.

M brings a challenge to the view of the House of Shammai about using the past tense, *created*, in connection with the light. If creation is completed, then the blessing for wine is rightly, "Who created the fruit of the vine." This poses no problem to the Hillelites. The answer is that there is a difference between the creation of wine and that of fire. When you compare this primitive analysis of the Shammaite position with the better developed and more interesting one in the Babylonian Talmud, you will see what might have been done on this question.

O–P then brings in a passage (from the Tosefta) only remotely connected to the foregoing. It refers to the creation of fire and the mule (!). Then the mention of the mule involves us in a long discussion of how various hybrids are created and of how to identify their constituent elements. DD brings us back to the fire, and KK–LL gloss the issue but not the story.

Nothing before us has been generated by the Palestinian Talmud's editors themselves for the analysis of our Mishnah. Everything derives from some other corpus of materials. We have here a little anthology of pertinent sayings and stories, by contrast to the discussions of the earlier sections of the Mishnah, in which we discern a sustained effort to develop original inquiries.

אֵין מְבָרְכִין עַל הַנֵּר וְעַל הַבְּשָׂמִים שֶׁל גּוֹיִם וְעַל הַנֵּר
וְעַל הַבְּשָׂמִים שֶׁל מֵתִים וְעַל הַנֵּר וְעַל הַבְּשָׂמִים שֶׁלִּפְנֵי
עֲבוֹדָה זָרָה וְאֵין מְבָרְכִין עַל הַנֵּר עַד שֶׁיֵּאוֹתוּ
לְאוֹרוֹ: גמ' תְּנָא רַבִּי יַעֲקֹב קוֹמֵי רַבִּי יִרְמִיָּה מְבָרְכִין
עַל הַבְּשָׂמִים שֶׁל גּוֹיִם. מָהוּ פְּלִיג. קַיּוֹמוּנֶה בְּמַעֲשָׂיו

לִפְנֵי חֲנוּתוֹ. עֲשָׂשִׁית אַף עַל פִּי שֶׁלֹּא כָבָת מְבָרְכִין
עָלֶיהָ. נֵר בְּתוֹךְ חֵיקוֹ אוֹ בְּתוֹךְ פָּנָס אוֹ בְּתוֹךְ
אַסְפַּקְלַרְיָא רוֹאֶה אֶת הַשַּׁלְהֶבֶת וְאֵינוֹ מִשְׁתַּמֵּשׁ
לְאוֹרָהּ מִשְׁתַּמֵּשׁ לְאוֹרָה וְאֵינוֹ רוֹאֶה אֶת הַשַּׁלְהֶבֶת
לְעוֹלָם אֵין מְבָרְכִין עָלֶיהָ עַד שֶׁיִּהְיֶה רוֹאֶה אֶת
הַשַּׁלְהֶבֶת וּמִשְׁתַּמֵּשׁ לְאוֹרָהּ. חֲמִשָּׁה דְבָרִים נֶאֶמְרוּ
בְגַחֶלֶת וַחֲמִשָּׁה בְשַׁלְהֶבֶת: גַּחֶלֶת שֶׁל הַקֹּדֶשׁ מוֹעֲלִין
בָּהּ וְהַשַּׁלְהֶבֶת לֹא נֶהֱנִין וְלֹא מוֹעֲלִין. גַּחֶלֶת שֶׁל
עֲבוֹדָה זָרָה אֲסוּרָה וְשַׁלְהֶבֶת מוּתֶּרֶת. הַמּוּדָּר הֲנָאָה
מֵחֲבֵירוֹ אָסוּר בְּגַחַלְתּוֹ וּמוּתָּר בְּשַׁלְהַבְתּוֹ. הַמּוֹצִיא
אֶת הַגַּחֶלֶת לִרְשׁוּת הָרַבִּים חַיָּיב וְהַשַּׁלְהֶבֶת פָּטוּר.
מְבָרְכִין עַל הַשַּׁלְהֶבֶת וְאֵין מְבָרְכִין עַל הַגַּחֶלֶת. רַבִּי
חִיָּיא בַּר אָשֵׁי בְּשֵׁם רַב: אִם הָיוּ גֶחָלִים לוֹחֲשׁוֹת
מְבָרְכִין. רַבִּי יוֹחָנָן דִּקְרָצִיוֹן בְּשֵׁם רַבִּי נָחוּם בַּר סִימָאי:
בִּלְבַד הַנִּקְטֶפֶת.

**8:6. They do not bless the light or spices of gentiles,
nor the light or spices of the dead, nor the light or
spices which are before an idol. They do not bless the
light until they make use of its illumination.**

A. R. Jacob taught before R. Jeremiah, "They do bless
the spices of gentiles."

B. *What is the difference* [between this view and the
Mishnah's]?

C. *We explain that the latter refers to the* gentile's deeds
before his own store [while the Mishnah refers to a
banquet].

D. Even though it has not gone out [but burned the
entire Sabbath], they may bless [the light of] a lantern
[because no prohibited work has been done by its light].

E. As regards a flame in the folds of one's garment, in
a lamp, or in a mirror, if one sees the flame but does not

make use of its light, or makes use of its light but not see the flame, one may not bless it. [One may bless] only when one may see the flame and makes use of the light.

F. Five things were said in regard to the burning coal, and five with regard to the flame.

1. A coal of the sanctuary is subject to the law of sacrilege, but a flame is neither used for pleasure nor subject to the law of sacrilege.

2. A burning coal used for idolatry is prohibited, but a flame is permitted.

3. He who vows not to have enjoyment from his fellow may not use his burning coal, but may use his flame.

4. He who brings a coal out to the public way [on the Sabbath] is liable, but if he brings a flame, he is not liable.

5. They bless the flame, but not the burning coal.

G. R. Hiyya bar Ashi in the name of Rav said, "If the coals were glowing, they may bless them."

H. R. Yohanan of Kerasion in the name of R. Nahum bar Simai [said], "On condition that it was cut off." [That is, the flame was shooting up from the coal.]

A–C produces a rule contrary to that printed in the Mishnah: One *may* bless the spices of gentiles. The Mishnah is understood to refer to a banquet—just as in the Babylonian discussion— while Jacob's view alludes to the spices belonging to a private person. These are not necessarily used for idolatrous purposes.

D tells us that a flickering lantern which has burned the entire Sabbath may be blessed; nothing forbidden has been done in its light. This is all we have as an equivalent to the Babylonian Talmud's full discussion of whether or not a candle has "rested" on the Sabbath.

E cites the Tosefta, and F is a group of five rules which make the same point about the coal and the flame. The one is material, the other immaterial. The fourth is contradicted in the

Babylonian Talmud, which therefore presumably does not know this list; if it did, someone would have remarked on the contradiction.

תְּנֵי: גּוֹי שֶׁהִדְלִיק מִיִשְׂרָאֵל וְיִשְׂרָאֵל שֶׁהִדְלִיק מִגּוֹי
נִיחָא. גּוֹי שֶׁהִדְלִיק מִיִשְׂרָאֵל מֵעַתָּה אֲפִילוּ גּוֹי מִגּוֹי.

I. *It was taught:*

J. Now the [light of] a gentile who kindled [a light from the flame of] an Israelite, and an Israelite who kindled [a light from the flame of a gentile]—*this poses no problems.*

K. But [the light of] a gentile who kindled [a light from the flame of] an Israelite [may be blessed]. If so, even [the flame of] a gentile who kindled from a gentile [should be allowed].

The problem is the same as that posed in the Babylonian Talmud. What is the reason you may not kindle a flame from one kindled by a gentile from a gentile, if you *may* do so from a flame kindled by an Israelite from a gentile?

אַשְׁכַּח תְּנֵי גּוֹי מִגּוֹי אֵין מְבָרְכִין.

L. *It is indeed taught:* They do *not* bless [a light kindled by] a gentile from a gentile.

The solution to the problem is no solution at all. It simply reasserts the original proposition.

רַבִּי אַבָּהוּ בְּשֵׁם רַבִּי יוֹחָנָן: מָבוֹי שֶׁכּוּלוֹ גוֹיִם וְיִשְׂרָאֵל
אֶחָד דָּר בְּתוֹכוֹ וְיָצָא מִשָּׁם הָאוֹר מְבָרְכִין עָלֶיהָ בִּשְׁבִיל
אוֹתוֹ יִשְׂרָאֵל שֶׁשָּׁם.

M. R. Abbahu in the name of R. Yohanan [said,] "As to an alleyway which is populated entirely by gentiles with a single Israelite living in its midst—if the light comes from there, they may bless it on account of that one Israelite who lives there."

Yohanan will now be cited in a saying, which, in concrete
terms, repeats the principle already established in general language, that you may say a blessing over something which is
used for its normal purpose. But you may not recite a blessing
over something which is used for some abnormal purpose—
spices used for cleaning clothes, for example.

רַבִּי אַבָּהוּ בְּשֵׁם רַבִּי יוֹחָנָן: אֵין מְבָרְכִין לֹא עַל
הַבְּשָׂמִים שֶׁל לֵילֵי שַׁבָּת בִּטְבֶרְיָא וְלֹא עַל הַבְּשָׂמִים
שֶׁל מוֹצָאֵי שַׁבָּת בְּצִיפּוֹרִין. וְלֹא עַל הַנֵּר וְלֹא עַל
הַבְּשָׂמִים שֶׁל אוֹר עֶרֶב שַׁבָּת בְּצפּוֹרִין. שֶׁאֵינָן עֲשׂוּיִין
אֶלָּא לְדָבָר אַחֵר. וְלֹא עַל הַנֵּר וְהַבְּשָׂמִים שֶׁל מֵתִים.
רַבִּי חִזְקָיָה וְרַבִּי יַעֲקֹב בַּר אַחָא בְּשֵׁם רַבִּי יוֹסֵי בֵּי רַבִּי
חֲנִינָא: הָדָא דַאת אָמַר: בִּנְתוּנִים לְמַעֲלָה מִמִּטָּתוֹ
שְׁלַמֵּת. אֲבָל אִם הָיָה נְתוּנִים לִפְנֵי מִטָתוֹ שְׁלַמֵּת
מְבָרְכִין. אֲנִי אוֹמֵר לִכְבוֹד הַחַיִּים הֵן עֲשׂוּיִן. וְלֹא עַל
הַנֵּר וְלֹא עַל הַבְּשָׂמִים שֶׁל עֲבוֹדָה זָרָה. וְלֹא הִיא שֶׁל
גּוֹיִם הִיא שֶׁל עֲבוֹדָה זָרָה. תִּיפְתַּר בַּעֲבוֹדָה זָרָה שֶׁל
יִשְׂרָאֵל.

N. R. Abbahu in the name of R. Yohanan [said], "They
do not bless either the spices on Sabbath evenings in
Tiberias or the spices on Saturday nights in Sepphoris,
or the light or the spices on Friday mornings in Sepphoris, for these all are prepared only for another purpose
[cleaning clothes]."

O. **Nor over the light or spices of the dead.**

P. R. Hezekiah and R. Jacob b. Aha in the name of R.
Yosé b. R. Hanina [said], "This refers to the following
case: 'When they are placed over the bed of the dead.
But if they are placed before the bed of the dead, they
may be blessed [that is, a blessing may be recited over
them].'"

Q. "[For] I say, they are prepared for the purposes of the living."

R. **Nor the light nor the spices of idolatry.**

S. But is not that of gentiles the same as that of idolatry? [Why repeat the same rule?]

T. Interpret it as applying to an Israelite idol.

I–L quotes and examines the Tosefta's rule. M gives a law contrary to the Babylonian Talmud's tradition formulated in the style of the Mishnah, called a *baraita*, which held a *majority* must be Israelites before the flame may be blessed. Again it seems this rule cannot have been known to the Babylonian editors.

In N we have the same view as above: People in Galilee would use spice for cleaning clothes; therefore, you may not bless the spice at the times at which it is used for that purpose.

O goes back over the law that you have to use a light for its normal purpose, not for the honor of a corpse.

R–T raises a good problem in literary analysis. The Mishnah seems to repeat itself. The solution is routine.

אֵין מְבָרְכִין עַל הַנֵּר עַד שֶׁיֵּאוֹתוּ לְאוֹרוֹ. דָּרַשׁ רַבִּי זְעֵירָא בְּרֵיהּ דְּרַבִּי אַבָּהוּ: וַיַּרְא אֱלֹהִים אֶת הָאוֹר כִּי טוֹב וְאַחַר כָּךְ וַיַּבְדֵּל אֱלֹהִים בֵּין הָאוֹר וּבֵין הַחֹשֶׁךְ. אָמַר רַבִּי בְּרֶכְיָה: כָּךְ דָּרְשׁוּ שְׁנֵי גְדוֹלֵי עוֹלָם רַבִּי יוֹחָנָן וְרַבִּי שִׁמְעוֹן בֶּן לָקִישׁ: וַיַּבְדֵּל אֱלֹהִים אַבְדָּלָה וַדַּאי. רַבִּי יְהוּדָה בֵּי רַבִּי סִימוֹן אָמַר: הִבְדִּילוֹ לוֹ. וְרַבָּנָן אָמְרִין: הִבְדִּילוֹ לַצַּדִּיקִים לֶעָתִיד לָבוֹא. מָשְׁלוּ מָשָׁל לְמָה הַדָּבָר דּוֹמֶה? לְמֶלֶךְ שֶׁהָיוּ לוֹ שְׁנֵי אִסְטְרַטֵיגִין זֶה אוֹמֵר: אֲנִי מְשַׁמֵּשׁ בַּיּוֹם, וְזֶה אוֹמֵר: אֲנִי מְשַׁמֵּשׁ בַּיּוֹם, קָרָא לָרִאשׁוֹן וְאָמַר לוֹ: פְּלוֹנִי הַיּוֹם יְהֵא תְחוּמְךָ. קָרָא לַשֵּׁנִי וְאָמַר לוֹ: פְּלוֹנִי הַלַּיְלָה יְהֵא תְחוּמְךָ. הֲדָא הוּא דִכְתִיב וַיִּקְרָא אֱלֹהִים לָאוֹר יוֹם וְגוֹ' לָאוֹר אָמַר לוֹ הַיּוֹם יְהֵא תְּחוּמְךָ וְלַחֹשֶׁךְ אָמַר לוֹ הַלַּיְלָה יְהֵא

תְּחוּמְךָ. אָמַר רַבִּי יוֹחָנָן: הוּא שֶׁאָמַר הַקָּדוֹשׁ בָּרוּךְ
הוּא לְאִיּוֹב: הַמִּיָּמֶיךָ צִוִּיתָ בּוֹקֶר יִדַּעְתָּ הַשַּׁחַר
מְקוֹמוֹ — יָדַעְתָּ אֵי זֶה מְקוֹמוֹ שֶׁל אוֹר שֵׁשֶׁת יְמֵי
בְרֵאשִׁית אֵיכָן נִגְנַז? אָמַר רַבִּי תַּנְחוּמָא אֲנָא אַמְרִית
טַעְמָא: יוֹצֵר אוֹר וּבוֹרֵא חוֹשֶׁךְ עוֹשֶׂה שָׁלוֹם מְשַׁיְּצָא
עוֹשֶׂה שָׁלוֹם בֵּינֵיהֶן. אֵין מְבָרְכִין עַל הַנֵּר עַד שֶׁיֵּאוֹתוּ
לְאוֹרוֹ רַב אָמַר יֵאוֹתוּ וּשְׁמוּאֵל אָמַר יֵעוֹתוּ. מָאן דַּאֲמַר
יֵאוֹתוּ אַךְ בְּזֹאת נֵאוֹתָה לָכֶם. מָאן דַּאֲמַר יֵעוֹתוּ,
לָדַעַת לָעוּת אֶת יָעֵף דָּבָר. תַּמָּן תְּנִינַן: כֵּיצַד מְעַבְּרִין
אֶת הֶעָרִים? רַב אָמַר: מְאַבְּרִין. וּשְׁמוּאֵל אָמַר:
מְעַבְּרִין. מָאן דַּאֲמַר מְאַבְּרִין מוֹסִיפִין לָהּ אֵבֶר. מָאן
דַּאֲמַר מְעַבְּרִין כְּאִשָּׁה עוּבָּרָה. תַּמָּן תְּנִינַן: לִפְנֵי אֵידֵיהֶן
שֶׁלַּגּוֹיִם. רַב אָמַר עֵידֵיהֶן וּשְׁמוּאֵל אָמַר אֵידֵיהֶן. מָאן
דַּאֲמַר אֵידֵיהֶן כִּי קָרוֹב יוֹם אֵדָם. וּמָאן דַּאֲמַר עֵידֵיהֶן
וְעֵידֵיהֶם הֵמָּה בַּל יִרְאוּ וּבַל יֵדְעוּ לְמַעַן יֵבֹשׁוּ. מָאן
מְקַיֵּם שְׁמוּאֵל טַעְמָא דְּרַב? וְעֵידֵיהֶם הֵמָּה שֶׁהֵן
עֲתִידִין לְבַיֵּישׁ אֶת עוֹבְדֵיהֶן לְיוֹם הַדִּין. אֵין מְבָרְכִין
עַל הַנֵּר עַד שֶׁיֵּאוֹתוּ לְאוֹרוֹ. רַב יְהוּדָה בְּשֵׁם שְׁמוּאֵל:
כְּדֵי שֶׁיְּהוּ נָשִׁים טַוּוֹת לְאוֹרוֹ. אָמַר רַבִּי יוֹחָנָן: כְּדֵי
שֶׁתְּהֵא עֵינוֹ רוֹאָה מַה בְּכוֹס וּמַה בַּקְּעָרָה. אָמַר רַב
חֲנִינָא: כְּדֵי שֶׁיְּהֵא יוֹדֵעַ לְהַבְחִין בֵּין מַטְבֵּעַ לְמַטְבֵּעַ.
תָּנֵי רַבִּי אוֹשַׁעְיָא: אֲפִילוּ טְרֵיקְלִין עֶשֶׂר עַל עֶשֶׂר
מְבָרְכִין. רַבִּי זְעֵירָא מְקָרֵב קָמֵיהּ בּוּצִינָא. אָמְרִין לֵיהּ
תַּלְמִידָיו רַבִּי מָה אַתְּ מַחְמִיר עָלֵינוּ הָא תְּנֵי רַבִּי
אוֹשַׁעְיָא אֲפִילוּ טְרֵיקְלִין עֶשֶׂר עַל עֶשֶׂר מְבָרְכִין:

**They do not bless the light until they make use of its
illumination.**

A. R. Zeira son of R. Abbahu expounded, "'And God
saw the light, that it was good' [Genesis 1:4]. And

afterward, 'And God divided the light from the darkness'" [Genesis 1:5]. [That is, first it was seen and used, then comes the *Havdalah*.]

B. R. Berekiah said, "Thus the two great men of the world [age], R. Yohanan and R. Simeon b. Laqish, expounded: 'And God divided—a certain division.'" [That is, he did so literally.]

C. R. Judah b. R. Simon said, "They divided for Him."

D. And the rabbis say, "They divided for the righteous who were destined to come into the world.

E. "They drew a parable: To what is the matter to be likened? To a king who has two generals. This one says, 'I shall serve by day,' and this one says, 'I shall serve by day.'

F. "He calls the first and says to him, 'So-and-so, the day will be your division.'

G. "He calls the second and says to him, 'So-and-so, the night will be your division.'

H. "That is the meaning of what is written, 'And God called the light day, and the darkness he called night.'

I. "To the light he said, 'The day will be your province.' And to the darkness he said, 'The night will be your province.'"

J. R. Yohanan said, "This is what the Holy One, blessed be He, said to Job [Job 38:12], 'Have you commanded the morning since your days began, and caused the dawn to know its place?'

K. "What is the place of the light of the six days of creation—where was it hidden?"

L. R. *Tanhuma said, "I give the reason:* 'Who creates light and makes darkness, and makes peace' [Isaiah 45:7]. When he went forth, he made peace between them."

M. **They do not bless the light until they make use of its illumination.**

N. Rav said, "They *use* [spelled with an *'alef*]."

O. And Samuel said, "They *enjoy* [spelled with an *'ayin*]."

P. He who said "they *use*" [may draw support from the following]:

Q. "Only on this condition will we *consent* to you" [Genesis 34:15].

R. He who said *"enjoy"* [may draw support from the following]:

S. "How to sustain with a word him that is weary" [Isaiah 50:4].

T. There we have learned: "How do they extend (M'BR) the Sabbath limits of cities?"

U. Rav said, *"Add"* [*'alef*].

V. And Samuel said, *"Increase"* [*'ayin*].

W. He who said it is with an *'alef* means they add a limb to it.

X. He who said it is with an *'ayin* means it is [increased] like a pregnant woman.

Y. There we learned, "Before the festivals ('YD) of gentiles."

Z. Rav said, *"Testimonies"* [*'ayin*].

AA. And Samuel said, *"Festivals"* [*'alef*].

BB. He who said it is with an *'alef* [may cite this verse], "For near is the day of their calamity ['YD]" [Deuteronomy 32:35].

CC. He who said it is with an *'ayin* [may cite], "Their testimonies neither see nor know, that they may be put to shame" [Isaiah 44:9].

DD. How does Samuel deal with the reason of Rav? [He may say,] "And their *testimonies* are destined to *shame* those who keep them on the day of judgment."

EE. **They do not bless the light until they have made use of its illumination.** [How much illumination must there be?]

FF. R. Judah in the name of Samuel said, "So that women may spin by its light."

GG. R. Yohanan said, "So that one's eye can see what is in the cup and what is in the saucer."

HH. R. Hanina said, "So that one may know how to distinguish one coin from another."

II. R. Oshaia taught, "Even [if the flame is in] a hall ten-by-ten, they may say the blessing."

JJ. *R. Zeira drew near the lamp. His disciples said to him, "Rabbi, why do you rule so stringently for us? Lo, R. Oshaia taught, 'One may bless even in a hall ten-by-ten.'"*

The point of A is that Scripture itself implies you must actually use the light before saying *Havdalah*. It refers to God's "saying *Havdalah*"—that is, making a division—only after he had looked at the light.

B then introduces a story about why the light was divided from the darkness.

M–DD is a collection of three examples of disputes between Rav and Samuel, early third-century Babylonian masters, about whether words are spelled with the *'alef* or the *'ayin*, both evidently silent letters in Babylonia, not distinguished from each other in pronunciation. The first concerns the spelling of the word *use* in our Mishnah; the difference produces variations in meanings, *use* versus *enjoy*. Each then is given a Scripture in which his spelling of the word appears. The second has to do with extending the Sabbath limits of a city; the *'alef* spelling of the word in question produces the meaning of *increase-by-adding-on*, augment; and the *'ayin* spelling produces the meaning of *increase-from-within*, expand. The final example has to do with the word for festival employed for gentile festivals. The *'alef* spelling yields a play on words, for, spelled with an *'alef*, the word means both "festival" and "calamity"; the *'ayin* spelling means "testimony."

EE–JJ illuminate the rule about using the illumination. How is this defined? The answers are routine. Oshaia's interpretation in II is not much different, except that he evidently regards as adequate the light available at a still greater distance from the flame. The story that follows provides a different literary and formal setting for the citation of Oshaia's rule.

מִי שֶׁאָכַל וְשָׁכַח וְלֹא בֵּירַךְ — בֵּית שַׁמַּאי אוֹמֵר יַחֲזוֹר
לִמְקוֹמוֹ וִיבָרֵךְ. וּבֵית הֶלֵּל אוֹמְרִים יְבָרֵךְ בְּמָקוֹם
שֶׁנִּזְכַּר. וְעַד מָתַי מְבָרֵךְ עַד כְּדֵי שֶׁיִּתְעַכֵּל הַמָּזוֹן
שֶׁבְּמֵעָיו: גמ' רַבִּי יוֹסְטָא בַּר שׁוֹנַם אָמַר: תְּרֵין
אָמוֹרִין חַד אָמַר טַעֲמוֹן דְּבֵית שַׁמַּאי וְחַד אָמַר טַעֲמוֹן
דְּבֵית הֶלֵּל.

8:7. He who ate and forgot and did not bless—

The House of Shammai say, "He should go back to his place and bless."

And the House of Hillel say, "He may bless in the place in which he remembered."

"Until when may he say the blessing? Until the food has been digested in his bowels."

A. *R. Yusta b. Shunam said, "[There are] two authorities. One gives the reason of the House of Shammai and the other the reason of the House of Hillel."*

Instead of a debate, we shall have a simple statement of the positions of the respective Houses. But the actual opinions are more fully articulated in the Babylonian Talmud. The Shammaites say you would take some trouble for material things, so you should also take some trouble for the divinity. The Hillelites say you do not put people to too much trouble.

מָאן דַּמַר טַעֲמוֹן דְּבֵית שַׁמַּאי אִילּוּ שָׁכַח שָׁם כִּיס
אֲבָנִים טוֹבוֹת וּמַרְגָּלִיּוֹת שֶׁמָּא לֹא הָיָה חוֹזֵר וְנוֹטֵל
כִּיסוֹ אַף הָכָא יַחֲזוֹר לִמְקוֹמוֹ וִיבָרֵךְ. מָאן דַּמַר טַעֲמְהוֹן
דְּבֵית הֶלֵּל אִילּוּ פּוֹעֵל עוֹשֶׂה בְּרֹאשׁ הַדֶּקֶל אוֹ בְּתוֹךְ
הַבּוֹר שֶׁמָּא מַטְרִיחִין שֶׁיַּחֲזוֹר לִמְקוֹמוֹ וִיבָרֵךְ אֶלָּא
מְבָרֵךְ בְּמָקוֹם שֶׁנִּזְכַּר אַף הָכָא מְבָרֵךְ בְּמָקוֹם שֶׁנִּזְכַּר.
עַד מָתַי הוּא מְבָרֵךְ?

B. *"The one who gives the reason of the House of Shammai* [says], 'If he had forgotten a purse of precious stones

and pearls there, would he not go back and take his
purse? *So too* let him go back to his place and bless.'

C. "*The one who gave the reason of the House of Hillel* [states],
'If he were a worker on the top of the palm or down in
a pit, would you trouble him to go back to his place
and bless? But he should bless in the place where he
remembers [to do so]. *Here too* let him bless in the place
where he remembers.'"

D. **Until when does he recite the blessing?**

The Mishnah will be defined in concrete terms. How long is
a person liable to say a blessing? If he forgets after a certain
time, he surely is not going to be expected to say the Grace.
The definitions are reasonable.

רַבִּי חִיָּא בְּשֵׁם שְׁמוּאֵל: עַד שֶׁיִּתְעַכֵּל הַמָּזוֹן בְּמֵעָיו
וַחֲכָמִים אוֹמְרִים: כָּל זְמַן שֶׁהוּא צָמֵא מֵחֲמַת אוֹתוֹ
סְעוּדָה. רַבִּי יוֹחָנָן אָמַר: עַד שֶׁיִּרְעַב:

E. R. Hiyya in the name of Samuel says, "Until the
food has been digested in his bowels."

F. And the sages say, "So long as he is thirsty on
account of that meal."

G. R. Yohanan says, "Until he becomes hungry again."

The "reasons" of A–C and the definitions of D–G do not
greatly differ from what we shall see in the Babylonian *Gemara*.

בָּא לָהֶן יַיִן אַחַר הַמָּזוֹן וְאֵין שָׁם אֶלָּא אוֹתוֹ הַכּוֹס —
בֵּית שַׁמַּאי אוֹמְרִים: מְבָרֵךְ עַל הַיַּיִן וְאַחַר כָּךְ מְבָרֵךְ
עַל הַמָּזוֹן. וּבֵית הִלֵּל אוֹמְרִים: מְבָרֵךְ עַל הַמָּזוֹן וְאַחַר
כָּךְ מְבָרֵךְ עַל הַיַּיִן. עוֹנִין אָמֵן אַחַר יִשְׂרָאֵל מְבָרֵךְ וְאֵין
עוֹנִין אָמֵן אַחַר כּוּתִי מְבָרֵךְ עַד שֶׁיִּשְׁמַע כָּל הַבְּרָכָה:
גמ' אָמַר רַבִּי בָּא עַל יְדֵי שֶׁהִיא בְּרָכָה קְטַנָּה שֶׁמָּא
יִשְׁכַּח וְיִשְׁתֶּה. בְּרַם הָכָא עַל יְדֵי שֶׁהִיא מְשׁוּלֶּשֶׁת עַל
הַכּוֹס אֵינוֹ שׁוֹכֵחַ. הָא אַחַר יִשְׂרָאֵל עוֹנִין אָמֵן אַף עַל

פִּי שֶׁלֹּא שָׁמַע. לֹא כֵן תְּנֵי: שָׁמַע וְלֹא עָנָה יָצָא עָנָה
וְלֹא שָׁמַע לֹא יָצָא.

8:8. If wine came to them after the food, and there is
there only one cup—

The House of Shammai say, "He blesses the wine and
afterward blesses the food."

And the House of Hillel say, "He blesses the food and
afterward blesses the wine."

They answer *Amen* after an Israelite who blesses, and
they do not answer *Amen* after a Samaritan who blesses
until the entire blessing has been heard.

A. R. Ba said, "Because it is a brief blessing, he may
forget and drink the wine. But because it is joined to the
[blessings for] cup, he will not forget."

B. **After an Israelite they answer *Amen*,** even though
he has not heard [the Grace]. Has it not been taught, "If
he heard [the Grace] and did not answer, he has carried
out his obligation [to say Grace]. If he answered [*Amen*]
and did not hear [the Grace], he has not carried out his
obligation."

The problem is already familiar. We assume the man has
eaten, but has heard only part of the grace. But he has to hear
the whole of the prayer if he is to have carried out his obligation
to say the Grace after Meals. The solution is simple. As before,
we have made the wrong assumption. In fact, the man did not
participate in the meal, so is not obligated at all. Yet, we are
taught, he still is supposed to respond with *Amen*.

חִיָּיא בְּרֵיה דְּרַב אָמַר: בְּשֶׁלֹּא אָכַל עִמָּהֶן כְּזַיִת. הָכָא
מַתְנִיתָא תְּנֵי שָׁמַע וְלֹא עָנָה יָצָא עָנָה וְלֹא שָׁמַע לֹא
יָצָא.

C. Hiyya the son of Rav said, "[The Mishnah speaks
of him who] did not eat with them as much as an olive's
bulk."

D. *So too it has been taught*: If he heard and did not answer, he has carried out his obligation. If he answered and did not hear, he has not carried out his obligation.

Now Rav is going to refine the foregoing rule.

רַב בְּשֵׁם אַבָּא בַר חָנָה וְאִית דָּאמְרִי לַהּ אַבָּא בַר חָנָה בְּשֵׁם רַב: וְהוּא שֶׁעָנָה רָאשֵׁי פְּרָקִים. רַבִּי זְעֵירָא בָּעֵי הֵי אִינִין רָאשֵׁי פְּרָקִים? הַלְלוּ יָהּ הַלְלוּ עַבְדֵי ה' הַלְלוּ אֶת שֵׁם ה'.

E. Rav in the name of Abba bar Hanna [said], *and some say Abba bar Hanna in the name of Rav* [said], "And this applies to a case in which he answered at the chapter [paragraph] headings."

F. *R. Zeira asked, "What are these chapter headings?"*

G. "Praise the Lord, praise the servants of the Lord, praise the name of the Lord" [Psalm 113:1].

Hiyya b. Abba will now explain the rule given at the outset, that merely hearing the Grace after Meals, without answering *Amen*, is sufficient to carry out one's obligation in that connection.

בְּעוֹן קוֹמֵי רַבִּי חִיָּיא בַר אַבָּא מִנַּיִן שֶׁאִם שָׁמַע וְלֹא עָנָה יָצָא?

H. *They asked before R. Hiyya b. Abba, "How do we know that, if one heard and did not answer [Amen], he has carried out his obligation?"*

Hiyya's answer draws upon the actual deeds of the rabbis of the day.

אָמַר מִן מָה דַאֲנַן חָמֵי רַבָּנָן רַבְרְבַיָּא עָבְדִין כֵּן אִינּוּן קַיְימִין בְּצִיבּוּרָא דְּאִילֵּין אָמְרִין דֵּין: בָּרוּךְ הַבָּא. וְאִילֵּין אָמְרִין: בְּשֵׁם ה'. וְאִילֵּין וְאִילֵּין יוֹצְאִין יְדֵי חוֹבָתָן. תַּנִי

רַב אוֹשַׁעְיָא: עוֹנֶה הוּא אָדָם אָמֵן אֲפִילוּ לֹא אָכַל
וְאֵינוּ אוֹמֵר "נְבָרֵךְ שֶׁאָכַלְנוּ מִשֶּׁלוֹ" אֶלָּא אִם כֵּן אָכַל.

I. *He said, "From what we have seen the great rabbis doing, so
they do in public, for they say this*: 'Blessed is he that comes.'
And the others say, 'In the name of the Lord.' *And both groups
thus* complete their obligation."

J. R. Oshaia taught, "A man responds *Amen,* even
though he has not eaten, and he does not say, 'Let us
bless him of whose bounty we have eaten,' unless he
actually ate."

We have a new tradition—several types of *Amen*s. These will
be listed, then explained.

תְּנֵי: אֵין עוֹנִין אָמֵן יְתוּמָה וְלֹא אָמֵן קְטוּפָה וְלֹא אָמֵן
חֲטוּפָה. בֶּן עַזַּאי אוֹמֵר: הָעוֹנֶה אָמֵן יְתוּמָה יִהְיוּ בָּנָיו
יְתוּמִים, חֲטוּפָה יִתְחַטְּפוּ שְׁנוֹתָיו, קְטוּפָה תִּקָּטֵף
נִשְׁמָתוֹ. אֲרוּכָה מַאֲרִיכִין לוֹ יָמָיו וּשְׁנוֹתָיו בְּטוֹבָה. אֵיזוֹ
הִיא אָמֵן יְתוּמָה? אָמַר רַב הוּנָא: דֵּין דִּיתֵיב לְמִיבָרָכָה
וְהוּא עָנָה וְלֹא יָדַע לְמָה הוּא עָנָה. תְּנָא: גּוֹי שֶׁבֵּירַךְ
אֶת הַשֵּׁם עוֹנֶה אַחֲרָיו אָמֵן. אָמַר רַבִּי תַּנְחוּם: אִם
בֵּירַכְךָ גּוֹי עֲנֵה אַחֲרָיו אָמֵן דִּכְתִיב: בָּרוּךְ תִּהְיֶה מִכָּל
הָעַמִּים. גּוֹי אֶחָד פָּגַע אֶת רַבִּי יִשְׁמָעֵאל וּבֵירְכוּ. אָמַר
לֵיהּ: כְּבָר מִלְּתָךְ אֲמִירָה. פָּגַע אַחֲרִינָא וְקִילְלוּ. אָמַר
לֵיהּ: כְּבָר מִילְּתָךְ אֲמִירָה. אָמְרוּ לוֹ תַּלְמִידָיו: רַבִּי
כְּמָה דַאמַרְתְּ לְהָדֵין אֲמַרְתְּ לְהָדֵין. אֲמַר לוֹן: כֵּן כְּתִיב:
אוֹרְרֶיךָ אָרוּר וּמְבָרְכֶיךָ בָּרוּךְ:

K. *It has been taught,* They do not respond with an
orphaned *Amen,* a cut-off *Amen,* or a hasty *Amen.*

L. Ben Azzai says, "If one answers an orphaned *Amen,*
his sons will be orphans. A cut-off one—his years will
be cut off. A hasty one—his soul will be cut down. A

long one—his days and years will be lengthened with goodness."

M. What is an orphaned *Amen?*

N. R. Huna said, *"This refers to a person who sat down to bless,* and he answered, but did not know to what [prayer] he answered [*Amen*]."

O. It was taught: If a gentile who blessed the divine name, they answer *Amen* after him.

P. R. Tanhum said, "If a gentile blesses you, answer after him *Amen, as it is written,* 'Blessed will you be by all the peoples'" [Deuteronomy 7:14].

Q. A gentile met R. Ishmael and blessed him. He said to him, *"You have already been answered."*

R. *Another met him* and cursed him. He said to him, *"You have already been answered."*

S. His disciples said to him, *"Rabbi, how could you say the same to both?"* He said to them, "Thus it is written in Scripture: 'Those that curse you will be cursed, and those that bless you will be blessed'" [Genesis 27:29].

The story about Ishmael calls to mind the very different formulation of the same attitude, that Israel is not wholly powerless in the face of the gentiles. God has already decided the relationships between Israel and the peoples of the world. If a gentile blesses you and treats you kindly, it is because God has ordained the peoples will bless Israel. If a gentile curses you ("anti-semitism") or pushes you around, this too has been taken care of by God: That man will be cursed. So whatever happens—in the village as much as in the heavens—reveals the plan and will of God. Nothing that takes place, whether the setting of the sun in the skies or the gesture of good will in the streets, whether in nature or in "history," to use grand, if inappropriate language, falls outside the realm of Torah.

Ba's explanation in A stands all by itself. Without some sort of commentary or explanation, one should have difficulty knowing what point Ba intends to make. The contrast to the

Babylonian version of the same explanation will be striking indeed. There we shall see what has led us to this little "explanation." In fact, Ba's saying comes at the end of, and summarizes, a considerable discussion.

The same pattern recurs in B. We are not told the problem, only the solution, given by Hiyya. E–H further illuminate the problem of saying *Amen* at the Grace after Meals. K–N give three examples of unsatisfactory *Amens,* and O–S conclude the chapter with a little story.

The difference between the last half of the Palestinian Talmud and the equivalent discussions of the same Mishnahs in the Babylonian Talmud is striking. In some instances the very same issues are raised. But while the Babylonian Talmud spells things out in detail, the Palestinian one supplies only enigmatic sayings.

A still more striking difference is in the failure of the Palestinian Talmud's editors to make much of the materials they do cite. Analyses, critical or otherwise, are few and far between. Normally, the editor simply tosses in a saying pertinent to the Mishnaic law, or at least relevant to its theme, and that completes his *Gemara.*

The Babylonian Talmud not only is tightly organized, but also excludes materials not closely pertinent to the Mishnah. The Palestinian one by contrast includes a wide range of stories and sayings remotely connected to the Mishnah's original concerns.

That is not to suggest the Palestinian Talmud is uninteresting. Its discrete stories reveal the mind of the rabbis who told them. One may learn a good deal about how they imagined the process of the creation of the world, for instance; or about how they envisioned the worldly relationships among imperial authorities. The exegeses of texts show how the rabbis understood Scriptures. The little collections of *'alef-'ayin* wordplays of Rav and Samuel are important evidence about how words were pronounced. In their own context, however, when properly set alongside the Mishnah passages to which they are pertinent, they yield considerable differences in the interpretation of the meaning of the Mishnah's language. Here they do not.

The primary problem for us is whether now one can attempt to enter the discussions of the Palestinian Talmud. The answer clearly is that one cannot. The materials may be elucidated by scholars of exegesis and used by historians. The one thing one cannot do is join the conversation, because, as is already clear, the discussion in the latter part of the chapter lacks a concern for logical inquiry and rational criticism. One can hardly call it a conversation at all. It is an anthology of useful information, nothing more. In the Babylonian Talmud and in the first part of the chapter before us, one may indeed attempt to work out and master technicalities, because these provide the where-withal for understanding something beyond the technicalities. The rest of the Palestinian Talmud just now reviewed consists of little more than details, some charming, some esoteric, but all episodic and none suggestive of anything beyond itself. One cannot regard the materials of the Palestinian Talmud as very "Talmudic" at all.

CHAPTER 5

The Babylonian Talmud

Introducing the Babylonian Talmud

Because of its vastness and depths the Babylonian Talmud is aptly compared to an "ocean." It is a compilation of law and lore created by Palestinian and Babylonian rabbis between the late first and seventh centuries A.D. From that time onward it has been studied partly as a source of practical law but mainly for the pleasure of joining in the discussions commenced within its pages. Commentaries laid open and added to its complexities; codes systematized and updated its laws. What is remarkable is devotion to the study of the Talmud not only by legal specialists and religious virtuosi, but by ordinary Jews living commonplace lives. Knowledge of Talmudic literature and ability to enter into issues first raised in arguments of the Talmud furthermore served as the measure not only of intellect but of piety and virtue, of holiness. This invitation to learning how to live and why extended over twenty centuries. The entire tradition rested on the Hebrew Scriptures and other sacred literature going back for another ten.

What made the Talmud so engaging as to retain the interest of one generation after another, so fascinating as to form the focus of interest for ordinary men, not merely learned specialists? The answer is the Talmudic argument and its mode of inquiry, an applied rationality. The Talmud compelled interest because its problems were worldly and accessible, its mode of argument open to participation by any person willing to reason, and its logic relevant to, and persuasive in, many and varied circumstances. People studied the Talmud because they could themselves join fully—in both intellect and feeling—in its arguments. They could attempt first to master and unravel them, then to reshape and revise them, and, perhaps, finally even to improve upon them, and in consequence repair the conduct of their own lives. Study of the Talmud therefore supplied the opportunity for reason to do its work, for the mind to be stretched and to move, and for the disciplined intellect to exercise itself through clean, sustained, and rigorous argumentation. Nor should the aesthetic pleasure of Talmudic learning be ignored. For those to whom beauty consists in order, architectonic clarity, and elegant structure, the Talmudic argument, with its balance, brilliance, clarity, completeness, and frequent elegance, constitutes a thing of splendor.

The Talmud is not an ordinary document from antiquity, interesting primarily to historians or lawyers (in Jewish courts) or theologians. It is fully pertinent to people without scholarly concerns. Like other great and abiding literature, the Talmud, for all its remoteness, its alien idiom and arcane data, has the capacity to win attention because of its timelessness, therefore its permanent pertinence to one generation after another. It lies open to the participation of minds with concerns quite different from those of its original authorities and with interests shaped by a world remote from that in which it was created. Because of its mode of critical thought and argumentation, the Talmud therefore preserves enduring intellectual vitality. The argument and counterargument, thesis and refutation, which constitute Talmudic dialectic—these are the ongoing foci of personal interest. So long as new minds reflect upon the old issues in new ways, but within the ancient disciplines of practical reason, the argument never ends.

To understand the Talmud, therefore, it is not enough to quote, or make anthologies of, its stories and sayings, to survey its laws and cases, to praise its wisdom. Were the Talmud merely a series of compilations of stories and laws, it would not warrant study in its own terms and language. Scholars of history, law, and philology, not to mention theology and the history of religions, might recover and present in the contemporary mode of learned discourse whatever is worthwhile in its pages. Because the Talmud is essentially a set of highly disciplined arguments effected through sustained criticism, it is to be confronted in its own language. Its mode of thinking remains apposite to contemporary ways of reasoning and reflection. Introducing the Talmud requires mapping out the arguments, not merely citing the conclusions. It cannot be learned except by a deeply personal engagement to its inner movements, by a love of its learned meanings—and, moreover, by an effort to reconstruct those meanings for oneself and not merely to repeat them. There is no end to Talmudic argument; it is part of the unending life, a maze of continuities. The Talmud is an astonishing variety of links in the chain of Jewish wisdom.

Yet, as I stressed, what is important in the Talmud is not simply the elegance and beauty of its mode of argument. What is remarkable is that, for many generations, people could perceive not mere beauty, but holiness, in the criticism and arguments of the Talmudic authorities. And that is what requires attention. The rabbis are not forerunners of merely rational professors, but are holy men. But what is it about rational inquiry that is holy? This is the question to confront us on every page. The answer is that the working of the human intellect is perceived to be the counterpart of the divine. What makes us human is our minds, our ability to be mindful and thoughtful, different from animals, which lack consciousness. But humanity is most mindful when we take seriously the ideas of our fellows, when we exercise power of concentration to take account of, to criticize, and to respond to ideas held by others. Reason joins each to the other and all to God. It establishes the tie between heaven and earth.

This is an extraordinary conviction, expressed to begin with
in the mythic picture of God's studying Torah along with
Moses and the heavenly academy, of the rabbi's imitating God
through his learning of the law. But the myth speaks of a
deeper reality. It is not merely a pious fable. It conveys the
stubborn conviction of the rabbis that the give-and-take of
argument represents us at our most human and speaks to God
at his most accessible. This conviction makes the Talmud more
than a document in the history of rationality. It renders it an
open book for those seeking a faith through understanding, yet
surpassing understanding. And to the contemporary intellectual, it is a peculiarly pertinent and strangely open mode of
faith—belief in the one thing intellectuals vividly perceive and
cultivate, their minds, but belief, too, in the *sanctity* of the
exercise of the intellect. Surely without the Talmud the intellectual knows this: All that is worthwhile derives from the
active intellect, in the curious communication of people who
take one another seriously enough to engage in argument.

Talmudic faith is accessible precisely because it is expe-
rienced even before articulation. Yet what makes that expe-
rienced faith *Talmudic* is the apprehension of the transcendent,
the view that sustained criticism bears otherworldly meanings.
I shall claim, without apology, that those meanings constitute
the vindication of the intellect, its consecration. People able to
give their lives to thought and its expression cannot remain
indifferent to the ways in which, within the Talmud, their
devotion constitutes an adumbration of the sacred. All this is
spelled out in the concluding chapter.

Where to Begin?

Every Talmudic tractate—there are thirty-seven of them in
the Babylonian Talmud—begins on page 2; there are no page 1s
because there is no beginning. Wherever you start your study,
you will feel you have joined a conversation which began long
before you came along. A great many facts will be taken for

granted, and these have to be learned before a discussion begins to make sense. Principles established somewhere else are always assumed within a given argument; you have to master those principles. Information not fully articulated is going to be cited. Finally, Talmudic argument presupposes modes of thought which are everywhere present but never wholly explained. Distinctions and rational considerations have to be assimilated. We might, to be sure, begin with a generalized discussion of the fundamentals of an argument, but such an analysis would produce useless abstractions. Since the Talmudic structures exhibit thoroughgoing consistency, you may apply to nearly every page what you have learned on nearly every other page of your study. The best way to study, therefore, is inductively, to proceed from one concrete problem to the next, carrying forward the generalizations and modes of argumentation already mastered, certain that they will recur time and again. That is how we shall proceed, for no Talmudic passage is better than any other; all passages are both constructed in a consistent pattern and equally typical and suggestive of the whole. Since there is no beginning—or ending—we may just as well jump into the middle.

A Page of the Talmud

A page of the Talmud is called a folio (Hebrew: *daf* from the Akkadian word for tablet), of which the obverse is designated A, the reverse, B (Hebrew for a side: *amud*, column). The pages (32-33) before us are Babylonian Talmud, Tractate of Blessings (*Berakhot*) 51b and 52a; the next side is 52b. The section marked I contains the Mishnah; II, the *Gemara*, the text of the Talmud which we shall study verbatim. Section III contains the phrase-by-phrase commentary of Rabbi Solomon bar Isaac, known as Rashi (R[abbi] Sh[elomo] [ben] Y[ishaq]), who lived, mainly in Troyes, France, from 1040 to 1105.

Rashi is one of the towering figures in the history of Judaism because he composed immensely influential commentaries for

OUR GEMARA

הדרן עלך שלשה שאכלו

הדרן עלך שלשה שאכלו

אלו דברים שבין בית שמאי ובין בית הלל בסעודה ב"ש אומרים מברך על היום ואח"כ מברך על היין בית הלל אומרים מברך על היין ואח"כ מברך על היום

nearly the whole of the Hebrew Bible and the Babylonian
Talmud. His commentaries exhibit such lucidity and peda-
gogic deftness that the texts which they serve are not to be
approached except through Rashi. But everyone may study
them with Rashi. The commentary to the Pentateuch is popular, addressed to the ordinary pious man. That to the Talmud
is wide-ranging and sophisticated, written for the scholar, but
still a paradigm of effective pedagogy. So Rashi had the ability
to find appropriate language for many audiences. His unex-
celled mastery of the whole of rabbinic literature, moreover,
meant that he could bring to bear in the elucidation of a given
problem virtually all available information. His step-by-step
commentary on the dialectic of the Talmudic argument stresses
the importance of the course of argument itself, not simply the
practical conclusions. Finally, his pedagogical sense told him
what was important for the student at any particular point and
what could be omitted. The comments always are adequate,
never excessive; they are glosses, not separate monographs;
precise, subtle, remarkably concise, tasteful and selective, they
are appropriate to the context. Many later authorities wrote
commentaries on his commentaries, both in Scripture and in
Talmud; none improved on his style or replaced him.

The most important of these supercommentaries, designated
as IV, is the *Tosafot*, supplements or additions to Rashi's
commentary (not to be confused with the Tosefta, the supplement to the Mishnah). The *Tosafot* are printed on the outer
margin, opposite Rashi's commentary. The work of the Tosafists, of addition and criticism, began when Rashi completed
his; the first ones in fact were his sons-in-law and grandsons.
Their work was chiefly to gloss Rashi. But the project of commenting on antecedent comments gradually was superseded by
another task: the active criticism of any and all authority—
including Rashi's—and the development of the law through
the extension to new problems of established principles. This
work took the form not of continuous commentary, but of

essays on specific problems. The first Tosafists were French; many of the later ones lived in the German Rhineland. Their work ended in the early fourteenth century. The writing of *Tosafot* in France ceased with the destruction of the Talmud in the reign of Louis IX ("Saint Louis"), regarded in the history of Talmudic texts as an exceptional calamity for his systematic destruction of Talmuds found in the libraries, Jewish and otherwise, in his kingdom.

These are the four main components of a page of the Babylonian Talmud. Printed texts today include numerous other commentaries and aids to understanding; most are printed as appendices to the several tractates. The work of nearly fifteen centuries and countries from the Euphrates to the Atlantic and from the Sahara to the Baltic Sea and as far east as the Dnieper—all will be contained within the standard printed texts. We shall concentrate, however, on the Babylonian Talmud as explained by Rashi.

We continue to study together (the right word is "learn") the eighth chapter of the tractate of Blessings, which in the Babylonian Talmud covers two and a half folios. Our task is simply to read the chapter in its entirety, step by step and line by line. We shall ask for information external to the analysis and argument only so far as it is intrinsic to the task of "learning." Our primary problem is not what the chapter teaches us about history of the Jews or of Judaism, theology, history of religions, philology, or related sciences. We simply want to know, What does the chapter say? How does it go about its business? and What is "Talmudic" about the Talmud? For history or philology the Talmud is a source among other sources. For us the Talmud's the thing. At the end we shall read the chapter as a whole, secure in our understanding of its parts. As we know, our chapter consists of two parts, a pericope of Mishnah, and its accompanying Babylonian *Gemara*. The Mishnah is a law-code. The *Gemara*, as we shall soon see, is essentially a wide-ranging, but tightly organized, commentary on that law code.

The Gemara

The *Gemara,* the part of the Babylonian Talmud serving as a commentary to the Mishnah, is generally supposed to be the product of approximately three centuries of work, from ca. A.D. 200 to ca. 500. These are conventional dates; we actually do not know either when the study of the Mishnah was reduced to formal commentaries, on the one side, or when the work of Talmudic creativity came to an end, and commentary on the now-completed Talmud began, on the other. Nor do we have a clear picture of the authorities, dates, and method of the final redaction of the Babylonian Talmud; it seems likely to assign the last stages of the work to the sixth and seventh centuries.

Gemara comes from the Aramaic verb to learn or study. *Gemara* is interpreted as the interpretation—"the learning"— or commentary on the Mishnah. What is marked as *Gemara* in the Talmud was in earlier times designated simply *Talmud,* from the Hebrew verb "to study," thus just as with the Aramaic word, "study of the Mishnah," or commentary. We shall use the two words interchangeably, for they are equivalent to each other. A master of the post-Mishnaic age, responsible for the Talmud, is called *Amora* (plural: *Amoraim*), meaning speaker, lecturer, or interpreter.

We have Babylonian Talmud for the larger part of the Mishnah, thirty-seven of the sixty-three tractates. But the whole of the order on Seeds (*Zera'im*), except Blessings (*Berakhot*), and the whole of the order on Purities (*Toharot*), except Menstrual Laws (*Niddah*), lack Talmud, possibly because the agricultural and purity laws had no bearing on Babylonian Jewish life. As a foreign, thus unholy land, Babylonia was not liable to the agricultural offerings required in Scripture, and of course it was unclean to begin with. But we have a full Talmud for Holy Things (*Qodashim*) while there was no Temple in Babylonia, nor did anyone suppose there ever would be. So that reason for the absence of many tractates is insufficient, yet we have no better one.

The Babylonian *Gemara* began as a commentary on the

Mishnah of Judah the Patriarch. The work of commentary and exegesis commenced as soon as the Mishnah and its accompanying cognate traditions (Tosefta and the like) reached the Babylonian rabbinical academies. The first generation tended to concentrate on providing simple comments and explanations—exegeses—of Mishnaic laws. The next generation of masters was apt to take as its task the identification of the authorities behind the various rulings of the Mishnah, the elucidation of the principles behind their rulings, the discovery of internal contradictions, in detail or in principle, in the Mishnaic corpus. For this purpose the non-Mishnaic traditions bearing Tannaitic authority, such as those found in the Tosefta or redacted outside of both the Mishnah and the Tosefta, called *baraita* (plural: *beraitot*) or "external tradition," were extremely useful. After the turn of the fourth century, the main efforts ceased to focus upon the Mishnah and its exegesis, for much had been accomplished. The center of interest was rather upon the larger principles and generalizations contained within the law. The effort now was to organize and harmonize the fundamental principles of the whole system of the rabbinic law. The work of the fifth, sixth, and seventh centuries is before us: putting together the whole work of Mishnah commentary and legal inquiry into well-organized, literarily sophisticated, unitary discussions, and the combination of these many discussions into the final *Gemara*. In the Palestinian Talmud we saw what the Babylonian Talmud would have looked like had the work of the last two centuries been omitted. While the Palestinian Talmud is a compendium of sayings and stories, the Babylonian Talmud transcends mere antiquarianism. It is a work of powerful, vigorous logic and continuous criticism, and that is why it is challenging and interesting, not merely informative.

Some More Essential Facts

The Talmud takes for granted thorough knowledge of the system of cultic purity alluded to above. Let us review some more facts necessary for understanding what is to follow.

First, cultic impurity is acquired by contact with either a primary or a secondary source of uncleanness, called a "father" or a "child," or "offspring" of uncleanness, respectively. In the first category is contact with a corpse, a person suffering a flux, a leper, and the like. Objects made of metal, wood, leather, bone, cloth, or sacking become fathers of uncleanness if they touch a corpse.

Foodstuffs and liquids are susceptible to uncleanness. But they, as offspring of uncleanness, will not render other food-stuffs unclean in the same remove of uncleanness which they themselves suffer. Foodstuffs furthermore will not make vessels or utensils unclean. But liquids made unclean by a father of uncleanness will do so if they touch the inner side of the vessel. That is, if they fall into the contained space of an earthenware vessel, they make the whole vessel unclean.

Now there are four removes of uncleanness in all. Food or liquid which touches the original father of uncleanness incurs *first* remove of uncleanness. If food touches a person or vessel made unclean by a primary source of uncleanness, it is unclean in the *second* remove of uncleanness. Food that touches *second* remove of uncleanness incurs *third* remove of uncleanness, and food that touches *third* remove of uncleanness incurs *fourth* remove of uncleanness. But, as we noticed, liquids touching either a primary source of uncleanness (father) or something unclean in the first or second remove of uncleanness (offspring) are regarded as unclean in the first remove. They *are* able to make something else unclean. If, therefore, the outer side of a vessel is made unclean by a liquid—thus is unclean in the second remove—and another liquid touches the outer side, the other liquid incurs not second, but first remove of uncleanness.

As to the hands, they are regarded as perpetually in a second remove of uncleanness. But you can cover your hands with a napkin and not wash them to prevent their imparting uncleanness, as Rav did.

Heave-offering—food raised up for priestly use only—unclean in the third remove of uncleanness and Holy Things (that is

things belonging to the cult) in the fourth remove of uncleanness do not make other things unclean—whether liquids or
food.

What is the point of these degrees of uncleanness? As we now
know, the Pharisees made every effort to eat their ordinary food
in a state of cultic purity. Whatever makes food unclean will
have to be avoided; food which suffers first or second remove of
uncleanness therefore is not acceptable. But the difference
between removes is important. For first remove of uncleanness
in common food will convey uncleanness. But while food
unclean in the second remove of uncleanness will be unaccept-
able, it will *not* convey uncleanness, that is, third remove of
uncleanness. But it will render Heave-offering *unfit*.

A further practical consideration affects the priestly offerings.
It was the practice to give to the priests the dues the Scriptures
had assigned to them. Heave-offering of the crop, among other
things, had to be preserved and consumed in a state of cultic
purity. As we just saw, it could be made unfit and unclean by a
first, and unfit by a second remove of uncleanness. If it touches
something unclean in the third remove it is made unfit, but
itself will not impart fourth remove of uncleanness.

Finally, a person had to be concerned for the cleanness of the
Temple cult. A Holy Thing suffering first, second, or third
remove of uncleanness is unclean and conveys uncleanness; if
it is unclean in the fourth remove, it is invalid for the cult but
does not convey uncleanness. It is thus *much* more susceptible
than noncultic things.

For example, common food which suffers second remove of
uncleanness will render Heave-offering *invalid* (unfit in the
third remove). We already know that it makes liquid unclean
in the first remove. Likewise, Heave-offering in a third remove
of uncleanness will make Holy Things invalid and put them
into the fourth remove of uncleanness. But—a further com-
plication—if common food is prepared in conditions of cleanness which befit Heave-offering, and it then suffers third
remove of uncleanness, it becomes invalid *like* Heave-offering,

in the same condition, at the same degree of susceptibility. If it touches a Holy Thing, it does not impart fourth remove of uncleanness. On the other hand, if common food is prepared in conditions of cleanness as would be appropriate for Holy Things, its third remove of uncleanness is regarded as clean, as is normal with common food. The processes by which things lose their uncleanness—rites of purification—do not play a role in our chapter of the Talmud.

This matter of preparing food in accord with rules still more strict than those that normally apply once more reminds us of the "realized-as-if" mentality with which we deal. These are ordinary folk pretending to be priests. They are Jews in exile from the holy land pretending to be living on the sacred and cultically pure soil. They are common people eating in their hovels, pretending to be eating a meal in the Temple in Jerusalem at the table of the Lord. But, we remind ourselves, the Temple was in ruins. To the Jewish nation the city was closed and forbidden. They could come only annually, and then to mourn. To the exiles at hand, the Land was a long way off. In the misery of their poverty, the people could at best imagine a better house, a table of marble, a meal of meat and wine and fine bread. And what effected the magical transformation of the profane into the holy, and the miserable into the magnificent? It was keeping rules, material and real taboos, which would apply if the observant person were what he or she were not. All of this is captured in the rather odd and puzzling notion that if one intentionally preserves the cleanness of a piece of bread in accord with the unusually strict laws applicable not to common food to be kept cultically clean, but to priestly rations ("Heave-offering") or even to Holy Things, then the status of the ordinary bread changes. It now does not become what it is not. But it ceases to be what it was. It does not become priestly rations or enter into the status of Holy Things, suitable for God's table, but it no longer is mere, ordinary bread, for a common person eating food, in a state of cultic cleanness—but not in the Temple, not in Jerusalem, not as a priest. So how we think changes how things are, and what we think has an effect upon reality. And all of this why? To reaffirm that Israel, the people, attaining cultic cleanness, remains God's holy people—in all its misery and humiliation and disappointment and defeat.

So for our purpose, we have to imagine people eating their meals with the concern for cultic cleanness uppermost in mind. Every aspect of the ritual of the meal—the Grace before Meals (generally said with bread, "Blessed are you, Lord our God, king of the world, who brings forth bread from the earth"), the Grace after Meals ("Blessing of Food," the process by which the hands are washed before and after eating), and the like— every aspect is going to be guided by considerations of cultic purity. The food must be preserved from the various sources which may make it unclean. Remember, we are not talking about the acceptability of foods as permitted or prohibited in Scriptures. A cow, properly slaughtered, is *kosher,* that is, fit or acceptable. But its flesh may receive cultic impurity and therefore may become unclean. Bread will be *kosher.* But the Jews whose laws are before us still will not eat it if it is *unclean.*

One last point: There is nothing material, or intrinsic, in cultic purity or impurity. We are not dealing with a belief that something—a demon or devil—really enters into the food and renders it unclean or unfit. Purity and impurity constitute a set of highly complex relationships. But these relationships have nothing to do with the physical world; they are wholly abstract. A great deal depends upon intention and purpose, circumstance and time. For instance, a vessel which is not entirely completed may touch a corpse and yet remain clean. For it is not susceptible to receive uncleanness until it both has been entirely finished, and its owner regards it as completed. A common person is normally regarded as unclean, for he does not observe the various taboos. But during a religious festival, he is regarded as clean. If the outer side of a vessel becomes unclean by a liquid, and food touches the outer side, it remains clean, for a vessel whose outer side alone is unclean does not render food unclean.

But if the food is a Holy Thing, it *is* unclean. So you might have two identical substances in different categories—one may be ordinary food or even Heave-offering, the other a Holy Thing; both touch the same outer side of the same vessel. The one is clean, the other unclean! Clearly, everything is relative to everything else.

It remains to observe that while first- and second-century authorities probably did observe these laws, we have very little evidence of their persistence in later times in the holy land; and in Babylonia everything was, as I said, unclean to begin with. So the theories before us revolve around matters which to begin with were entirely theoretical, a highly intellectual, utterly unworldly enterprise—a manifestly appropriate, fictitious refuge for the defeated people. The Irish and the Scots went to America. For a long time, the Jews went to the Talmud.

The Elements of the Chapter

My translation follows the standard printed text, checked against the manuscript known as Codex Munich (95), which dates from 1343, the only manuscript in existence containing the complete text of the Babylonian Talmud. A facsimile edition was printed in Jerusalem in 1971, so the manuscript is now widely available and convenient for everyday use. I further referred to Maurice Simon, *Berakoth, Translated into English with Notes, Glossary, and Indices.** As before, we shall first examine the text by units, and afterward see how it has been put together as a whole.

The Babylonian Talmud is written in two languages, Hebrew and Aramaic. (Three-fourths of the Palestinian Talmud is in Hebrew.) The use of the one rather than the other is by no means accidental. Normally, though not always, the sayings attributed to the Tannaim and statements of normative law will be in Hebrew. The comments and analyses of the Amoraim and stories will be in Aramaic. And the editors' own remarks

*London, 1948: Soncino Press.

will be in Aramaic. To signify the differences, which are very important, Hebrew will be in regular type, Aramaic in italics. Boldfaced type is used for citations from the Mishnah and the Tosefta, which stand at the head of the major divisions of the chapter. I shall cite the *Gemara* in small sections and comment on each. Then I shall review and comment upon a complete set of arguments or inquiries. Finally, at the end, we shall reread the chapter as a whole and examine its total literary characteristics, seen as a unity.

תָּנוּ רַבָּנָן : דְּבָרִים שֶׁבֵּין בֵּית שַׁמַּאי וּבֵית הַלֵּל בִּסְעָדָה:
בֵּית שַׁמַּאי אוֹמְרִים : "מְבָרֵךְ עַל הַיּוֹם וְאַחַר כָּךְ מְבָרֵךְ
עַל הַיַּיִן, שֶׁהַיּוֹם גּוֹרֵם לַיַּיִן שֶׁיָּבֹא וּכְבָר קָדַשׁ הַיּוֹם
וַעֲדַיִן יַיִן לֹא בָא." וּבֵית הַלֵּל אוֹמְרִים : "מְבָרֵךְ עַל הַיַּיִן
וְאַחַר כָּךְ מְבָרֵךְ עַל הַיּוֹם, שֶׁהַיַּיִן גּוֹרֵם לִקְדֻשָּׁה
שֶׁתֵּאָמֵר. דָּבָר אַחֵר : בִּרְכַּת הַיַּיִן תְּדִירָה וּבִרְכַּת הַיּוֹם
אֵינָה תְּדִירָה. תָּדִיר וְשֶׁאֵינוּ תָּדִיר – תָּדִיר קוֹדֵם."
וַהֲלָכָה כְּדִבְרֵי בֵּית הַלֵּל. | אחר גג

[51b] *Gemara: A. Our rabbis have taught:*

B. **The things which are between the House of Shammai and the House of Hillel in** [regard to] **a meal:**

The House of Shammai say, "One blesses over the day and afterward blesses over the wine, for the day causes the wine to come, and the day has already been sanctified, while the wine has not yet come."

And the House of Hillel say, "One blesses over the wine and afterward blesses over the day, for the wine causes the Sanctification to be said.

"Another matter: The blessing over the wine is perpetual, and the blessing over the day is not perpetual. Between that which is perpetual and that which is not perpetual, that which is perpetual takes precedence."

And the law is in accordance with the words of the House of Hillel.

The *Gemara* opens with a simple citation of the Tosefta we have already studied. It then proceeds to analyze the passage.

מַאי "דָּבָר אַחֵר"?

C. *What is the purpose of* "another matter"?

The first peculiarity is simply the second "reason" assigned to the Hillelites. Why should we require *two* reasons for their position, while we have only one for the Shammaites?

וְכִי תֵימָא: הָתָם תַּרְתֵּי וְהָכָא חֲדָא, הָכָא נַמֵּי תַּרְתֵּי
נִינְהוּ: בִּרְכַּת הַיַּיִן תְּדִירָה וּבִרְכַּת הַיּוֹם אֵינָה תְּדִירָה.
תָּדִיר וְשֶׁאֵינוּ תָּדִיר — תָּדִיר קֹדֶם.

If you should say that there [in regard to the Tosefta's report of the opinion of the House of Shammai] *two* [reasons are given], *and here* [in regard to the Tosefta's report of the opinion of the House of Hillel] *one, here too* [in respect to the House of Hillel], *there are two* [reasons, the second being]: "The blessing of the wine is perpetual and the blessing of the day is not perpetual. That which is perpetual takes precedence over that which is not perpetual."

The *Gemara* reads into the Shammaite saying two separate reasons, and so explains that in order to balance those two reasons, the Hillelites likewise are given two.

וַהֲלָכָה כְּדִבְרֵי בֵּית הַלֵּל.

D. "And the law is in accord with the opinion of the House of Hillel."

The statement of the final decision is cited from Tosefta, but this poses a new problem. For the law normally will follow the Hillelites. Why say so?

— פְּשִׁיטָא, דְּהָא נָפְקָא בַּת קוֹל.

This is obvious [that the law is in accord with the House of Hillel], *for the echo has gone forth* [and pronounced from

heaven the decision that the law follows the opinion of
the House of Hillel.]

Now the question is spelled out. In rabbinic lore, it was
believed that a few years after the destruction of the Temple in
70, a heavenly echo had announced that the law follows the
House of Hillel. Since that is the established and well-known
fact, why is it necessary to say so in this particular setting?

אִיבָּעֵית אֵימָא: קֹדֶם בַּת קוֹל. וְאִיבָּעֵית אֵימָא: לְאַחַר
בַּת קוֹל, וְרַבִּי יְהוֹשֻׁעַ הִיא, דְּאָמַר: "אֵין מַשְׁגִּיחִין בְּבַת
קוֹל."

*Schechtr
"the
daughtr-
voice"*

E. *If you like, I can argue that* [this was stated] before the
echo.

F. *And if you like, I can argue that* it was after the echo,
and [the passage is formulated in accord with the] opinion of [52a] R. Joshua, who stated, "They do not pay
attention to an echo [from heaven]."

Two answers are given. The first is that the final decision
was formulated before the echo had been heard, the second,
that it came afterward but accords with the view of those who
nonetheless deny supernatural intervention into the formulation of the law, for instance, Joshua b. Hananiah, who lived at
that time and was alleged to have rejected the testimony of
supernatural signs.

Let us review the whole pericope.

The Talmud opens with a citation (A) of the Tosefta's parallel to the Mishnah. Our chapter consistently supplements the
Mishnah with the Tosefta, primarily in order to analyze the
latter. The Tosefta is cited with the introduction of A, a fixed
formula which indicates that a Tannaitic source, that is, an
authority of the Mishnah's times, is quoted. Other such
formulae include *We have learned,* the formula for introducing
a citation to the Mishnah, *It has been taught,* introducing a
teaching attributed to the authority of Tannaim, though not
necessarily to a specific Mishnaic teacher. These Aramaic for-

mulae function like footnotes, providing information on the source of, or type of authority behind, materials cited in the text.

B simply cites the Tosefta we have already examined. Then C undertakes the analysis of the passage. The explanation and elucidation are ignored; it is assumed that these are clear. What C wants to know is why the House of Hillel give two reasons for their opinion. The "two reasons" of the Shammaites are ① the wine is brought on account of the Sabbath, and ② it is already the Sabbath, yet the wine is still lacking. The Hillelites' reason then is cited without comment.

D continues the analysis of the Toseftan passage. The statement that the law follows the House of Hillel is regarded as obvious, since normally that is so. The presupposition of the Talmud is that nothing will be stated which is obvious; redundancy, it goes without saying, will not occur. But the Talmud also objects to the inclusion of well-known facts. This is regarded as bad style. The reference to the "echo which has gone forth" alludes to a story about the House of Shammai's and the House of Hillel's debating for three years, until Heaven intervened with the divine announcement, delivered by an echo, that both Houses possess the words of the living God, but the law follows the House of Hillel. Supernatural intervention into legal matters is commonplace. The Talmud was created in a world which took for granted that Heaven cared about, therefore influenced or interfered in, the affairs of men, particularly the affairs of the people of Israel, and especially those of the rabbis, who were believed to study Torah on earth exactly as it was studied by Moses "our rabbi" in the Heavenly Academy.

E provides a simple, "historical" answer: D was included before the echo had delivered its message. F then gives a somewhat more substantial response: Some rabbis opposed accepting supernatural signs of the determination of the law by Heaven. Chief among these is Joshua b. Hananiah (ca. A.D. 90), who, when presented by Eliezer b. Hyrcanus with supernatural evidence in behalf of the latter's position, proclaimed, "It—the

Torah—is not in heaven" (Deuteronomy 30:12). D thus is credited to Joshua, who would not accept the heavenly decision and therefore had to provide earthly counsel based on reason.

The foregoing issue, about whether supernatural intervention may determine a moot point of law, raises a very large question. It is, What are the limits of Talmudic supernaturalism? Where does the force of reason and logic end, and the power of Heaven begin? On the one side is the view of Joshua. God has given the Torah to man. It now is in man's hands to do with as he finds reasonable. Reason becomes the way of continuing, of elaborating revelation. The Torah lays forth the principles of rational inquiry. Once set forth, these will work their own way. The processes of thought no longer are subject to the modulation of revelation—for they themselves continue the process of revelation. If you want to know what God now wants, you turn not to prayer or to the expectation of miraculously imparted inspiration or insight. You turn rather to the laws already revealed, laws of substance and laws of reason, and you think further according to rational principles about these laws. On the other side is the view of Eliezer. God not only revealed the Torah in times past. He continues to reveal, he himself. You cannot close off the possibility of divine participation in the arguments of men, of rabbis. If you do, you say God is no longer interested. He has wound up the watch; now let it run on. That is not so. God so loved Israel that he gave to them his Torah. He continues to love Israel—that is shown by his punishing them for their transgressions, a sign he will reward them for their regeneration and repentance. So he may, too, continue to give them Torah, instruction. The arguments of rabbis on earth are heard and joined by God and the angels in heaven. What prevents the heavenly party from intervening in the affairs of the earthly one? It is not easy to resolve this question, for within it are fundamental issues facing religious people.*

* I remind the reader that the persistent reference to God as he, and to man, is not my choice but my effort to replicate the frame of reference of those whose

It remains to observe that Hebrew is consistently used in the
formulation of the normative law, and Aramaic is equally consistently used for the discussion and analysis of the law. The
Palestinian Talmud's pattern is similar. This pattern is repeated
throughout our chapter. I shall point to its significance in the
last chapter. The Aramaic is the rhetoric and the reasoning, the
Hebrew is the facts, the building blocks of inquiry.

וְסָבְרִי בֵּית שַׁמַּאי דְּבִרְכַּת הַיּוֹם עֲדִיפָא?

(A) *And is it the reasoning of the House of Shammai that the*
blessing of the day is more important?

When you examine the position of the House of Shammai,
which rule that you bless the day and then the wine, it appears
that they regard the day as more important than the wine, so it
takes precedence.

וְהָתַנְיָא: "הַנִּכְנָס לְבֵיתוֹ בְּמוֹצָאֵי שַׁבָּת — מְבָרֵךְ עַל
הַיַּיִן וְעַל הַמָּאוֹר וְעַל הַבְּשָׂמִים וְאַחַר כָּךְ אוֹמֵר
הַבְדָלָה וְאִם אֵין לוֹ אֶלָּא כּוֹס אֶחָד — מַנִּיחוֹ לְאַחַר
הַמָּזוֹן וּמְשַׁלְשְׁלָן כֻּלָּן לְאַחֲרָיו."

But has a Tanna not taught: "He who enters his house at
the close of the Sabbath blesses over the wine and the
light and the spices and afterward he says *Havdalah.* And
if he has only one cup, he leaves it for after the food and
then says the other blessings in order after it." [*Havdalah*
is the blessing of the day, yet comes last!]

We presently assume that the House of Shammai stand
behind the cited tradition. Then the tradition contradicts their
position that the day takes precedence.

---

views are described and summarized. This disclaimer and apology must be
kept in mind throughout. Any other policy would misrepresent the state of
affairs in the world subject to analysis and interpretation—and misstate the
problem to be solved in our own world.

וְהָא מִמַּאי דְּבֵית שַׁמַּאי הִיא, דִּלְמָא בֵּית הִלֵּל הִיא!

(B.) But lo, on what account [do you say] this is the view of the House of Shammai? Perhaps it is the House of Hillel['s opinion]?

The obvious solution is to assign the cited tradition to the House of Hillel. But this solution is forthwith challenged.

לָא סָלְקָא דַעְתָּךְ, דְּקָתָנֵי מָאוֹר וְאַחַר כָּךְ בְּשָׂמִים,
וּמַאן שְׁמַעַתְּ לֵיהּ דְּאִית לֵיהּ הַאי סְבָרָא? בֵּית שַׁמַּאי;
דְּתַנְיָא, אָמַר רַבִּי יְהוּדָה: לֹא נֶחְלְקוּ בֵּית שַׁמַּאי וּבֵית
הִלֵּל עַל הַמָּזוֹן שֶׁבַּתְּחִלָּה וְעַל הַבְדָּלָה שֶׁהִיא בַּסּוֹף,
עַל מָה נֶחְלְקוּ? עַל הַמָּאוֹר וְעַל הַבְּשָׂמִים — בֵּית
שַׁמַּאי אוֹמְרִים: מָאוֹר וְאַחַר כָּךְ בְּשָׂמִים, וּבֵית הִלֵּל
אוֹמְרִים: בְּשָׂמִים וְאַחַר כַּךְ מָאוֹר.

(C.) Let [such a thought] not enter your mind, for the Tanna teaches: "Light and afterward spices." And of whom have you heard who holds this opinion? The House of Shammai, as a Tanna has taught:

R. Judah said, "The House of Shammai and the House of Hillel did not differ concerning the [blessing of the] food, that it is at first, and Havdalah, that is at the end.

"Concerning what did they dispute? Concerning the light and the spices.

"For the House of Shammai say, 'Light and afterward spices.'

"And the House of Hillel say, 'Spices and afterward light.'"

The House of Shammai are shown to stand behind the foregoing tradition. Judah's version, quoted in Tosefta, is that the Houses agree that Havdalah comes at the end. The Shammaites say the right order is light, then spices. So they *must* stand behind the tradition which contradicts the view that the day takes precedence—and thus are shown not consistent!

Shammai shown inconsistent

וּמִמַּאי דְּבֵית שַׁמַּאי הִיא וְאַלִּיבָּא דְּרַבִּי יְהוּדָה, דִּילְמָא
בֵּית הֶלֵּל הִיא וְאַלִּיבָּא דְּרַבִּי מֵאִיר!

(D.) *And on what account* [do you suppose that] *it is the
House of Shammai as* [interpreted by] *R. Judah? Perhaps it is* [a
teaching in accord with] *the House of Hillel* [as interpreted
by] *R. Meir?*

The solution to this problem is that Judah's version of the
House of Shammai's position is not the only one. We have
another, which is Meir's and opposite—the House of Shammai
will say light comes after the spices. So the originally cited
tradition does not belong to the Shammaites at all.

לָא סָלְקָא דַעְתָּךְ, דְּקָתָנֵי הָכָא בְּמַתְנִיתִין, בֵּית שַׁמַּאי
אוֹמְרִים: נֵר וּמָזוֹן בְּשָׂמִים וְהַבְדָּלָה, וּבֵית הֶלֵּל
אוֹמְרִים: נֵר וּבְשָׂמִים מָזוֹן וְהַבְדָּלָה; וְהָתַם בַּבָּרַיְיתָא
קָתָנֵי: אִם אֵין לוֹ אֶלָּא כּוֹס אֶחָד — מַנִּיחוֹ לְאַחַר
הַמָּזוֹן וּמְשַׁלְשְׁלָן כֻּלָּן לְאַחֲרָיו, שְׁמַע מִינָהּ דְּבֵית שַׁמַּאי
הִיא וְאַלִּיבָּא דְּרַבִּי יְהוּדָה.

(E.) *Do not let such a thing enter your mind, for lo, a Tanna
teaches here in our Mishnah:* The House of Shammai say,
"Light and food and spices and *Havdalah*."

And the House of Hillel say, "Light and spices, food
and *Havdalah*."

But there, in the baraita, *lo he has taught:* "If he has only
one cup, he leaves it for after the food and then says the
other blessings in order after it."

*From this it is to be inferred that it is the House of Shammai's
teaching, according to the* [interpretation] *of R. Judah.*

We may now demonstrate that that original tradition, in A,
has to belong to the House of Shammai. But no matter how
you solve that problem, you still have the House of Shammai's

ruling that the wine takes precedence over the day, and this
contradicts their ruling that the day takes precedence over the
wine.

וּמִכָּל מָקוֹם קַשְׁיָא!

(F.) *In any event there is a problem* [for the House of Shammai now give precedence to reciting a blessing for the
wine over blessing the day].

We shall now solve the problem by distinguishing between
the two contradictory rulings. One deals with the advent of the
Sabbath, the other with the end of the Sabbath. These should
not be regarded as comparable, for they have different traits.
The difference will be spelled out.

*advent
vs.
end.*

קָא סָבְרִי בֵּית שַׁמַּאי: שָׁאנֵי עַיּוּלֵי יוֹמָא מֵאַפּוֹקֵי יוֹמָא, עַיּוּלֵי יוֹמָא — כְּמָה דִמְקַדְּמִינַן לֵיהּ עֲדִיף, אַפּוֹקֵי יוֹמָא — כְּמָה דִמְאַחֲרִינַן לֵיהּ עֲדִיף, כִּי הֵיכִי דְּלָא לֶהֱוֵי עֲלָן כְּמַשּׂוּי.

*The House of Shammai suppose that the coming of the holy day is
to be distinguished from its leaving. As to the coming of the* [holy]
*day, the earlier one may bring it in, the better. As to the leaving of
the festival day, the later one may take leave of it, the better, so that it
should not seem to us as a burden.*

One central interest of criticism is the examination of the
whole of a given philosophy, to see that the parts are harmonious with one another. The Talmud's criticism of antecedent
traditions therefore compares the suppositions of a master in
one ruling with those evident in his rulings on other matters. A
review of the pericope shows how this criticism takes shape. In
A the conclusion is reached from the House of Shammai's
statement that the Sabbath Day takes precedence over the wine;
the blessing of the day—Sanctification—is more important. A
contrary viewpoint, assumed to be held by the House of

Shammai, is immediately cited (as we surmised in examining the Tosefta, above), to the effect that the blessing of the Day— *Havdalah*—comes last, not first.

The best answer is that it is not the opinion of the House of Shammai at all. B states exactly that. But C then rejects this response. Judah's tradition on the pertinent dispute between the Houses is that all parties agree *Havdalah* comes at the end. The tradition is cited in full. To this, D replies that Judah's tradition is not the only one concerning the opinions of the Houses on this question. His contemporary, Meir, had a different tradition, which assigned the cited passage to the House of Hillel. But, more decisive still, E points out that the Mishnah before us is consistent with Judah's picture of the opinion of the House of Shammai, which places *Havdalah* at the end.

F then points out the question is still a very real one; however you assign the authority for the tradition, the House of Shammai is still represented as giving precedence to the wine over the day. <u>The solution has to be to distinguish between the beginning of the Sabbath, when the Sanctification will take precedence, and the end of the Sabbath, when wine comes first.</u> The distinction then is drawn between the start of the Sabbath, which one wants to move up if one can, and the end of the Sabbath, when one wants to delay matters, so that the Sabbath may be extended, rather than concluded in unseemly haste.

The upshot is that the position of the House of Shammai no longer will consistently favor first blessing the day. Circumstances change, and the Shammaites' opinion will change accordingly. So the introductory question is now answered in the negative. The argument, however, is so constructed as, first, to take account of all possible conditions according to the authorities behind them; second, to examine the reliability of the foregoing distinctions; and finally, to provide a new basis for argument, this time distinguishing among the situations represented by superficially contradictory laws.

וְסָבְרִי בֵּית שַׁמַּאי בִּרְכַּת הַמָּזוֹן טְעוּנָה כּוֹס ? וְהָא תְּנַן :
בָּא לָהֶם יַיִן לְאַחַר הַמָּזוֹן, אִם אֵין שָׁם אֶלָּא אוֹתוֹ

כּוֹס — בֵּית שַׁמַּאי אוֹמְרִים: מְבָרֵךְ עַל הַיַּיִן וְאַחַר כָּךְ
מְבָרֵךְ עַל הַמָּזוֹן;

A. *And do the House of Shammai hold the opinion that* Grace
requires a cup [of wine]? *And lo, we have learned:* [If] wine
came to them after the food, and there is there only that
cup, the House of Shammai say, "He blesses over the
wine and afterward blesses over the food." [So Grace is
said *without* the cup.]

In the tradition we cited above, we saw that the House of
Shammai say if the man has only one cup of wine, he holds it
until after he eats, then says the blessing of the food with that
cup. This seems to suggest that one must have wine for saying
the blessing of food after meals. The position of the House of
Shammai will now be investigated on the question of whether
one must have and drink a cup of wine in connection with the
Grace after Meals.

מַאי לָאו דִּמְבָרֵךְ עִילָוֵיהּ וְשָׁתֵי לֵיהּ! לָא, דִּמְבָרֵךְ
עִילָוֵיהּ וּמַנַּח לֵיהּ. וְהָאֲמַר מָר: הַמְבָרֵךְ צָרִיךְ שֶׁיִּטְעַם!
דְּטָעֵים לֵיהּ.

B. *Does this not mean that he blesses it and drinks* [it]?
No. He blesses it and leaves it.
C. But has not a master said, "He that blesses must
[also] taste [it]."
He does taste it.

Now we ask, does the aforecited tradition not mean that the
man says the blessing for the wine, then drinks the wine before
the Grace after Meals? The answer is that the man does *not*
have to drink the wine on the occasion of the Grace after Meals.
But this is immediately challenged. A person has, after all, to
make use of the thing he has blessed. So we suppose the man
does taste the wine.

וְהָאֲמַר מָר: טְעָמוֹ — פְּגָמוֹ! דְּטָעֵים לֵיהּ בִּידֵיהּ.

D. And has not a master said, "Tasting it is spoiling it."

He tastes it with his hand [finger].

If we agree the man does taste the wine, then he is supposed to have spoiled it, so it cannot be used again.

וְהָאֲמַר מָר: כּוֹס שֶׁל בְּרָכָה צָרִיךְ שִׁעוּר, וְהָא קָא פָּחֵית לֵיהּ מִשִּׁעוּרֵיהּ! דְּנָפִישׁ לֵיהּ טְפֵי מִשִּׁעוּרֵיהּ.

E. And has not a master said, "The cup of blessing requires a [fixed] measure." *And lo, he diminishes it from its fixed measure.*

[We speak of a situation in which] *he has more than the fixed measure.*

If we say the man merely tastes the wine with his finger, then we still have a problem, because he is supposed to have a full measure of wine, and here he no longer has a full measure. The solution is that we posit the man has more than enough wine.

וְהָא "אִם אֵין שָׁם אֶלָּא אוֹתוֹ כּוֹס" קָתָנֵי! תְּרֵי לָא הָוֵי וּמֵחַד נָפִישׁ.

F. But lo, has it not been taught: "If there is there *only* that cup" . . . [so he has no more].

G. *There is not enough for two, but more than enough for one.*

The solution that the man has more than enough wine is contrary to the original case, which specifies he has only a single cup, in full, but fixed measure. So we posit he has a bit more than a single cup.

וְהָא תָּנֵי רַבִּי חִיָּא, בֵּית שַׁמַּאי אוֹמְרִים: מְבָרֵךְ עַל הַיַּיִן וְשׁוֹתֵהוּ וְאַחַר כָּךְ מְבָרֵךְ בִּרְכַּת הַמָּזוֹן! אֶלָּא, תְּרֵי תַנָּאֵי וְאַלִּיבָּא דְּבֵית שַׁמַּאי.

H. *And has not R. Hiyya taught:* The House of Shammai say, "He blesses over the wine and drinks it, and afterward he says Grace."

i.e.,
a
contrad.

I. Then we have two Tannas' [traditions] in respect to the opinion of the House of Shammai.

The foregoing solutions are not possible. We have a tradition from Hiyya that explicitly states the man must drink the wine and then say Grace. The only way out is to suppose we have two contradictory traditions in the name of the House of Shammai. Now let us reconsider the entire argument.

The position of the House of Shammai is further investigated, a curious inquiry, considering that the practical law follows the House of Hillel. The issue is whether the Shammaites require that one have a cup of wine before saying Grace after Meals. The thrust of the argument is to show that this is *not* the opinion of the House of Shammai.

A cites the primary datum, the Mishnah 8:8B, then makes the point explicit. The Mishnah seems to specify that the man says the blessing, drinks the wine, and *then* says the Grace. But this is rejected: The blessing is said for the wine, then the wine is left over. C objects that this procedure is contrary to law. This is answered: He does taste the wine, but does not finish the whole cup. D objects to this procedure too. But, it is explained, the tasting is with a finger. E still again objects to the new theory of what is to be done, for the wine has to fill the cup. But the cup is more than full. F points out this contradicts the original statement. To this G replies there is more than one cup, less than two. Then H provides a definitive statement: The House of Shammai explicitly rule one *does* drink the wine, which means the Grace after Meals does *not* require a cup of wine in addition. The only possible solution is given in I: We have contradictory opinions attributed to the House of Shammai.

Clearly, the construction is "artificial." The series of questions is asked in full awareness of the consequent replies. A simple construction would have given A, then H–I. But, as we see, the Talmud normally prefers to lay out and explore all possible routes through an inquiry. The simple and definitive answer is the least likely to come at the outset. Rather, the

argument will move from point to point, back and forth, before
it is allowed to close with a simple solution.

"בֵּית שַׁמַּאי אוֹמְרִים" וְכוּלֵי. תְּנוּ רַבָּנָן, בֵּית שַׁמַּאי
אוֹמְרִים: נוֹטְלִין לַיָּדַיִם וְאַחַר כָּךְ מוֹזְגִין אֶת הַכּוֹס,
שֶׁאִם אַתָּה אוֹמֵר "מוֹזְגִין אֶת הַכּוֹס תְּחִלָּה"", גְּזֵרָה
שֶׁמָּא יְטַמְאוּ מַשְׁקִין שֶׁאֲחוֹרֵי הַכּוֹס מֵחֲמַת יָדָיו, וְיַחְזְרוּ
וִיטַמְּאוּ אֶת הַכּוֹס.

*now begin
ritual
defilement
+
its
transmission*

The House of Shammai say [They wash the hands
and afterward mix the cup] . . .
A. *Our rabbis have taught:*
**The House of Shammai say, "They wash the hands
and afterward mix the cup, for if you say they mix the
cup first,** [against this view is] **a** [precautionary] **decree
to prevent the liquids on the outer sides of the cup,
which are unclean by reason of his hands'** [touching
them], **from going back and making the cup unclean."**

The Tosefta pertinent to the Mishnah is simply cited.

וְלִיטַמּוּ יָדַיִם לַכּוֹס!

B. *But will not the hands make the cup itself unclean* [without
reference to the liquids]?

Now the problem is raised: Whether or not there are liquids,
why will the *hands* themselves not make the cup unclean? The
question is asked as if we did not know the following answer.
But as a matter of fact, what follows is established law:

יָדַיִם שְׁנִיּוֹת הֵן, וְאֵין שֵׁנִי עוֹשֶׂה שְׁלִישִׁי בְּחֻלִּין אֶלָּא
עַל יְדֵי מַשְׁקִין.

The hands are in the second remove of uncleanness,
and the [object unclean in] the second remove of uncleanness cannot [then] render [another object unclean]
in the third [remove] in respect to profane foods [but

only to Heave-offering]. But [this happens] only by
means of liquids [unclean in the first remove].

The answer simply reviews the well-known law. Something
unclean in the second remove of uncleanness cannot make
another object unclean so far as ordinary food in concerned.
This is done only by means of liquids, which are always
unclean in the first remove and therefore render food unclean.

וּבֵית הַלֵּל אוֹמְרִים : מוֹזְגִין אֶת הַכּוֹס וְאַחַר כָּךְ נוֹטְלִין
לַיָּדַיִם, שֶׁאָם אַתָּה אוֹמֵר "נוֹטְלִין לַיָּדַיִם תְּחִלָּה", גְּזֵרָה
שֶׁמָּא יִטָּמְאוּ מַשְׁקִין שֶׁבַּיָּדַיִם מֵחֲמַת הַכּוֹס, וְיַחְזְרוּ
וִיטַמְּאוּ אֶת הַיָּדַיִם.

**C. And the House of Hillel say, "They mix the cup
and afterward wash the hands, for if you say they wash
the hands first,** [against this view is] **a** [precautionary]
decree lest the liquids which are [already] **on the hands
become unclean on account of the cup and go and render
the hands unclean."**

We turn to the opinion of the House of Hillel.

וְנִיטַמֵּי כוֹס לַיָּדַיִם! אֵין כְּלִי מְטַמֵּא אָדָם.

D. *But will not the cup* [itself] *make the hands unclean?*
A vessel cannot render a man unclean.

The question addressed to the House of Shammai is repeated
to the House of Hillel, which also have to answer it. The
answer is simply that a man is *not* made unclean by a vessel,
but only by something unclean from a primary source [father]
of uncleanness. Everyone knows that!

וְנִיטַמֵּי לַמַּשְׁקִין שֶׁבְּתוֹכוֹ! הָכָא — בִּכְלִי שֶׁנִּטְמְאוּ
אֲחוֹרָיו בְּמַשְׁקִין עָסְקִינַן, דְּתוֹכוֹ טָהוֹר וְגַבּוֹ טָמֵא;
דִּתְנַן: כְּלִי שֶׁנִּטְמְאוּ אֲחוֹרָיו בְּמַשְׁקִין — אֲחוֹרָיו
טְמֵאִים, תּוֹכוֹ וְאָגְנוֹ וְאָזְנוֹ וְיָדָיו טְהוֹרִין, נִטְמָא
תּוֹכוֹ — נִטְמָא כֻּלּוֹ.

E. *But will they* [the hands] *not render the liquids which are in it* [the cup] *unclean?*

Here we are dealing with a vessel the outer part of which has been made unclean by liquid. The inner part is clean but the outer part is unclean. *Thus we have learned:*

[If] a vessel is made unclean on the outside by liquid, the outside is unclean, [52b] but its inside and its rim, handle, and haft are clean. If, however, the inside is unclean, the whole [cup] is unclean.

Now comes the problem of the liquid, just as with the Shammaites. Will not the liquid in the cup be made unclean? The answer is that we distinguish among the parts of a cup. The outer part is regarded as separate from the inner part. If the outer part is unclean, the inner part remains clean. But if the inner part is unclean, however, the whole is regarded as unclean. And this is an established tradition.

בְּמַאי קָא מִיפַּלְגִי?

E. *What, then, do they* [the Houses] *dispute?*

If so, what can the issue possibly be on which the Houses are supposed to differ? What we originally supposed to be under discussion is obviously not at issue at all.

בֵּית שַׁמַּאי סָבְרִי: אָסוּר לְהִשְׁתַּמֵּשׁ בִּכְלִי שֶׁנִּטְמְאוּ אֲחוֹרָיו בְּמַשְׁקִין, גְּזֵרָה מִשּׁוּם נִיצוֹצוֹת, וְלֵיכָא לְמִגְזַר שֶׁמָּא יִטָּמְאוּ הַמַּשְׁקִין שֶׁבַּיָּדַיִם בַּכּוֹס,

The House of Shammai hold that it is prohibited to make use of a vessel whose outer parts are unclean by liquids, as a decree on account of the drippings. [There thus is] *no* [reason] *to decree* lest the liquids on the hands be made unclean by the cup.

The House of Shammai say we take precautions about a vessel whose outer part is unclean by liquids. Since we do take such a precaution, we do not have to worry that the liquid on

the hands is going to be affected by the cup, for the cup to
begin with is *not* going to be unclean.

וּבֵית הִלֵּל סָבְרִי: מְתָּר לְהִשְׁתַּמֵּשׁ בִּכְלִי שֶׁנִּטְמְאוּ
אֲחוֹרָיו בְּמַשְׁקִין, אָמְרִי: נִיצוֹצוֹת לָא שְׁכִיחִי, וְאִיכָּא
לְמֵיחַשׁ שֶׁמָּא יִטָּמְאוּ מַשְׁקִין שֶׁבַּיָּדַיִם מֵחֲמַת הַכּוֹס.

And the House of Hillel reckon that it is permitted to make
use of a vessel whose outer part is made unclean by
liquids, *for drippings are unusual. But there is reason to take care*
lest the liquids which are on the hands may be made
unclean by the cup.

The Hillelites say you may make use of a cup which is wet
and unclean on the outside. <u>Drippings are not commonplace.</u>
But you do have to worry about the liquid on the hands, which
may be made unclean by the cup. The difference, therefore,
concerns the sort of precautions one takes in respect to the cup.
This is a far cry from our original supposition. It strongly
suggests the later authorities were not entirely clear about what
had originally bothered the Houses and led to their contradictory rulings.

don't worry over rarity

דָּבָר אַחֵר: תֵּכֶף לִנְטִילַת יָדַיִם סְעָדָה.

G. **Another matter: [So that] immediately upon the
washing of the hands [may come] the meal [itself].**

We return to the Tosefta and cite its second reason for the
Hillelite position.

מַאי "דָּבָר אַחֵר"? הָכִי קָאָמְרִי לְהוּ בֵּית הִלֵּל לְבֵית
שַׁמַּאי: לְדִידְכוּ דְּאָמְרִיתוּ "אָסוּר לְהִשְׁתַּמֵּשׁ בִּכְלִי
שֶׁאֲחוֹרָיו טְמֵאִין" דְּגָזְרִינַן מִשּׁוּם נִיצוֹצוֹת, אֲפִלּוּ הָכִי
הָא עֲדִיפָא, דְּתֵכֶף לִנְטִילַת יָדַיִם סְעָדָה.

What is the reason for this additional explanation?
This is what the House of Hillel said to the House of Shammai:

Hillel given 2ⁿᵈ opinion, but our view is better, cuz meal follows immd. aftr wash

"According to your reasoning, in saying that it is prohibited to make use of a cup whose outer parts are unclean, *we decree on account of the drippings. But even so,* [our opinion] *is better, for* **immediately upon the washing of the hands [should come] the meal.**"

Now we explain why the second reason is given. No matter what you say, the Hillelite ruling is better, for it is appropriate that one start the meal immediately after washing hands.

To review the entire argument: Once again, the Talmud focuses upon the Tosefta, ignoring the simpler formulation of the law by the Mishnah. B and D are matched: The same question is directed toward each House. Each is assumed to have good, logical reasons for its opinion. The House of Shammai say a person washes the hands to keep the liquid on the outside of the cup from being made unclean by them. If touched by the unclean hands, the liquid would then go and make the cup itself unclean. But asks B, why should the hands themselves not make the cup unclean? This question feigns ignorance of the well-known law, immediately following, about the hands' remove of uncleanness. Obviously, the person who raised the question knew the answer, which was a commonplace, so asking the question represents a rhetorical and pedagogical device. The question is asked so that the information may be imparted in a pertinent way. The hands cannot make the cup unclean. But they can make liquid unclean, and in a first remove of uncleanness at that, so liquid will affect the cup.

The Hillelites then have to explain why the cup cannot make the hands unclean. The vessel is no different from the hands. Now in E a further, obvious question is raised: Will not the unclean liquid on the outside of the cup make the liquid *in* the cup unclean?

But the answer is equally obvious: No, the liquid on the outside has no affect on the liquid inside. (E is greatly augmented in the Palestinian version.)

Having elucidated the pertinent laws through questions and answers, the Talmud has now to explain the issue between the

Houses. It is shown to be considerably less obvious than we
had originally supposed. The House of Shammai say that,
whatever the law may be, you should not use a cup the outer
part of which is unclean by liquids lest the liquids drip. Since
such a cup will not be used, however, then you do not have to
worry about the cup's making the hands unclean. The House
of Hillel say such a vessel may be used; therefore, you have to
take care lest the liquid on the hands be made unclean by the
cup.

G then explains why the House of Hillel are given a second
reason: We take account of your view, but ours is better overall,
because the meal should follow immediately upon the washing
of the hands.

"בֵּית שַׁמַּאי אוֹמְרִים: מְקַנֵּחַ" וְכוּלֵי. תְּנוּ רַבָּנָן, בֵּית
שַׁמַּאי אוֹמְרִים: מְקַנֵּחַ יָדָיו בַּמַּפָּה וּמַנִּיחָהּ עַל הַשֻּׁלְחָן,
שֶׁאִם אַתָּה אוֹמֵר "עַל הַכֶּסֶת", גְּזֵרָה שֶׁמָּא יִטָּמְאוּ
מַשְׁקִין שֶׁבַּמַּפָּה מֵחֲמַת הַכֶּסֶת, וְיַחְזְרוּ וִיטַמְּאוּ אֶת
הַיָּדַיִם.

*next,
towel
(EL AM
961)*

**The House of Shammai say, "He dries his hand on the
napkin . . ."**

A. *Our rabbis have taught:*

**The House of Shammai say, "He wipes his hands with
the napkin and lays it on the table, for if you say, 'on
the cushion,' [that view is wrong, for it is a precaution-
ary] decree lest the liquids which are on the napkin
become unclean on account of the cushion and go back
and render the hands unclean."**

Again we begin simply by citing the Tosefta pertinent to the
Mishnah. We then analyze it according to the positions of each
House, just as we did above.

וּנְטַמְיֵיהּ כֶּסֶת לַמַּפָּה! אֵין כְּלִי מְטַמֵּא כְּלִי.

B. *And will not the cushion* [itself] *render the napkin unclean?*
A vessel cannot make a vessel unclean.

The first, obvious question is: <u>Why should we *not* worry
about the cushion?</u> Will it not make the napkin unclean? The
obvious answer is that it cannot.

וּנְטַמְיֵיהּ כֶּסֶת לְגַבְרָא גוּפֵיהּ! אֵין כְּלִי מְטַמֵּא אָדָם.

And will not the cushion [itself] *make the man unclean?*
A vessel cannot make a man unclean.

The second, still obvious question is, Will the cushion not
make the man unclean? And the answer is equally obvious—it
really is the same as the one in regard to the cushion. The
principle is no different.

וּבֵית הִלֵּל אוֹמְרִים : עַל הַכֶּסֶת, שֶׁאִם אַתָּה אוֹמֵר "עַל
הַשֻּׁלְחָן", גְּזֵרָה שֶׁמָּא יִטָּמְאוּ מַשְׁקִים שֶׁבַּמַּפָּה מֵחֲמַת
הַשֻּׁלְחָן, וְיַחְזְרוּ וִיטַמְּאוּ אֶת הָאֹכָלִין.

C. **And the House of Hillel say, "'On the cushion,'
for if you say, 'on the table,'** [that opinion is wrong, for
it is a] **decree lest the liquids become unclean on account
of the table and go and render the food unclean."**

We turn to the opinion of the House of Hillel, as elaborated
by the Tosefta.

וּלְטַמֵּא שֻׁלְחָן לָאֳכָלִין שֶׁבְּתוֹכוֹ! הָכָא בְּשֻׁלְחָן שֵׁנִי
עָסְקִינַן, וְאֵין שֵׁנִי עוֹשֶׂה שְׁלִישִׁי בְּחֻלִּין אֶלָּא עַל יְדֵי
מַשְׁקִין.

But will not the table render the food which is on it unclean?
We here deal with a table which is unclean in the second remove,
and something unclean in the second remove does not
render something unclean in the third remove in respect
to unconsecrated food, except by means of liquids [which
are always unclean in the first remove].

If we do not worry about the cushion, why should we not
worry about the table? Will the table not make the food

unclean? So why the concern about the cushion, which is a minor matter, if the table on which the food is set itself will make the food unclean! The answer is that the table is unclean in the second remove (like the hands) and does not make the food unclean. Only a wet table will do that, and we take for granted our table is dry.

בְּמַאי קָמִיפַּלְגִי? בֵּית שַׁמַּאי סָבְרִי: אָסוּר לְהִשְׁתַּמֵּשׁ
בְּשֻׁלְחָן שֵׁנִי, גְּזֵרָה מִשּׁוּם אוֹכְלֵי תְרוּמָה;

D. *What* [principle] *do they dispute?*
The House of Shammai reckon that it is prohibited to make use of a table unclean in the second remove, as a decree on account of those who eat Heave-offering [which is rendered unfit by an object unclean in the second remove].

Once again, we have to discover the principle on which the Houses disagree. It is the status of the *table*. The House of Shammai say you cannot use a table unclean in the second remove. The reason is that, while ordinary food will not be affected by such a table, Heave-offering, which is a priestly gift, *is* going to be made unfit by it. We worry therefore about the priests who may be eating Heave-offering. Their food will be made unfit by the table unclean in the second remove.

וּבֵית הִלֵּל סָבְרִי: מֻתָּר לְהִשְׁתַּמֵּשׁ בְּשֻׁלְחָן שֵׁנִי, אוֹכְלֵי
תְרוּמָה זְרִיזִין הֵם.

And the House of Hillel reckon that it is permitted to make use of a table unclean in the second remove, for those who eat Heave-offering [the priests] are careful.

The Hillelites are more practical here. They say that people who eat Heave-offering are used to taking precautions to preserve its fitness against second remove of uncleanness. Ordinary folk may make use of a table unclean in the second remove, and priests are not going to stumble thereby.

EL Am trans: "Secular things" = חֻלִּין

דָּבָר אַחֵר: אֵין נְטִילַת יָדַיִם לְחֻלִּין מִן הַתּוֹרָה.

NB the motive principle

E. Another matter: There is no Scriptural requirement to wash the hands before eating unconsecrated
food. (

Again we have a second reason. This one is important, however, for it reviews the principles on which the reasons just
now given actually are based. Hands are unclean in the second
remove. They will not make ordinary food unclean, therefore
unfit. So a man really does not have to wash his hands before
eating unconsecrated, that is, ordinary food.

מַאי "דָּבָר אַחֵר"? הָכִי קָאָמְרִי לְהוּ בֵּית הִלֵּל לְבֵית
שַׁמַּאי: וְכִי תֵּימְרוּ, מַאי שְׁנָא גַּבֵּי אֳכָלִין דְּחָיְישִׁינַן,
וּמַאי שְׁנָא גַּבֵּי יָדַיִם דְּלָא חָיְישִׁינַן? אֲפִלּוּ הָכִי הָא
עֲדִיפָא, דְּאֵין נְטִילַת יָדַיִם לְחֻלִּין מִן הַתּוֹרָה, מוּטָב
שֶׁיִּטָּמְאוּ יָדַיִם דְּלֵית לְהוּ עִקָּר מִדְּאוֹרָיְיתָא, וְאַל יִטָּמְאוּ
אֳכָלִים דְּאִית לְהוּ עִקָּר מִדְּאוֹרָיְיתָא.

What is the purpose of "another explanation"?
This is what the House of Hillel said to the House of Shammai: If
you ask what is the difference in respect to food, concerning which we
take care, and in respect to the hands, concerning which we do not
take care—even in this regard [our opinion] *is preferable, for*
there is no Scriptural requirement concerning the washing of the hands before eating unconsecrated food.
It is better that the hands should be made unclean, *for*
there is no Scriptural basis for [washing] *them,* and let not the
food be made unclean, *concerning which there is a Scriptural*
basis [for concern about its uncleanness].

Why do the Hillelites need this other reason? The food has to
be protected; the hands do not form an equally serious consideration. Therefore, we take care to protect the food, but we are
not so concerned about the hands.

Notice the highly formal pattern according to which the

several arguments we have reviewed are constructed. It is aston-
ishingly consistent. We are now well aware that our chapter of
the Talmud is constructed according to a simple but rigid
pattern. First, the Tosefta will be cited, then the opinions of
each House will be tested against certain obvious considerations; third, the underlying principle at issue will be spelled
out, and that issue will be remote from the original terms of the
argument; fourth, the second reason of the House of Hillel will
be turned into a full argument against the House of Shammai,
thus shown not irrelevant or tacked on, but central to the issue.

A–C thus are not much different from what has already been
examined. D then brings the issue of the sort of table one may
use, parallel to the foregoing, in which the condition of the
cup is debated. Finally, in E, the House of Hillel is made to
claim a distinction between the food and the hands. But, be
that as it may, the Hillelites say their position is better, for
what Scripture requires has to be done.

At this point we probably could construct our own Talmud,
at least in the model of the present form. The rhetorical and
critical principles are sufficiently clear so that, given other
materials such as those before us, we might apply them on our
own within the established pattern. And it would be legitimate.
How so? Let me explain.

To understand the concept of ongoing argument, we note
the introduction of an interesting distinction between the law
decreed by Scripture, which is at a higher status, and the law
decreed by scribes, sages, or rabbis, which is at a lesser status.
One of the principal distinctions operative in the thought of
the sages of the Babylonian Talmud is before us. When we can
show that a law derives from Scripture, we know that that law
must be rigidly enforced. And, to the contrary, what scribes or
sages or rabbis decree may be set aside, the one being divine,
the other merely useful. In making such a distinction, the
Talmudic rabbis recognize that, in addition to the Torah
revealed by God to Moses at Sinai, there are secondary additions
and accretions to the law, contributed by authorities later on,

in accord with their reasoning and their understanding of the requirements of the world and the age. The unfolding of the law therefore goes forward through both reason and the good judgment of the astute sage. The conception that the canon of revelation closed at Sinai proves alien to the sages at hand; to them revelation by God to Moses at Sinai goes forward in the processes of argument and judgment carried on by sages in the chain of tradition. So the canon, the basket, of Judaism remains forever open to new canonical—authoritative—doctrines of law and theology.

"בֵּית שַׁמַּאי אוֹמְרִים: מְכַבְּדִין" וְכוּלֵי. תָּנוּ רַבָּנָן, בֵּית שַׁמַּאי אוֹמְרִים: מְכַבְּדִין אֶת הַבַּיִת וְאַחַר כָּךְ נוֹטְלִין לַיָּדַיִם, שֶׁאִם אַתָּה אוֹמֵר "נוֹטְלִין לַיָּדַיִם תְּחִלָּה", נִמְצָא אַתָּה מַפְסִיד אֶת הָאֳכָלִין.

The House of Shammai say, "They clean the house and afterward wash the hands . . ."

A. *Our rabbis have taught:*

The House of Shammai say, "They clean the house and afterward wash the hands, for if you say, 'They wash the hands first,' it turns out that you spoil the food."

Once again we investigate the reasons behind the rulings of the two Houses. We begin with the Shammaites. They say you should sweep up first so that you will not moisten, therefore ruin, the crumbs of food.

אֲבָל נְטִילַת יָדַיִם לְבֵית שַׁמַּאי תְּחִלָּה — לָא סְבִירָא לְהוּ, מַאי טַעֲמָא? מִשּׁוּם פֵּרוּרִין.

B. *But the House of Shammai do not reckon that one washes the hands first.*

What is the reason?

On account of the crumbs.

The reason is now spelled out, as if it were not already clear.
You do not first wash your hands, so that water will not spill
onto the remaining food.

וּבֵית הִלֵּל אוֹמְרִים: אִם שַׁמָּשׁ תַּלְמִיד חָכָם הוּא, נוֹטֵל
פֵּרוּרִין שֶׁיֵּשׁ בָּהֶן כַּזַּיִת וּמַנִּיחַ פֵּרוּרִין שֶׁאֵין בָּהֶן כַּזַּיִת.

C. And the House of Hillel say, "If the servant is a
disciple of a sage, he takes the crumbs which are as large
as an olive [in bulk] and leaves the crumbs which are not
so much as an olive [in bulk]."

The opinion of the House of Hillel now is cited, and its
pertinence to the opinion of the House of Shammai is taken for
granted. The Hillelites say there is not going to be food left
over to be spoiled by the water. In that case, the two Houses are
in agreement.

— מְסַיַּע לֵיהּ לְרַבִּי יוֹחָנָן, דַּאֲמַר רַבִּי יוֹחָנָן: פֵּרוּרִין
שֶׁאֵין בָּהֶם כַּזַּיִת — מֻתָּר לְאַבְּדָן בַּיָּד.

D. (This view supports the opinion of R. Yohanan, for R.
Yohanan said, "Crumbs which are not an olive in bulk
may be deliberately destroyed.")

This is the first interpolation from a later authority we have
seen. Yohanan's saying is cited because it is relevant to what
has been said, but it does not fit into the established construction. It breaks what has been until now a perfect structure.
Yohanan lived two centuries after the Houses, ca. A.D. 250, in
the land of Israel.

— בְּמַאי קָמִיפַּלְגִי? בֵּית הִלֵּל סָבְרִי: אָסוּר לְהִשְׁתַּמֵּשׁ
בְּשַׁמָּשׁ עַם הָאָרֶץ, וּבֵית שַׁמַּאי סָבְרִי: מֻתָּר לְהִשְׁתַּמֵּשׁ
בְּשַׁמָּשׁ עַם הָאָרֶץ.

E. In what do they differ?
The House of Hillel reckon that it is prohibited to employ a

servant who is an ignorant man, *and the House of Shammai reckon that* it is permitted to employ a servant who is an ignorant man.

The issue between the Houses is now made explicit. They differ not about spoiling food, but about the conditions of the meal. An ignorant man will not know he should collect the crumbs of a certain size. The Hillelites say you will not have such a servant to begin with, so you do not have to worry about the crumbs. The Shammaites say you may. All of this looks to be much after the fact.

אָמַר רַבִּי יוֹסֵי בַּר חֲנִינָא אָמַר רַב הוּנָא: בְּכוּלֵּיהּ פִּרְקִין הֲלָכָה כְּבֵית הִלֵּל, בַּר מֵהָא דַּהֲלָכָה כְּבֵית שַׁמַּאי; וְרַבִּי אוֹשַׁעְיָא מַתְנֵי אִיפְּכָא, וּבְהָא נַמֵּי הֲלָכָה כְּבֵית הִלֵּל.

F. R. Yosé bar Hanina said in the name of R. Huna, "In our entire chapter the law is in accord with the House of Hillel, excepting this matter, in which the law is in accord with the House of Shammai."

And R. Oshaia taught the matter contrariwise. And in this matter too the law is in accord with the House of Hillel.

Apart from D, which is an obvious interpolation, and F, which provides a general ruling on the final decision of the law, the construction before us is consistent with the foregoing. B explains the position of the House of Shammai, E draws the obvious conclusion that the Houses differ about exactly what their original sayings make clear is their disagreement.

new pericope

"בֵּית שַׁמַּאי אוֹמְרִים: נֵר וּמָזוֹן" וְכוּלֵּי.

The House of Shammai say, "Light and food . . ."

We cite a new Mishnaic paragraph. Instead of analyzing it, we shall first review a repertoire of pertinent stories. But the stories lead to the sort of inquiry we have just now completed. The form is different, but the point of analysis is not: Just what traditions belong to the respective Houses, and what are the reasons behind the traditions, or how are they accurately to be assigned? The story concerns two fourth-century masters and how they said the *Havdalah* blessings.

[Marginal note: no Mishn. + Toseft now]

רַב הוּנָא בַּר יְהוּדָה אִיקְּלַע לְבֵי רָבָא, חַזְיֵיהּ לְרָבָא דִּבְרִיךְ אַבְּשָׂמִים בְּרֵישָׁא, אָמַר לֵיהּ: מִכְּדֵי בֵּית שַׁמַּאי וּבֵית הִלֵּל אַמָּאוֹר לָא פְּלִיגִי, דְּתַנְיָא, בֵּית שַׁמַּאי אוֹמְרִים: נֵר וּמָזוֹן בְּשָׂמִים וְהַבְדָּלָה, וּבֵית הִלֵּל אוֹמְרִים: נֵר וּבְשָׂמִים מָזוֹן וְהַבְדָּלָה! עָנֵי רָבָא בָּתְרֵיהּ: זוֹ דִּבְרֵי רַבִּי מֵאִיר, אֲבָל רַבִּי יְהוּדָה אוֹמֵר: לֹא נֶחְלְקוּ בֵּית שַׁמַּאי וּבֵית הִלֵּל עַל הַמָּזוֹן שֶׁהוּא בַּתְּחִלָּה וְעַל הַבְדָּלָה שֶׁהִיא בַּסּוֹף, עַל מָה נֶחְלְקוּ? עַל הַמָּאוֹר וְעַל הַבְּשָׂמִים, שֶׁבֵּית שַׁמַּאי אוֹמְרִים: עַל הַמָּאוֹר וְאַחַר כָּךְ בְּשָׂמִים, וּבֵית הִלֵּל אוֹמְרִים: בְּשָׂמִים וְאַחַר כָּךְ מָאוֹר; וְאָמַר רַבִּי יוֹחָנָן: נָהֲגוּ הָעָם כְּבֵית הִלֵּל אַלִּיבָּא דְּרַבִּי יְהוּדָה.

[Marginal note: Rava]

A. *R. Huna bar Judah happened by the house of Rava. He saw that Rava blessed the spices first.*

He said to him, "Now the House of Shammai and the House of Hillel did not dispute concerning the light, [it should come first].

"*For it was taught:* The House of Shammai say, 'Light, and food, spices, and *Havdalah*,' and the House of Hillel say, 'Light, and spices, and food, and *Havdalah*.'"

[Marginal note: Rava explains issues betw. houses]

Rava answered him, "This is the opinion [= version] *of R. Meir, but R. Judah says,* 'The House of Shammai and the House of Hillel did not differ concerning the food, that it comes first, and concerning the *Havdalah*, that it is at the end.

"'Concerning what did they differ?'

"'Concerning the light and the spices.'

"For the House of Shammai say, 'The light and afterward the spices.'

"And the House of Hillel say, 'The spices and afterward the light.'"

B. And R. Yohanan said, "The people were accustomed to act in accord with the House of Hillel *as presented by* R. Judah."

The Mishnah and Tosefta now fade into the background. The law is taken for granted, and its practical application comes to the fore. The story, concerning fourth-century Babylonian Amoraim, shows, however, that accurate traditions were earnestly sought out. Rava is able to show Huna that he has acted in accord with a sound version of the Houses' opinions. B is an independent saying, substantiating the action of Rava by pointing out that the ordinary folk likewise did as Judah said the House of Hillel had ruled.

The search for, and analysis of, accurate versions of what is attributed to the earlier authorities is a primary trait of the Talmudic argument. We discern no vested interests in a given version; if it can be shown that there are several views of what an earlier master had taught, then all have to be taken into account. The critical and rational spirit of Talmudic inquiry is revealed in many different ways; this is one of the most characteristic.

new pericope

"בֵּית שַׁמַּאי אוֹמְרִים: שֶׁבָּרָא" וְכוּלֵי.

The House of Shammai say, "Who created . . ."

Once again, we begin with a citation of the Mishnah. Then the fourth-century authorities will try to explain the difference between the Houses.

אָמַר רָבָא: בְּ"בָּרָא" כּוּלֵי עָלְמָא לָא פְּלִיגִי דִּבְרָא
מַשְׁמַע, כִּי פְּלִיגִי — בְּ"בוֹרֵא", בֵּית שַׁמַּאי סָבְרִי:

"בּוֹרֵא" — דַּעֲתִיד לְמִבְרָא, וּבֵית הִלֵּל סָבְרִי: "בּוֹרֵא"
נַמֵּי דִּבְרָא מַשְׁמַע.

Sham: past tense

A. Rava said, "*Concerning the word* 'bara' [created], *everyone agrees that* 'bara' *implies* [the past tense]. *They differ concerning* 'boré' [creates]. *The House of Shammai reckon that* 'boré' *means* 'Who will create in the future.' *And the House of Hillel reckon that* 'boré' *also means what was created* [in the past]."

Rava claims that the issue is the meaning of the present-tense form of the verb *boré*, who creates. The Shammaites say *boré* refers to creation in the future. The House of Hillel say that the participle *boré* may refer also to creation in the past.

מְתִיב רַב יוֹסֵף: "יוֹצֵר אוֹר וּבוֹרֵא חֹשֶׁךְ", "יוֹצֵר הָרִים
וּבֹרֵא רוּחַ", "בּוֹרֵא הַשָּׁמַיִם וְנוֹטֵיהֶם"!

present participles referring to acts of creation: grammat evidence

B. *R. Joseph objected,* "'Who forms light and creates darkness' [Isaiah 45:7], 'Creates mountains and forms the wind' [Amos 4:13], 'Who creates the heavens and spreads them out'" [Isaiah 42:5].

Joseph rejects the Shammaite position out of hand. We have numerous examples of the use of the form *boré* to refer to what was done in the long-distant past. The Shammaites cannot have held otherwise, for they are presumed to be as well informed as the Hillelites.

אֶלָּא אָמַר רַב יוֹסֵף: בְּ"בָּרָא" וּ"בוֹרֵא" כּוּלֵי עָלְמָא לָא
פְּלִיגִי דִּבְרָא מַשְׁמַע, כִּי פְּלִיגִי — בְּ"מָאוֹר" וּ"מְאוֹרֵי",
דְּבֵית שַׁמַּאי סָבְרִי: חֲדָא נְהוֹרָא אִיכָּא בְּנוּרָא, וּבֵית
הִלֵּל סָבְרִי: טוּבָא נְהוֹרֵי אִיכָּא בְּנוּרָא.

"But," R. Joseph said, "*Concerning* 'bara' *and* 'boré' *everyone agrees that* [the words] *refer to the past. They differ as to whether one should say* 'light' *or* 'lights.'"

this is the real problem: lights

"The House of Shammai reckon there is one light in the fire."
"And the House of Hillel reckon there are many lights in the fire."

Joseph provides a better interpretation of the difference between the Houses. They are supposed to have agreed on the meaning of the verb "to create." That is no problem. The issue is whether one speaks of *light* or *lights*. And that devolves upon the nature of fire. Then the editor of the *Gemara* supplies a Tannaitic tradition in support of Joseph's interpretation of the dispute. The curious thing, of course, is that the Houses *do* differ about *creates* vs. *created* [*boré/bara*], as much as about *light/lights*, but no one is able to explain that difference!

Joseph ignores it cuz cant figure it

תַּנְיָא נַמֵי הָכֵי, אָמְרוּ לָהֶם בֵּית הִלֵּל לְבֵית שַׁמַּאי:
הַרְבֵּה מְאוֹרוֹת יֵשׁ בָּאוֹר.

C. *We have a Tannaitic teaching along the same lines:*
The House of Hillel say to the House of Shammai, "There are many illuminations in the light."

To review the whole: Rava explains the issue between the Houses. The House of Shammai prefer the past tense, *who created,* for the blessing is on account of the fire which has already been created in the past. The present participle, *boré,* may imply the present or the future tense. The House of Shammai therefore reject the present participial form of the verb "create," for, as stated, the blessing is for fire already created. The House of Hillel reject this view—so Rava. In B, Joseph proves the difference cannot be as Rava suggests, for Scripture contains present participles referring to the very acts of creation which, everyone knows, took place in the long-distant past. That is the reason Joseph quotes the several Scriptures before us. These constitute solid grammatical evidence.

The Houses therefore cannot be thought to have differed on that issue, for the House of Shammai know Scriptures. The difference between the Houses, rather, is about whether one says *light* or *lights*. The House of Shammai prefer the singular, the House of Hillel, the plural, for the reasons given. C then gives us a formulation, attributed to a Tannaitic authority, of the same issue; it looks like a fragment of a larger debate between the Houses. But we have no further evidence of the rest of the debate. And Joseph does not account for the obvious fact that the Houses *do* differ about *created* vs. *create;* since he cannot find a rational basis for the difference, he simply prefers to ignore the evidence that there was one. Bad form indeed!

"אֵין מְבָרְכִין" כּוּלֵי.

A blessing is not said . . .

The Mishnah is cited in abbreviated form. The rule is that you may not say a blessing either over the light or over the spices of gentiles.

בִּשְׁלָמָא נֵר — מִשּׁוּם דְּלָא שָׁבַת, אֶלָּא בְּשָׂמִים מַאי טַעֲמָא לָא?

A. *Certainly,* [in the case of] *the light* [of idolators, one should not say a blessing] *because it did not rest on the Sabbath. But what is the reason that for spices* [one may] not say [the blessing]?

We take for granted that there is a good reason for not blessing the light of the gentiles. But why should you not bless over their spices? Rav will provide the answer.

אָמַר רַב יְהוּדָה אָמַר רַב: הָכָא בִּמְסִבַּת עוֹבְדֵי כּוֹכָבִים עָסְקִינַן, מִפְּנֵי שֶׁסְּתָם מְסִבַּת עוֹבְדֵי כּוֹכָבִים לַעֲבוֹדָה זָרָה הִיא.

R. Judah said in the name of Rav, *"We here deal with a banquet held by idolators,* because the run-of-the-mill banquet held by idolators is for the sake of idolatry."

Rav's reason is that whenever spices are used, it is going to be for idolatrous purposes.

הָא מִדְּקָתָנֵי סֵיפָא: אֵין מְבָרְכִין לֹא עַל הַנֵּר וְלֹא עַל
הַבְּשָׂמִים שֶׁל עֲבוֹדָה זָרָה, מִכְּלָל דְּרֵישָׁא לָאו בַּעֲבוֹדָה
זָרָה עָסְקִינַן!

B. *But since it has been taught at the end of the clause,* "Or
over the light or spices of idolatry," *we must infer that the
beginning of the clause does not deal with idolatry.*

Mish. only
repeats
for
pedag.
purposes

Rav's reason is challenged. The Mishnah already includes a
reference to the spices used for idolatrous purposes. So the first
reference must be to something other than spices used for gentile worship, for the Mishnah does not repeat itself.

אָמַר רַב חֲנִינָא מִסּוּרָא: "מַה טַעַם" קָאָמַר, מַה טַעַם
אֵין מְבָרְכִין לֹא עַל הַנֵּר וְלֹא עַל הַבְּשָׂמִים שֶׁל עוֹבְדֵי
כּוֹכָבִים וּמַזָּלוֹת? מִפְּנֵי שֶׁסְּתָם מְסִבַּת עוֹבְדֵי כּוֹכָבִים
לַעֲבוֹדָה זָרָה.

C. R. Hanina from Sura said, "What is the reason is
what it explains, namely, what is the reason that they do
not bless the light or spices of idolators? Because the
run-of-the-mill banquet held by idolators is for the sake
of idolatry."

Hanina's explanation is not a bad one. The Mishnah will
sometimes give a rule, then spell it out. In effect Hanina says
the Mishnah sometimes will repeat itself—just like modern
writers—for the purpose of making clear the meaning only
implied in what is said just once. Repetition is not always for
the sake of introducing a new point; it sometimes serves pedagogical purposes.

To review the whole: The simple rule given in the Mishnah
is examined. The reason taken for granted in respect to the
gentile's light in fact has not yet been adduced; it will come
later on. The issue of spices is raised, and this permits Rav's
comment on the Mishnah to be stated: The idolators' spice
normally serves their cult. The language of Rav's saying is

curious. It begins in Aramaic ("we deal here"), but then the substantive rule ("because . . .") is given in concise, Mishnaic Hebrew, again as though cited from some already known formula. B then challenges Rav's interpretation of the Mishnah by analyzing the language of the Mishnah itself, a fair test. Since the latter part of the rule explicitly refers to idolatry, it may be assumed that the former part does *not* deal with idolatry, contrary to Rav's assertion. Hanina in C explains the Mishnah's language in another way. The first clause is expanded by the second, which provides the reason. But this seems forced.

תְּנוּ רַבָּנָן: אוֹר שֶׁשָּׁבַת — מְבָרְכִין עָלָיו, וְשֶׁלֹּא שָׁבַת — אֵין מְבָרְכִין עָלָיו. (מַאי שָׁבַת) וּמַאי לֹא שָׁבַת?

Our rabbis have taught:

A. One may bless a light which has rested on the Sabbath, but one may not bless a light which has not rested on the Sabbath.

B. *And what is the meaning of* "which has not rested on the Sabbath"?

We earlier alluded to the light "which has not rested on the Sabbath." What can this possibly mean?

אִי נֵימָא, לֹא שָׁבַת מֵחֲמַת מְלָאכָה אֲפִלּוּ מִמְּלָאכָה דְהֶיתֵּרָא,

[53a] *Shall we say* it has not rested on the Sabbath on account of the work [which has been done with it, including] even work which is permitted?

The obvious answer is posited. Work has been done by this light. But what sort of work? Some things, after all, may be done on the Sabbath.

וְהָתַנְיָא: אוֹר שֶׁל חַיָּה וְשֶׁל חוֹלֶה — מְבָרְכִין עָלָיו!

[margin note:] raises alternatives in Ⓑ and dismisses them in Ⓒ–Ⓓ

necess.
wrk

C. *And has it not been taught:* They do bless light [kindled on the Sabbath for] a woman in confinement or a sick person.

We continue to belabor the obvious. There is work you may do by a light on the Sabbath—for example, tending to the needs of sick people.

אָמַר רַב נַחְמָן בַּר יִצְחָק: מַאי שָׁבַת? שֶׁשָּׁבַת מֵחֲמַת מְלֶאכֶת עֲבֵרָה.

D. R. Nahman bar Isaac said, *"What is the meaning of* 'which enjoyed Sabbath-rest'? Which enjoyed Sabbath rest on account of work the doing of which is a transgression [on the Sabbath]."

Nahman bar Isaac now says what was clear at the outset. The light has been used for prohibited work.

תַּנְיָא נַמֵּי הָכֵי: עֲשָׁשִׁית שֶׁהָיְתָה דּוֹלֶקֶת וְהוֹלֶכֶת כָּל הַיּוֹם כֻּלּוֹ — לְמוֹצָאֵי שַׁבָּת מְבָרְכִין עָלֶיהָ.

E. *We have learned likewise in a* baraita:
They may bless a lamp which has been burning throughout the day to the conclusion of the Sabbath.

At the end we cite a *baraita,* that is, a tradition attributed to the second-century masters, the Tannaim, which reinforces our conclusion.

Let us review the argument as a whole. The Talmud introduces materials pertinent to the theme of the Mishnah, but not directly alluded to in the Mishnah's own laws. The first item has to do with the Sabbath-rest of flame; this will recur in the next pericope. A gives the rule, then B begins the analysis. Obviously, the question of what one might possibly mean by a flame's "resting on the Sabbath" has to be answered. But the analysis is obtuse: Do we mean to exclude even light which has served a permissible purpose? Obviously not. C then explains the question: There are things you may do with the light on the Sabbath. Nahman bar Isaac, in D, then says what everyone knows to begin with, and the *baraita*, E, is cited to show that his interpretation has excellent precedent. Here again the artifice of the editor accounts for what must otherwise appear to be a foolish inquiry into obvious things. The editor wishes to make a simple distinction about blessing light which has not rested on the Sabbath. So instead of citing E, he raises in B the possible alternatives and in C–D dismisses them, one by one.

תָּנוּ רַבָּנָן: נָכְרִי שֶׁהִדְלִיק מִיִּשְׂרָאֵל וְיִשְׂרָאֵל שֶׁהִדְלִיק
מִנָּכְרִי — מְבָרְכִין עָלָיו, נָכְרִי מִנָּכְרִי — אֵין מְבָרְכִין
עָלָיו.

Our rabbis have taught:
A. They bless [a light] kindled by a gentile from an Israelite, or by an Israelite from a gentile, but they do not bless [a light] kindled by a gentile from a gentile.

We now begin the analysis of a new teaching, one which specifies which light may, and which may not, be blessed.

מַאי שְׁנָא נָכְרִי מִנָּכְרִי דְלָא — מִשּׁוּם דְּלָא שָׁבַת,

B. *What is the reason one does not do so* [from a light kindled by] *a gentile from a gentile?*
Because it did not enjoy Sabbath-rest.

First we have a repetition of what we already know. You cannot bless a light of a gentile because it did not "enjoy Sabbath-rest."

אִי הָכֵי, יִשְׂרָאֵל מִנָּכְרִי נַמִּי הָא לָא שָׁבַת!

C. *If so, lo,* [a light kindled by] *an Israelite from a gentile also has not enjoyed Sabbath-rest.*

We challenge that reason, which cannot be sufficient, for an Israelite may kindle from a gentile. So the Israelite's light has its beginning in a flame which did not "enjoy Sabbath-rest"!

וְכִי תֵּימָא, הָךְ אִיסּוּרָא אֲזַל לֵיה וְהָא אַחֲרִינָא הוּא
וּבִידָא דְיִשְׂרָאֵל קָא מִתְיַלְּדָא, אֶלָּא הָא דְתַנְיָא:
הַמּוֹצִיא שַׁלְהֶבֶת לִרְשׁוּת הָרַבִּים — חַיָּב, אַמַּאי חַיָּב?
מַה שֶּׁעָקַר לֹא הִנִּיחַ וּמַה שֶּׁהִנִּיחַ לֹא עָקַר!

D. *And if you say this prohibited* [light] *has vanished, and the
one* [in hand] *is another and was born in the hand of the Israelite,*
[how will you deal] *with this teaching?*

He who brings out a flame to the public way [on the
Sabbath] is liable [for violating the Sabbath rule against
carrying from private to public property].

Now why should he be liable? What he raised up he did not
put down, and what he put down he did not raise up.

One solution is to posit that the light of the gentile has
vanished, and in the Israelite's hand is a new light. But that
solution is impossible. For the law explicitly takes for granted
the "unity" of a flame. You cannot take something out from
private property to the public road on the Sabbath. If you take
out a flame, you are liable for punishment. But if the flame you
put down is different, you should not be liable, as is clearly
explained.

אֶלָּא, לְעוֹלָם דְּאִיסּוּרָא נַמֵּי אִיתֵיה, וְכִי קָא מְבָרֵךְ —
אַתּוֹסֶפְתָּא דְּהֶתֵּירָא קָא מְבָרֵךְ.

E. *But* [we must conclude] *that the prohibited* [flame] *is
present, but when he blesses, it is over the additional* [flame], *which
is permitted, that he blesses.*

The best solution is that in addition to the original flame
there is a further, also additional flame, which has begun after
the prohibited flame, and that is the part which one is allowed
to bless.

אִי הָכֵי, נָכְרִי מִנָּכְרִי נַמֵּי!

F. *If so, a gentile*['s flame kindled] *from a gentile*['s flame]
also [should be permitted].

That is a good solution, it is now argued, but it should likewise apply to a gentile's flame kindled from a gentile's flame. That too is a new flame, or there is an additional part which is not prohibited. That is the point of F.

אֵין הָכֵי נַמֵּי, גְּזֵרָה מִשּׁוּם נָכְרִי רִאשׁוֹן וְעַמּוּד רִאשׁוֹן.

That is true, but [it is prohibited by] *decree, on account of the original gentile and the original flame* [of light kindled on the Sabbath by the gentile].

We explicitly agree that the same principle applies, but we take extra precautions in regard to the gentile's flame.

We shall see how the argument is put together as a whole. The earlier discussion assumes greater importance. It has prepared the way for the substantive analysis before us. (A) provides the important rule about not blessing a light kindled by a gentile from a gentile's light. (B) gives the reason, which we already knew from the antecedent pericope. But this reason is flawed, for the light kindled by an Israelite from a gentile is in the same category as one kindled by a gentile from a gentile; neither one has rested on the Sabbath. (D) then presses the question home. The obvious answer is that the light is changing, therefore the Israelite may use the gentile's light, since it is not the same one that has been improperly used on the Sabbath.

But that answer is impossible, for we have a teaching which explicitly rejects the distinction between the original light and the one now in hand. On the Sabbath a person is not supposed to move something from the private to the public domain. We are explicitly informed that that rule applies to a flame. But if the flame changes in character, then why should a person be prohibited from moving it? What he takes up in the private domain is not the same flame as he puts down in the public domain. (E) then draws the necessary inference, the prohibited flame (which has "worked," not rested, on the Sabbath) indeed is present. But *together* with it is additional flame, produced by the original. It is that part of the flame which one may bless.

(F) is absolutely necessary. If so, we cannot distinguish

between an Israelite's kindling from a gentile's flame, and a
gentile's doing so. (G) provides the answer. Logically, one
cannot. But the gentile's flame is prohibited because of its
illicit origin. On this Rashi comments, "If you permit a flame
in the case of a gentile who kindled from a gentile after dark,
one will end up blessing a light in the case of a gentile who
kindled while it was still the Sabbath day; and it is that very
light itself, to which no further light has been added, that one
might then bless right after dark."

Once again, let us stand back from the materials before us
and ask about their place within the larger Talmudic interpretation and construction of reality. The first thing we notice is
that the Jews take for granted they may make some decisions in
respect to gentiles. They may decide whether or not to make
use of light kindled by gentiles or reflected from their homes.
Now to the gentiles it can hardly have mattered whether or not
Jews say blessings over their candles, or sniff their incense, or
sip their wine. Being people of good will, they will not have
objected to the Jews' doing so. But what difference can it make
to them if the Jews do not? To the Jews that decision is represented as a matter of some weight, as if it truly matters.

That representation revises the realities of power confronting
Israel. It imparts to the Jews' decisions in respect to the gentiles
an importance quite incommensurate with either the character
of those decisions or the worldly power of the Jews who made
them. And lending importance to what one does—whether
known or not—with the gentile's flame is part of a much larger
tendency of the rabbis. That tendency was to interpret what the
people did in terms of a much larger, grander scale of transcendent values than might be implied by the significance of
the actions themselves.

The Jews did not have much say about their own fate. The
power available within the Jewish community was derivative,
episodic, and inconsequential. It derived from the wishes of
men and from forces external to Jewry. What Jews did, did not
make a great deal of difference in the larger world in which

they found themselves. All they could really control, in the end, was their private affairs. So the rabbis made the issues of those humble lives into matters of enormous cosmic consequence. The placing of a napkin expressed a grand, invisible concern for the unseen relationships of purity and impurity. And placing the napkin in the correct way assured that the man would be clean, just like a priest in the holy Temple. It expressed the view that here is not an ordinary man, eating his piece of bread and drinking his beer in a little hovel in the hot and dusty Babylonian plains. Here is a priest. The hovel is the Temple. The table is the altar. God is being worshiped and served. What incongruity between the reality and the interpretation of reality! That is the glory of religion.

By this point in our consideration of the details of the laws and how they were decided, it is easy to forget the larger context in which they are set to make sense. But the trivialities are commensurate, as I said, to the power in the hands of the Jews, to the sorts of things they actually could decide and control. What the rabbis accomplished was to impart to these trivialities so great an importance that ordinary folk could conceive themselves significant beyond their perceived weakness. If the Jews could not determine the natural course of history, the rabbis would teach them about their power in the supernatural structure of reality. That is the importance of the messianic claim made in behalf of keeping the "Torah of Moses our rabbi" by the rabbis themselves.

So said one of them, "If Israel obeys the will of their Father in Heaven, then no nation or race can rule over them." "When Israel casts words of Torah to the ground, the heathen are able to decree and carry out their decrees." "When the haughty people will disappear within Israel, then the haughty gendarmes will disappear among the Iranians." These words are not idle homilies. They provide the key to understanding why such stress was laid upon the legal and social reformation of Israel. It is through the concrete achievement of the teachings of the Torah, here and now, that the rabbis intended to bring redemption. Defining the will of God in terms of deeds people actually could do, expressing "Torah" in matters of the household and the hearth—these were ways to make concrete, therefore open to attainment, the large and weighty promises of the prophets. If all you can do is decide what food you will eat and how you will consume it, or whether or not you will recite a blessing over a candle lit by a gentile, then you are fortunate indeed to believe your decision bears consequence even for the cosmic order of being. True, you may be deluded. But the ultimate test of the rabbis' convictions is yet to come.

תָּנוּ רַבָּנָן: הָיָה מְהַלֵּךְ חוּץ לַכָּרָךְ וְרָאָה אוֹר, אִם רֹב
נָכְרִים — אֵינוֹ מְבָרֵךְ, אִם רֹב יִשְׂרָאֵל — מְבָרֵךְ. הָא
גּוּפָא קַשְׁיָא! אָמְרַתְּ: אִם רֹב נָכְרִים — אֵינוֹ מְבָרֵךְ,
הָא מֶחֱצָה עַל מֶחֱצָה — מְבָרֵךְ, וְהַדַּר תָּנֵי: אִם רֹב
יִשְׂרָאֵל — מְבָרֵךְ, הָא מֶחֱצָה עַל מֶחֱצָה — אֵינוֹ
מְבָרֵךְ! בְּדִין הוּא דַּאֲפִלּוּ מֶחֱצָה עַל מֶחֱצָה נַמֵּי מְבָרֵךְ,
וְאַיְּידֵי (דְּתְנָא) רֵישָׁא "רֹב נָכְרִים", תְּנָא סֵיפָא "רֹב
יִשְׂרָאֵל".

Our rabbis have taught:

A. [If] one was walking outside of the village and saw a light, if the majority [of the inhabitants of the village] are gentiles, he does not bless it. If the majority are Israelites, he blesses it.

B. *Lo, the statement is self-contradictory. You have said,* "If the majority are gentiles, he does not bless it." *Then if they are evenly divided, he may bless it.*

But then it teaches, "If the majority are Israelites, he may bless." *Then if they are evenly divided, he may not bless it.*

C. *Strictly speaking, even if they are evenly divided, he may bless. But since in the opening clause* [the language is], "The majority are gentiles," *in the concluding clause,* [the same language is used:] "The majority are Israelites."

The *baraita,* or Tannaitic tradition, A, is subjected to the sort of quibble for which the Talmud is (unjustly) famous. What is the rule if the inhabitants were evenly divided? The implication of the first half of the rule is that one may bless the light; of the second, one may not. C then reduces the quibble; it is a matter of the language used in the tradition. The formulation will be consistent, even though it may produce an (immaterial) measure of obscurity. The Palestinian Talmud explicitly rejects this tradition and says if only one Jew is present, the light may be blessed.

תָּנוּ רַבָּנָן : הָיָה מְהַלֵּךְ חוּץ לַכְּרַךְ וְרָאָה תִּינוֹק וַאֲבוּקָה בְּיָדוֹ, בּוֹדֵק אַחֲרָיו, אִם יִשְׂרָאֵל הוּא – מְבָרֵךְ, אִם נָכְרִי הוּא – אֵינוֹ מְבָרֵךְ. מַאי אִירְיָא תִּינוֹק, אֲפִלּוּ גָּדוֹל נַמֵּי! אָמַר רַב יְהוּדָה אָמַר רַב: הָכָא בְּסָמוּךְ לִשְׁקִיעַת הַחַמָּה עָסְקִינַן, גָּדוֹל – מוֹכְחָא מִילְתָא דְּוַדַּאי נָכְרִי הוּא, תִּינוֹק – אֵימַר יִשְׂרָאֵל הוּא אִקְרִי וְנָקֵיט.

Our rabbis have taught:

A. [If] a man was walking outside of a village and saw a child with a torch in his hand, he makes inquiries about him. If he is an Israelite, he may bless [the light]. If he is a gentile, he may not bless.

B. *Why do we speak of a child? Even an adult also* [would be subject to the same rule].

C. *Rav Judah said in the name of Rav, "In this case we are dealing with* [a time] *near sunset. As to a gentile, it will be perfectly clear that he certainly is a gentile* [for an Israelite would not use the light immediately after sunset]. *If it is a child, I might say it is an Israelite child who happened to take up* [the torch]."

The analysis of the language of the *baraita* is consequential. The specification of "child" seems strange. Rav provides an

answer (more persuasive then than now): It will be obvious
whether an adult is gentile or Jewish, for, if he has a light right
after sunset, he assuredly is not a Jew. But a child might not be
so scrupulous.

תְּנוּ רַבָּנָן: הָיָה מְהַלֵּךְ חוּץ לַכְּרָךְ וְרָאָה אוֹר, אִם עָבֶה
כְּפִי הַכִּבְשָׁן — מְבָרֵךְ עָלָיו, וְאִם לָאו — אֵינוֹ מְבָרֵךְ
עָלָיו.

> *Our rabbis have taught:*
> A. [If] one was walking outside of a village and saw a
> light, if it was as thick as the opening of a furnace, he
> may bless it, and if not, he may not bless it.

The decisive principle is that you must bless a flame only if
it is used for the purpose of light. But if a light does not serve
for illumination, but for some other, extraneous purpose, it
cannot serve for the blessing in *Havdalah*. We shall now consider a whole series of contradictory opinions, and each is going
to be resolved in the same way. If you say one may bless such-
and-such a light, it is because it is used for illumination. If you
say one may not, it is because the light is not used for illumination, but for some other purpose.

תְּנֵי חֲדָא: אוֹר שֶׁל כִּבְשָׁן — מְבָרְכִין עָלָיו, וְתַנְיָא
אִידָךְ: אֵין מְבָרְכִין עָלָיו! לָא קַשְׁיָא: הָא בַּתְחִלָּה, הָא
לְבַסּוֹף. תְּנֵי חֲדָא: אוֹר שֶׁל תַּנּוּר וְשֶׁלַּכִּירַיִם — מְבָרְכִין
עָלָיו, וְתַנְיָא אִידָךְ: אֵין מְבָרְכִין עָלָיו! לָא קַשְׁיָא: הָא
בַּתְחִלָּה, הָא לְבַסּוֹף.

> B. *One Tanna* [authority] [says], "They may bless the
> light of a furnace," *and another Tanna* [says], "They may
> not bless it."
> C. *There is no difficulty. The first speaks at the beginning* [of
> the fire], *the other at the end.*

Here is the first such effort. The furnace may be blessed at
the outset, for the fire is large and does not serve only to heat

up the coals. At the end the flame is kept burning only to keep
the oven hot, in no sense for illumination.

תָּנֵי חֲדָא: אוֹר שֶׁל בֵּית הַכְּנֶסֶת וְשֶׁל בֵּית הַמִּדְרָשׁ —
מְבָרְכִין עָלָיו, וְתַנְיָא אִידָךְ: אֵין מְבָרְכִין עָלָיו! לָא
קַשְׁיָא: הָא דְאִיכָּא אָדָם חָשׁוּב, הָא דְלֵיכָּא אָדָם
חָשׁוּב.

D. *One authority says,* "They may bless the light of an
oven or a stove," *and another authority says,* "They may not
bless it."

*There is no problem. The former speaks of the beginning, the
latter of the end.*

E. *One authority says,* "They may bless the light of the
synagogue and the schoolhouse," *and another authority says,*
"They may not bless it."

There is no problem. The former speaks [of a case in which]
an important man *is present, the latter* [of a case in which]
an important man *is not present.*

Now we have a synagogue. If an important man is present,
the light is kindled in his honor, not for illumination. Where
the light is not for illumination, it may not be blessed.

וְאִי בָּעֵית אֵימָא: הָא וְהָא דְאִיכָּא אָדָם חָשׁוּב, וְלָא
קַשְׁיָא: הָא דְאִיכָּא חַזָּנָא, הָא דְלֵיכָּא חַזָּנָא.

F. *And if you want, I shall explain both teachings as applying to
a case in which* an important man *is present. There still is no
difficulty. The former* [teaching speaks of a case in which]
there is a beadle [who eats in the synagogue], *the latter in
which there is none.*

We begin to make things still more complicated. What is
decisive is not the important person's presence, but the beadle.
Perhaps the light comes from the fire kindled by the beadle by
which to eat his food. Then it may be blessed.

The last case involves moonlight. If there is moonlight, then
the light is not kindled for illumination.

וְאִי בָּעֵית אֵימָא: הָא וְהָא דְּאִיכָּא חַזָּנָא, וְלָא קַשְׁיָא:
הָא דְּאִיכָּא סַהֲרָא, וְהָא דְּלֵיכָּא סַהֲרָא.

G. *And if you want, I shall explain both teachings as applying to
a case in which a beadle is present. There still is no difficulty. The
former teaching* [speaks of a case in which] *there is moonlight,
the latter in which there is no moonlight.*

We shall review the argument as a whole: A takes for granted
a person may bless the light of a furnace. B informs us some say
he may not do so, and C resolves the contradiction. The
authorities do not really differ from one another. At the outset
the furnace, presumed to be for the burning of lime, is lit to
burn the lime, therefore it may not be used. Afterward it is kept
lit for the purpose of light, so it may be used. D and E follow
the same pattern. The oven is lit for cooking; the light may not
be blessed. It is kept lit for the light; now the illumination is
acceptable for the blessing. In E the problem again is the purpose for which the light is kindled. If an important person—
this is a technical term, referring to a distinguished Talmudic
authority—is present, the light is kindled in *his* honor, not for
light, and may not be blessed. Otherwise, it may be blessed.
The principle here is the same as applies to not blessing light
or spices prepared for the dead.

F then is an elegant spinning out of the possibilities of the
synagogue. If an important man is present, it may still be
permitted to bless the light; if there is a beadle, it is permitted,
for he eats in the synagogue and may have kindled the flame
for light to eat by. Or both traditions speak of a case in which
there are a beadle *and* an important man; if there is moonlight,
the lights in the synagogue are for the important man, not the
beadle's meal, and it is prohibited. This sort of thing can produce an infinite number of further qualifications; it is an open-
ended progression. But when I spoke of the Talmud as a continuing conversation, this is not what I meant.

[margin note: both mean beadle: former is moon, latter, not]

תָּנוּ רַבָּנָן: הָיוּ יוֹשְׁבִין בְּבֵית הַמִּדְרָשׁ וְהֵבִיאוּ אוֹר
לִפְנֵיהֶם, בֵּית שַׁמַּאי אוֹמְרִים: כָּל אֶחָד וְאֶחָד מְבָרֵךְ
לְעַצְמוֹ, וּבֵית הִלֵּל אוֹמְרִים: אֶחָד מְבָרֵךְ לְכֻלָּן, מִשּׁוּם
שֶׁנֶּאֱמַר: "בְּרָב־עָם הַדְרַת־מֶלֶךְ". בִּשְׁלָמָא בֵּית הִלֵּל
מְפָרְשִׁי טַעֲמָא, אֶלָּא בֵּית שַׁמַּאי מַאי טַעֲמָא? קָסָבְרִי:
מִפְּנֵי בִּטּוּל בֵּית הַמִּדְרָשׁ. תַּנְיָא נַמִּי הָכִי: שֶׁל בֵּית רַבָּן
גַּמְלִיאֵל לֹא הָיוּ אוֹמְרִים "מַרְפֵּא" בְּבֵית הַמִּדְרָשׁ, מִפְּנֵי
בִּטּוּל בֵּית הַמִּדְרָשׁ.

Our rabbis have taught:

(A.) [If] they were sitting in the schoolhouse, and light was brought before them—

The House of Shammai say, "Each one blesses for himself."

And the House of Hillel say, "One blesses for all of them, as it is said, 'In the multitude of people is the King's glory'" [Proverbs 14:28].

B. *Certainly* [we can understand the position of the House of Hillel because] *the House of Hillel explain their reason.*

But what is the reason of the House of Shammai?

They reckon [it as they do] *on account of* [avoiding] *interruption in* [Torah-study] *in the schoolhouse.*

C. *We have a further Tannaitic tradition to the same effect:*

The members of the house of Rabban Gamaliel did not say [the blesssing], "Good health" [after a sneeze] in the schoolhouse on account of the interruption [of study] in the schoolhouse.

The "reason" of the House of Hillel is a gloss; the Shammaite saying has not been glossed, so the Talmud asks for their reason. A *baraita* tells us that the same consideration was important to Gamaliel, toward the end of the first century. By now it is commonplace to expect that after an Amoraic discussion of a Tannaitic tradition, a further Tannaitic saying will be adduced in evidence of the correctness of the Amoraic interpretation. Here again we conclude that if the Tannaitic saying was known at the outset, the pericope has been constructed so as to give full expression to the Amoraic analysis before the decisive evidence is adduced.

"אֵין מְבָרְכִין לֹא עַל הַנֵּר וְלֹא עַל הַבְּשָׂמִים שֶׁל מֵתִים".
מַאי טַעֲמָא? נֵר — לִכְבוֹד הוּא דַּעֲבִידָא, בְּשָׂמִים —
לְעַבּוֹרֵי רֵיחָא הוּא דַּעֲבִידִי.

They say a blessing neither on the light nor on the spices of the dead . . .

    A. *What is the reason?*
    The light is made for the honor [of the deceased], *the spices to remove the bad smell.*

The principle, already established, that you bless light only if it is used for its normal purpose as illumination, is extended to spices. The light is not for illumination, but for the honor of the corpse. The spices are not for the pleasure of their scent, but as a deodorant.

אָמַר רַב יְהוּדָה אָמַר רַב: כֹּל שֶׁמּוֹצִיאִין לְפָנָיו בַּיּוֹם
וּבַלַּיְלָה — אֵין מְבָרְכִין עָלָיו, וְכֹל שֶׁאֵין מוֹצִיאִין לְפָנָיו
אֶלָּא בַּלַּיְלָה — מְבָרְכִין עָלָיו.

    B. Rav Judah in the name of Rav said, "[Light made for] whoever [is of such importance that] they take out [a light] before him both by day and by night is not blessed. [And light made for] whoever [is not important, so that] they take out [a light] before him only by night, is blessed."

Rav gives the same principle as was applied in the earlier discussion. But he applies that principle to the light kindled in honor of the corpse. Much depends upon the importance of the corpse. Rav explains the several distinctions.

אָמַר רַב הוּנָא: בְּשָׂמִים שֶׁל בֵּית הַכִּסֵּא, וְשֶׁמֶן הֶעָשׂוּי
לְהַעֲבִיר אֶת הַזֻּהֲמָא — אֵין מְבָרְכִין עָלָיו.

C. R. Huna said, "They do not bless spices of the privy and oil made to remove the grease."

remove smell

Huna's is an independent saying, which applies the same principle to other cases. But then we challenge the entire principle: Do we say things must be used only for their primary purpose? But we have a contrary rule.

לְמֵימְרָא, דְּכָל הֵיכָא דְּלָאו לְרֵיחָא עֲבִידָא — לָא
מְבָרְכִין עֲלֵויהּ, מוֹתִיבִי: הַנִּכְנַס לַחֲנוּתוֹ שֶׁל בַּשָּׂם וְהֵרִיחַ
רֵיחַ, אֲפִלּוּ יָשַׁב שָׁם כָּל הַיּוֹם כֻּלּוֹ — אֵינוֹ מְבָרֵךְ אֶלָּא
פַּעַם אֶחָד, נִכְנַס וְיָצָא נִכְנַס וְיָצָא — מְבָרֵךְ עַל כָּל
פַּעַם וָפַעַם, וְהָא הָכָא דְּלָאו לְרֵיחָא הוּא דַּעֲבִידָא
וְקָמְבָרֵךְ!

D. *Does this saying imply that wherever [spice] is not used for smell, they do not bless over it? It may be objected:*

He who enters the stall of a spice dealer and smells the odor, even though he sat there all day long, blesses only one time. He who enters and goes out repeatedly blesses each time.

And lo, here is a case in which it is not used for the scent, and still he blesses.

the contrary: spice dealer (abnormal?)

We have a rule which seems to contradict the established principle. How can a law for a specific case contradict the general principle governing the determination of all laws? The solution is simple: The case is not exceptional at all.

אִין, לְרֵיחָא נַמֵּי הוּא דַּעֲבִידָא, כִּי הֵיכִי דְּנוֹרְחוּ אֱינָשֵׁי
וְנֵיתוּ וְנִזְבּוּן מִינֵּיהּ.

oh, but not so contrary (nb: normal)

E. *Yes, but it also is used for the odor—so that people will smell and come and purchase it.*

The Mishnah is supplied with a rational basis. As is already obvious, the issue will be whether the spice or light is prepared for its normal use, in which case it may be blessed, or for some extrinsic purpose, in which case it may not be blessed.

ask class: What is this basis?

The material to be blessed thus must be used in a normal way.
A explains that the light and spices are in abnormal usage.
B brings us back to the problem reviewed above, concerning
blessing light of a furnace, oven, stove, or synagogue; the
principle has not changed, and the applications here are not
original. Rav in B simply says what was already clear in the
Mishnah as interpreted in A.

C introduces new materials, which illustrate the same principle. Then D raises the fundamental challenge to all of the
foregoing, though it responds directly to C. If spice is not used
for its odor, are we not to bless it? The objection draws on a
rule which takes for granted, in both of its cases, that one does
bless the odor of the spice in a spice-dealer's stall. And, it is
made explicit, that is not used for the scent. It is for sale. E says
the odor is not secondary, for in order for people to buy the
spice, they want to smell it.

New
pericope

תְּנוּ רַבָּנָן: הָיָה מְהַלֵּךְ חוּץ לַכָּרָךְ וְהֵרִיחַ רֵיחַ, אִם רֹב
עוֹבְדֵי כּוֹכָבִים — אֵינוֹ מְבָרֵךְ, אִם רֹב יִשְׂרָאֵל —
מְבָרֵךְ; רַבִּי יוֹסֵי אוֹמֵר: אֲפִלּוּ רֹב יִשְׂרָאֵל נַמֵּי אֵינוֹ
מְבָרֵךְ, מִפְּנֵי שֶׁבְּנוֹת יִשְׂרָאֵל מְקַטְּרוֹת לִכְשָׁפִים. אַטּוּ
כּוּלְּהוּ לִכְשָׁפִים מְקַטְּרָן?! הֲוָה לֵיהּ מִיעוּטָא לִכְשָׁפִים
וּמִיעוּטָא נַמֵּי לְגַמֵּר אֶת הַכֵּלִים, אִשְׁתְּכַח. רוּבָּא דְּלָאו
לְרֵיחָא עֲבִיד, וְכָל רוּבָּא דְּלָאו לְרֵיחָא עֲבִיד — לָא
מְבָרֵךְ.

אָמַר רַבִּי חִיָּא בַּר אַבָּא אָמַר רַבִּי יוֹחָנָן: הַמְהַלֵּךְ בְּעַרְבֵי
שַׁבָּתוֹת בִּטְבֶרְיָא וּבְמוֹצָאֵי שַׁבָּתוֹת בְּצִפּוֹרֵי וְהֵרִיחַ
רֵיחַ — אֵינוֹ מְבָרֵךְ, מִפְּנֵי שֶׁחֶזְקָתוֹ — אֵינוֹ עָשׂוּי אֶלָּא
לְגַמֵּר בּוֹ אֶת הַכֵּלִים.

תְּנוּ רַבָּנָן: הָיָה מְהַלֵּךְ בְּשׁוּק שֶׁל עוֹבְדֵי כּוֹכָבִים וּמַזָּלוֹת,
נִתְרַצָּה לְהָרִיחַ הֲרֵי זֶה חוֹטֵא.

Our rabbis have taught:
A. If one was walking outside of a village and smelled

a scent, if most of the inhabitants are idolators, he does not bless it. If most are Israelites, he blesses it.

R. Yosé says, "Even if most are Israelites, he *still* may not bless, because Israelite women use incense for witchcraft."

B. *But do they "all" burn incense for witchcraft!*   *i. e. "surely not!"*
A small part is for witchcraft, and a small part is also for scenting garments, which yields a larger part not used for scent, and wherever the majority [of the incense] *is not used for scent, one does not bless it.*

C. R. Hiyya bar Abba said in the name of R. Yohanan, "He who walks on the eve of the Sabbath in Tiberias and at the end of the Sabbath in Sepphoris and smells an odor does not bless it, because it is presumed to have been made only to perfume garments."

D. *Our rabbis taught:* If one was walking in the gentiles'   ) continues
market and was pleased to scent the spices, he is a sinner.   ) A

The rules in A are further elaborations of the foregoing principle. It is taken for granted that the scent is from incense used for idolatry. Yosé adds that Israelite women also make illicit use of spices. B then asks (incredulously) whether it is alleged that *all* Israelite women practice witchcraft. The answer is that some goes for that purpose, some for finishing garments, leaving only a minor part of the spices to be used for scent alone. The use of spices for cleaning garments is then illustrated by C. D is tacked on, but it is a continuation of A.

We notice that the rabbis are not unaware of the religious practices of the ordinary folk, just as they take account of the Samaritans' views. On the contrary, the pages of the Talmud reveal an endless conflict between the rabbis and other Jews. Here we find the laconic observation, not accompanied by cries of wrath or woe, that Jewish women practice witchcraft. What is meant by "witchcraft" is of no consequence to us. What is striking is that the rabbis' formulation of the law is going to take account of the unpleasant or distasteful doings of other Jews. They are not attempting to create laws for angels, beings without the impulse to do evil, without the pressures and needs of fleshly, frail mortals. They legislate so as to form a perfect society, a people made in the model of the Torah. But they do so in full awareness that the people to be perfected and regenerated are flesh and blood, unreliable, impetuous, credulous, doubting, human. And so too are the rabbis themselves.

That is what makes the effort noble: the capacity to face up to people's ornery or slovenly ways, yet to want to make them something more and better. And what makes the hope real and plausible is the means chosen for the task, the instrument of law and lawful ordering of the behavior and beliefs of the folk. What finally gives the rabbis their optimistic willingness to struggle with people who are assumed to practice witchcraft is their faith in three things: God, who made the people what they are; the Torah, which has the power to change and reshape them; and the Jews themselves, who come from worthy fathers and mothers, people who could make a golden calf, but who also could say, "We shall do and obey."

[handwritten margin note: new pericope]

"וְאֵין מְבָרְכִין עַל הַנֵּר עַד שֶׁיֵּאוֹתוּ". אָמַר רַב יְהוּדָה אָמַר רַב: לֹא "יֵאוֹתוּ" יֵאוֹתוּ מַמָּשׁ, אֶלָּא כָּל שֶׁאִלּוּ עוֹמֵד בְּקָרוֹב וּמִשְׁתַּמֵּשׁ לְאוֹרָה, וַאֲפִלּוּ בְּרָחוּק מָקוֹם. וְכֵן אָמַר רַב אָשֵׁי: בְּרָחוּק מָקוֹם שָׁנִינוּ.

[handwritten margin note: at least, be able to use it]

(53b) **They do not recite a blessing over the light until it has been used . . .**

A. Rav Judah said in the name of Rav, "Not that he has actually used it, but if anyone stood near enough so that he might use the light, even at some distance, [he may say the blessing]."

B. So too R. Ashi said, "We have learned this teaching even [concerning] those at some distance."

Rav and Ashi both interpret the original rule about using the light. It is not that you have actually to make use of the light. But you have to be *able* to use it. We shall now have an objection, based on a Toseftan tradition:

מוֹתִיבִי: הָיְתָה לוֹ נֵר טְמוּנָה בְּחֵיקוֹ אוֹ בְּפָנָס, אוֹ
שֶׁרָאָה שַׁלְהֶבֶת וְלֹא נִשְׁתַּמֵּשׁ לְאוֹרָהּ, אוֹ נִשְׁתַּמֵּשׁ
לְאוֹרָהּ וְלֹא רָאָה שַׁלְהֶבֶת — אֵינוֹ מְבָרֵךְ עַד שֶׁיִּרְאֶה
שַׁלְהֶבֶת וְיִשְׁתַּמֵּשׁ לְאוֹרָהּ:

BUT:

C. *It was objected* [on the basis of the following teach-
ing]: If one had a light hidden in the folds of his cloak or
in a lamp, or saw the flame but did not make use of its
light, or made use of the light but did not [actually] see
the flame, he may not say the blessing. [He may say the
blessing only when] he [both] sees the flame and uses its
light.

↳that is,

Rav's and Ashi's principle thus contradicts the rule that you
have got both to see the flame and to use the light. We shall
apply that rule to show the contradiction to Rav's and Ashi's
interpretation of the Mishnah.

בִּשְׁלָמָא מִשְׁתַּמֵּשׁ לְאוֹרָהּ וְלֹא רָאָה שַׁלְהֶבֶת —
מַשְׁכַּחַתְּ לָהּ דְּקָיְימָא בְּקֶרֶן זָוִית, אֶלָּא רָאָה שַׁלְהֶבֶת
וְלֹא נִשְׁתַּמֵּשׁ לְאוֹרָהּ הֵיכֵי מַשְׁכַּחַתְּ לָהּ? לַאו דִּמְרַחֲקָא!

Certainly one finds cases in which one may use the light and
not see the flame. *This may be when the light is in a corner.*
But where do you find a case in which one may see the flame
and not make use of its light. *Is it not when he is at a distance?*

*ie: can't
see it
directly*

If you examine the cases to which the Toseftan tradition may
refer, you come to one which has to stand against the principle
of Rav and Ashi. A person may both use the light and not see
the flame. But when can you see the flame but not use it?
Surely that is when you are at a distance. And so Ashi and Rav
are wrong, for the case implied by the Tosefta contradicts their
interpretation of the Mishnah. But no, we have a way out of
that dilemma:

*thus
Ashi +
Rav
wrong?*

↓

*no:
the issue
is amt.
of lite,
not &
distance*

לָא, כְּגוֹן דְּעָמְיָא וְאָזְלָא.

D. *No, it is when the flame keeps on flickering.*

Rav's comment on the Mishnah is important: The law is not
to be interpreted literally to mean that the light has *actually*
been used. It merely must be *possible* to use it, whether one
actually does so or not.

The objection of C is serious. The several cases listed in the
Tosefta's tradition seem to include one involving light at some
distance. D replies that the cases involve not distance but the
quality of the light itself. This satisfactorily takes care of the
potential challenge to Rav's interpretation.

C–D are a good example of the Talmud's testing its interpretation of the Mishnah against potentially contradictory cases
or rules. The authority of Rav, the first great Babylonian
Talmudic authority, along with Samuel, and founder of the
study of the Mishnah in Babylonia, is insufficient against contrary evidence or reason. Reason, not authority, consensus, or
appeal to piety, is decisive.

NB

תָּנוּ רַבָּנָן: גֶּחָלִים לוֹחֲשׁוֹת — מְבָרְכִין עֲלֵיהֶן,
אוֹמְמוֹת — אֵין מְבָרְכִין עֲלֵיהֶן. הֵיכִי דָמֵי לוֹחֲשׁוֹת?
אָמַר רַב חִסְדָּא: כֹּל שֶׁאִלּוּ מַכְנִיס לְתוֹכָן קֵיסָם וְדוֹלֶקֶת
מֵאֵלֶיהָ.

אִיבַּעְיָא לְהוּ: אוֹמְמוֹת אוֹ עוֹמְמוֹת? תָּא שְׁמַע, דְּאָמַר
רַב חִסְדָּא בַּר אַבְדִּימֵי: "אֲרָזִים לֹא־עֲמָמֻהוּ בְּגַן־
אֱלֹהִים".

A. *Our rabbis have taught:*
They may say a blessing over glowing coals, but not
over dying coals ['*omemot*].

B. *What is meant by* glowing coals?
R. Hisda said, "If one puts a chip into them and it
kindles on its own, [these are] all [glowing coals]."

linguistic problem answered w/ Scrip. prf txt

C. *It was asked: Is the word* '*omemot* ['*alef*] *or* '*omemot*
['*ayin*]?
Come and hear, for R. Hisda b. Abdimi said, "The cedars in
the garden of God could not darken ['*amamuhu*] it"
[Ezekiel 31:8].

> answer is ~~alef~~ *ayin*, even tho alef is
> used in question

The elucidation of the *baraita* poses no difficulties. The word for glowing coals is *'omemot*, spelled with an *'alef*, one of two Hebrew letters not sounded in Babylonia (called "silent" letters). C then asks for the spelling of the word: with an *'alef*, or with an *'ayin*? Evidence is drawn from Scripture. But the *baraita* uses an *'alef*—it has not been corrected to conform to the result of the *Gemara*'s discussion!

> וְרָבָא אָמַר: יֵאוֹתוּ מַמָּשׁ. וְכַמָּה? אָמַר עוּלָא: כְּדֵי
> שֶׁיַכִּיר בֵּין אִיסָר לְפוּנְדְּיוֹן, חִזְקִיָּה אָמַר: כְּדֵי שֶׁיַכִּיר בֵּין
> מְלוּזְמָא שֶׁל טְבֶרְיָא לִמְלוּזְמָא שֶׁל צִפּוֹרִי. רַב יְהוּדָה
> מְבָרֵךְ אַדְּבֵי אַדָּא דַּיָּילָא. רָבָא מְבָרֵךְ אַדְּבֵי גּוּרְיָא בַּר
> חָמָא. אַבַּיֵי מְבָרֵךְ אַדְּבֵי בַּר אֲבוּהּ.
> אָמַר רַב יְהוּדָה אָמַר רַב: אֵין מְחַזְרִין עַל הָאוֹר כְּדֶרֶךְ
> שֶׁמְּחַזְרִין עַל הַמִּצְוֹת. אָמַר רַבִּי זֵירָא: מֵרִישׁ הֲוָה
> מְהַדְרַנָא, כֵּיוָן דִּשְׁמַעְנָא לְהָא דְּרַב יְהוּדָה אָמַר רַב,
> אֲנָא נַמֵּי לָא מְהַדַּרְנָא, אֶלָּא אִי מִקְּלַע לִי מִמֵּילָא —
> מְבָרֵיכְנָא.

A. And Rava said, "He must make actual use of it."

B. *And how* [near must one be]?

Ulla said, "So that he may make out the difference between an *issar* and a *pundion* [two small coins]."

Hezekiah said, "So that he may make out the difference between a *meluzma* [a weight] of Tiberias and one of Sepphoris."

C. *Rav Judah would say the blessing* [for the light of the] *house of Adda the waiter* [which was nearby].

Rava would say the blessing [for the light of the] *house of Guria bar Hama.*

Abbaye would say the blessing [for the light of the] *house of Bar Abbuha.*

D. R. Judah said in the name of Rav, "They do not go looking for the light in the way they go looking for [means to carry out other] commandments."

> R. Zera said, "At the outset, I used to go looking [for light].
> Now that I have heard this teaching of R. Judah in the name of Rav,
> I too will not go searching, but if one comes my way, I shall say the
> blessing over it."

Rava's opinion, A, brings us back to the interpretation of the
Mishnah: People bless the light once it has been used. Rav has
been quoted by Rav Judah, a master in the generation preceding Rava, that you do not have to make actual use of the fire.
Rava says you must really use it. Then how near must you be?
The question in effect pertains to the opinions of both Rav and
Rava. B provides two answers, then C gives three examples of
the actual practice of important masters. The assumption is
that the practice of a rabbi is as adequate evidence of what to do
as the theoretical statement of a law. The rabbi is a living
commentary on the Torah.

D contains a further ruling of Rav Judah in Rav's name:
You do not have to take the trouble to find the fire. Then Zera's
saying is given to make clear that once an authority has given
his opinion, others may take advantage of its leniency. But you
must take the trouble of finding the means of carrying out
other commandments.

new
peric.

"מִי שֶׁאָכַל" וְכוּלֵי.

He who ate [and did not say Grace] . . .

We cite the Mishnah once again. If a person forgot to say
Grace, and so goes away from the place where he ate, does he
have to go back to recite the Grace? Or may he say it wherever
he remembers? The Hillelites take the latter, lenient position,
the Shammaites the former, strict one.

אָמַר רַב זְבִיד, וְאִיתֵּימָא רַב דִּימִי בַּר אַבָּא: מַחֲלֹקֶת
בְּשָׁכַח, אֲבָל בְּמֵזִיד — דִּבְרֵי הַכֹּל יַחֲזֹר לִמְקוֹמוֹ
וִיבָרֵךְ.

A. R. Zevid, and some say, R. Dimi bar Abba, said,
"The dispute [between the Houses] applies to a case of

forgetfulness, but in a case in which a person deliberately [omitted Grace], all agree that he should return to his place and say the blessing."

Zevid now tries to clarify what is at issue. He says the Houses differ concerning a person who forgot to say Grace. But if a person deliberately omitted the prayer, he is required to go back to where he ate.

פְּשִׁיטָא, "וְשָׁכַח" תְּנַן!

This is perfectly obvious. It is [explicitly] *taught, "And he forgot."*

The *Gemara* points out that Zevid's interpretation is not necessary. The Mishnah has already stated what he claims is "his" interpretation. So we have to explain what Zevid's interpretation was meant to imply.

מַהוּ דְּתֵימָא הוּא הַדִּין אֲפִלוּ בְּמֵזִיד, וְהַאי דְּקָתָנֵי
"וְשָׁכַח" — לְהוֹדִיעֲךָ כֹּחָן דְּבֵית שַׁמַּאי, קָמַשְׁמַע לָן.

B. *What might you have said? That is the rule even where it was intentional, but the reason that the Tanna taught, "And he forgot," is to tell you how far the House of Shammai was willing to go* [in requiring the man to go back to where he ate. They did so even if a man accidentally forgot]. *Thus we are taught* [the contrary. If one forgot, unintentionally, he must go back].

Zevid's effort at defining the issue between the Houses proves hopeless. What he says is at issue is explicitly stated in the Mishnah itself. B then tries to straighten things out.

תַּנְיָא,   new peric.

A. *It was taught:*

The *baraita* now provides a dialogue between the Houses, supplementing their simple disagreement about the rule. This

Continues issue of forgetting

is a kind of debate. Each side makes clear the advantage of its own viewpoint and the disadvantage of that of the opposition.

אָמְרוּ לָהֶם בֵּית הִלֵּל לְבֵית שַׁמַּאי: לְדִבְרֵיכֶם, מִי שֶׁאָכַל בְּרֹאשׁ הַבִּירָה וְשָׁכַח וְיָרַד וְלֹא בֵרַךְ, יַחֲזֹר לְרֹאשׁ הַבִּירָה וִיבָרֵךְ? אָמְרוּ לָהֶן בֵּית שַׁמַּאי לְבֵית הִלֵּל: לְדִבְרֵיכֶם, מִי שֶׁשָּׁכַח אַרְנָקִי בְּרֹאשׁ הַבִּירָה, לֹא יַעֲלֶה וְיִטְּלֶנָּה?! לִכְבוֹד עַצְמוֹ הוּא עוֹלֶה, לִכְבוֹד שָׁמַיִם לֹא כָּל שֶׁכֵּן.

The House of Hillel said to the House of Shammai, "According to your opinion, someone who ate on the top of the Temple Mount and forgot and went down without saying Grace should go back to the top of the Mount and say the blessing."

The House of Shammai said to the House of Hillel, "According to your opinion, someone who forgot a purse on the top of the Temple Mount would not go back and retrieve it.

"For his own sake, he [assuredly] will go back. For the sake of Heaven [should he] not all the more so [go back]?"

After the debate the editor provides a couple of stories to make the point that people who are strict with themselves are rewarded, but those who are slovenly in the performance of their religious duties are punished supernaturally.

הָנְהוּ תְּרֵי תַּלְמִידֵי, חַד עֲבִיד בְּשׁוֹגֵג כְּבֵית שַׁמַּאי וְאַשְׁכַּח אַרְנְקָא דְּדַהֲבָא, וְחַד עֲבִיד בְּמֵזִיד כְּבֵית הִלֵּל וְאַכְלֵיהּ אַרְיָא.

רַבָּה בַּר בַּר חָנָה הֲוָה קָאָזֵל בְּשַׁיָּירְתָּא, אֲכַל וְאִשְׁתְּלִי וְלָא בָרֵיךְ. אֲמַר, הֵיכִי אֶעֱבֵיד? אִי אָמִינָא לְהוּ "אַנְשַׁאי לְבָרֵךְ", אָמְרִי לִי: בָּרֵיךְ, כָּל הֵיכָא דִּמְבָרְכַתְּ לְרַחֲמָנָא מְבָרְכַתְּ: מוּטָב דְּאָמִינָא לְהוּ "אַנְשַׁאי יוֹנָה דְּדַהֲבָא".

אָמַר לְהוּ: אַנְטְרוּ לִי, דְּאַנְשַׁאי יוֹנָה דְּדַהֲבָא, אֲזֵיל
וּבָרֵיךְ וְאַשְׁכַּח יוֹנָה דְּדַהֲבָא.

B. *There were these two disciples. One did it* [forgot Grace]
accidentally, and, following the rule of the House of Shammai,
[went back to bless], *and found a purse of gold. And one did it*
deliberately [omitted Grace], *and following the rule of the House*
of Hillel [did not go back to say it], *and a lion ate him.*

C. *Rabbah bar bar Hanna was traveling in a caravan. He ate*
and was sated but [forgot and] *did not say Grace.*

He said, "What shall I do? If I tell the men [of the caravan
with me] *that I forgot to bless, they will say to me, 'Bless here.*
Wherever you say *the blessing, you are saying the blessing to the*
Merciful [God].' *It is better that I tell them I have forgotten a golden*
dove."

So he said to them, "Wait for me, for I have forgotten a golden
dove."

He went back and blessed and found a golden dove.

Ordinary folk are presumed to be uninterested in the Houses'
rules. Now the Talmud will explain a detail in the foregoing
story about Rabbah. The dove is an important symbol in his
story. Why?

וּמַאי שְׁנָא יוֹנָה? דִּמְתִילֵי כְּנֶסֶת יִשְׂרָאֵל לְיוֹנָה, דִּכְתִיב:
"כַּנְפֵי יוֹנָה נֶחְפָּה בַכֶּסֶף וְאֶבְרוֹתֶיהָ בִּירַקְרַק חָרוּץ",
מַה־יּוֹנָה אֵינָה נִצּוֹלֶת אֶלָּא בִּכְנָפֶיהָ, אַף יִשְׂרָאֵל אֵינָן
נִצּוֹלִין אֶלָּא בְּמִצְוֹת.

D. *And why was a dove so important?*

Because the community of Israel is compared to a dove, as it is
written, "The wings of the dove are covered with silver,
and her pinions with the shimmer of gold" [Psalm 68:14].
Just as the dove is saved only by her wings, so Israel is
saved only by the commandments.

To review: The little debate between the Houses, A, leaves
the Shammaites with the last word, therefore in the winning

[margin notes: *aggadah adduced to make halakha*; *why a dove?* ↓ *universal symbol now*] position. Each side takes the position of the other to its logical extreme. But the Hillelites can only point up the Shammaites' severity, while the Shammaites produce a theological absurdity out of the Hillelite position. B then tells a story showing that true piety is rewarded. In this case the disciple who did not say the prayer accidentally, not intentionally, nonetheless followed the Shammaite rule and was rewarded. The disciple who deliberately neglected the Grace and said it in some other place was eaten by a lion. The story of the good disciple is then topped by Rabbah bar bar Hanna, who went to some trouble to return to the place in which he had eaten, though he cannot be thought to have deliberately moved on to say Grace in some other place. He was appropriately rewarded. Then the key detail in that story is explained.

new peric

"עַד אֵימָתַי הוּא" וְכוּלֵי. כַּמָּה שָׁעוּר עִכּוּל? אָמַר רַבִּי יוֹחָנָן: כָּל זְמַן שֶׁאֵינוֹ רָעֵב, וְרֵישׁ לָקִישׁ אָמַר: כָּל זְמַן שֶׁיִּצְמָא מֵחֲמַת אֲכִילָתוֹ. אֲמַר לֵיהּ רַב יֵימָר בַּר שְׁלֶמְיָא לְמָר זוּטְרָא, וְאָמְרִי לָהּ רַב יֵימָר בַּר שִׁיזְבִי לְמָר זוּטְרָא: מִי אֲמַר רֵישׁ לָקִישׁ הָכִי? וְהָאֲמַר רַב אַמִּי אָמַר רֵישׁ לָקִישׁ: כַּמָּה שָׁעוּר עִכּוּל? כְּדֵי לְהַלֵּךְ אַרְבַּע מִילִין! לָא קַשְׁיָא: כַּאן בַּאֲכִילָה מְרֻבָּה, כַּאן בַּאֲכִילָה מְעֶטֶת.

Until when can he say the Grace? Until the food is digested in his bowels . . .

A. How long does it take to digest the food?

R. Yohanan said, "As long as one is no longer hungry."

small meal

Resh Laqish said, "As long as one [still] is thirsty on account of his meal."

B. *R. Yemar bar Shelamia said to Mar Zutra—and some say, Rav Yemar bar Shizbi said to Mar Zutra—"Did Resh Laqish really say this? And did not R. Ammi say in the name of Resh Laqish,*

big meal

'How long does it take to digest a meal? The time it takes to go four miles.'"

There is no problem: Here [we speak of] a big meal, there [we speak of] a small meal.

A comments on the Mishnah, B then analyzes A in terms of
other sayings of the master represented therein. Resh Laqish
has two explanations for the Mishnah, and these have to be
distinguished, therefore harmonized. It takes a walk of four
miles to digest a big meal, and the end of thirst marks the
digestion of a small one.

"בָּא לָהֶם יַיִן" וְכוּלֵי.   new
peri.

If wine came to them . . .

Once more we return to the Mishnah. The citation is abbre-
viated. You will want to reread the entire paragraph of the   NB
Mishnah. We are going to analyze only the part about saying
Amen after an Israelite, but not after a gentile or a Samaritan.

לְמֵימְרָא, דְּיִשְׂרָאֵל אַף עַל גַּב דְּלֹא שָׁמַע כֻּלָּהּ בְּרָכָה
עוֹנֶה, וְכִי לֹא שָׁמַע הֵיכִי נָפֵיק?

A. *This implies that in the case of an Israelite*['s saying
Grace], *even though one has not heard the entire blessing, he responds* [*Amen*].
But if he has not heard [the whole Grace], *how can he have
performed his duty by doing so* [assuming he has eaten also?
For he has to hear the entire Grace to carry out his
obligation to say Grace].

What good does it do to respond *Amen* if a person has not
heard the whole Grace? That does not relieve you of the obligation to say Grace. Hiyya will now explain that we have made a
false assumption. The man did *not* eat with the party. He came
later. He should still say *Amen*.

אָמַר חִיָּא בַּר רַב: בְּשֶׁלֹּא אָכַל עִמָּהֶן. וְכֵן אָמַר רַב
נַחְמָן אָמַר רַבָּה בַּר אֲבוּהּ: בְּשֶׁלֹּא אָכַל עִמָּהֶן.

B. Hiyya bar Rav said, "[We speak of a case] in which
he did not eat with them."
So too did R. Nahman say in the name of Rabbah bar

Abbuha, "[We speak of a case] in which he did not eat with them."

We introduce a new question: Is it better to say Grace in behalf of the whole assembly, or simply to answer *Amen?* We have two examples of rabbis' advice to their sons to try to have the honor of saying Grace in behalf of the whole company, rather than simply answering *Amen.*

אֲמַר לֵיה רַב לְחִיָּא בְּרֵיה: בְּרִי, חֲטוֹף וּבָרֵיךְ. וְכֵן אֲמַר
רַב הוּנָא לְרַבָּה בְּרֵיה: חֲטוֹף וּבָרֵיךְ. לְמֵימְרָא, דִּמְבָרֵךְ
עֲדִיף מִמַּאן דְּעָנֵי "אָמֵן", וְהָתַנְיָא, רַבִּי יוֹסֵי אוֹמֵר:
גָּדוֹל הָעוֹנֶה "אָמֵן" יוֹתֵר מִן הַמְבָרֵךְ! אֲמַר לֵיה רַבִּי
נְהוֹרַאי: הַשָּׁמַיִם! כֵּן הוּא; תֵּדַע, שֶׁהֲרֵי גּוּלְיָרִין יוֹרְדִין
וּמִתְגָּרִין [בַּמִּלְחָמָה] וְגִבּוֹרִים יוֹרְדִין וּמְנַצְּחִין. תַּנָּאֵי
הִיא, דְּתַנְיָא: אֶחָד הַמְבָרֵךְ וְאֶחָד הָעוֹנֶה "אָמֵן"
בְּמַשְׁמַע, אֶלָּא שֶׁמְּמַהֲרִין לַמְבָרֵךְ יוֹתֵר מִן הָעוֹנֶה
"אָמֵן".

C. *Rav said to Hiyya his son, "My son, seize* [the cup] *and bless."*

So did R. Huna say to Rabbah his son, "Seize and bless."

D. *This implies that he who says the blessing is better than he who answers* "Amen." *But has it not been taught:*

R. Yosi says, "The one who answers *Amen* is greater than the one who says the blessing."

R. Nehorai said to him, "By heaven! It is so. You should know it, for behold, common soldiers go ahead and open the battle, but the heroes go in and win it."

E. *It is a matter of dispute between Tannaim, as it has been taught:*

Both the one who says the blessing and the one who answers *Amen* are implied [in the Scripture (Nehemiah 9:5)]. But the one who says the blessing is more quickly [answered] than he who answers *Amen.*

Let us review the whole. A thus assumes that the Israelite has eaten. He therefore responds *Amen* to Grace in order to carry out his obligation to say Grace. The question follows, How may he do so, for he has to hear the entire prayer? The Mishnah states one may say *Amen* even having heard only part of it. B gives the obvious answer. The man did not eat at all. A could have been replaced by, "And this speaks of a case in which he did not eat." Further discussion would have been unnecessary, but then the reason for the gloss would have been left unarticulated. So for the sake of a clear statement of the operative considerations, the question had to be fully stated.

C is unrelated to the foregoing. A cup of wine is brought in preparation for the Grace after Meals. Rav and Huna advise their sons to make every effort to take the cup, so as to recite Grace for the rest of the assembled group. D then asks the obvious question: Is the reason for this advice that it is better to say the prayer than to respond to it? But the contrary is stated. E settles the matter, as we by now have come to expect. Some people hold one opinion, some people hold the other.

The reference in E is to Nehemiah 9:5, "Stand up and bless the Lord your God from everlasting to everlasting. Blessed be thy glorious name which is exalted above all blessing and praise." The first part is understood to have been stated by the one who says the blessing, the last by the one who answers *Amen.* Both therefore are equally represented in the blessing.

The larger issue in E is whether it is better to perform a religious action or to stand by and let someone else do it for you. The rabbis, for their part, claim no special role in the liturgical life. A prayer or a blessing said by a rabbi is not more pleasing to God than one said by an ordinary person. The rabbi has no special religious duties not incumbent upon everybody else. He also has no privileges or rights which others do not enjoy. He sees himself as a Jew like any other. And he wants the other to be like him. So he is not willing to claim that someone—even a rabbi—has a priestly function which pleases God especially, or that someone else—a "layman"— who stands by and forms part of the larger community, is less important to God. The priesthood of all Israel, which is expressed in the rules about cleanness at the table, also forms the basis for the rule before us. Everyone is as good as everyone else. No special sanctity is imputed to the one who prays in behalf of the community. Anyone may do so, if he knows the way. To be sure, the rabbis will teach the right way. But after learning Torah properly, the disciple also is a rabbi.

New peric.

בָּעֵי מִינֵיהּ שְׁמוּאֵל מֵרַב: מַהוּ לַעֲנוֹת "אָמֵן" אַחַר
תִּינוֹקוֹת שֶׁל בֵּית רַבָּן? אֲמַר לֵיהּ: אַחַר הַכֹּל עוֹנִין
"אָמֵן" חוּץ מִתִּינוֹקוֹת שֶׁל בֵּית רַבָּן, הוֹאִיל וּלְהִתְלַמֵּד
עֲשׂוּיִין. וְהָנֵי מִילֵי בִּדְלָא עִידָּן מִפְטָרַיְיהוּ, אֲבָל בְּעִידָּן
מִפְטָרַיְיהוּ — עוֹנִין.

A. *Samuel asked Rav,* "Should one answer *Amen* after [the blessings of] children in the schoolhouse?"

He said to him, "They answer *Amen* after everyone except children in the schoolhouse, since they are [saying blessings solely] for the sake of learning."

B. *And this applies when it is not the time for them to say the* "Haftarah," *but in the time to say* "Haftarah," *they do respond* [*Amen*].

Since the subject of saying *Amen* is introduced, a further issue is raised and settled, then the rule is further analyzed in B. The point is that in the school the blessings are said only as an exercise and do not require *Amen*. But the blessings for Scriptural readings by children—as in reading in the prophets' writings, the *Haftarah*—are responded to.

New peric.

תָּנוּ רַבָּנָן: שֶׁמֶן מְעַכֵּב אֶת הַבְּרָכָה, דִּבְרֵי רַבִּי זִילַאי;
רַבִּי זִיוַאי אוֹמֵר: אֵינוֹ מְעַכֵּב; רַבִּי אַחָא אוֹמֵר: שֶׁמֶן
טוֹב מְעַכֵּב;

Our rabbis have taught:

A. "The absence of oil holds up the blessing [Grace]," the words of Rabbi Zilai.

R. Zivai says, "It does not hold it up."

R. Aha says, "[The absence of] good oil holds it up."

We have three possible opinions on whether you have to have oil with which to clean the hands before one says Grace. Zilai says you have to have oil. Zivai says you do not have to have oil. Aha says you have to have good oil—the most extreme position. Now we shall have a parallel opinion, that you have to clean the hands, but there is no reference to the question of oil.

רַבִּי זְהֻמַאי אוֹמֵר: כְּשֵׁם שֶׁמְּזֹהָם פָּסוּל לַעֲבוֹדָה, כָּךְ יָדַיִם מְזֹהָמוֹת פְּסוּלוֹת לִבְרָכָה. אָמַר רַב נַחְמָן בַּר יִצְחָק: אֲנָא לָא זִילַאי וְלָא זִיוַאי וְלָא זְהֻמַאי יָדַעְנָא, אֶלָּא מַתְנִיתָא יָדַעְנָא; דְּאָמַר רַב יְהוּדָה אָמַר רַב, וְאָמְרִי לָהּ בְּמַתְנִיתָא תְּנָא: "וְהִתְקַדִּשְׁתֶּם" — אֵלּוּ מַיִם רִאשׁוֹנִים, "וִהְיִיתֶם קְדֹשִׁים" — אֵלּוּ מַיִם אַחֲרוֹנִים, "כִּי קָדוֹשׁ" — זֶה שֶׁמֶן, "אֲנִי ה' אֱלֹהֵיכֶם" — זוֹ בְּרָכָה.

R. Zuhamai says, "Just as a dirty person [*mezuham*] is unfit for the Temple service, so dirty hands are unfit for the blessing."

B. *R. Nahman bar Isaac said, "I know neither Zilai nor Zivai nor Zuhamai. But I know a teaching which R. Judah said in the name of Rav, and some say it was taught as a* baratia:

"'And be you holy' [Leviticus 20:7]—this refers to washing the hands before the meal."

"'And you shall be holy'—this refers to the washing after the meal."

"'For holy'—this refers to the oil."

"'Am I the Lord your God'—this refers to the blessing [Grace]."

Nahman rejects the foregoing rulings, but instead is going to cite an exegesis of Leviticus 20:7 which proves that you *do* have to have oil before blessing the food after the meal. The exegesis explicitly says one must first wash, then put oil on his hands, and finally say Grace. This means that, according to Nahman, the position of Zilai, Aha, and Zuhamai is correct, because a tradition bearing the authority of the Tannaim has shown that rule derives from Scripture itself—the highest authority of all.

The teachings about oil are in the names of authorities unknown to Nahman, and at least one of them, Zuhamai, seems to be a play on the word "dirty," so the whole tradition may be spurious. Rav's exegesis, however, introduces the same requirement: One must have oil before saying the Grace after Meals.

The exegesis of the Scripture, B, involves the allegorical interpretation of each of its parts in terms of some other system of values or religious practices. The elements of "sanctification" ("You shall be holy") are taken to mean, or are applied to, the rite of eating a meal—a fitting conclusion to the chapter.

The Chapter As a Whole

Having examined the Babylonian Talmud's individual units of tradition, we shall review the chapter as a whole. The natural divisions are set by the Mishnah's paragraphs. The whole *Gemara* now will be clearly seen as an extended, well-organized commentary on the Mishnah and on some elements of its accompanying Tosefta. Very little occurs, the theme of which could not have been predicted on the basis of the two earlier documents. The neatly ordered chapter splits naturally into four divisions; first, the discussion of some, though not all, of the disputes between the Houses, then, in the next three, the elucidation of the other parts of the Mishnah and related Tosefta.

I
THE HOUSES' DISPUTES

[51b] *Gemara: Our rabbis have taught:*

The things which are between the House of Shammai and the House of Hillel in [regard to] **a meal:**

The House of Shammai say, "One blesses over the day and afterward blesses over the wine, for the day causes the wine to come, and the day has already been sanctified, while the wine has not yet come."

And the House of Hillel say, "He blesses over the wine and afterward blesses over the day, for the wine causes the Sanctification to be said.

"Another matter: The blessing over the wine is perpetual, and the blessing over the day is not perpetual. Between that which is perpetual and that which is not perpetual, that which is perpetual takes precedence."

And the law is in accordance with the words of the House of Hillel.

What is the purpose of "another matter"?

If you should say that there [in regard to the opinion of the House of Shammai] *two* [reasons are given] *and here* [in regard to the opinion of the House of Hillel] *one, here too* [in respect to the House of Hillel], *there are two* [reasons, the second being]: "The blessing of the wine is perpetual and the blessing of the day is not perpetual. That which is perpetual takes precedence over that which is not perpetual."

And the law is in accord with the opinion of the House of Hillel.

This is obvious [that the law is in accord with the House of Hillel], *for the echo has gone forth* [and pronounced from heaven the decision that the law follows the opinion of the House of Hillel].

If you like, I can argue that [this was stated] before the echo.

And if you like, I can argue that it was after the echo, and [the passage is formulated in accord with the] opinion of [52a] R. Joshua, who stated, "They do not pay attention to an echo [from heaven]."

And is it the reasoning of the House of Shammai that the blessing of the day is more important?

But has a Tanna not taught: "He who enters his house at the close of the Sabbath blesses over the wine and the light and the spices and afterward he says *Havdalah.* And if he has only one cup, he leaves it for after the food and then says the other blessings in order after it." [*Havdalah* is the blessing of the day, yet comes last!]

But lo, on what account [do you say] *this is the view of the House of Shammai? Perhaps it is the House of Hillel*['s opinion]?

Let [such a thought] *not enter your mind, for the Tanna teaches:* "Light and afterward spices." *And of whom have you heard who holds this opinion?* The House of Shammai, *as a Tanna has taught:*

R. Judah said, "The House of Shammai and the House of Hillel did not differ concerning the [blessing of the] food, that it is at first, and the *Havdalah,* that it is at the end.

"Concerning what did they dispute? Concerning the light and the spices.

"For the House of Shammai say, 'Light and afterward spices.'

"And the House of Hillel say, 'Spices and afterward the light.'"

And on what account [do you suppose that] *it is the House of Shammai as* [interpreted by] *R. Judah? Perhaps it is* [a teaching in accord with] *the House of Hillel* [as interpreted by] *R. Meir?*

Do not let such a thing enter your mind, for lo, a Tanna teaches here in our Mishnah: The House of Shammai say, "Light and food and spices and *Havdalah.*"

And the House of Hillel say, "Light and spices, food and *Havdalah.*"

But there, in the "baraita," *lo he has taught:* "If he has only one cup, he leaves it for after the food and then says the other blessings in order after it."

From this it is to be inferred that it is the House of Shammai's teaching, according to the [interpretation] *of R. Judah.*

In any event there is a problem [for the House of Shammai now give precedence to reciting a blessing for the wine over blessing the day].

The House of Shammai suppose that the coming of the holy day is to be distinguished from its leaving. As to the coming of the [holy] *day, the earlier one may bring it in, the better. As to the leaving of the festival day, the later one may take leave of it, the better, so that it should not seem to us as a burden.*

And do the House of Shammai hold the opinion that Grace requires a cup [of wine]? *And lo, we have learned:* [If] wine came to them after the food, and there is there only that cup, the House of Shammai say, "He blesses over the wine and afterward blesses over the food." [So Grace is said *without* the cup.]

Does this not mean that he blesses it and drinks [it]?

No. He blesses it and leaves it.

But has not a master said, "He that blesses must [also] taste [it]."

He does taste it.

And has not a master said, "Tasting it is spoiling it."

He tastes it with his hand [finger].

And has not a master said, "The cup of blessing requires a [fixed] measure." *And lo, he diminishes it from its fixed measure.*

[We speak of a situation in which] *he has more than the fixed measure.*

But lo, has it not been taught: If there is there *only* that cup . . . [so he has no more].

There is not enough for two, but more than enough for one.

And has not R. Hiyya taught: The House of Shammai say, "He blesses over the wine and drinks it, and afterward he says Grace."

Then we have two Tannas' [traditions] in respect to the opinion of the House of Shammai.

The House of Shammai say [They wash the hands and afterward mix the cup] . . .

Our rabbis have taught:

The House of Shammai say, "They wash the hands and afterward mix the cup, for if you say they mix the cup first, [against this view is] **a** [precautionary] **decree to prevent the liquids on the outer sides of the cup, which are unclean by reason of his hands'** [touching them], **from going back and making the cup unclean."**

But will not the hands make the cup itself unclean [without reference to the liquids]?

The hands are in the second remove of uncleanness, and the [object unclean in] the second remove of uncleanness cannot [then] render [another object unclean] in the third [remove] in respect to profane foods, [but only to Heave-offering]. But [this happens] only by means of liquids [unclean in the first remove].

And the House of Hillel say, "They mix the cup and afterward wash the hands, for if you say they wash the hands first, [against this view is] **a** [precautionary] **decree lest the liquids which are** [already] **on the hands become unclean on account of the cup and go and render the hands unclean."**

But will not the cup [itself] *make the hands unclean?*

A vessel cannot render a man unclean.

But will they [the hands] *not render the liquids which are in it* [the cup] *unclean?*

Here we are dealing with a vessel the outer part of which has been made unclean by liquid. The inner part is clean but the outer part is unclean. *Thus we have learned:*

[If] a vessel is made unclean on the outside by liquid, the outside is unclean, [52b] but its inside and its rim, handle, and haft are clean. If, however, the inside is unclean, the whole [cup] is unclean.

What, then, do they [the Houses] *dispute?*

The House of Shammai hold that it is prohibited to make use of a vessel whose outer parts are unclean by liquids, as a decree on account of the drippings. [There is] *no* [reason] *to decree* lest the liquids on the hands be made unclean by the cup.

And the House of Hillel reckon that it is permitted to make use of a vessel whose outer part is made unclean by liquids, *for drippings are unusual. But there is reason to take care* lest the liquids which are on the hands may be made unclean by the cup.

Another matter: [So that] **immediately upon the washing of the hands** [may come] **the meal** [itself].

What is the reason for this additional explanation?

This is what the House of Hillel said to the House of Shammai: "According to your reasoning, in saying that it is prohibited to make use of a cup whose outer parts are unclean, *we decree on account of the drippings. But even so,* [our opinion] *is better,* for **immediately upon the washing of the hands** [should come] **the meal."**

The House of Shammai say, "He dries his hand on the napkin . . ."

Our rabbis have taught:

The House of Shammai say, "He wipes his hands with the napkin and lays it on the table, for if you say, 'on the cushion,' [that view is wrong, for it is a precautionary] **decree lest the liquids which are on the napkin become unclean on account of the cushion and go back and render the hands unclean."**

And will not the cushion [itself] *render the napkin unclean?*

A vessel cannot make a vessel unclean.

And will not the cushion [itself] *make the man unclean?*

A vessel cannot make a man unclean.

And the House of Hillel say, "'On the cushion,' for if you say, 'on the table,' [that opinion is wrong, for it is a] decree lest the liquids become unclean on account of the table and go and render the food unclean."

But will not the table render the food which is on it unclean?

We here deal with a table which is unclean in the second remove, and something unclean in the second remove does not render something unclean in the third remove in respect to unconsecrated food, except by means of liquids [which are always unclean in the first remove].

What [principle] *do they dispute?*

The House of Shammai reckon that it is prohibited to make use of a table unclean in the second remove, as a decree on account of those who eat Heave-offering [which is rendered unfit by an object unclean in the second remove].

And the House of Hillel reckon that it is permitted to make use of a table unclean in the second remove, for those who eat Heave-offering [the priests] are careful.

Another matter: There is no Scriptural requirement to wash the hands before eating unconsecrated food.

What is the purpose of "another explanation"?

This is what the House of Hillel said to the House of Shammai: If you ask what is the difference in respect to food, concerning which we take care, and in respect to the hands, concerning which we do not take care—even in this regard [our opinion] *is preferable,* for there is no Scriptural requirement concerning the washing of the hands before eating unconsecrated food.

It is better that the hands should be made unclean, *for there is no Scriptural basis for* [washing] *them,* and let not the food be made unclean, *concerning which there is a Scriptural basis* [for concern about its uncleanness].

The House of Shammai say, "They clean house and afterward wash the hands . . ."

Our rabbis have taught:

The House of Shammai say, "They clean the house and afterward wash the hands, for if you say, 'They wash the hands first,' it turns out that you spoil the food."

But the House of Shammai do not reckon that one washes the hands first.

What is the reason?

On account of the crumbs.

And the House of Hillel say, "If the servant is a disciple of a sage, he takes the crumbs which are as large as an olive [in bulk] and leaves the crumbs which are not so much as an olive [in bulk]."

(*This view supports the opinion of R. Yohanan, for* R. Yohanan said, "Crumbs which are not an olive in bulk may be deliberately destroyed.")

In what do they differ?

The House of Hillel reckon that it is prohibited to employ a servant who is an ignorant man, *and the House of Shammai reckon that* it is permitted to employ a servant who is an ignorant man.

R. Yosé bar Hanina said in the name of R. Huna, "In our entire chapter the law is in accord with the House of Hillel, excepting this matter, in which the law is in accord with the House of Shammai."

And R. Oshaia taught the matter contrariwise. And in this matter too the law is in accord with the House of Hillel.

The House of Shammai say, "Light and food . . ."

R. Huna bar Judah happened by the house of Rava. He saw that Rava blessed the spices first.

He said to him, "Now the House of Shammai and the House of Hillel did not dispute concerning the light, [it should come first].

"For it was taught: The House of Shammai say, 'Light, and food, spices, and *Havdalah,'* and the House of Hillel say, 'Light, and spices, and food, and *Havdalah.'*

Rava answered him, "This is the opinion [= version] *of R. Meir, but R. Judah says,* 'The House of Shammai and the House of Hillel did not differ concerning the food, that it

comes first, and concerning the *Havdalah*, that it is at the
end.

"'Concerning what did they differ?'

"'Concerning the light and the spices.'

"For the House of Shammai say, 'The light and afterward the spices.'

"And the House of Hillel say, 'The spices and afterward the light.'"

And R. Yohanan said, "The people were accustomed
to act in accord with the House of Hillel *as presented by* R.
Judah."

The House of Shammai say, "Who created . . ."

Rava said, "*Concerning the word 'bara' [created] everyone
agrees that 'bara' implies* [the past tense]. *They differ concerning
'boré' [creates]. The House of Shammai reckon that 'boré' means,
'Who will create in the future.' And the House of Hillel reckon that
'boré' also means what was created* [in the past]."

R. Joseph objected, "'Who forms light and creates darkness' [Isaiah 45:7], 'Creates mountains and forms the
wind' [Amos 4:13], 'Who creates the heavens and spreads
them out'" [Isaiah 42:5].

"But," R. Joseph said, "*Concerning 'bara' and 'boré' everyone agrees that* [the words] *refer to the past. They differ as to
whether one should say 'light' or 'lights.'*

"*The House of Shammai reckon there is one light in the fire.*

"*And the House of Hillel reckon that there are many lights in the
fire.*"

We have a Tannaitic teaching along the same lines:

The House of Hillel said to the House of Shammai,
"There are many illuminations in the light."

The Talmud to this point is constructed of a series of
inquiries which follow a single pattern. The structure is tight,
and the argument orderly and logical. The whole set of elements is put together with little artifice; the Mishnah is cited,
then the same inquiry recurs, time and again. Only the very

last item—"Who created"—breaks the orderly sequence. And this element is ignored in Tosefta.

The second and third divisions of the chapter are thematically well integrated, though the same forms are not so consistently followed as earlier. The theme now is the light and the spices. After the Mishnah is analyzed, a series of *beraitot,* Tannaitic traditions mostly found in Tosefta, is introduced and analyzed, one by one.

II
THE LIGHT AND THE SPICES

A blessing is not said . . .

Certainly, [in the case of] *the light* [of idolators, one should not say a blessing] *because it did not rest on the Sabbath. But what is the reason that for spices* [one may not say the blessing]?

R. Judah said in the name of Rav, "*We here deal with a banquet held by idolators,* because the run-of-the-mill banquet held by idolators is for the sake of idolatry."

But since it has been taught at the end of the clause, "Or over the light or spices of idolatry," *we must infer that the beginning of the clause does not deal with idolatry.*

R. Hanina from Sura said, "What is the reason is what it explains, namely, what is the reason that they do not bless the light or spices of idolators? Because the run-of-the-mill banquet held by idolators is for the sake of idolatry."

Our rabbis have taught:

One may bless a light which has rested on the Sabbath, but one may not bless a light which has not rested on the Sabbath.

And what is the meaning of "which has not rested on the Sabbath"?

[53a] *Shall we say* it has not rested on the Sabbath on

account of the work [which has been done with it, including] even work which is permitted?

And has it not been taught: They do bless the light [kindled on the Sabbath for] a woman in confinement or a sick person.

R. Nahman bar Isaac said, *"What is the meaning of* 'which enjoyed Sabbath-rest'? Which enjoyed Sabbath-rest on account of work, the doing of which is a transgression [on the Sabbath]."

We have learned likewise in a baraita:

They may bless a lamp which has been burning throughout the day to the conclusion of the Sabbath.

Our rabbis have taught:

They bless [a light] kindled by a gentile from an Israelite, or by an Israelite from a gentile, but they do not bless [a light] kindled by a gentile from a gentile.

What is the reason one does not do so [from a light kindled by] a gentile from a gentile?

Because it did not enjoy Sabbath-rest.

If so, lo, [a light kindled by] *an Israelite from a gentile also has not enjoyed Sabbath-rest.*

And if you say this prohibited [light] *has vanished, and the one* [in hand] *is another and was born in the hand of the Israelite,* [how will you deal] *with this teaching?*

He who brings out a flame to the public way [on the Sabbath] is liable [for violating the Sabbath rule against carrying from private to public property].

Now why should he be liable? What he raised up he did not put down, and what he put down he did not raise up.

But [we must conclude] *that the prohibited* [flame] *is present, but when he blesses, it is over the additional* [flame], *which is permitted, that he blesses.*

If so, a gentile['s flame kindled] *from a gentile*['s flame] *also* [should be permitted].

That is true, but [it is prohibited by] *decree, on account of the original gentile and the original flame* [of light kindled on the Sabbath by the gentile].

Our rabbis have taught:
[If] one was walking outside of the village and saw a light, if the majority [of the inhabitants of the village] are gentiles, he does not bless it. If the majority are Israelites, he blesses it.

Lo, the statement is self-contradictory. You have said, "If the majority are gentiles, he does not bless it." Then if they were evenly divided, he may bless it.

But then it teaches, "If the majority are Israelites, he may bless." Then if they are evenly divided, he may not bless it.

Strictly speaking, even if they are evenly divided, he may bless. But since in the opening clause [the language is], "The majority are gentiles," *in the concluding clause,* [the same language is used:] "A majority are Israelites."

Our rabbis have taught:
[If] a man was walking outside of a village and saw a child with a torch in his hand, he makes inquiries about him. If he is an Israelite, he may bless [the light]. If he is a gentile, he may not bless.

Why do we speak of a child? Even an adult also [would be subject to the same rule].

Rav Judah said in the name of Rav, "In this case we are dealing with [a time] *near sunset. As to a gentile, it will be perfectly clear that he certainly is a gentile* [for an Israelite would not use the light immediately after sunset]. *If it is a child, I might say it is an Israelite child who happened to take up* [the torch]."

Our rabbis have taught:
[If] one was walking outside of a village and saw a light, if it was as thick as the opening of a furnace, he may bless it, and if not, he may not bless it.

One Tanna [authority] [says], "They may bless the light of a furnace," *and another Tanna* [says], "They may not bless it."

There is no difficulty. The first speaks at the beginning [of the fire], *the other at the end.*

One authority says, "They may bless the light of an oven or a stove," *and another authority says,* "They may not bless it."

There is no problem. The former speaks of the beginning, the latter of the end.

One authority says, "They may bless the light of the synagogue and the schoolhouse," *and another authority says,* "They may not bless it."

There is no problem. The former speaks [of a case in which] an important man *is present, the latter* [of a case in which] an important man *is not present.*

And if you want, I shall explain both teachings as applying to a case in which an important man *is present. There still is no difficulty. The former* [teaching speaks of a case in which] *there is a beadle* [who eats in the synagogue], *the latter in which there is none.*

And if you want, I shall explain both teachings as applying to a case in which a beadle is present. There still is no difficulty. The former teaching [speaks of a case in which] *there is moonlight, the latter in which there is no moonlight.*

Our rabbis have taught:

[If] they were sitting in the schoolhouse, and light was brought before them—

The House of Shammai say, "Each one blesses for himself."

And the House of Hillel say, "One blesses for all of them, as it is said, 'In the multitude of people is the King's glory'" [Proverbs 14:28].

Certainly [we can understand the position of the House of Hillel because] *the House of Hillel explain their reason.*

But what is the reason of the House of Shammai?

They reckon [it as they do] *on account of* [avoiding] *interruption in* [Torah study] *in the schoolhouse.*

We have a further Tannaitic tradition to the same effect:

The members of the house of Rabban Gamaliel did not say [the blessing] "Good health" [after a sneeze] in the schoolhouse on account of the interruption [of study] in the schoolhouse.

They say a blessing neither on the light nor on the spices of the dead . . .

What is the reason?

The light is made for the honor [of the deceased], *the spices to remove the bad smell.*

Rav Judah in the name of Rav said, ["Light made for] whoever [is of such importance that] they take out [a light] before him both by day and by night is not blessed. [And light made for] whoever [is not important, so that] they take out [a light] before him only by night, is blessed."

R. Huna said, "They do not bless spices of the privy and oil made to remove the grease."

Does this saying imply that wherever [spice] *is not used for smell, they do not bless over it? It may be objected:*

He who enters the stall of a spice dealer and smells the odor, even though he sat there all day long, blesses only one time. He who enters and goes out repeatedly blesses each time.

And lo, here is a case in which it is not used for the scent, and still he blesses.

Yes, but it also is used for the odor—so that people will smell and come and purchase it.

Our rabbis have taught:

If one was walking outside of a village and smelled a scent, if most of the inhabitants are idolators, he does not bless it. If most are Israelites, he blesses it.

R. Yosé says, "Even if most are Israelites, he *still* may not bless, because Israelite women use incense for witchcraft."

But do they "all" burn incense for witchcraft!

A small part is for witchcraft, and a small part is also for scenting garments, which yields a larger part not used for scent, and wherever the majority [of the incense] is not used for scent, one does not bless it.

R. Hiyya bar Abba said in the name of R. Yohanan, "He who walks on the eve of the Sabbath in Tiberias and at the end of the Sabbath in Sepphoris and smells an odor does not bless it, because it is presumed to have been made only to perfume garments."

Our rabbis taught: If one was walking in the gentiles' market and was pleased to scent the spices, he is a sinner.

III

USING THE LIGHT

[53b] **They do not recite a blessing over the light until it has been used . . .**

Rav Judah said in the name of Rav, "Not that he has actually used it, but if anyone stood near enough so that he might use the light, even at some distance, [he may say the blessing]."

So too R. Ashi said, "We have learned this teaching even [concerning] those at some distance."

It was objected [on the basis of the following teaching]: If one had a light hidden in the folds of his cloak or in a lamp, or saw the flame but did not make use of its light, or made use of the light but did not [actually] see the flame, he may not say the blessing. [He may say the blessing only when] he [both] sees the flame and uses its light.

Certainly one finds cases in which one may use the light and not see the flame. *This may be when the light is in a corner.*

But where do you find a case in which one may see the flame and not make use of its light? *Is it not when he is at a distance?*

No, it is when the flame keeps on flickering.

Our rabbis have taught:

They may say a blessing over glowing coals, but not over dying coals (*'omemot*).

What is meant by glowing coals?

R. Hisda said, "If one puts a chip into them and it kindles on its own, [these are] all [glowing coals]."

It was asked: Is the word 'omemot ['alef] *or* 'omemot ['ayin]?

Come and hear, for R. Hisda b. Abdimi said, "'The cedars in the garden of God could not darken ['*amamuhu*] it'" [Ezekiel 31:8].

And Rava said, "He must make actual use of it."

And how [near must one be]?

Ulla said, "So that he may make out the difference between an *issar* and a *pundion* [two small coins]."

Hezekiah said, "So that he may make out the difference between a *meluzma* [a weight] of Tiberias and one of Sepphoris."

Rav Judah would say the blessing [for the light of the] *house of Adda the waiter* [which was nearby].

Rava would say the blessing [for the light of the] *house of Guria bar Hama.*

Abbaye would say the blessing [for the light of the] *house of Bar Abbuha.*

R. Judah said in the name of Rav, "They do not go looking for the light in the way they go looking for [means to carry out other] commandments."

R. Zera said, "At the outset, I used to go looking [for light]. *Now that I have heard this teaching of R. Judah in the name of Rav, I too will not go searching, but if one comes my way, I shall say the blessing over it."*

The first problem of part II concerns the light and spices of gentiles. The sequence begins with Rav's interpretation of the

Mishnah's referent. Then we have a series of *beraitot,* introduced by *Our rabbis have taught.* Each is analyzed in sequence. The point of analysis is, What is the reason for the rule? When a reason is adduced, the next question is, Is the reason logical and harmonious with other laws? Finally, where possible, a further Tannaitic teaching is introduced in support of the accepted interpretation. The sequence, after the discussion of the light and spices of idolatry, is as follows: (1) a light which has not rested on the Sabbath; then (2) a light kindled by an Israelite (or a gentile) from a light which has not rested on the Sabbath; then (3) further examples of the light of gentiles— (4) the light of a village, (5) a child carrying a torch.

Since light is under discussion, a new problem occurs: Does one bless light seen from a distance? The first issue is light from a furnace, then from a synagogue. Once the schoolhouse is introduced, light brought to the schoolhouse is naturally going to be discussed; here the issue is drawn from the life of study.

We then turn to the Mishnah on the light and spices of the dead. The issue is whether these are used for their normal purpose, in which case they may be blessed. Once that principle is laid down, further examples are analyzed, beginning with incense smelled from afar.

The unit concludes with an analysis of a new Mishnah, this one on using the light. Rav Judah in Rav's name says one does not have actually to use the light. There follows a brief interpolation, then comes Rava's opinion, pertinent to the Mishnah, that one does have to make actual use of the light. Afterward we define the distance one may stand from a light and still be able to make use of it. Finally comes another interpolation, this in the name of the first master, Rav Judah in the name of Rav.

IV

FORGETTING GRACE. AMEN.

He who ate [and did not say Grace] . . .

R. Zevid, and some say, R. Dimi bar Abba, said, "The dispute [between the Houses] applies to a case of forgetfulness, but in a case in which a person deliberately [omitted Grace], all agree that he should return to his place and say the blessing."

This is perfectly obvious. It is [explicitly] *taught,* "And he forgot."

What might you have said? That is the rule even where it was intentional, but the reason that the Tanna taught, "And he forgot," *is to tell you how far the House of Shammai were willing to go* [in requiring the man to go back to where he ate. They did so even if a man accidentally forgot]. *Thus we are taught* [the contrary. Even if one forgot, unintentionally, he must go back].

It was taught:

The House of Hillel said to the House of Shammai, "According to your opinion, someone who ate on the top of the Temple Mount and forgot and went down without saying Grace should go back to the top of the Mount and say the blessing."

The House of Shammai said to the House of Hillel, "According to your opinion, someone who forgot a purse on the top of the Temple Mount would not go back and retrieve it.

"For his own sake, he [assuredly] will go back. For the sake of Heaven [should he] not all the more so [go back]?"

There were these two disciples. One did it [forgot Grace] *accidentally, and, following the rule of the House of Shammai,* [went back to bless], *and found a purse of gold. And one did it deliberately* [omitted Grace], *and following the rule of the House of Hillel* [did not go back to say it], *and a lion ate him.*

Rabbah bar bar Hanna was traveling in a caravan. He ate and was sated but [forgot and] *did not say Grace.*

He said, "What shall I do? If I tell the men [of the caravan with me] *that I forgot to bless, they will say to me, 'Bless here. Wherever you say the blessing, you are saying the blessing to the Merciful* [God].' *It is better that I tell them I have forgotten a golden dove."*

So he said to them, "Wait for me, for I have forgotten a golden dove."

He went back and blessed and found a golden dove.

And why was a dove so important?

Because the community of Israel is compared to a dove, as it is written, "The wings of the dove are covered with silver, and her pinions with the shimmer of gold" [Psalm 68:14]. Just as the dove is saved only by her wings, so Israel is saved only by the commandments.

Until when can he say the Grace? Until the food is digested in his bowels . . .

How long does it take to digest the food?

R. Yohanan said, "As long as one is no longer hungry."

Resh Laqish said, "As long as one [still] is thirsty on account of his meal."

R. Yemar bar Shelamia said to Mar Zutra—and some say, Rav Yemar bar Shizbi said to Mar Zutra—"Did Resh Laqish really say this? And did not R. Ammi say in the name of Resh Laqish, 'How long does it take to digest a meal? The time it takes to go four miles.'"

There is no problem: Here [we speak of] a big meal, there [we speak of] a small meal.

If wine came to them . . .

This implies that in the case of an Israelite['s saying Grace], even though one has not heard the entire blessing, he responds [*Amen*].

But if he has not heard [the whole Grace], *how can he have performed his duty by doing so* [assuming he has eaten also? For he has to hear the entire Grace to carry out his obligation to say Grace.]

Hiyya bar Rav said, "[We speak of a case] in which he did not eat with them."

So too did R. Nahman say in the name of Rabbah bar Abbuha, "[We speak of a case] in which he did not eat with them."

Rav said to Hiyya his son, "My son, seize [the cup] *and bless."*

So did R. Huna say to Rabbah his son, "Seize and bless."

This implies that he who says the blessing is better than he who answers Amen. *But has it not been taught:*

R. Yosé says, "The one who answers *Amen* is greater than the one who says the blessing."

R. Nehorai said to him, "By heaven! It is so. You should know it, for behold, common soldiers go ahead and open the battle, but the heroes go in and win it."

It is a matter of dispute between Tannaim, as it has been taught:

Both the one who says the blessing and the one who answers *Amen* are implied [in the Scripture (Nehemiah 9:5)]. But the one who says the blessing is more quickly [answered] than he who answers *Amen.*

Samuel asked Rav, "Should one answer [*Amen*] after [the blessings of] children in the schoolhouse?"

He said to him, "They answer *Amen* after everyone except children in the schoolhouse, since they are [saying blessings solely] for the sake of learning."

And this applies when it is not the time for them to say the "Haftarah," *but in the time to say* "Haftarah," *they do respond* [*Amen*].

Our rabbis have taught:

"The absence of oil holds up the blessing [Grace]," the words of Rabbi Zilai.

R. Zivai says, "It does not hold it up."

R. Aha says, "[The absence of] good oil holds it up."

R. Zuhamai says, "Just as a dirty person [*mezuham*] is unfit for the Temple service, so dirty hands are unfit for the blessing."

R. Nahman Bar Isaac said, "I know neither Zilai nor Zivai nor Zuhamai. But I know a teaching which R. Judah said in the name of Rav, and some say it was taught as a 'baraita':

"'And be you holy' [Leviticus 20:7]—this refers to washing the hands before the meal.

"'And you shall be holy'—this refers to the washing after the meal.

"'For holy'—this refers to the oil.

"'Am I the Lord your God'—this refers to the blessing [Grace]."

The final unit is introduced by the analysis of the Houses' differences about what to do if one has forgotten to say Grace after Meals. After Zevid's abortive gloss, we have discrete materials—the fragment of a debate, then stories illustrative of the principles of the debate, but all in favor of the stand of the House of Shammai. The Mishnaic teaching about digesting the food is then explained. Finally, the question of responding *Amen* raised in the Mishnah is worked out, but only in one detail, an Israelite's saying *Amen* at the end of Grace. The little story about answering *Amen* after school children treats a problem related in theme, but not in principle. Finally, a further addition, about oil in connection with the Grace after Meals, permits the conclusion of the chapter on an exalted note.

The Four Modes of Criticism

We see that the chapter is tightly organized according to the themes of the Mishnah to which it is a commentary. It contains remarkably little extraneous material; almost everything in the chapter is pertinent to the themes of the Mishnah. Most materials are relevant not only in substance, but in detail. The editors had to work with discrete materials—the Mishnah, the Tosefta in its several elements, opinions of Amoraim from Rav in the early third century to Ashi in the fifth, not to mention teachings of Tannaim from the first and second centuries, stories about rabbis, Scriptural exegeses, parables, legends. Considering the hodgepodge of materials handed on for five centuries, beginning with a barely intelligible mnemonic list possibly dating to pre-70 times, we can hardly fail to be astonished at the neat, orderly, thematically logical, and pedagogically illuminating arrangement accomplished by the editors. They have not only brought good order to chaos. They have done so in such a way that the critical interest of the reader is maintained, his or her powers to participate in the argument enhanced.

For what is *Talmudic* about the chapter before us, Talmudic and not merely encyclopedic and antiquarian, is the persistence of the spirit of criticism in four modes: (1) abstract, rational criticism of each tradition in sequence and of the answers hazarded to the several questions; (2) historical criticism of sources and their (un)harmonious relationship; (3) philological and literary criticism of the meanings of words and phrases; and (4) practical criticism of what people actually do in order to carry out their religious obligations.

It goes without saying that these four modes of criticism are peculiarly contemporary. Careful, skeptical examination of answers posed to problems is utterly commonplace to modern men and women. Historical criticism of sources, which does not gullibly accept whatever is alleged as fact, is the beginning of historical study. Philological study of the origins and meanings of words, literary criticism of the style of expression—these are familiar. Finally, we take for granted that it is normal to examine people's actions against some large principle of behavior. These are traits of inquiry which are both Talmudic and routinely modern.

What makes them different from modern modes of thought? It is the remarkable claim that in the give and take of argument, in the processes of criticism, you do something transcendent, more than this-worldly. I cannot overemphasize how remarkable is the combination of rational criticism and supernatural value attached to that criticism. You simply cannot understand the Talmud and take seriously its claim upon modern men and women without confronting the otherworldly context in which this so completely secular thinking goes forward. The claim is that in seeking reason and order, you serve God. But what are we to make of that claim? Does lucid thinking bring heavenly illumination? How can people suggest so?

Perhaps the best answer may be sought in your own experience. Whence comes insight? Having put everything together in a logical and orderly way, we sometimes find ourselves immobilized. We know something, but we do not know what it means, what it suggests beyond itself. We sometimes catch an unexpected insight and come in some mysterious way to a comprehension of a whole which exceeds the sum of its parts. And we cannot explain how we have seen what, in a single instant, stuns us by its ineluctable rightness, fittingness—by the unearned insight, the inexplicable understanding. For the rabbis that stunning moment of rational insight comes with *siyyata dishamaya,* the help of Heaven. The charisma imparted by the rabbinic imagination to the brilliant man is not different in substance from the moral authority and spiritual dignity imparted by contemporary intellectuals to the great minds of the age. The profound honor to be paid to the intellectual paragons—the explorers of the unknown, the men and women of courage to doubt the accepted truths of the hour—is not much different from the deference shown by the disciple to the rabbi. So the religious experience of the rabbi and the secular experience of the intellectual differ not in quality. They gravely differ in the ways by which we explain and account for that experience. Still, in reflecting upon the commonalities of experience, we are enabled to enter into the curious mode of religiosity discovered within the Talmud. That accounts for our capacity to follow the primary question of the Talmud:

Why are things as you claim? Perhaps they are just the opposite.

The persistent issue is, What is the reason for the ruling? Once reasons are adduced, they may be criticized and replaced. Changing situations may produce new reasons and end the pertinence of old ones. Just as the argument moves from point to point, so it remains open-ended. Not only new data, but also new intelligence and ideas may be introduced to change the course of the legal discussion. Thus the editors of the Talmud have turned materials of merely historical interest and authority into a living and vigorous discussion of wholly contemporary concern, vivid so long as the living choose to engage their minds with the ideas and the reasoning of the long-dead.

It must have taken considerable courage to criticize an authoritative law code, the Mishnah, and its accompanying supplement, the Tosefta. It would have been pious merely to accept those laws and digest them for future generations to memorize and copy. Judah the Patriarch, called "our holy rabbi," and those whose traditions he organized and handed on were very ancient authorities. Two or three centuries later the prestige of the Mishnah, regarded, as we saw, as the "Oral Torah" revealed by Moses at Sinai, was considerable. To ask for reasons, to criticize those reasons, to seek contradictions, to add to the law, to revise or even reject what the ancients had said—these were acts of men who had no equivalent claim either to firsthand knowledge of the Oral Torah or to the sanctity and prestige of the Tannaim. Yet that is exactly what the Amoraim did. And they did so in such a way as to revise everything that had gone before, to place upon the whole heritage of the past the indelible and distinct, unmistakable stamp of their own minds.

The reason is that the Amoraim did not confuse respect with servility. They carefully nurtured the disciples' critical and creative faculties. Gibbon said (probably unfairly) of the Byzantine schools, "Not a single composition of history, philosophy, or literature has been saved from oblivion by the intrinsic beauties of style, or sentiment, or original fancy, or even of successful imitation." By contrast, the Babylonian Talmud is the product not of servility to the past or of dogmatism in the present, but of an exceptionally critical, autonomous rationalism and an utterly independent spirit. The Amoraim gave to pedantry a cool welcome. Clearly, to them mere learning was insufficient. Not what one knew, but what he could do with what he knew was decisive. The authority and approbation of the elders were set aside by the critical accomplishments of the newest generation. In the fullest sense, the Amoraim were not traditionalists. They took the laws and traditions of the early generations into their care, respectfully learning them, reverently handing them on. But these they thoroughly digested and made their own. Their minds were filled with the learning of the ancients. But their rational wisdom and unrelenting criticism were wholly their own.

CHAPTER 6

Talmudic Thinking and Us

The Talmud we have studied records not only laws, but the processes by which laws are uncovered. By describing those processes, the rabbis propose to resolve the tension between ordinary life and logic. Using the data deriving from revealed laws of cultic purity and liturgy, the Talmud engages in the give-and-take of argument about what one is obligated to do and not do in eating a meal. The argument develops its themes through inquiry into fundamental, unifying principles and their application of those to ordinary affairs. Humble matters of where one puts his napkin are shown to reveal such underlying principles. These are then subjected to analysis and produce a search for still more basic, and ultimately unifying conceptions. The primary convictions which generate this search for hidden unities are that God is one, creation derives from the single, omnipotent and omnipresent Creator, and Torah expresses God's wholly self-consistent will. We deal, therefore, with the intellectual effects of the fundamental conviction of monotheism.

The conceptions turned up by the rabbis' quest for the principles to guide everyday deeds prove to be highly relative and abstract. For nothing is more abstract than the nonmaterial, or supramaterial, laws of purity and impurity. So even the placing of a napkin at a meal is turned into a sacred discipline for living, a discipline which requires that logic and order everywhere prevail, and demands, as I said, that concerns for a vast world of unseen, well-regulated, and highly principled relationships of sanctity come to bear. Thoughtless action is elevated, sanctified, made worthy of thought, and is shown to bear heavy consequences. Thus, as Judah Goldin says, "Study, interpretation, debate are the discipline for living; without them no right action is likely. . . ."*

The Talmud is a fundamentally nonhistorical document. It does not appeal to the authority of the past. The argument, though unfolding by generations of rabbis, is not about the authority and biography of the ancients, but about their timeless, impersonal reasons for ruling as they do. The participants in the argument sometimes are named, but the most interesting constructions are given anonymously: "What is the reason of the House of Shammai?" "Do not the House of Shammai and the House of Hillel agree with R. Yosé and R. Meir, respectively?" These elegant structures are not assigned to specific authorities, because to the Talmud the time and place, name and occupation of the authority behind an inquiry are of no great interest. Logic and criticism are not bound to specific historical or biographical circumstances. Therefore, the principles of orderly, disciplined, holy life are not reduced to the personalities or situations of the men who laid down or discovered those principles.

Talmudic thinking stands over against historical and psychological interpretation because of its preference for finding abstraction and order in concrete, perennial problems of daily life. What counts is reason, ubiquitous, predominant, penetrating. The object of reason is twofold: first, the criticism of the given by the criterion of fundamental principles of order; and second, the demonstration of the presence within commonplace matters of transcendent considerations. Casuistical controversy over trivialities does not always link up to a tran-

* The Living Talmud (N.Y., 1957: Mentor, New American Library), p. 15.

scendent concern for the sacred; but it always is meant to. For the ultimate issue is how to discover the order of the well-ordered existence and well-correlated relationships; and the prevalent attitude is perfect seriousness (not specious solemnity) about life, human intentions, and actions.

The presupposition of the Talmudic approach to life is that order is better than chaos, reflection than whim, decision than accident, ratiocination and rationality than witlessness and force. The only admissible force is the power of fine logic, ever refined against the gross matter of daily living. The sole purpose is so to construct the discipline of everyday life and to pattern the relationships among men that all things are intelligible, well-regulated, trustworthy—and sanctified. The Talmud stands for the perfect intellectualization of life, that is, the subjection of life to rational study. For nothing is so trivial as to be unrelated to some conceptual, abstract principle. If the placing of a napkin or the washing of the hands is subject to critical analysis, what can be remote from the Talmud's rigorous inquiry? But the mode of inquiry is not ours alone. We are made in God's image. And that part of us which is like God is not corporeal. It is the thing which separates humanity from beast: the mind, consciousness. When we use our minds, we are acting like God. That surely is a conviction uncharacteristic of modern intellectuals, yet at the heart of Talmudic intellectuality.

The Talmud's conception of us is obvious: We think, therefore we and what we do are worth taking seriously. We will respond to reason and subject ourselves to discipline founded upon criticism. Our response will consist in self-consciousness about all we do, think, and say. To be sure, humanity is dual, we are twin things, ready to do evil and ready to do good. The readiness is not all, though some now think so. Beyond readiness there is mindfulness. As the Talmudic warning about not interrupting one's study even to admire a tree—that is, nature—makes clear, we cannot afford even for one instant to break off from consciousness, to open ourselves to what appears then to be "natural"; to be mindless is to lose touch with revealed order and revealed law, the luminous disciplines of the sacred.

Nor is the ultimate issue of humanity solely ethical; it is holiness. To be sure, one must do the good, but Torah encompasses more than ethical behavior. The good is more than the moral; it is also the well-regulated conduct of matters to which morality is impertinent. The whole person, private and public, is to be disciplined. Etiquette (who blesses first) is blended with theology—the imitation of God's behavior at the end of the first Sabbath; furthermore with something one might call metaphysics—the composition of the flame; and finally with social law—relationships with sages, on the one side, and idolators, on the other. Other examples of the Talmud would have laid greater stress on different aspects of behavior and belief; monumental discussions of civil obligations, torts and damages, for example, might well have been cited. But these would have produced a picture not much different, except in substance, from the one yielded by the Talmud's investigations into how a meal is conducted. For no limits are set to the methods of exploring reason and searching for order. Social order with its concomitant ethical concern is no more important than the psychic order of the individual, with its full articulation in the "ritual" life. All reality comes under the discipline of the critical intellect, all is capable of sanctification.

The Talmud's single-minded pursuit of unifying truths itself constitutes its primary discipline. But the discipline does not derive from the perception of unifying order in the natural world. It comes, rather, from the lessons imparted supernaturally in the Torah. The sages perceived the Torah not as a mélange of sources and laws of different origins, but as a single, unitary document, a corpus of laws reflective of an underlying ordered will. The Torah revealed the way things should be, just as the rabbis' formulation and presentation of their laws tell how things should be, whether or not that is how they actually are done. The order derives from the plan and will of the Creator of the world, the foundation of all reality. The Torah was interpreted by the Talmudic rabbis to be the architect's design for reality: God looked into the Torah and created the world, just as an architect follows his prior design in raising a building. A single, whole Torah—in two forms, oral and written, to be sure—underlay the one, seamless reality of the world. The search for the unities hidden by the pluralities of the trivial world, the supposition that some one thing is revealed by many things—these represent, as I said, in intellectual form the theological and metaphysical conception of a single, unique God, creator of heaven and earth, revealer of one complete Torah, guarantor of the unity and ultimate meaning of all the human actions and events that constitute history. On that account the Talmud links the private deeds of individuals to a larger pattern, provides a large and general "meaning" for small, particular, trivial doings.

Behind this conception of the unifying role of reason and the integrating force of criticism lay the conviction that God supplies the model for our minds, therefore, we, through reasoning in the Torah's laws, may penetrate into God's intent and plan. The rabbis of the Talmud believed they studied Torah as God did in heaven; their schools were conducted like the academy on high. They performed rites just as God performed rites, wearing fringes as did he, putting on phylacteries just as God put on phylacteries. In studying Torah they besought the heavenly paradigm revealed by God "in his image" and handed down from Moses and the prophets to their own teachers. If the rabbis of the Talmud studied and realized the divine teaching of Moses, whom they called "our rabbi," it was because the order they would impose upon earthly affairs would replicate on earth the order they perceived from heaven, the rational construction of reality. It is Torah which reveals the mind of God, the principles by which he shaped reality. So studying Torah is not merely imitating God, who does the same, but is a way to the apprehension of God and the attainment of the sacred. The modes of argument are holy because they lead from earth to heaven, as prayer or fasting or self-denial cannot. Reason is the way, God's way, and the holy man is therefore he who is able to think clearly and penetrate profoundly into the mysteries of the Torah and, especially, of its so very trivial laws. In context those trivialities contain revelation.

To the Talmudic way of thinking a person is liberated, not imprisoned, by reason, which opens the way to true creativity, that is, the work of finding, or imposing, form and order upon chaos. The wherewithal of creativity is triviality—that by now is obvious—and what is to be done with triviality is to uncover, within or beyond the simple things of chaos, the order, the complex structure, the coherence of the whole. What is concrete therefore is subordinate to what is abstract. It is the construction of the larger reality that reveals the traits of that reality. And to the Talmudic rabbi, the most interesting aspect of reality is the human and the societal: the village, the home, the individual. Talmudic Judaism, because of its stress on what and how one eats and drinks, has been called a religion of pots and pans. And so it is, if not that alone, for its raw materials are the irreducible atoms of concrete life. But these come at the beginning; they stand prior to what will become of them, are superficial by contrast to what lies beneath them, to what they adumbrate.

What is to be done with these atoms, these smallest building blocks of reality? The answer now is evident: They are to be subjected to control, the person to self-control. All impulses are to be carefully regulated in accord with the divine plan for reality. All are good and may be holy when so ordered, evil when not. The robust sexuality of the Talmudic laws of marital relations testifies to the rabbis' seriousness and matter-of-factness about what today is highly charged material. For one thing, they consistently referred to a couple's having intercourse "all night long" and promised sons and other blessings to those who engaged in sexual relations two (or more) times in succession—the more the better.

So the regulation of impulse was the opposite of its suppression; it was its liberation. But what was done had to be done rightly, had to be sanctified; the nuptial bed was the right circumstance. To be sure, appropriate social and legal regulations brought the couple to their bed; but (in theory at least), if an unmarried man, legally permitted to marry his beloved, engaged in sexual relations with an unmarried woman, the couple thereby consummated a legitimate marriage-union and were regarded as fully and legally married in all respects. It is assumed that a man does not enter sexual relations lightly or licentiously. It is taken for granted that people intend to do the right thing. Again, the time had to be right. The Torah prohibited sexual relations during a woman's menstrual cycle. Then not during that cycle relations are to be encouraged. The circumstances then had to be discussed: Is it better in the light or in the dark? Is it all right in not completely private conditions? The pious would have relations in the dark; the ultra-pious would drive away even flies and mosquitoes. So the course of law rolls on, regulating what is natural and enhancing it through good order, bringing to consciousness what is beneath the surface, through the therapy of public analysis and reasoned inquiry legitimizing what otherwise might be repressed. It is not unimportant that the Talmudic tractate on betrothals is called "sanctification."

Certainly, the Talmudic way of thinking appeals to, and itself approves, the cultured over the uncultured, those capable of self-conscious criticism over those too dull to think. "An ignorant man cannot be pious." Fear of sin without wisdom is worthless. The sages encouraged the articulate over the inarticulate: "The shy person cannot learn." For the give-and-take of argument, one cannot hang back out of feigned or real bashfulness. Reason makes individuals equals and reveals their inequalities. Reason is not a quirk of personality, but a trait of mind, therefore must be shamelessly and courageously drawn out. The ideal is one for intellectuals, devoted to words and the expression, or reduction, of reality to the abstractions constituted by words.

Notice, for example, how few are the simple, declarative

sentences we saw in our chapter of the Talmud; the primary mode of expression is those joining-parts of language which link thought to thought, or set thought against thought: "But," "However," "Do you reason so?" "What is the presupposition?" What is Talmudic about the Talmud is expressed in the Aramaic mortar, not in the Hebrew stones. The near-grunts of the uneducated, "I want this," "I do that," "That is my opinion"—these are virtually absent in the extended discourse. The argument is expressed in terse, apocopated phrases, moving almost too rapidly for the ordinary ear to grasp.

What is Talmudic, too, is perpetual skepticism, expressed in response to every declarative sentence or affirmative statement. Once one states that matters are so, it is inevitable that he will find as a response: "Why do you think so?" or "Perhaps things are the opposite of what you say?" or "How can you say so when a contrary principle may be adduced?" Articulation, forthrightness, subtle reasoning but lucid expression, skepticism— these are the traits of intellectuals, not of untrained and undeveloped minds, nor of neat scholars, capable only to serve as curators of the past, but not as critics of the present.

Above all, Talmudic thinking rejects gullibility and credulity. It is, indeed, peculiarly modern in its systematic skepticism, its testing of each proposition, not to destroy but to refine what people suppose to be so. As we have seen time and again, the Talmud's first question is not "*Who* says so?" but "Why?" "What is the reason of the House of Shammai?" In the Talmudic approach to thought, faith is restricted to ultimate matters, to the fundamental principles of reality beyond which one may not penetrate. Akabya warned to try to find out whence one comes and whither one is going. The answers will yield humility. But humility in the face of ultimate questions is not confused with servility before the assertions, the truth-claims, of putative authorities, ancient or modern, who are no more than mortal.

Since the harvest of learning is humility, however, the more one seeks to find out, the greater will be one's virtue. And the way to deeper perception lies in skepticism about shallow assertion. One must place as small a stake as possible in the acceptance of specific allegations. The fewer vested convictions, the greater the chances for wide-ranging inquiry. But while modern skepticism may yield—at least in the eye of its critics—corrosive and negative results, Talmudic skepticism produces measured, restrained, and limited insight. The difference must be in the open-endedness of the Talmudic inquiry: nothing is ever left as a final answer, a completed solution. The fruit of insight is inquiry; the result of inquiry is insight, in endless progression. The only road closed is the road back, to the unarticulated, the unconscious, and the unself-conscious. For once consciousness is achieved, a reason spelled out, one cannot again pretend there is no reason, and nothing has been articulated. For the Talmud the alternatives are not faith or nihilism, but reflection or dumb reflex, consciousness or animal instinct. Humanity, in God's image, has the capacity to reflect and to criticize. All an animal can do is act and respond. And a person may be holy or unholy. An animal can only be clean or unclean—a considerable difference.

That is why energy, the will to act, has to be channeled and controlled by law. You are what you do. Therefore, deed without deliberation is not taken seriously. Examination of deeds takes priority over mere repetition of what works or feels good. For this purpose, genius is insufficient, cleverness is irrelevant. What is preferred is systematic and orderly consideration, step by step, of the principles by which one acts. The human problem in the Talmudic conception is not finding the motive force to do, but discovering the restraint to regulate that protean force. In the quest for restraint and self-control, the primal energies will ensure one is not bored or lacking in purpose. For the Talmudic mode of thought perceives a perpetual tension between energy and activity, on the one side, and reflection on the other. To act without thought comes naturally, is contrary, therefore, to the fact of revealed discipline. The drama of the private life consists in the struggle between will and intellect, action and reflection. If the Talmud is on the side of the intellect and reflection, it is because the will and action require no allies. The outcome will be determined, ultimately, by force of character and intellect, these together. And the moot issue is not how to repress, but how to reshape, the primal energy.

Yet it is an error to focus so one-sidedly upon the Talmudic mind and so to ignore the other formative force in culture, the community. The Talmud, for its part, fully recognizes the social forces, the pressures to conform and to follow established custom and habit. That is why so much attention centers upon people's doing things together. The Talmudic rabbis exhibit keen awareness that restraint is societal before it is personal; community takes priority over individuality and gives the private person nearly the whole of the structure of symbols and values that render living meaningful. "Give me fellowship, or give me death," said one of them.

The "meal" we analyzed in some detail is assumed to be a public occasion; there is nothing private about it. When people eat, it is taken for granted that they eat together and follow publicly known regulations; that is why there are such regulations. The more important parts of the Talmud, furthermore, deal with civil regulations: What to do if an ox gores another ox? How to divide a disputed prayer shawl? How to litigate a contested will, in which the material results affect the disposition of a palm tree or a tiny bit of land?

The Talmudic rabbis are well aware that society forms the individual. If a sage seeks to create a disciplined individual, whose life is regulated by revealed law, he must give priority to the regulation of the society which forms the ground of individual existence. And to regulate society, he must concentrate upon the conflicts among men, the conflicting claims to unimportant things which, all together, will add up to justice and make possible dignity and autonomy. It is through law that you will revise habit, establish good customary behavior. It is through a lawful society that you will create an environment naturally productive of restraint and rational manners. If, therefore, it is correct to claim that what is Talmudic about the Talmud is the application of reason and criticism to concrete and practical matters, then the Talmud is at its core an instrument for the regulation of society in the most humble and workaday sense of the words.

To be sure, to regulate society you must have access to the institutions that exercise and confer legitimate power, and the Talmudic rabbis knew the importance of various sorts of power. They understood, first of all, the intrinsic power of law itself, which rendered unnecessary constant, *ad hoc* intervention of puissant authority into routine affairs. Once law has established how things should be done, the enforcement of the law becomes necessary only in exceptional circumstances. In normal ones the law itself ensures its own enforcement, for most people most of the time are law-abiding.

The Talmudic rabbis, second, actively sought access to the instrumentalities of Jewish autonomous government made available by the authorities of Roman Palestine and Iranian Babylonia. If the imperial regimes were content to have the Jews regulate their own affairs and fundamentally disinterested in meddling in ritual and community regulations, the rabbis were eager to take over the institutions authorized to regulate the people's lives. They worked their way into these institutions, formed by the Patriarch of Palestine and the Exilarch of Babylonia, and made themselves the chief agents for the day-to-day government of the local communities. So far as the state stood behind the Jewish community's officials, the rabbis enjoyed the benefit of state power and therefore mastered the intricacies of politics.

Third, the Talmudic rabbis exercised moral authority sufficient to make people do what the rabbis wanted without the intervention of secular authorities. That moral authority was based upon multiform foundations.

Let me list them. First, the rabbi was understood to have

mastery of the divine revelation and unique access to part of it, the Oral Torah handed down from Sinai. So his rule was according to heavenly principles.

Second, the rabbi was seen as himself paradigmatic of the Torah's image of man. Therefore, what he did was revelatory. Common folk who proposed to obey the will of God as the rabbis explained it would not have to be coerced to do what the rabbis said. They might just as well imitate the rabbi, confident that he did what he did in order to imitate Moses "our rabbi" and God, Moses' rabbi. The Talmud we have studied is full of stories of what individuals said and did on specific occasions. In some instances the abstract law is conveyed by such stories. In most others, the point of the story is to show, by relating the rabbi's deed, what the law is, how one should conduct himself. These are not "political" stories, yet they have a pronouncedly political result, for the story influences behavior no less than a court decree shapes action.

Finally, among the rabbis were some who could exercise miraculous and even supernatural powers. A modern anthropologist having spent a few years in Talmudic circles to study the social role of the rabbi might well call his book, "The Lawyer-Magicians of Babylonia." But the exercise of supernatural power, the ability to appeal to the fantasies of ordinary folk—fantasies the rabbis themselves certainly shared—these too constituted a kind of "moral authority." Curiously, it was intellectual achievement that produced theurgical power. The righteous were believed to have the creative power of God: "If a righteous man desires it, he can create a world." And why should the rabbi not have such power, given his knowledge of the Torah, which contained the plan and pattern for God's own creation of this world? Learning reshaped a man into the likeness of God and therefore endowed him with God's powers of creation. In a secular sense, belief in the supernatural consequences of the supernatural power of mastery of Torah traditions and reasoning about them produced a practical power considerably more efficient than political instrumentalities in moving people to do the right thing. The charisma represented by brilliance in reasoning and argument was affective outside of the circle of intellectuals, just as it is today, but with better reason then. So the luminous becomes numinous.

One can hardly refer to politics without alluding, as well, to the construction of the family, the relationship of father to son. Here Talmudic rabbis discerned a tension and resolved it in their own favor. They took for granted the primacy of the father in the formation of the personality of the child and the shape of the family. At the same time they claimed they, as masters of Torah, should shape personality and provide the model for the family. They admitted that the father brought the child into this world. But, they quickly added, the sage brings him into the next world, therefore is entitled to the honor owing from the child to the father. The sage is better than the father, above the father, just as God is the ultimate father of the child and giver of his life. If, therefore, a son sees the ass of his father struggling under his load, and at the same time he sees the ass of his sage about to stumble, he helps the ass of his rabbi, then that of his father, for the one has brought him into this world, the other, eternity. Just as the rabbi placed his rule over that of the state and the state's functionaries, the patriarch and exilarch, so he sought to take precedence over the primary component of the community, the family, by laying claim to the position of the father.

In larger terms the effort to replace the father by the rabbi symbolizes a struggle equivalent to the effort to replace the concrete, this-worldly government of ordinary officials by the nonnatural or supernatural authority of the rabbi, qualified by learning of the Torah and capacity to reason about it. The Roman authority and his representative in Jewry ruled through force or the threat of force. The rabbinical figure compelled obedience through moral authority, through the capacity to persuade and to demonstrate, through affective example, what the law required. Both political and familial life thus were to be rendered something other than what seemed natural or

normal. Everyone could understand the authority of the gen-
darme, the priority of the father. But to superimpose the rabbi
both in politics and in the family represented a redefinition of the
ordinary sense of politics and the plain, accepted meaning of
the family. It made both into something abstract, subject to a
higher level of interpretation, than an ordinary person might
readily perceive. Political life to the rabbi was not merely a
matter of the here and now, nor was the family what it seemed.
Both were to be remodeled in the image of Heaven, according
to the pattern of the Torah. That is to say, they were to be
restructured according to the underlying principles of reality
laid down by the divine plan as undercovered by rational
inquiry. Society was to be made to conform to the heavenly
definition of the good community; the family was to be revised
according to the supernatural conception of who the father
really was: God and God's surrogate, the rabbi—man most
closely conforming to his image.

The Talmudic stress upon criticism, therefore, produced a
new freedom of construction, the freedom to reinterpret reality
and to reconstruct its artifacts upon the basis of well-analyzed,
thoroughly criticized principles revealed through the practical
reason of the sages. Once a person is free to stand apart from
what is customary and habitual, to restrain energies and
regulate them, he or she attains the higher freedom to revise the
given, to reinterpret established perceptions of reality and the
institutions which give them effect. This constitutes, to begin
with, the process of the mind's focusing upon unseen relationships and the formation of imposed, nonmaterial and nonnatural considerations.

We recall in this connection the purity laws, which play so
considerable a role in the rabbis' regulation of eating (and
other fundamental things, for instance, sexual relations). Those
laws seem to have comprised and created a wholly abstract set
of relationships, a kind of non-Euclidean geometry of the
levitical realm. Yet such high abstractions are brought down to
earth to determine in what order one washes his hands and

picks up a cup of wine, or, as noted, where one puts his napkin. So what is wholly relative and entirely a matter of theory, not attached to concrete things, transforms trivialities. It affects, indeed generates, the way one does them. It transforms them into issues of some consequence, by relating them to the higher meanings (to be sure, without much rational, let alone material substance) associated with the pure and the impure. The purity laws stand at the pinnacle of Talmudic abstraction and ratiocination.

We may supply a social explanation for the intellectuality and abstraction of the Talmudic rabbis' approach to reality. They themselves stood apart from the larger Jewish society, much as the Jews stood apart from the gentile majority. Their intent was to reshape and improve society. But they were different from other men because of their learning and intellect. They lived in this world, but in another too, one in which, for example, the unseen realities and unfelt relationships of purity and impurity were taken so seriously as to determine behavior in the world of material realities and perceived, concrete relationships. They stood apart not because they alone believed in God, for everyone did, or because they alone revered the Torah, for they were not alone, but because they alone conceived it possible for man to elevate himself heavenward through Torah, rationally apprehended. They participated in the history of this world, but were aware of the precariousness and imperfection of this world when perceived and measured by the standard of the next.

Their capacity to criticize therefore derived from their detachment. They knew that what is now is not necessarily whatever was or what must always be. Able to stand apart because of the perspective of distance attained through rational criticism of the practical life, they realized people have choices they themselves may not perceive. There have been and are now other ways of conducting life and living with others, of building society and creating culture, than those the ordinary people supposed were normative. Able to criticize from the perspective of a transcendent perception of the principles of being, the rabbis could evaluate what others took for granted, could see the given as something to be elevated and transcended.

In a word, the Talmud is a document created by the intellect devoted to morality and seeking sanctity. It takes for granted that humanity's primary capacity is to think; it therefore is to be taken with utmost seriousness. The Talmud endures as a monument to intellectualism focused upon the application of practical rationality to society. It pays tribute, on every page, to the human potential to think morally, yet without lachrymose sentimentality, to reflect about fundamentals and basic principles, yet for concrete purposes and with ordinary society in mind. The good, well-regulated society will nurture disciplined, strong character. The mighty man—"one who overcomes his impulses"—will stand as a pillar of the good society. This is what I understand as the result of the intellectual activity of the moral intellect. Reason, criticism, restraint, and rational exchange of ideas—these are not data for the history of Talmudic literature alone. The Talmud itself testifies to their necessary consequences for the personality and for society alike.

What are we to make of the Talmudic approach to life? How shall we appropriate the Talmud's moral intellectualism for contemporary sensibility?

Perhaps you think I have claimed too much for the Talmudic way, but I fear I have claimed too little. For what the Talmud accomplished in the formation of a specific civilization—that of the Jewish people—was to lay the foundations for a society capable of rational, supple response to an irrational situation. The Jews lived as aliens, so they created a homeland wherever they found themselves. They effectively and humanely governed themselves without the normal instruments of government, lacking much of a bureaucracy, having no consequential power at all. They created not one culture but multiple cultures, all of them quintessentially "Jewish," out of the materials of many languages, societies, sorts of natural environment, histories, and traditions. The Talmud's construction of a world of ideas and sacred principles, corresponding to, but transcendent of, reality is a paradigm of the Jews' capacity to reinterpret reality and reconstruct culture in age succeeding age, their nonmaterial power fully, rigorously, and robustly to live the life of the mind. Beyond the Jews' capacity for fantasy—after all, not unique to them—was their power to reflect, reconsider, stand back from reality, and revise its interpretation. This, it now is clear, is the end result of a society which trained its young in the Talmud and rewarded its mature and old men alike for lifelong devotion to its study.

It was the rationality and intellectuality of the Jews' culture which led them to a way of living with one another not in perfect harmony—they were flesh and blood—but in mighty restraint and mutual respect. The inner life of the Jewish community was so organized that the people might conflict with one another, yet not through the totally free expression of the impulse toward mutual annihilation. Renunciation of brute power, affirmation of the force of ideas and reason—these represented the Jews' discovery. They cannot claim to have uncovered these principles, but they most rightly do claim meaningfully to have effected them in the formation of their community life and the establishment of their protean culture. Reason applied to practical affairs through the acute inquiry of Talmudic argument—this I think accounts for the Jews' capacity for so many centuries to accommodate themselves to a situation of worldly powerlessness. For they knew ideas could be powerful; criticism could constitute a great force in society; and, in the end, the sword, once sheathed, could change nothing, but an idea, once unleashed, could so persist as to move people to move the world.

The Talmud lays the foundation for the rational, therefore the moral culture. I refer to Philip Rieff, who speaks of the functions of culture: "(1) to organize the moral demands men make upon themselves in a system of symbols that make men intelligible and trustworthy to each other, thus rendering also

the world intelligible and trustworthy; (2) to organize the
expressive remissions by which men release themselves, in some
degree, from the strain of conforming to the controlling
symbolic, internalized variant readings of culture that constitute individual character."* Clearly, the Talmud exhibits the
capacity to organize "the moral demands" of people into a
system of orderly, integrated symbols. These take the form of
actions to be taken, others to be rejected. The degree of order
and integration depends upon the rabbis' success in locating
the fundamental principles which draw together and show the
interrelationships among discrete actions.

But what is the form of the "expressive remissions"? How
does the Talmud make room for individual character? The
answer lies in the Talmud's stress on the reasons for its rules.
Once the reason is made known, one makes room for contrary
reason, for reason to reject or revise the established rule. Not
only do individuals have the place to differ, but they also have
the power through criticism to move the entire community to
appropriate what to begin with expressed private judgment,
individuality. This I think is not only to the advantage of the
individual, but also fundamentally therapeutic for the community as a whole.

Now for contemporary humanity the Talmud presents formidable criticism, for by it the value, "follow your own
impulse"—utter subjectivism in all things—is rejected. The
Talmud gives contrary advice. "Tame your impulse," regulate,
restrain, control energies through the self-imposition of the
restraining rule of law. At the same time, the Talmud demands
that a person *not* do "his own thing" alone, but persuade
others to make what is "his own" into what is to be shared by
all. The Talmud therefore subjects the individual to restraints
on pure individuality, while opening for individuality the
possibility of moral suasion of the community at large. "Unre-

---

* *The Triumph of the Therapeutic. Uses of Faith after Freud* (N.Y., 1966:
Harper & Row), p. 232.

strained" and "individualism" therefore are set over against "regulated" and "rationality," for it is rationality which overcomes the isolation of the individual, connecting one mind to another through the mediating way of reason. Through the imposition of rational, freely adopted rules, one restrains those destructive elements of the personality which potentially are damaging for both the individual and the community.

To be sure, the supernatural framework of Talmudic religion cannot claim a serious hearing among Jews who stand at a distance from the traditional world of faith, let alone among gentiles. But the Talmud serves a good purpose nonetheless, for it contains within its pages a detailed demonstration of how practical reason may be applied to humble affairs. As a whole document within the multiform historical civilizations of the Jewish people, it testifies to the concrete possibilities of rational and critical approaches to human affairs. This it does not only in generalities, but in strikingly trivial details. The course of the Talmudic argument shows it is possible committedly, involvedly, to argue about changing hypotheses, to pay serious attention to culturally neutral matters, and to find important principles in ordinary affairs. In a way, the Talmudic rabbi takes a clinical attitude toward his own ideas, and certainly toward those of his fellows. They are there for analysis, not for either gullible acceptance or utter rejection. The purpose of the analysis, moreover, is not final commitment to some one conclusion, but provisional decision for laying the way open to further inquiry.

The open-ended character of the Talmudic argument impressed us earlier. Now its very contemporary pertinence becomes clear. Since one expects no final solutions, we must be prepared for a succession of intermediate, provisional ones. We learn, therefore, the discipline of commitment within open-mindedness, the capacity to hold conviction loosely, to refrain from imposing on the other person the task of verifying, by assenting to, one's own deeply held convictions. It is the undogmatic quality of Talmudic discourse which contemporaries might well learn to emulate. They will do so when their commitment is to method rather than to its results, and when the method, or mode, of thought recovers the form prefigured in the Talmud: above all, skepticism, criticism, easy and free movement.

The tradition of Talmudic learning prepared the Jews for the modern situation and even in premodern times carried within itself the qualities we now associate with modernity. So far as modernity requires us to take this world seriously, the Talmud met the requirements of modernity. So far as modernity is characterized by cosmopolitanism and the relativity of values, the Talmud, which could be both studied and realized in many countries and various cultures, prepared the Jews for the modern situation. By its stress on the unfolding possibilities of reason and by its relentless testing of all propositions against the measure of skeptical reason, the Talmud prepared the Jews to recognize the relativity of successive truth claims, the probability that each would in its term have to give way to the next. A trait of modernity is the denial of the ultimacy of any values. To be sure, the Talmud affirmed the Torah and the final truth of all contained therein. But so far as the ideas were perceived as human, not divine, the Talmud spurned the claim that any insight might endure beyond its capacity to be shown to be reasonable. Later, when *all* ideas were perceived as human, the Talmud's fundamental attitude was simply extended to areas where it formerly had been absent. The Talmud's persistent dubiety disciplined the Jewish intellectual to speculate about the unthinkable—"Perhaps things are the opposite of what they seem?"—to investigate the forbidden, to reconsider the commonplace, and so to reshape reality.

The Talmud thus taught its disciples to deny the need they must have felt, the need to judge all values, all assertions, all theories by their own, particular, self-authenticating system of thought. The Talmud prepared its students to see as merely transitory and useful artifacts and ideas the world understood to be absolute and perfected. The Talmud disciplined its devotees to preserve a thoroughly skeptical attitude toward the perfections of the hour. It imparted the view that reality—the immutable truths of others—was something to be criticized, and imparted the humility likewise to perceive one's own.

So, in the end, the Talmud raised abiding skepticism about what people offered as salvation, as final solutions to the problems of the human condition. The Talmudist did not expect final solutions, was trained to ask simple, therefore devastating questions about their finality. So the Talmud readied the Jews for the modern situation of doubt, of provisional truths and hypotheses subject to testing and revision. True, the Talmud did come to decisions. But these were in matters of detail. No one ever resolved any of the really interesting questions of logic and skeptical reasoning. The Talmudic rabbi remained open to the good insights that might come, denying at the same time the finality of what was already present. This gave him the freedom to criticize the Mishnah, the *Gemara*, Rashi, and whatever was to come thereafter. The Talmudist could deny the present achievements of the mind because he hoped for ultimately better ones.

The Jews, disciplined in the Talmud's mode of thought, could accommodate themselves to the modern world's relativization of values precisely because they had already seen the vision of greater perfection than what was originally present. The Talmud produced an activist tradition of people interested in daily affairs and in their proper regulation, a tradition which told people they were partners in the task of perfecting the world under the dominion of God. If the world is perceived to be insufficient and incomplete, it is our task to help complete it. If people saw values as in a measure relative to the situation of specific groups, if they understood reason to be something provisional and transitory, the Talmud taught the Jews their duty was to criticize and purify their ideas by skeptical criteria, at once most ancient and still not wholly realized.

Finally, the Talmud taught the Jews not to be terrified by the necessity to face, and to choose among, a plurality of uncertain alternatives in an insecure world. The Talmud testified that people must choose, if tentatively and for a time only, among competing interpretations, so that the law might in fact be applied, and the ordinary folk might know what to do. So the Talmud forced choices, in a tentative and austere spirit, among the many truths available to reasonable folk. It insisted one cannot be paralyzed before contrary claims and equally persuasive reasons. The House of Shammai and the House of Hillel both laid claim to sound law and excellent reasoning; neither party could be shown inferior to the other in critical acumen. But a choice had to be made. If heaven had to resolve the formidable problem of choice, it set a good example and did not have to intervene again.

The Talmud taught that we must end up doing some one thing when faced with conflicting choices. Values may be relative, but we must choose some ideal by which to guide our lives. People could not endure in indecision. They have to decide to be more than nothing in particular, for their capacity for rational thought is insufficient without an equivalent ability to make and carry out rational decision. The best proof of the duty to make reasonable decisions among unreasonable alternatives was the Jews themselves, who, because of their international character and their memories of many lands and empires, saw the world in all its complex plurality. But they also chose to form the most vivid and intense of all groups, to sustain what is, after all, one of the most particular of all literary traditions, the Talmud itself. Yet they did so in full knowledge that their group was not coextensive with society, and that their Talmudic tradition did not contain everything worth knowing about the right way of living life.

So the Talmud imparted the lesson that humanity may face a relativity of values, but in the end must choose life in some specific place, among some particular group of people. In the end you do put your napkin on the cushion—or the table. The values that shape those lives are not relative to the conditions in which they are lived. When all values are seen to be relative and all reasons may be criticized with equally good reason, that is when people most need the fellowship produced by access to a common, deeply held and widely shared, discipline of thinking. The conclusions will vary; the mode of thought and argumentation must then be constant and enduring.

Having emphasized the priority of making difficult choices, we come to the final, peculiarly modern, trait of the Talmudic mind, one that has recurrently impressed us: its pragmatism. In offering Talmudic pragmatism as peculiarly modern, I do not mean to suggest that, because it is modern, the Talmud is therefore vindicated. I mean the very opposite. What makes it possible for contemporary men and women to reach out to the Talmud's power to transcend and reconstruct reality is their pragmatism and willingness to cope with details and to take seriously the trivialities of ordinary life. Because of the very secularity, the seriousness about worldly things, characteristic of our own day, we are able to understand the importance of the Talmud's lessons about the criticism and regulation of worldly things. What shall we say of a tradition of thought that laid greatest emphasis upon deed, upon a pattern of actions and a way of living, but that it is pragmatic? What shall we say of a perspective upon the world that focused on practical reason, but that it is worldly? What shall we conclude of a religious language that called honesty or charity a *kiddush hashem,* a sanctification of God's name, but that it is deeply secular? A legal system whose deepest concerns were for the detailed articulation of the this-worldly meaning of love for one's neighbor here and now is one which long ago brought the Jews into the pragmatic, this-worldly framework of modernity.

That is why the Talmud not only relates to the contemporary world, but may stand in judgment of it. And it surely will judge a world willing to reduce man to part of himself, to his impulses and energies. It will judge an age prepared to validate the unrestrained expression of those energies as the ultimate, legitimate adumbration of what is individual about the person, as though he had no mind, no strength of rational thought. It will condemn a world of enthusiasts who make an improvement and call it redemption, come up with a good idea and, without the test of skeptical analysis, pronounce salvation. The Talmud shows a better way: It demonstrates that humanity has the capacity to assess the unredemption of the world, to perceive the tentativeness of current solutions to enduring problems, and at the same time to hope for sanctification and work for salvation. It is this unfulfilled yet very vivid evaluation of the world, the power to take the world so seriously as to ask searching questions about its certainties, which, I think, explains the Jew's capacity to love so much, and yet to doubt; to hold the world very near and close, with open arms. The Jew has been taught by the Talmud to engage realistically in the world's tasks, to do so with a whole heart, yet without the need, or even the power, to regard completion of those tasks as the threshold of a final and completed fulfillment of history.

Because of its mode of thinking, the Talmud teaches us to take seriously the wide range of worldly problems without expecting that in solving them—provisionally, let alone finally—they might save the world. If Jews have found the modern situation congenial and congruent to their perception of humanity, it is because the Talmud, writ large across the traditional culture of the Jewish people, had uniquely prepared them for the conditions of modernity, readied them not only to participate in those conditions, but deeply and unstintingly to criticize them, and, finally, in full rationality to reform them.

But to undertake reform through Talmudic modes of thought and analysis, we have, to begin with, to reconsider what makes those modes more than merely an expression of practical reason, but an expression of the transcendent which is in ourselves. We cannot ask the Talmud to vindicate itself by our standards. We have to bring to bear upon our perceptions of ourselves the Talmud's critique, *its* sacred image of us. To begin with it asks, What say you of the human condition? What is man, but that God is mindful of him? If all we are and ever shall be is here and now, if our minds are merely useful and our capacity to think entirely a secular virtue, then the Talmudic mode of reform is unavailable to us. If through our strength of reason we pursue the profound rationality which underlies, gives unity, and imparts meaning to existence, and if through our power of reflection we then undertake the reconstruction of reality, the interpretation of what is in terms of what can and should be, then we shall have already entered into the Talmudic situation. But when we do, we shall thereby have undertaken all the Talmud knows as the discipline of the sacred. We shall, in other words, have renewed the experience of sanctification both *through* the intellect and *of* the intellect. That experience is open when the pages of the Talmud lie before us, but becomes consequential when the Talmud's perceptions of life and interpretations of society come to possess us. I therefore speak, without shame, of religious experience, indeed of the turning toward God which the sages called *teshuvah*, insufficiently translated as repentance, but truly meaning *turning*. The way of Talmudic piety and spirituality has been the path of saints, a path each chose—and may choose again—in full rationality, at life's turning.

Hebrew Text of
Talmudic Passages

The Mishnah

אֵלוּ דְבָרִים שֶׁבֵּין בֵּית שַׁמַּאי וּבֵית הִלֵּל בַּסְעוּדָה. בֵּית שַׁמַּאי
אוֹמְרִים: מְבָרֵךְ עַל הַיוֹם, וְאַחַר כָּךְ מְבָרֵךְ עַל הַיַּיִן. וּבֵית
הִלֵּל אוֹמְרִים: מְבָרֵךְ עַל הַיַּיִן, וְאַחַר כָּךְ מְבָרֵךְ עַל הַיוֹם.
בֵּית שַׁמַּאי אוֹמְרִים: נוֹטְלִין לַיָּדַיִם, וְאַחַר כָּךְ מוֹזְגִין אֶת
הַכּוֹס. וּבֵית הִלֵּל אוֹמְרִים: מוֹזְגִין אֶת הַכּוֹס, וְאַחַר כָּךְ
נוֹטְלִין לַיָּדַיִם.
בֵּית שַׁמַּאי אוֹמְרִים: מְקַנֵּחַ יָדָיו בַּמַּפָּה, וּמַנִּיחָהּ עַל הַשֻּׁלְחָן.
וּבֵית הִלֵּל אוֹמְרִים: עַל הַכֶּסֶת.
בֵּית שַׁמַּאי אוֹמְרִים: מְכַבְּדִין אֶת הַבַּיִת, וְאַחַר כָּךְ נוֹטְלִין
לַיָּדַיִם. וּבֵית הִלֵּל אוֹמְרִים: נוֹטְלִין לַיָּדַיִם, וְאַחַר כָּךְ מְכַבְּדִין
אֶת הַבַּיִת.
בֵּית שַׁמַּאי אוֹמְרִים: נֵר, וּמָזוֹן, וּבְשָׂמִים, וְהַבְדָּלָה. וּבֵית
הִלֵּל אוֹמְרִים: נֵר, וּבְשָׂמִים, וּמָזוֹן, וְהַבְדָּלָה. בֵּית שַׁמַּאי
אוֹמְרִים: "שֶׁבָּרָא מְאוֹר הָאֵשׁ"; וּבֵית הִלֵּל אוֹמְרִים: "בוֹרֵא
מְאוֹרֵי הָאֵשׁ".
אֵין מְבָרְכִין לֹא עַל הַנֵּר, וְלֹא עַל הַבְּשָׂמִים שֶׁל גּוֹיִם, וְלֹא
עַל הַנֵּר, וְלֹא עַל הַבְּשָׂמִים שֶׁל מֵתִים, וְלֹא עַל הַנֵּר, וְלֹא עַל

הַבְּשָׂמִים שֶׁלִּפְנֵי עֲבוֹדָה זָרָה. אֵין מְבָרְכִין עַל הַנֵּר עַד
שֶׁיֵּאוֹתוּ לְאוֹרוֹ.

מִי שֶׁאָכַל וְשָׁכַח וְלֹא בֵּרֵךְ — בֵּית שַׁמַּאי אוֹמְרִים: יַחֲזֹר
לִמְקוֹמוֹ וִיבָרֵךְ. וּבֵית הִלֵּל אוֹמְרִים: יְבָרֵךְ בִּמְקוֹם שֶׁנִּזְכַּר. עַד
אֵימָתַי הוּא מְבָרֵךְ? עַד כְּדֵי שֶׁיִּתְעַכֵּל הַמָּזוֹן שֶׁבְּמֵעָיו.
בָּא לָהֶם יַיִן לְאַחַר הַמָּזוֹן, וְאֵין שָׁם אֶלָּא אוֹתוֹ הַכּוֹס —
בֵּית שַׁמַּאי אוֹמְרִים: מְבָרֵךְ עַל הַיַּיִן, וְאַחַר כָּךְ מְבָרֵךְ עַל
הַמָּזוֹן. וּבֵית הִלֵּל אוֹמְרִים: מְבָרֵךְ עַל הַמָּזוֹן, וְאַחַר כָּךְ
מְבָרֵךְ עַל הַיַּיִן. עוֹנִין אָמֵן אַחַר יִשְׂרָאֵל הַמְבָרֵךְ, וְאֵין עוֹנִין
אָמֵן אַחַר הַכּוּתִי הַמְבָרֵךְ, עַד שֶׁיִּשְׁמַע כָּל הַבְּרָכָה.

The Tosefta

גּוֹי הַמְבָרֵךְ בַּשֵּׁם עוֹנִין אַחֲרָיו אָמֵן, אֶת הַשֵּׁם אֵין עוֹנִין
אַחֲרָיו אָמֵן, עַד שֶׁיִּשְׁמַע אֶת כָּל הַבְּרָכָה.   דְּבָרִים שֶׁבֵּין
בֵּית שַׁמַּאי לְבֵית הִלֵּל בַּסְּעוּדָה. בֵּית שַׁמַּאי אוֹמְרִין: מְבָרֵךְ עַל
הַיּוֹם וְאַחַר כָּךְ מְבָרֵךְ עַל הַיַּיִן, שֶׁהַיּוֹם גּוֹרֵם לַיַּיִן שֶׁיָּבֹא,
וּכְבָר קָדַשׁ הַיּוֹם וַעֲדַיִין יַיִן לֹא בָּא. וּבֵית הִלֵּל אוֹמְרִין: מְבָרֵךְ
עַל הַיַּיִן וְאַחַר כָּךְ מְבָרֵךְ עַל הַיּוֹם, שֶׁהַיַּיִן גּוֹרֵם לִקְדוּשַׁת
הַיּוֹם שֶׁתֵּאָמֵר. דָּבָר אַחֵר בִּרְכַּת הַיַּיִן תְּדִירָה וּבִרְכַּת הַיּוֹם
אֵינָהּ תְּדִירָה. וַהֲלָכָה כְּדִבְרֵי בֵּית הִלֵּל.   בֵּית שַׁמַּאי אוֹמְרִין
נוֹטְלִין לַיָּדַיִם וְאַחַר כָּךְ מוֹזְגִין אֶת הַכּוֹס, שֶׁמָּא נִטְמְאוּ
מַשְׁקִין שֶׁבַּאֲחוֹרֵי הַכּוֹס מֵחֲמַת הַיָּדַיִם וְיַחְזְרוּ וִיטַמְּאוּ אֶת
הַכּוֹס. בֵּית הִלֵּל אוֹמְרִין: אֲחוֹרֵי הַכּוֹס לְעוֹלָם טְמֵאִין. דָּבָר
אַחֵר אֵין נְטִילַת יָדַיִם אֶלָּא סָמוּךְ לַסְּעוּדָה. מוֹזְגִין אֶת הַכּוֹס
וְאַחַר כָּךְ נוֹטְלִין לַיָּדַיִם.   בֵּית שַׁמַּאי אוֹמְרִין: מְקַנֵּחַ יָדוֹ
בַּמַּפָּה וּמַנִּיחָהּ עַל הַשֻּׁלְחָן, שֶׁמָּא נִטְמְאוּ מַשְׁקִין שֶׁבַּמַּפָּה
מֵחֲמַת הַכֶּסֶת וְיַחְזְרוּ וִיטַבְּלוּ אֶת הַיָּדַיִם. בֵּית הִלֵּל אוֹמְרִין:
סָפֵק מַשְׁקִין לַיָּדַיִם טָהוֹר. דָּבָר אַחֵר אֵין נְטִילַת יָדַיִם לְחוּלִּין,
אֶלָּא מְקַנֵּחַ יָדָיו בַּמַּפָּה וּמַנִּיחָהּ עַל הַכֶּסֶת, שֶׁמָּא נִטְמְאוּ

מַשְׁקִין שֶׁבַּמַּפָּה מֵחֲמַת הַשֻּׁלְחָן וְיַחְזְרוּ וִיטַמְּאוּ אֶת
הָאוֹכָלִים.   בֵּית שַׁמַּאי אוֹמְרִין: מְכַבְּדִין אֶת הַבַּיִת, מִפְּנֵי
אוֹבְדָן שֶׁל אוֹכָלִים, וְאַחַר כָּךְ נוֹטְלִין לַיָּדַיִם, בֵּית הִלֵּל
אוֹמְרִין: אִם הָיָה שַׁמָּשׁ תַּלְמִיד חָכָם מְלַקֵּט פֵּרוּרִין שֶׁיֵּשׁ בָּהֶן
כַּזַּיִת. וְנוֹטְלִין לַיָּדַיִם וְאַחַר כָּךְ מְכַבְּדִין אֶת הַבַּיִת.   בֵּית
שַׁמַּאי אוֹמְרִין: אוֹחֵז כּוֹס יַיִן בִּימִינוֹ וְשֶׁמֶן עָרֵב בִּשְׂמֹאלוֹ,
מְבָרֵךְ עַל הַיַּיִן וְאַחַר כָּךְ מְבָרֵךְ עַל הַשֶּׁמֶן. וּבֵית הִלֵּל אוֹמְרִין:
אוֹחֵז שֶׁמֶן עָרֵב בִּימִינוֹ וְכוֹס יַיִן בִּשְׂמֹאלוֹ, מְבָרֵךְ עַל הַשֶּׁמֶן
וְטָחוּ בְּרֹאשׁ הַשַּׁמָּשׁ. אִם הָיָה שַׁמָּשׁ תַּלְמִיד חָכָם (מְלַקֵּט
פֵּירוּרִין) טָחוּ בַּכּוֹתֶל, לְפִי שֶׁאֵין שֶׁבַח תַּלְמִיד חָכָם שֶׁיֵּצֵא
מְבוּסָם.   אָמַר רַבִּי יְהוּדָה: לֹא נֶחְלְקוּ בֵּית שַׁמַּאי וּבֵית
הִלֵּל עַל בִּרְכַּת הַמָּזוֹן שֶׁהִיא בַתְּחִלָּה וְעַל הַבְדָּלָה שֶׁהִיא
בַסּוֹף, עַל מָה נֶחְלְקוּ? עַל הַמָּאוֹר וְעַל הַבְּשָׂמִים, שֶׁבֵּית
שַׁמַּאי אוֹמֵר: מָאוֹר וְאַחַר כָּךְ בְּשָׂמִים, וּבֵית הִלֵּל אוֹמֵר:
בְּשָׂמִים וְאַחַר כָּךְ מָאוֹר. הַנִּכְנָס לְתוֹךְ בֵּיתוֹ בְּמוֹצָאֵי שַׁבָּת,
מְבָרֵךְ עַל הַיַּיִן וְעַל הַמָּאוֹר וְעַל הַבְּשָׂמִים, וְאוֹמֵר הַבְדָּלָה.
וְאִם אֵין לוֹ אֶלָּא כּוֹס אֶחָד מַנִּיחוֹ לְאַחַר הַמָּזוֹן וּמְשַׁלְשְׁלָן
כּוּלָּן אַחֲרָיו. אוֹמֵר הַבְדָּלָה בְּמוֹצָאֵי שַׁבָּת, וּבְמוֹצָאֵי יוֹם
טוֹב, וּבְמוֹצָאֵי יוֹם הַכִּפּוּרִים, וּבְמוֹצָאֵי שַׁבָּת לְיוֹם טוֹב,
וּבְמוֹצָאֵי יוֹם טוֹב לְחוּלוֹ שֶׁל מוֹעֵד. הָרָגִיל אוֹמֵר הַבְדָּלוֹת
הַרְבֵּה, וְשֶׁאֵינוֹ רָגִיל אוֹמֵר אוֹ אַחַת אוֹ שְׁתַּיִם. בְּבֵית הַמִּדְרָשׁ
בֵּית שַׁמַּאי אוֹמֵר: אֶחָד מְבָרֵךְ לְכוּלָּן. וּבֵית הִלֵּל אוֹמֵר: כָּל
אֶחָד וְאֶחָד מְבָרֵךְ לְעַצְמוֹ.   הָיָה לוֹ נֵר טָמוּן בְּתוֹךְ חֵיקוֹ,
אוֹ בְתוֹךְ הַפָּנָס, רוֹאֶה אֶת הַשַּׁלְהֶבֶת וְאֵין מִשְׁתַּמֵּשׁ לְאוֹרָהּ,
מִשְׁתַּמֵּשׁ לְאוֹרָהּ וְאֵין רוֹאֶה אֶת הַשַּׁלְהֶבֶת, אֵין מְבָרֵךְ עַד
שֶׁיִּהְיֶה רוֹאֶה אֶת הַשַּׁלְהֶבֶת וּמִשְׁתַּמֵּשׁ לְאוֹרָהּ. עֲשָׂשִׁית אַף
עַל פִּי שֶׁלֹּא כָבְתָה מְבָרֵךְ עָלֶיהָ. נֵר שֶׁל גּוֹיִם אֵין מְבָרְכִין
עָלָיו. יִשְׂרָאֵל שֶׁהִדְלִיק מִגּוֹי, וְגוֹי שֶׁהִדְלִיק מִיִּשְׂרָאֵל, מְבָרֵךְ
עָלָיו.

The Palestinian Talmud

אֵלּוּ דְבָרִים שֶׁבֵּין בֵּית שַׁמַּאי וּבֵית הִלֵּל בַּסְּעוֹדָה. בֵּית שַׁמַּאי
אוֹמְרִים: מְבָרֵךְ עַל הַיּוֹם וְאַחַר כָּךְ מְבָרֵךְ עַל הַיַּיִן וּבֵית הִלֵּל
אוֹמְרִים: מְבָרֵךְ עַל הַיַּיִן וְאַחַר כָּךְ מְבָרֵךְ עַל הַיּוֹם:
גמ' מָה טַעֲמְהוֹן דְּבֵית שַׁמַּאי? שֶׁקְּדוּשַׁת הַיּוֹם גָּרְמָה לַיַּיִן
שֶׁיָּבוֹא וּכְבָר נִתְחַיֵּיב בִּקְדוּשַׁת הַיּוֹם עַד שֶׁלֹּא בָּא הַיַּיִן. מָה
טַעֲמְהוֹן דְּבֵית הִלֵּל? שֶׁהַיַּיִן גּוֹרֵם לִקְדוּשַׁת הַיּוֹם שֶׁתֵּאָמֵר.
דָּבָר אַחֵר הַיַּיִן תָּדִיר וּקְדוּשָׁה אֵינָהּ תְּדִירָה. אָמַר רַבִּי יוֹסֵי:
מִדִּבְרֵי שְׁנֵיהֶן יַיִן וְהַבְדָּלָה הַיַּיִן קוֹדֶם. כְּלוּם טַעֲמְהוֹן דְּבֵית
שַׁמַּאי אֶלָּא שֶׁקְּדוּשַׁת הַיּוֹם גָּרְמָה לַיַּיִן שֶׁיָּבוֹא וְכָאן הוֹאִיל
וְלֹא אַבְדָּלָה גָּרְמָה לַיַּיִן שֶׁיָּבוֹא הַיַּיִן קוֹדֶם? כְּלוּם טַעֲמְהוֹן
דְּבֵית הִלֵּל אֶלָּא שֶׁהַיַּיִן תָּדִיר וּקְדוּשָׁה אֵינָהּ תְּדִירָה וְכָאן
הוֹאִיל וְהַיַּיִן תָּדִיר וְאַבְדָּלָה אֵינָהּ תְּדִירָה הַיַּיִן קוֹדֶם? אָמַר
רַבִּי מָנָא: מִדִּבְרֵי שְׁנֵיהֶן יַיִן וְאַבְדָּלָה, אַבְדָּלָה קוֹדֶמֶת. כְּלוּם
טַעֲמְהוֹן דְּבֵית שַׁמַּאי אֶלָּא שֶׁכְּבָר נִתְחַיֵּיב בִּקְדוּשַׁת הַיּוֹם עַד
שֶׁלֹּא בָּא הַיַּיִן וְכָאן הוֹאִיל וְנִתְחַיֵּיב בְּהַבְדָּלָה עַד שֶׁלֹּא בָּא
הַיַּיִן אַבְדָּלָה קוֹדֶמֶת? כְּלוּם טַעֲמְהוֹן דְּבֵית הִלֵּל אֶלָּא שֶׁהַיַּיִן
גּוֹרֵם לִקְדוּשַׁת הַיּוֹם שֶׁתֵּאָמֵר וְכָאן הוֹאִיל וְאֵין הַיַּיִן גּוֹרֵם
לָאַבְדָּלָה שֶׁתֵּאָמֵר, אַבְדָּלָה קוֹדֶמֶת. אָמַר רַבִּי זְעֵירָא: מִדִּבְרֵי
שְׁנֵיהֶן מַבְדִּילִין בְּלֹא יַיִן וְאֵין מְקַדְּשִׁין אֶלָּא בְּיַיִן. הִיא דַעְתֵּיהּ
דְּרַבִּי זְעֵירָא דְּרַבִּי זְעֵירָא אָמַר: מַבְדִּילִין עַל הַשֵּׁכָר וְאַזְלִין
מִן אֲתַר לַאֲתַר מִשּׁוּם קְדוּשָׁה. אָמַר רַבִּי יוֹסֵי בְּרַבִּי: נְהִיגִין
תַּמָּן בְּמָקוֹם שֶׁאֵין יַיִן שְׁלִיחַ צִיבּוּר עוֹבֵר לִפְנֵי הַתֵּיבָה וְאוֹמֵר
בְּרָכָה אַחַת מֵעֵין שֶׁבַע וְחוֹתֵם בִּמְקַדֵּשׁ יִשְׂרָאֵל וְאֶת יוֹם
הַשַּׁבָּת. וְקַשְׁיָא עַל דְּבֵית שַׁמַּאי: בְּלֵילֵי שַׁבָּת הֵיךְ עֲבִידָה?
הָיָה יוֹשֵׁב וְאוֹכֵל בְּעֶרֶב שַׁבָּת וְחָשְׁכָה לֵילֵי שַׁבָּת וְאֵין שָׁם
אֶלָּא אוֹתוֹ הַכּוֹס. אַתְּ אָמַר מַנִּיחוֹ לְאַחַר הַמָּזוֹן וּמְשַׁלְשֵׁל
כּוּלָּם עָלָיו? מָה נַפְשָׁךְ? יְבָרֵךְ עַל הַיּוֹם? הַמָּזוֹן קוֹדֵם. יְבָרֵךְ
עַל הַמָּזוֹן? הַיַּיִן קוֹדֵם. יְבָרֵךְ עַל הַיַּיִן? הַיּוֹם קוֹדֵם. נִשְׁמְעִינָה

מִן הָדָא: בָּא לָהֶן יַיִן אַחַר הַמָּזוֹן וְאֵין שָׁם אֶלָּא אוֹתוֹ
הַכּוֹס — אָמַר רַבִּי בָּא עַל יְדֵי שֶׁהוּא בְּרָכָה קְטַנָּה, שֶׁמָּא
יִשְׁכַּח וְיִשְׁתֶּה. בְּרַם הָכָא מִכֵּיוָן שֶׁהוּא מְשַׁלְשֵׁל עַל יְדֵי
הַכּוֹס אֵינוֹ שׁוֹכֵחַ. כֵּיצַד יַעֲשׂוּ עַל דִּבְרֵי בֵית שַׁמַּאי? יְבָרֵךְ עַל
הַמָּזוֹן תְּחִילָּה וְאַחַר כָּךְ מְבָרֵךְ עַל הַיּוֹם, וְאַחַר כָּךְ עַל הַיַּיִן.
וְקַשְׁיָא עַל דִּבְרֵי בֵית הַלֵּל: בְּמוֹצָאֵי שַׁבָּת הֵיךְ עֲבִידָה? הָיָה
יוֹשֵׁב וְאוֹכֵל בְּשַׁבָּת וְחָשְׁכָה מוֹצָאֵי שַׁבָּת וְאֵין שָׁם אֶלָּא
אוֹתוֹ הַכּוֹס — אַתְּ אָמַר מַנִּיחוֹ לְאַחַר הַמָּזוֹן וּמְשַׁלְשֵׁל כּוּלָּן
עָלָיו? מָה נַפְשָׁךְ? יְבָרֵךְ עַל הַיַּיִן? הַמָּזוֹן קוֹדֵם. יְבָרֵךְ עַל
הַמָּזוֹן? הַנֵּר קוֹדֵם. יְבָרֵךְ עַל הַנֵּר? הַבְדָּלָה קוֹדֶמֶת. נִשְׁמְעִינָה
מִן הָדָא: אָמַר רַבִּי יְהוּדָה: לֹא נֶחְלְקוּ בֵּית שַׁמַּאי וּבֵית הַלֵּל
עַל בִּרְכַּת הַמָּזוֹן שֶׁהוּא בַּתְּחִילָּה וְלֹא עַל הַבְדָּלָה שֶׁהִיא
בַּסּוֹף. עַל מָה נֶחְלְקוּ? עַל הַנֵּר וְעַל הַבְּשָׂמִים שֶׁבֵּית שַׁמַּאי
אוֹמְרִים: בְּשָׂמִים וְאַחַר כָּךְ נֵר, וּבֵית הַלֵּל אוֹמְרִים: מָאוֹר
וְאַחַר כָּךְ בְּשָׂמִים. ר' בָּא וְרַב יְהוּדָה הֲלָכָה כְּמִי שֶׁהוּא אוֹמֵר
בְּשָׂמִים וְאַחַר כָּךְ נֵר. כֵּיצַד יַעֲשֶׂה עַל דִּבְרֵי בֵית הַלֵּל? יְבָרֵךְ
עַל הַמָּזוֹן תְּחִילָּה וְאַחַר כָּךְ יְבָרֵךְ עַל הַיַּיִן וְאַחַר כָּךְ עַל הַנֵּר.
יוֹם טוֹב שֶׁחָל לִהְיוֹת בְּמוֹצָאֵי שַׁבָּת — רַבִּי יוֹחָנָן אָמַר:
יקנ"ה יַיִן קִידּוּשׁ נֵר הַבְדָּלָה. חָנִין בַּר בָּא אָמַר בְּשֵׁם רַב: יַיִן
קִידּוּשׁ נֵר הַבְדָּלָה סוֹכָּה וּזְמַן. רַבִּי חֲנִינָא אָמַר: ינה"ק.
שְׁמוּאֵל לָא אָמַר כַּהֲדָא דְּרַבִּי חֲנִינָא דַּאֲמַר רַבִּי אָחָא בְּשֵׁם
רַבִּי יְהוֹשֻׁעַ בֶּן לֵוִי: מֶלֶךְ יוֹצֵא וְשִׁלְטוֹן נִכְנָס מַלְוִין אֶת הַמֶּלֶךְ
וְאַחַר כָּךְ מַכְנִיסִין אֶת הַשִּׁלְטוֹן. לֵוִי אָמַר: ינה"ק מִסְתַּבְרָא
דְּלֵוִי אָמַר מֵעֵין שְׁנֵיהֶם. אָמַר רַבִּי זְעֵירָא בְּעָא קוֹמֵי רַבִּי
יוֹסֵי: הֵיךְ עוֹבְדִין עוֹבָדָא? אֲמַר לֵיהּ: כְּרַב וּכְרַבִּי יוֹחָנָן. וְכֵן
נְפַק עוֹבָדָא כְּרַב וּכְרַבִּי יוֹחָנָן וְרַבִּי אַבָּהוּ כַּד הֲוָה אָזֵיל
לִדְרוֹמָה הֲוָה עָבֵיד כְּרַבִּי חֲנִינָא וְכַד הֲוָה נָחֵית לִטְבֶרְיָא הֲוָה
עָבֵיד כְּרַבִּי יוֹחָנָן דְּלָא מִפְלָג עַל בַּר נָשׁ בְּאַתְרֵיהּ. עַל דַּעְתֵּיהּ
דְּרַבִּי חֲנִינָא נִיחָא. וְקַשְׁיָא יוֹחָנָן: עַל דְּרַבִּי יוֹחָנָן אִילוּ בִּשְׁאָר
יְמוֹת הַשָּׁנָה אֵינוֹ מְבָרֵךְ עַל הַנֵּר שֶׁלֹּא יִכְבֶּה וְכָא מְבָרֵךְ עַל

הַנֵּר שֶׁלֹּא יִכְבֶּה. מָה עֲבַד לֵיהּ רַבִּי יוֹחָנָן? מִכֵּיוָן שֶׁיֵּשׁ לוֹ יַיִן אֵין נֵרוֹ כוֹבֶה. וִיבָרֵךְ עַל הַנֵּר בַּסּוֹף? שֶׁלֹּא לַעֲקוֹר זְמַן הַשַּׁבָּתוֹת הַבָּאוֹת:

הֲלָכָה ב מתני' בֵּית שַׁמַּאי אוֹמְרִים נוֹטְלִין לַיָּדַיִם וְאַחַר כָּךְ מוֹזְגִין אֶת הַכּוֹס וּבֵית הִלֵּל אוֹמְרִים מוֹזְגִין הַכּוֹס תְּחִילָּה וְאַחַר כָּךְ נוֹטְלִין לַיָּדַיִם: **גמ'** מָן טַעֲמְהוֹן דְּבֵית שַׁמַּאי? שֶׁלֹּא יִטַּמְאוּ מַשְׁקִין שֶׁבַּאֲחוֹרֵי הַכּוֹס מִיָּדָיו וְיַחְזְרוּ וִיטַמְּאוּ אֶת הַכּוֹס. מָה טַעֲמְהוֹן דְּבֵית הִלֵּל? לְעוֹלָם אֲחוֹרֵי הַכּוֹס טְמֵאִין. דָּבָר אַחֵר: אֵין נְטִילַת יָדַיִם אֶלָּא סָמוּךְ לִבְרָכָה. רַבִּי בִּיבָן בְּשֵׁם רַבִּי יוֹחָנָן: אָתְיָא דְּבֵית שַׁמַּאי כְּרַבִּי יוֹסֵי וּדְבֵית הִלֵּל כְּרַבִּי מֵאִיר דִּתְנֵינָן תַּמָּן: רַבִּי מֵאִיר אוֹמֵר לַיָּדַיִם טֻמְאוֹת וּטְהוֹרוֹת. אָמַר רַבִּי יוֹסֵי: לָא אֲמַרָן אֶלָּא לַיָּדַיִם טְהוֹרוֹת בִּלְבַד. רַבִּי יוֹסֵי בְּשֵׁם רַבִּי שַׁבְּתַי וְרַבִּי חִיָּיא בְּשֵׁם רַבִּי שִׁמְעוֹן בֶּן לָקִישׁ: לְחַלָּה וְלִנְטִילַת יָדַיִם אָדָם מְהַלֵּךְ אַרְבַּע מִילִין. רַבִּי אַבָּהוּ בְּשֵׁם רַבִּי יוֹסֵי בֵּי רַבִּי חֲנִינָא: הָדָא דַּאֲמַר: לְפָנָיו, אֲבָל לְאַחֲרָיו אֵין מַטְרִיחִין עָלָיו. שׁוֹמְרֵי גִּנּוֹת וּפַרְדֵּיסִים מָה אַתְּ עֲבַד לְהוֹן כִּלְפְנֵיהֶן כִּלְאַחֲרֵיהֶן? נִשְׁמְעִינָהּ מִן הָדָא: הָאִשָּׁה יוֹשֶׁבֶת וְקוֹצָה חַלָּתָהּ עֲרוּמָּה מִפְּנֵי שֶׁהִיא יְכוֹלָה לְכַסּוֹת אֶת עַצְמָהּ אֲבָל לֹא הָאִישׁ. וְהָדָא אִשָּׁה לֹא בְּתוֹךְ הַבַּיִת הִיא יוֹשֶׁבֶת וְאַתְּ אָמַר אֵין מַטְרִיחִין עָלֶיהָ. וְכָאן אֵין מַטְרִיחִין עָלָיו. תְּנֵי מַיִם שֶׁלִּפְנֵי הַמָּזוֹן רְשׁוּת וְשֶׁלְּאַחַר הַמָּזוֹן חוֹבָה. אֶלָּא שֶׁבָּרִאשׁוֹנִים נוֹטֵל וּמַפְסִיק, וּבַשְּׁנִיִּים נוֹטֵל וְאֵינוּ מַפְסִיק. מָה הוּא נוֹטֵל וּמַפְסִיק? רַבִּי יַעֲקֹב בַּר אָחָא אָמַר: נוֹטֵל וְשׁוֹנֶה. רַבִּי שְׁמוּאֵל בַּר יִצְחָק אָמַר בְּעִי נוֹטֵל וְשׁוֹנֶה וְאַתְּ אֲמַרְתְּ רְשׁוּת? אָמַר רַבִּי יַעֲקֹב בַּר אִידִי: עַל הָרִאשׁוֹנִים נֶאֱכָל בְּשַׂר חֲזִיר עַל הַשְּׁנִיִּים יָצְאָה אִשָּׁה מִבֵּיתָהּ וְיֵשׁ אוֹמְרִים שֶׁנֶּהֶרְגוּ עָלֶיהָ שְׁלֹשָׁה נְפָשׁוֹת. שְׁמוּאֵל סְלֵק לְגַבֵּי רַב. חֲמָא יָתֵיהּ אָכֵל בְּמַפָּה. אָמַר לֵיהּ: מַהוּ כֵן? אָמַר לִי: אִיסְתְּנֵיס אֲנִי. רַבִּי זְעֵירָא כַּד סְלֵיק לְהָכָא חֲמָא חֲמָא כָּהֲנַיָּא אָכְלִין בְּמַפָּה אֲמַר לְהוֹן: הָא אֲזִילָא הַהִיא דְּרַב וּשְׁמוּאֵל.

אֲתָא רַבִּי יוֹסֵי בַּר בַּר כָּהֲנָא בְּשֵׁם שְׁמוּאֵל: נְטִילַת יָדַיִם
לְחוּלִין. אֵין נְטִילַת יָדַיִם לִתְרוּמָה. רַבִּי יוֹסֵי אוֹמֵר: לִתְרוּמָה
וּלְחוּלִין. רַבִּי יוֹסֶה בְּשֵׁם רַבִּי חִיָּיא בַּר אַשִׁי וְרַבִּי יוֹנָה וְרַבִּי
חִיָּיא בַּר אַשִׁי בְּשֵׁם רַב: נְטִילַת יָדַיִם לִתְרוּמָה עַד הַפֶּרֶק
וּלְחוּלִין עַד קִשְׁרֵי אֶצְבְּעוֹתָיו. מֵיישָׁא בַּר בְּרֵיה דְּרַבִּי יְהוֹשֻׁעַ
בֶּן לֵוִי אָמַר: מַן דַּהֲוָה אָכֵל עִם סָבִי וְלָא מְשַׁטֵּף יְדוֹי עַד
הַפֶּרֶק לָא הֲוָה אָכֵל עִימֵּיה. רַב הוּנָא אָמַר: אֵין נְטִילַת יָדַיִם
אֶלָּא לְפַת בִּלְבַד. תַּנֵי רַבִּי הוֹשַׁעְיָא: כָּל דָּבָר שֶׁיֵּשׁ בּוֹ לִיכְלוּךְ
מַשְׁקֶה. רַבִּי זְעֵירָא אָמַר: אֲפִילוּ מְקַצֵּץ תּוּרְמוֹסִין הֲוָה נָטֵל
יְדֵיה. רַב אָמַר: נָטַל יָדָיו בַּשַּׁחֲרִית אֵין מַטְרִיחִין עָלָיו בֵּין
הָעַרְבַּיִם. רַבִּי אַבִּינָא מְפַקֵּיד לְחַמָּרֵיה: הֵן דְּאַתּוּן מַשְׁכְּחִין
מַיָּא נְסַבּוּן יְדֵיכוּן וּמִתְנֵי עַל כָּל יוֹמָא. רַבִּי זְעֵירָא סְלֵיק גַּבֵּיה
רַבִּי אַבָּהוּ לְקֵיסָרִין אַשְׁכְּחֵיה אָמַר: אֲזַל לְמֵיכוֹל, יְהַב לֵיה
עֲגוּלָה דִּיקְצֵי. אָמַר לֵיה: סַב בָּרֵיךְ. אָמַר לֵיה: בַּעַל הַבַּיִת
יוֹדֵעַ כֹּחוֹ שֶׁל כִּכָּרוֹ. מִן דַּאֲכַלוּן אָמַר לֵיה סַב בָּרֵיךְ אָמַר לֵיה
חֲכַם רַבִּי לְרַב הוּנָא אֶנָּשָׁא רַבָּה וְהוּא הֲוָה אָמַר: הַפּוֹתֵחַ
הוּא חוֹתֵם. מַתְנִיתָא פְּלִיגָא עַל רַב הוּנָא דְּתָנֵי: סֵדֶר נְטִילַת
יָדַיִם עַד חֲמִשָּׁא מַתְחִילִין מִן הַגָּדוֹל. יוֹתֵר מִיכָּן מַתְחִילִין מִן
הַקָּטוֹן בְּאֶמְצַע הַמָּזוֹן מַתְחִילִין מִן הַגָּדוֹל לְאַחַר הַמָּזוֹן
מַתְחִילִין מִן הַמְבָרֵךְ. לֹא שֶׁיַּתְקִינוּ עַצְמוֹ לַבְּרָכָה. אֵין תֵּימַר
הַפּוֹתֵחַ הוּא חוֹתֵם כְּבָר מוּתְקָן הוּא. אָמַר רַבִּי יִצְחָק: תִּפְתַּר
בְּאִילֵין דַּהֲוָה עֲלֵין קִיטְעִין קִיטְעִין וְלָא יָדְעִין מָה מְבָרְכָה:
הֲלָכָה ג מַתְנִי' בֵּית שַׁמַּאי אוֹמְרִים מְקַנֵּחַ יָדָיו בַּמַּפָּה
וּמַנִּיחָהּ עַל הַשֻּׁלְחָן וּבֵית הִלֵּל אוֹמְרִים עַל הַכֶּסֶת:
גְּמ' מַתְנִיתָא בְּשֻׁלְחָן שֶׁל שַׁיִשׁ וְשֶׁל פְּרָקִים שֶׁאֵינוּ מְקַבֵּל
טוּמְאָה. מָה טַעֲמוֹן דְּבֵית שַׁמַּאי? שֶׁלֹּא יִטַּמְאוּ מַשְׁקִין
שֶׁבַּמַּפָּה מִן הַכֶּסֶת וְיַחְזְרוּ וִיטַמְּאוּ אֶת יָדָיו. וּמָה טַעֲמוֹן
דְּבֵית הִלֵּל? לְעוֹלָם סָפֵק מַשְׁקִין לַיָּדַיִם טָהוֹר. דָּבָר אַחֵר:
אֵין יָדַיִם לְחוּלִין. וּכְבֵית שַׁמַּאי יֵשׁ יָדַיִם לְחוּלִין? תִּיפְתַּר אוֹ
כְּרַבִּי שִׁמְעוֹן בֶּן אֶלְעָזָר אוֹ כְּרַבִּי אֶלְעָזָר בֵּי רַבִּי צָדוֹק. כְּרַבִּי

שִׁמְעוֹן בֶּן אֶלְעָזָר דְּתָנֵי: רַבִּי שִׁמְעוֹן בֶּן אֶלְעָזָר אוֹמֵר מִשּׁוּם
רַבִּי מֵאִיר: הַיָּדַיִם תְּחִלָּה לְחוּלִּין וּשְׁנִיּוֹת לִתְרוּמָה. אוֹ כְּרַבִּי
אֶלְעָזָר בֵּי רַבִּי צָדוֹק דְּתָנֵינַן תַּמָּן: חוּלִּין שֶׁנַּעֲשׂוּ עַל גַּבֵּי
הַקּוֹדֶשׁ הֲרֵי אֵילוּ כְּחוּלִּין. רַבִּי אֶלְעָזָר בֵּי רַבִּי צָדוֹק אוֹמֵר:
הֲרֵי אֵילוּ כִּתְרוּמָה לְטַמֵּא שְׁנַיִם וּלְפָסוּל אֶחָד. תַּמָּן תְּנֵינַן:
הַסָּךְ שֶׁמֶן טָהוֹר נִטְמָא וְיָרַד וְטָבַל בֵּית שַׁמַּאי אוֹמְרִים אַף
עַל פִּי מְנַטֵּף טָהוֹר וּבֵית הִלֵּל אוֹמְרִים טָמֵא. וְאִם הָיָה שֶׁמֶן
טָמֵא מִתְּחִלָּתוֹ בֵּית שַׁמַּאי אוֹמְרִים כְּדֵי סִיכַת אֵבֶר קָטָן
וּבֵית הִלֵּל אוֹמְרִים מַשְׁקֶה טוֹפֵחַ. רַבִּי יְהוּדָה אוֹמֵר מִשּׁוּם
בֵּית הִלֵּל: טוֹפֵחַ וּמַטְפִּיחַ. מְחַלְּפַת שִׁיטָתְהוֹן דְּבֵית הִלֵּל.
תַּמָּן אָמְרִין טָמֵא וְהָכָא וְהָכָא אָמְרִין טָהוֹר. תַּמָּן בְּעֵינוֹ הוּא. וְהָכָא
בָּלוּעַ בַּמַּפָּה הוּא:

הלכה ד מתני' בֵּית שַׁמַּאי אוֹמְרִים: מְכַבְּדִין אֶת הַבַּיִת
וְאַחַר כָּךְ נוֹטְלִין לַיָּדַיִם. וּבֵית הִלֵּל אוֹמְרִים נוֹטְלִין לַיָּדַיִם
וְאַחַר כָּךְ מְכַבְּדִין אֶת הַבַּיִת: גמ' מָה טַעֲמְהוֹן דְּבֵית
שַׁמַּאי? מִפְּנֵי אוֹבְדַן אוֹכָלִין. וּמָה טַעֲמְהוֹן דְּבֵית הִלֵּל? אִם
הַשַּׁמָּשׁ פִּיקֵחַ הֲרֵי זֶה מַעֲבִיר פֵּרוּרִין פָּחוֹת מִכַּזַּיִת וְנוֹטְלִין
לַיָּדַיִם וְאַחַר כָּךְ מְכַבְּדִין אֶת הַבַּיִת:

הלכה ה מתני' בֵּית שַׁמַּאי אוֹמְרִים: נֵר מָזוֹן בְּשָׂמִים
וְהַבְדָּלָה. וּבֵית הִלֵּל אוֹמְרִים: נֵר וּבְשָׂמִים וּמָזוֹן וְהַבְדָּלָה.
בֵּית שַׁמַּאי אוֹמְרִים: שֶׁבָּרָא מְאוֹר הָאֵשׁ. וּבֵית הִלֵּל אוֹמְרִים:
בּוֹרֵא מְאוֹרֵי הָאֵשׁ: גמ' תָּנֵי: אָמַר רַבִּי יְהוּדָא לֹא נֶחְלְקוּ
בֵּית שַׁמַּאי וּבֵית הִלֵּל עַל הַמָּזוֹן שֶׁהוּא בַּתְּחִלָּה וְעַל הַבְדָּלָה
שֶׁהִיא בַסּוֹף. וְעַל מָה נֶחְלְקוּ? עַל הַמָּאוֹר וְעַל הַבְּשָׂמִים
שֶׁבֵּית שַׁמַּאי אוֹמְרִים בְּשָׂמִים וּמָאוֹר. וּבֵית הִלֵּל אוֹמְרִים
מָאוֹר וּבְשָׂמִים. רַבִּי בָּא וְרַב יְהוּדָא בְּשֵׁם רַב: הֲלָכָה כְּדִבְרֵי
מִי שֶׁאוֹמֵר בְּשָׂמִים וְאַחַר כָּךְ מָאוֹר. בֵּית שַׁמַּאי אוֹמְרִים:
כּוֹס בִּימִינוֹ וְשֶׁמֶן עָרֵב בִּשְׂמֹאלוֹ. אוֹמֵר עַל הַכּוֹס וְאַחַר כָּךְ
אוֹמֵר עַל שֶׁמֶן עָרֵב. בֵּית הִלֵּל אוֹמְרִים: שֶׁמֶן עָרֵב בִּימִינוֹ
וְכוֹס בִּשְׂמֹאלוֹ וְאוֹמֵר עַל שֶׁמֶן עָרֵב וְטָחוּ בְּרֹאשׁ הַשַּׁמָּשׁ.

אִם הָיָה שַׁמָּשׁ תַּלְמִיד חָכָם טָחוּ בַּכּוֹתַל. שֶׁאֵין שִׁבְחוֹ שֶׁל
תַּלְמִיד חָכָם לִהְיוֹת יוֹצֵא מְבוֹשָׁם. אַבָּא בַּר בַּר חַנָּא וְרַב
חוּנָא הֲווֹן יָתְבִין אָכְלִין וַהֲוָה רַבִּי זְעֵירָא קָאֵים וּמְשַׁמֵּשׁ
קוּמֵיהוֹן. עָלָה וְטָעֵין תַּרְוֵיהוֹן בַּחֲדָא יְדֵיהּ. אָמַר לֵיהּ אַבָּא
בַּר בַּר חַנָּא מָה יָדְךָ חוֹרִיתָא קְטַעוֹן ? וּכְעַס עִילָוֵי אַבּוּי. אָמַר
לֵיהּ לָא מִסְתָּךְ דְּאַתְּ רְבִיעַ וְהוּא קָאֵים מְשַׁמֵּשׁ. וְעוֹד דְּהוּא
כֹּהֵן וַאֲמַר שְׁמוּאֵל הַמִּשְׁתַּמֵּשׁ בַּכְּהוּנָה מָעַל. אַתְּ מֵיקֵל לֵיהּ.
גְּזֵירָה דְּהוּא רָבַע וְאַתְּ קָאֵים וּמְשַׁמֵּשׁ תַּחְתּוֹי. מִנַּיִן
הַמִּשְׁתַּמֵּשׁ בַּכְּהוּנָה מָעַל? רַבִּי אָחָא בְּשֵׁם שְׁמוּאֵל אָמַר:
וְאָמְרָה לָהֶן אַתֶּם קוֹדֶשׁ לה' וְהַכֵּלִים קוֹדֶשׁ מָה כֵּלִים
הַמִּשְׁתַּמֵּשׁ בָּהֶן מָעַל אַף הַמִּשְׁתַּמֵּשׁ בְּכֹהֲנִים מָעַל: [פִּיסְקָא
ב"שׁ אוֹמְרִים שֶׁבָּרָא וכו'.] עַל דַּעֲתְהוֹן דְּבֵית שַׁמַּאי: אֲשֶׁר
בָּרָא פְּרִי הַגֶּפֶן. עַל דַּעֲתֵיהוֹן דְּבֵית הִלֵּל: בּוֹרֵי פְּרִי הַגֶּפֶן. יַיִן
מִתְחַדֵּשׁ בְּכָל שָׁנָה וְשָׁנָה, הָאֵשׁ אֵינוֹ מִתְחַדֵּשׁ בְּכָל שָׁעָה.
הָאֵשׁ וְהַכִּלְאַיִם אַף עַל פִּי שֶׁלֹּא נִבְרְאוּ מְשֵׁשֶׁת יְמֵי בְּרֵאשִׁית
אֲבָל עָלוּ בַּמַּחֲשָׁבָה מְשֵׁשֶׁת יְמֵי בְרֵאשִׁית. הַכִּלְאַיִם וּבְנֵי
צִבְעוֹן אַיָּה וַעֲנָה הוּא עֲנָה אֲשֶׁר מָצָא אֶת הַיֵּמִים בַּמִּדְבָּר.
מָהוּ יֵמִים? רַבִּי יְהוּדָה בֶּן סִימוֹן אוֹמֵר: הֵמְיוֹנֵס וְרַבָּנָן
אָמְרִין: הֵימִים: חֶצְיוֹ סוּס וְחֶצְיוֹ חֲמוֹר. וְאֵילוּ הֵן הַסִּימָנִין:
אָמַר רַבִּי יְהוּדָה: כֹּל שֶׁאָזְנָיו קְטַנּוֹת אִמּוֹ סוּס וְאָבִיו חֲמוֹר.
גְּדוֹלוֹת אִמּוֹ חֲמוֹרָה וְאָבִיו סוּס. רַבִּי מָנָא מְפַקֵּד לְאִילֵּין
דְּנְשִׂיאָה: אֵין בָּעִיתוּן מִיזְבּוֹן מוּלְיוֹן תְּהוֹן זָבְנִין אִילֵּין
דְּאוּדְנֵיהוֹן דְּקִיקִין שֶׁאִמּוֹ סוּסָה וְאָבִיו חֲמוֹר. מֶה עָשָׂה צִבְעוֹן
וַעֲנָה זִימֵּן חֲמוֹרָה וְהֶעֱלָה עָלֶיהָ סוּס זָכָר וְיָצָא מֵהֶן פְּרְדָה.
אָמַר הַקָּדוֹשׁ בָּרוּךְ הוּא לָהֶם: אַתֶּם הֲבֵאתֶם לָעוֹלָם דָּבָר
שֶׁהוּא מַזִּיקָן. אַף אֲנִי מֵבִיא עַל אוֹתוֹ הָאִישׁ דָּבָר שֶׁהוּא
מַזִּיקוֹ. מֶה עָשָׂה הַקָּדוֹשׁ בָּרוּךְ הוּא זִימֵּן חֲכִינָה וְהֶעֱלָה
עָלֶיהָ חַרְדּוֹן וְיָצָא מִמֶּנָּה חֲבַרְבָּר. מִיָּמָיו לֹא יֹאמַר לְךָ אָדָם
שֶׁעֲקָצוֹ חֲבַרְבָּר וְחָיָה, נְשָׁכוֹ כֶּלֶב שׁוֹטֶה וְחָיָה שֶׁבְּעָטַתּוּ פְּרְדָה
וְחָיָה וּבִלְבָד פְּרְדָה לְבָנָה. הָאֵשׁ: רַבִּי לֵוִי בְּשֵׁם רַבִּי בְּזֵירָה:

שְׁלֹשִׁים וָשֵׁשׁ שָׁעוֹת שִׁימְּשָׁה אוֹתָהּ הָאוֹרָה שֶׁנִּבְרֵאת בַּיּוֹם
הָרִאשׁוֹן. שְׁתֵּים עֶשְׂרֵה בְּעֶרֶב שַׁבָּת וּשְׁתֵּים עֶשְׂרֵה בְּלֵיל
שַׁבָּת וּשְׁתֵּים עֶשְׂרֵה בְּשַׁבָּת. וְהָיָה אָדָם הָרִאשׁוֹן מַבִּיט בּוֹ
מִסּוֹף הָעוֹלָם וְעַד סוֹפוֹ כֵּיוָן שֶׁלֹּא פָּסְקָה הָאוֹרָה הִתְחִיל כָּל
הָעוֹלָם כּוּלּוֹ מְשׁוֹרֵר שֶׁנֶּאֱמַר: תַּחַת כָּל הַשָּׁמַיִם יִשְׁרֵהוּ לְמִי
שֶׁאוֹרוֹ עַל כַּנְפוֹת הָאָרֶץ. כֵּיוָן שֶׁיָּצֵאת שַׁבָּת הִתְחִיל מְשַׁמֵּשׁ
הַחוֹשֶׁךְ וּבָא וְנִתְיָרֵא אָדָם וְאָמַר אֵלּוּ הוּא שֶׁכָּתַב בּוֹ: הוּא
יְשׁוּפְךָ רֹאשׁ וְאַתָּה תְּשׁוּפֶנּוּ עָקֵב שֶׁמָּא בָּא לְנָשְׁכֵנִי וְאָמַר אַךְ
חֹשֶׁךְ יְשׁוּפֵנִי. אָמַר רַבִּי לֵוִי: בְּאוֹתוֹ שָׁעָה זִימֵּן הַקָּדוֹשׁ בָּרוּךְ
הוּא שְׁנֵי רְעָפִין וְהִקִּישָׁן זֶה לָזֶה וְיָצָא מֵהֶן הָאוֹר הָדָא הוּא
דִּכְתִיב וְלַיְלָה אוֹר בַּעֲדֵנִי וּבֵירַךְ עָלֶיהָ: בּוֹרֵא מְאוֹרֵי הָאֵשׁ.
שְׁמוּאֵל אָמַר: לְפִיכָךְ מְבָרְכִין עַל הָאֵשׁ בְּמוֹצָאֵי שַׁבָּתוֹת
שֶׁהִיא תְּחִילַת בְּרִיָּיתָה. רַב הוּנָא בְּשֵׁם רַבִּי אַבָּהוּ בְּשֵׁם רַבִּי
יוֹחָנָן: אַף בְּמוֹצָאֵי יוֹם הַכִּיפּוּרִים מְבָרֵךְ עָלֶיהָ שֶׁכְּבָר שָׁבַת
הָאוֹר כָּל אוֹתוֹ הַיּוֹם:
הלכה ו מתני׳ אֵין מְבָרְכִין עַל הַנֵּר וְעַל הַבְּשָׂמִים שֶׁל
גּוֹיִם וְעַל הַנֵּר וְעַל הַבְּשָׂמִים שֶׁל מֵתִים וְעַל הַנֵּר וְעַל
הַבְּשָׂמִים שֶׁלִּפְנֵי עֲבוֹדָה זָרָה וְאֵין מְבָרְכִין עַל הַנֵּר עַד
שֶׁיֵּאוֹתוּ לְאוֹרוֹ: גמ׳ תָּנָא רַבִּי יַעֲקֹב קוֹמֵי רַבִּי יִרְמְיָה
מְבָרְכִין עַל הַבְּשָׂמִים שֶׁל גּוֹיִם. מָהוּ פְּלִיג. קַיּוֹמוּנֶה בְּמַעֲשָׂיו
לִפְנֵי חֲנוּתוֹ. עֲשָׂשִׁית אַף עַל פִּי שֶׁלֹּא כָבַת מְבָרְכִין עָלֶיהָ. נֵר
בְּתוֹךְ חֵיקוֹ אוֹ בְּתוֹךְ פָּנָס אוֹ בְּתוֹךְ אַסְפַּקְלַרְיָא רוֹאֶה אֶת
הַשַּׁלְהֶבֶת וְאֵינוֹ מִשְׁתַּמֵּשׁ לְאוֹרָהּ מִשְׁתַּמֵּשׁ לְאוֹרָהּ וְאֵינוֹ
רוֹאֶה אֶת הַשַּׁלְהֶבֶת לְעוֹלָם אֵין מְבָרְכִין עָלֶיהָ עַד שֶׁיִּהְיֶה
רוֹאֶה אֶת הַשַּׁלְהֶבֶת וּמִשְׁתַּמֵּשׁ לְאוֹרָהּ. חֲמִשָּׁה דְבָרִים
נֶאֶמְרוּ בְּגַחֶלֶת וַחֲמִשָּׁה בְּשַׁלְהֶבֶת: גַּחֶלֶת שֶׁל הַקֹּדֶשׁ מוֹעֲלִין
בָּהּ וְהַשַּׁלְהֶבֶת לֹא נֶהֱנִין וְלֹא מוֹעֲלִין. גַּחֶלֶת שֶׁל עֲבוֹדָה זָרָה
אֲסוּרָה וְשַׁלְהֶבֶת מוּתֶּרֶת. הַמּוּדָּר הֲנָאָה מֵחֲבֵירוֹ אָסוּר
בְּגַחַלְתּוֹ וּמוּתָּר בְּשַׁלְהַבְתּוֹ. הַמּוֹצִיא אֶת הַגַּחֶלֶת לִרְשׁוּת
הָרַבִּים חַיָּיב וְהַשַּׁלְהֶבֶת פָּטוּר. מְבָרְכִין עַל הַשַּׁלְהֶבֶת וְאֵין

מְבָרְכִין עַל הַגַּחֶלֶת. רַבִּי חִיָּיא בַּר אָשֵׁי בְּשֵׁם רַב: אִם הָיוּ
גֶחָלִים לוֹחֲשׁוֹת מְבָרְכִין. רַבִּי יוֹחָנָן דְקִרְצִיוֹן בְּשֵׁם רַבִּי נָחוּם
בַּר סִימַאי: בִּלְבַד הַנְּקְטֶפֶת. תְּנֵי: גּוֹי שֶׁהִדְלִיק מִיִּשְׂרָאֵל
וְיִשְׂרָאֵל שֶׁהִדְלִיק מִגּוֹי נִיחָא. גּוֹי שֶׁהִדְלִיק מִיִּשְׂרָאֵל מֵעַתָּה
אֲפִילוּ גּוֹי מִגּוֹי. אַשְׁכַּח תְּנֵי גּוֹי מִגּוֹי אֵין מְבָרְכִין. רַבִּי אַבָּהוּ
בְּשֵׁם רַבִּי יוֹחָנָן: מָבוֹי שֶׁכּוּלּוֹ גּוֹיִם וְיִשְׂרָאֵל אֶחָד דָר בְּתוֹכוֹ
וְיָצָא מִשָׁם הָאוֹר מְבָרְכִין עָלֶיהָ בִּשְׁבִיל אוֹתוֹ יִשְׂרָאֵל שֶׁשָׁם.
רַבִּי אַבָּהוּ בְּשֵׁם רַבִּי יוֹחָנָן: אֵין מְבָרְכִין לֹא עַל הַבְּשָׂמִים שֶׁל
לֵילֵי שַׁבָּת בִּטְבֶרְיָא וְלֹא עַל הַבְּשָׂמִים שֶׁל מוֹצָאֵי שַׁבָּת
בְּצִיפּוֹרִין. וְלֹא עַל הַנֵּר וְלֹא עַל הַבְּשָׂמִים שֶׁל אוֹר עֶרֶב שַׁבָּת
בְּצִפּוֹרִין. שֶׁאֵינָן עֲשׂוּיִין אֶלָּא לְדָבָר אַחֵר. וְלֹא עַל הַנֵּר
וְהַבְּשָׂמִים שֶׁל מֵתִים. רַבִּי חִזְקִיָּה וְרַבִּי יַעֲקֹב בַּר אָחָא בְּשֵׁם
רַבִּי יוֹסֵי בֵּי רַבִּי חֲנִינָא: הָדָא דְאַתְּ אָמַר: בִּנְתוּנִים לְמַעֲלָה
מִמִּיטָתוֹ שֶׁלַּמֵּת. אֲבָל אִם הָיָה נְתוּנִים לִפְנֵי מִטָּתוֹ שֶׁלַּמֵּת
מְבָרְכִין. אֲנִי אוֹמֵר לִכְבוֹד הַחַיִּים הֵן עֲשׂוּיִן. וְלֹא עַל הַנֵּר
וְלֹא עַל הַבְּשָׂמִים שֶׁל עֲבוֹדָה זָרָה. וְלֹא הִיא שֶׁל גּוֹיִם הִיא
שֶׁל עֲבוֹדָה זָרָה. תִּיפְתַּר בַּעֲבוֹדָה זָרָה שֶׁל יִשְׂרָאֵל. אֵין
מְבָרְכִין עַל הַנֵּר עַד שֶׁיֵּאוֹתוּ לְאוֹרוֹ. דָרַשׁ רַבִּי זְעִירָא בְּרֵיהּ
דְרַבִּי אַבָּהוּ: וַיַּרְא אֱלֹהִים אֶת הָאוֹר כִּי טוֹב וְאַחַר כָּךְ וַיַּבְדֵּל
אֱלֹהִים בֵּין הָאוֹר וּבֵין הַחֹשֶׁךְ. אָמַר רַבִּי בְּרֶכְיָה: כָּךְ דָרְשׁוּ
שְׁנֵי גְדוֹלֵי עוֹלָם רַבִּי יוֹחָנָן וְרַבִּי שִׁמְעוֹן בֶּן לָקִישׁ: וַיַּבְדֵּל
אֱלֹהִים אַבְדָלָה וַדַּאי. רַבִּי יְהוּדָה בֵּי רַבִּי סִימוֹן אָמַר: הִבְדִּילוּ
לוֹ. וְרַבָּנָן אָמְרִין: הִבְדִּילוּ לַצַּדִּיקִים לֶעָתִיד לָבוֹא. מָשְׁלוּ
מָשָׁל לְמָה הַדָּבָר דוֹמֶה? לְמֶלֶךְ שֶׁהָיוּ לוֹ שְׁנֵי אִיסְטְרַטֵיגִין זֶה
אוֹמֵר: אֲנִי מְשַׁמֵּשׁ בַּיּוֹם, וְזֶה אוֹמֵר: אֲנִי מְשַׁמֵּשׁ בַּיּוֹם, קָרָא
לָרִאשׁוֹן וְאָמַר לוֹ: פְּלוֹנִי הַיּוֹם יְהֵא תְחוּמְךָ. קָרָא לַשֵׁנִי
וְאָמַר לוֹ: פְּלוֹנִי הַלַּיְלָה יְהֵא תְחוּמְךָ. הָדָא הוּא דִכְתִיב
וַיִּקְרָא אֱלֹהִים לָאוֹר יוֹם וְגו' לָאוֹר אָמַר לוֹ הַיּוֹם יְהֵא
תְחוּמְךָ וְלַחֹשֶׁךְ אָמַר לוֹ הַלַּיְלָה יְהֵא תְחוּמְךָ. אָמַר רַבִּי
יוֹחָנָן: הוּא שֶׁאָמַר הַקָּדוֹשׁ בָּרוּךְ הוּא לְאִיוֹב: הַמִיָּמֶיךָ צִוִּיתָ

בּוֹקֶר יָדַעְתָּ הַשַּׁחַר מְקוֹמוֹ — יָדַעְתָּ אֵי זֶה מְקוֹמוֹ שֶׁל אוֹר
שֵׁשֶׁת יְמֵי בְרֵאשִׁית אֵיכָן נִגְנַז? אָמַר רַבִּי תַּנְחוּמָא אֲנָא
אַמְרִית טַעְמָא: יוֹצֵר אוֹר וּבוֹרֵא חוֹשֶׁךְ עוֹשֶׂה שָׁלוֹם מְשִׁיצָא
עוֹשֶׂה שָׁלוֹם בֵּינֵיהֶן. אֵין מְבָרְכִין עַל הַנֵּר עַד שֶׁיֵּאוֹתוּ לְאוֹרוֹ
רַב אָמַר יֵאוֹתוּ וּשְׁמוּאֵל אָמַר יֵעוֹתוּ. מַאן דַּאֲמַר יֵאוֹתוּ אַךְ
בְּזֹאת נֵאוֹתָה לָכֶם. מַאן דַּאֲמַר יֵעוֹתוּ, לָדַעַת לָעוּת אֶת יָעֵף
דָּבָר. תַּמָּן תְּנִינָן: כֵּיצַד מְעַבְּרִין אֶת הֶעָרִים? רַב אָמַר:
מְאַבְּרִין. וּשְׁמוּאֵל אָמַר: מְעַבְּרִין. מַאן דַּאֲמַר מְאַבְּרִין
מוֹסִיפִין לָהּ אֵבֶר. מַאן דַּאֲמַר מְעַבְּרִין כְּאִשָּׁה עוּבָּרָה. תַּמָּן
תְּנִינָן: לִפְנֵי אִידֵיהֶן שֶׁלַּגּוֹיִם. רַב אָמַר עִידֵיהֶן וּשְׁמוּאֵל אָמַר
אֵידֵיהֶן. מַאן דַּאֲמַר אֵידֵיהֶן כִּי קָרוֹב יוֹם אֵידָם. וּמַאן דַּאֲמַר
עִידֵיהֶן וְעֵידֵיהֶם הֵמָּה בַּל יִרְאוּ וּבַל יֵדְעוּ לְמַעַן יֵבשׁוּ. מָאן
מְקַיֵּים שְׁמוּאֵל טַעְמָא דְרַב? וְעֵידֵיהֶם הֵמָּה שֶׁהֵן עֲתִידִין
לְבַיֵּישׁ אֶת עוֹבְדֵיהֶן לְיוֹם הַדִּין. אֵין מְבָרְכִין עַל הַנֵּר עַד
שֶׁיֵּאוֹתוּ לְאוֹרוֹ. רַב יְהוּדָה בְּשֵׁם שְׁמוּאֵל: כְּדֵי שֶׁיְּהוּ נָשִׁים
טָווֹת לְאוֹרוֹ. אָמַר רַבִּי יוֹחָנָן: כְּדֵי שֶׁתְּהֵא עֵינוֹ רוֹאָה מַה
בְּכוֹס וּמַה בַּקְּעָרָה. אָמַר רַב חֲנִינָא: כְּדֵי שֶׁיְּהֵא יוֹדֵעַ לְהַבְחִין
בֵּין מַטְבֵּעַ לְמַטְבֵּעַ. תְּנֵי רַבִּי אוֹשַׁעְיָא: אֲפִילוּ טְרִיקְלִין עֶשֶׂר
עַל עֶשֶׂר מְבָרְכִין. רַבִּי זְעֵירָא מְקָרֵב קַמֵּיהּ בּוּצִינָא. אָמְרִין
לֵיהּ תַּלְמִידָיו רַבִּי מָה אַתְּ מַחְמִיר עָלֵינוּ הָא תְּנֵי רַבִּי אוֹשַׁעְיָא
אֲפִילוּ טְרִיקְלִין עֶשֶׂר עַל עֶשֶׂר מְבָרְכִין:

הֲלָכָה ז מתני׳ מִי שֶׁאָכַל וְשָׁכַח וְלֹא בֵירַךְ — בֵּית שַׁמַּאי
אוֹמְרִים יַחֲזוֹר לִמְקוֹמוֹ וִיבָרֵךְ. וּבֵית הִלֵּל אוֹמְרִים יְבָרֵךְ בִּמְקוֹם
שֶׁנִּזְכַּר. וְעַד מָתַי מְבָרֵךְ עַד כְּדֵי שֶׁיִּתְעַכֵּל הַמָּזוֹן שֶׁבְּמֵעָיו:

גמ׳ רַבִּי יוֹסְטָא בַּר שׁוּנָם אָמַר: תְּרֵין אָמוֹרִין חַד אָמַר
טַעֲמוֹן דְּבֵית שַׁמַּאי וְחַד אָמַר טַעֲמוֹן דְּבֵית הִלֵּל. מַאן דַּמַר
טַעֲמוֹן דְּבֵית שַׁמַּאי אִילוּ שָׁכַח שָׁם כִּיס אֲבָנִים טוֹבוֹת
וּמַרְגָּלִיּוֹת שֶׁמָּא לֹא הָיָה חוֹזֵר וְנוֹטֵל כִּיסוֹ אַף הָכָא יַחֲזוֹר
לִמְקוֹמוֹ וִיבָרֵךְ. מַאן דַּמַר טַעֲמַהוֹן דְּבֵית הִלֵּל אִילוּ פוֹעֵל
עוֹשֶׂה בְּרֹאשׁ הַדֶּקֶל אוֹ בְּתוֹךְ הַבּוֹר שֶׁמָּא מַטְרִיחִין שֶׁיַּחֲזוֹר

לִמְקוֹמוֹ וִיבָרֵךְ אֶלָּא מְבָרֵךְ בִּמְקוֹם שֶׁנִּזְכַּר אַף הָכָא מְבָרֵךְ
בִּמְקוֹם שֶׁנִּזְכַּר. עַד מָתַי הוּא מְבָרֵךְ? רַבִּי חִיָּיא בְּשֵׁם שְׁמוּאֵל:
עַד שֶׁיִּתְעַכֵּל הַמָּזוֹן בְּמֵעָיו וַחֲכָמִים אוֹמְרִים: כָּל זְמַן שֶׁהוּא
צָמֵא מֵחֲמַת אוֹתוֹ סְעוּדָה. רַבִּי יוֹחָנָן אָמַר: עַד שֶׁיִּרְעַב:

הלכה ח מתני' בָּא לָהֶן יַיִן אַחַר הַמָּזוֹן וְאֵין שָׁם אֶלָּא
אוֹתוֹ הַכּוֹס — בֵּית שַׁמַּאי אוֹמְרִים: מְבָרֵךְ עַל הַיַּיִן וְאַחַר
כָּךְ מְבָרֵךְ עַל הַמָּזוֹן. וּבֵית הִלֵּל אוֹמְרִים: מְבָרֵךְ עַל הַמָּזוֹן
וְאַחַר כָּךְ מְבָרֵךְ עַל הַיַּיִן. עוֹנִין אָמֵן אַחַר יִשְׂרָאֵל מְבָרֵךְ וְאֵין
עוֹנִין אָמֵן אַחַר כּוּתִי מְבָרֵךְ עַד שֶׁיִּשְׁמַע כָּל הַבְּרָכָה:
גמ' אָמַר רַבִּי בָּא עַל יְדֵי שֶׁהִיא בְּרָכָה קְטַנָּה שֶׁמָּא יִשְׁכַּח
וְיִשְׁתֶּה. בְּרַם הָכָא עַל יְדֵי שֶׁהִיא מְשׁוּלְשָׁה עַל הַכּוֹס אֵינוֹ
שׁוֹכֵחַ. הָא אַחַר יִשְׂרָאֵל עוֹנִין אָמֵן אַף עַל פִּי שֶׁלֹּא שָׁמַע.
לֹא כֵן תְּנֵי: שָׁמַע וְלֹא עָנָה יָצָא עָנָה וְלֹא שָׁמַע לֹא יָצָא.
חִיָּיא בְּרֵיהּ דְּרַב אָמַר: בְּשֶׁלֹּא אָכַל עִמָּהֶן כְּזַיִת. הָכָא
מַתְנִיתָא תְּנֵי שָׁמַע וְלֹא עָנָה יָצָא עָנָה וְלֹא שָׁמַע לֹא יָצָא.
רַב בְּשֵׁם אַבָּא בַּר חַנָּה וְאִית דְּאָמְרִי לַהּ אַבָּא בַּר חַנָּה בְּשֵׁם
רַב: וְהוּא שֶׁעָנָה רָאשֵׁי פְּרָקִים. רַבִּי זְעִירָא בָּעֵי הֵי אִינּוּן
רָאשֵׁי פְּרָקִים? הַלְלוּ יָהּ הַלְלוּ עַבְדֵי ה' הַלְלוּ אֶת שֵׁם ה'.
בְּעוֹן קוֹמֵי רַבִּי חִיָּיא בַּר אַבָּא מִנַּיִן שֶׁאִם שָׁמַע וְלֹא עָנָה
יָצָא? אָמַר מִן מָה דַאֲנַן חָמֵי רַבָּנָן רַבְרְבַיָּא עָבְדִין כֵּן אִינּוּן
קַיְימִין בְּצִיבּוּרָא דְּאִילֵּין אָמְרִין דֵּין: בָּרוּךְ הַבָּא. וְאִילֵּין
אָמְרִין: בְּשֵׁם ה'. וְאִילֵּין וְאִילֵּין יוֹצְאִין יְדֵי חוֹבָתָן. תַּנֵּי רַב
אוֹשַׁעְיָא: עוֹנֶה הוּא אָדָם אָמֵן אֲפִילּוּ לֹא אָכַל וְאֵינוֹ אוֹמֵר
"נְבָרֵךְ שֶׁאָכַלְנוּ מִשֶּׁלּוֹ" אֶלָּא אִם כֵּן אָכַל. תְּנֵי: אֵין עוֹנִין
אָמֵן יְתוֹמָה וְלֹא אָמֵן קְטוּפָה וְלֹא אָמֵן חֲטוּפָה. בֶּן עַזַּאי
אוֹמֵר: הָעוֹנֶה אָמֵן יְתוֹמָה יִהְיוּ בָּנָיו יְתוֹמִים, חֲטוּפָה יִתְחַטְּפוּ
שְׁנוֹתָיו, קְטוּפָה תִּקָּטֵף נִשְׁמָתוֹ. אֲרוּכָה מַאֲרִיכִין לוֹ יָמָיו
וּשְׁנוֹתָיו בְּטוֹבָה. אֵיזוֹ הִיא אָמֵן יְתוֹמָה? אָמַר רַב הוּנָא: דֵּין
דִּיתִיב לְמִיבָרָכָה וְהוּא עָנָה וְלֹא יָדַע לְמָה הוּא עָנָה. תְּנָא:
גּוֹי שֶׁבֵּירַךְ אֶת הַשֵּׁם עוֹנֶה אַחֲרָיו אָמֵן. אָמַר רַבִּי תַּנְחוּם:

אִם בֵּירַכְךָ גּוֹי עֲנֵה אַחֲרָיו אָמֵן דִּכְתִיב: בָּרוּךְ תִּהְיֶה מִכָּל
הָעַמִּים. גּוֹי אֶחָד פָּגַע אֶת רַבִּי יִשְׁמָעֵאל וּבֵירְכוּ. אָמַר לֵיהּ:
כְּבָר מִלְּתָךְ אֲמִירָה. פָּגַע אַחֲרִינָא וְקִילְלוּ. אָמַר לֵיהּ: כְּבָר
מִילְתָךְ אֲמִירָה. אָמְרוּ לוֹ תַּלְמִידָיו: רַבִּי כְּמָה דַּאֲמַרְתְּ לְהָדֵין
אָמַרְתְּ לְהָדֵין. אָמַר לוֹן: כֵּן כְּתִיב: אוֹרְרֶיךָ אָרוּר וּמְבָרְכֶיךָ
בָּרוּךְ:

The Babylonian Talmud

תָּנוּ רַבָּנָן: דְּבָרִים שֶׁבֵּין בֵּית שַׁמַּאי וּבֵית הִלֵּל בִּסְעוֹדָה: בֵּית
שַׁמַּאי אוֹמְרִים: "מְבָרֵךְ עַל הַיּוֹם וְאַחַר כָּךְ מְבָרֵךְ עַל הַיַּיִן,
שֶׁהַיּוֹם גּוֹרֵם לַיַּיִן שֶׁיָּבֹא וּכְבָר קָדַשׁ הַיּוֹם וַעֲדַיִן יַיִן לֹא בָא."
וּבֵית הִלֵּל אוֹמְרִים: "מְבָרֵךְ עַל הַיַּיִן וְאַחַר כָּךְ מְבָרֵךְ עַל
הַיּוֹם, שֶׁהַיַּיִן גּוֹרֵם לְקַדֵּשָׁה שֶׁתֵּאָמֵר. דָּבָר אַחֵר: בִּרְכַּת הַיַּיִן
תְּדִירָה וּבִרְכַּת הַיּוֹם אֵינָהּ תְּדִירָה. תָּדִיר וְשֶׁאֵינוֹ תָּדִיר —
תָּדִיר קוֹדֶם." וַהֲלָכָה כְּדִבְרֵי בֵּית הִלֵּל.

מַאי "דָּבָר אַחֵר"? וְכִי תֵימָא: הָתָם תַּרְתֵּי וְהָכָא חֲדָא, הָכָא
נַמֵי תַּרְתֵּי נִינְהוּ: בִּרְכַּת הַיַּיִן תְּדִירָה וּבִרְכַּת הַיּוֹם אֵינָהּ
תְּדִירָה. תָּדִיר וְשֶׁאֵינוֹ תָּדִיר — תָּדִיר קָדֵם. וַהֲלָכָה כְּדִבְרֵי
בֵּית הִלֵּל. — פְּשִׁיטָא, דְּהָא נְפַקָא בַת קוֹל. אִיבָּעֵית אֵימָא:
קָדֵם בַּת קוֹל. וְאִיבָּעֵית אֵימָא: לְאַחַר בַּת קוֹל, וְרַבִּי יְהוֹשֻׁעַ
הִיא, דְּאָמַר: "אֵין מַשְׁגִּיחִין בְּבַת קוֹל."

וְסָבְרֵי בֵּית שַׁמַּאי דְּבִרְכַּת הַיּוֹם עֲדִיפָא? וְהָתַנְיָא: "הַנִּכְנָס
לְבֵיתוֹ בְּמוֹצָאֵי שַׁבָּת — מְבָרֵךְ עַל הַיַּיִן וְעַל הַמָּאוֹר וְעַל
הַבְּשָׂמִים וְאַחַר כָּךְ אוֹמֵר הַבְדָּלָה וְאִם אֵין לוֹ אֶלָּא כּוֹס
אֶחָד — מַנִּיחוֹ לְאַחַר הַמָּזוֹן וּמְשַׁלְשְׁלָן כֻּלָּן לְאַחֲרָיו." וְהָא
מִמַּאי דְּבֵית שַׁמַּאי הִיא, דִּלְמָא בֵּית הִלֵּל הִיא! לָא סָלְקָא
דַּעְתָּךְ, דְּקָתָנֵי מָאוֹר וְאַחַר כָּךְ בְּשָׂמִים, וּמַאן שְׁמַעַתְּ לֵיהּ
דְּאִית לֵיהּ הַאי סְבָרָא? בֵּית שַׁמַּאי; דְּתַנְיָא, אָמַר רַבִּי יְהוּדָה:
לֹא נֶחְלְקוּ בֵּית שַׁמַּאי וּבֵית הִלֵּל עַל הַמָּזוֹן שֶׁבַּתְּחִלָּה וְעַל

הַבְדָּלָה שֶׁהִיא בַסּוֹף, עַל מָה נֶחְלְקוּ? עַל הַמָּאוֹר וְעַל
הַבְּשָׂמִים — בֵּית שַׁמַּאי אוֹמְרִים: מָאוֹר וְאַחַר כָּךְ בְּשָׂמִים,
וּבֵית הִלֵּל אוֹמְרִים: בְּשָׂמִים וְאַחַר כַּךְ מָאוֹר. וּמַמַּאי דְּבֵית
שַׁמַּאי הִיא וְאַלִּיבָּא דְּרַבִּי יְהוּדָה, דִּילְמָא בֵּית הִלֵּל הִיא
וְאַלִּיבָּא דְּרַבִּי מֵאִיר! לָא סָלְקָא דַּעְתָּךְ, דְּקָתָנֵי הָכָא
בְּמַתְנִיתִין, בֵּית שַׁמַּאי אוֹמְרִים: נֵר וּמָזוֹן בְּשָׂמִים וְהַבְדָּלָה,
וּבֵית הִלֵּל אוֹמְרִים: נֵר וּבְשָׂמִים מָזוֹן וְהַבְדָּלָה; וְהָתָם
בַּבְּרַיְיתָא קָתָנֵי: אִם אֵין לוֹ אֶלָּא כּוֹס אֶחָד — מַנִּיחוֹ לְאַחַר
הַמָּזוֹן וּמְשַׁלְשְׁלָן כֻּלָּן לְאַחֲרָיו, שְׁמַע מִינָּה דְּבֵית שַׁמַּאי הִיא
וְאַלִּיבָּא דְּרַבִּי יְהוּדָה. וּמִכָּל מָקוֹם קַשְׁיָא! קָא סָבְרִי בֵּית
שַׁמַּאי: שָׁאנֵי עַיּוּלֵי יוֹמָא מֵאַפּוּקֵי יוֹמָא, עַיּוּלֵי יוֹמָא — כְּמָה
דִּמְקַדְּמִינַן לֵיהּ עֲדִיף, אַפּוּקֵי יוֹמָא — כְּמָה דִּמְאַחֲרִינַן לֵיהּ
עֲדִיף, כִּי הֵיכִי דְּלָא לֶהֱוֵי עֲלָן כְּמַשּׂוֹי. וְסָבְרִי בֵּית שַׁמַּאי
בִּרְכַּת הַמָּזוֹן טְעוּנָה כּוֹס? וְהָא תְּנַן: בָּא לָהֶם יַיִן לְאַחַר
הַמָּזוֹן, אִם אֵין שָׁם אֶלָּא אוֹתוֹ כּוֹס — בֵּית שַׁמַּאי אוֹמְרִים:
מְבָרֵךְ עַל הַיַּיִן וְאַחַר כָּךְ מְבָרֵךְ עַל הַמָּזוֹן; מַאי לַאו דִּמְבָרֵךְ
עִילָּוֵיהּ וְשָׁתֵי לֵיהּ! לָא, דִּמְבָרֵךְ עִילָּוֵיהּ וּמַנַּח לֵיהּ. וְהָאָמַר
מָר: הַמְבָרֵךְ צָרִיךְ שֶׁיִּטְעַם! דְּטָעֵים לֵיהּ. וְהָאָמַר מָר:
טְעָמוֹ — פְּגָמוֹ! דְּטָעֵים לֵיהּ בִּידֵיהּ. וְהָאָמַר מָר: כּוֹס שֶׁל
בְּרָכָה צָרִיךְ שִׁעוּר, וְהָא קָא פָּחֵית לֵיהּ מִשִּׁיעוּרֵיהּ! דְּנָפִישׁ
לֵיהּ טְפֵי מִשִּׁיעוּרֵיהּ. וְהָא "אִם אֵין שָׁם אֶלָּא אוֹתוֹ כּוֹס"
קָתָנֵי! תְּרֵי לָא הֲוֵי וּמֵחַד נָפִישׁ. וְהָא תָּנֵי רַבִּי חִיָּא, בֵּית
שַׁמַּאי אוֹמְרִים: מְבָרֵךְ עַל הַיַּיִן וְשׁוֹתֵהוּ וְאַחַר כָּךְ מְבָרֵךְ
בִּרְכַּת הַמָּזוֹן! אֶלָּא, תְּרֵי תַנָּאֵי וְאַלִּיבָּא דְּבֵית שַׁמַּאי.

"בֵּית שַׁמַּאי אוֹמְרִים" וְכוּלֵּי. תָּנוּ רַבָּנָן, בֵּית שַׁמַּאי אוֹמְרִים:
נוֹטְלִין לַיָּדַיִם וְאַחַר כָּךְ מוֹזְגִין אֶת הַכּוֹס, שֶׁאִם אַתָּה אוֹמֵר
"מוֹזְגִין אֶת הַכּוֹס תְּחִלָּה", גְּזֵרָה שֶׁמָּא יִטָּמְאוּ מַשְׁקִין
שֶׁאֲחוֹרֵי הַכּוֹס מֵחֲמַת יָדָיו, וְיַחְזְרוּ וִיטַמְּאוּ אֶת הַכּוֹס. וְלִיטַמּוּ
יָדַיִם לַכּוֹס! יָדַיִם שְׁנִיּוֹת הֵן, וְאֵין שֵׁנִי עוֹשֶׂה שְׁלִישִׁי בְּחֻלִּין
אֶלָּא עַל יְדֵי מַשְׁקִין. וּבֵית הִלֵּל אוֹמְרִים: מוֹזְגִין אֶת הַכּוֹס

וְאַחַר כָּךְ נוֹטְלִין לַיָּדַיִם, שֶׁאִם אַתָּה אוֹמֵר "נוֹטְלִין לַיָּדַיִם
תְּחִלָּה", גְּזֵרָה שֶׁמָּא יִטָּמְאוּ מַשְׁקִין שֶׁבַּיָּדַיִם מֵחֲמַת הַכּוֹס,
וְיַחְזְרוּ וִיטַמְּאוּ אֶת הַיָּדַיִם. וְנִיטַמֵּי כּוֹס לַיָּדַיִם! אֵין כְּלִי
מְטַמֵּא אָדָם. וְנִיטַמֵּי לַמַּשְׁקִין שֶׁבְּתוֹכוֹ! הָכָא — בִּכְלִי
שֶׁנִּטְמְאוּ אֲחוֹרָיו בְּמַשְׁקִין עָסְקִינַן, דְּתוֹכוֹ טָהוֹר וְגַבּוֹ טָמֵא;
דִּתְנַן: כְּלִי שֶׁנִּטְמְאוּ אֲחוֹרָיו בְּמַשְׁקִין — אֲחוֹרָיו טְמֵאִים,
תּוֹכוֹ וְאׇגְנוֹ וְאׇזְנוֹ וְיָדָיו טְהוֹרִין, נִטְמָא תוֹכוֹ — נִטְמָא כֻלּוֹ.
בְּמַאי קָא מִיפַּלְּגִי? בֵּית שַׁמַּאי סָבְרִי: אָסוּר לְהִשְׁתַּמֵּשׁ בִּכְלִי
שֶׁנִּטְמְאוּ אֲחוֹרָיו בְּמַשְׁקִין, גְּזֵרָה מִשׁוּם נִיצוֹצוֹת, וְלֵיכָּא
לְמִגְזַר שֶׁמָּא יִטָּמְאוּ הַמַּשְׁקִין שֶׁבַּיָּדַיִם בַּכּוֹס, וּבֵית הִלֵּל
סָבְרִי: מֻתָּר לְהִשְׁתַּמֵּשׁ בִּכְלִי שֶׁנִּטְמְאוּ אֲחוֹרָיו בְּמַשְׁקִין,
אָמְרִי: נִיצוֹצוֹת לָא שְׁכִיחִי, וְאִיכָּא לְמֵיחַשׁ שֶׁמָּא יִטָּמְאוּ
מַשְׁקִין שֶׁבַּיָּדַיִם מֵחֲמַת הַכּוֹס.

דָּבָר אַחֵר: תֵּכֶף לִנְטִילַת יָדַיִם סְעֻדָּה. מַאי "דָּבָר אַחֵר"? הָכִי
קָאָמְרִי לְהוּ בֵּית הִלֵּל לְבֵית שַׁמַּאי: לְדִידְכוּ דְּאָמְרִיתוּ "אָסוּר
לְהִשְׁתַּמֵּשׁ בִּכְלִי שֶׁאֲחוֹרָיו טְמֵאִין" דְּגָזְרִינַן מִשׁוּם נִיצוֹצוֹת,
אֲפִלּוּ הָכִי הָא עֲדִיפָא, דְּתֵכֶף לִנְטִילַת יָדַיִם סְעֻדָּה.

"בֵּית שַׁמַּאי אוֹמְרִים: מְקַנֵּחַ" וְכוּלֵי. תָּנוּ רַבָּנַן, בֵּית שַׁמַּאי
אוֹמְרִים: מְקַנֵּחַ יָדָיו בַּמַּפָּה וּמַנִּיחָהּ עַל הַשֻּׁלְחָן, שֶׁאִם אַתָּה
אוֹמֵר "עַל הַכֶּסֶת", גְּזֵרָה שֶׁמָּא יִטָּמְאוּ מַשְׁקִין שֶׁבַּמַּפָּה
מֵחֲמַת הַכֶּסֶת, וְיַחְזְרוּ וִיטַמְּאוּ אֶת הַיָּדַיִם. וּנְטַמְּיֵהּ כֶּסֶת
לַמַּפָּה! אֵין כְּלִי מְטַמֵּא כְּלִי. וּנְטַמְּיֵהּ כֶּסֶת לְגַבְרָא גּוּפֵיהּ!
אֵין כְּלִי מְטַמֵּא אָדָם. וּבֵית הִלֵּל אוֹמְרִים: עַל הַכֶּסֶת, שֶׁאִם
אַתָּה אוֹמֵר "עַל הַשֻּׁלְחָן", גְּזֵרָה שֶׁמָּא יִטָּמְאוּ מַשְׁקִים
שֶׁבַּמַּפָּה מֵחֲמַת הַשֻּׁלְחָן, וְיַחְזְרוּ וִיטַמְּאוּ אֶת הָאֳכָלִין. וּלְטַמֵּא
שֻׁלְחָן לָאֳכָלִין שֶׁבְּתוֹכוֹ! הָכָא בְּשֻׁלְחָן שֵׁנִי עָסְקִינַן, וְאֵין שֵׁנִי
עוֹשֶׂה שְׁלִישִׁי בְּחֻלִּין אֶלָּא עַל יְדֵי מַשְׁקִין. בְּמַאי קָמִיפַּלְגִי?
בֵּית שַׁמַּאי סָבְרִי: אָסוּר לְהִשְׁתַּמֵּשׁ בְּשֻׁלְחָן שֵׁנִי, גְּזֵרָה מִשׁוּם
אוֹכְלֵי תְרוּמָה; וּבֵית הִלֵּל סָבְרִי: מֻתָּר לְהִשְׁתַּמֵּשׁ בְּשֻׁלְחָן
שֵׁנִי, אוֹכְלֵי תְרוּמָה זְרִיזִין הֵם.

דָּבָר אַחֵר: אֵין נְטִילַת יָדַיִם לְחֻלִּין מִן הַתּוֹרָה. מַאי "דָּבָר

אַחֵר"? הָכֵי קָאָמְרִי לְהוּ בֵּית הִלֵּל לְבֵית שַׁמַּאי: וְכִי תֵימְרוּ,
מַאי שְׁנָא גַּבֵּי אֲכָלִין דְּחָיְישִׁינַן, וּמַאי שְׁנָא גַּבֵּי יָדַיִם דְּלָא
חָיְישִׁינַן? אֲפִלּוּ הָכֵי הָא עֲדִיפָא, דְּאֵין נְטִילַת יָדַיִם לְחֻלִּין מִן
הַתּוֹרָה, מוּטָב שֶׁיִּטָּמְאוּ יָדַיִם דְּלֵית לְהוּ עִקָּר מִדְּאוֹרָיְיתָא,
וְאַל יִטָּמְאוּ אֲכָלִים דְּאִית לְהוּ עִקָּר מִדְּאוֹרָיְיתָא.

"בֵּית שַׁמַּאי אוֹמְרִים: מְכַבְּדִין" וְכוּלֵּי. תָּנוּ רַבָּנָן, בֵּית שַׁמַּאי
אוֹמְרִים: מְכַבְּדִין אֶת הַבַּיִת וְאַחַר כָּךְ נוֹטְלִין לַיָּדַיִם, שֶׁאִם
אַתָּה אוֹמֵר "נוֹטְלִין לַיָּדַיִם תְּחִלָּה", נִמְצָא אַתָּה מַפְסִיד אֶת
הָאֳכָלִין. אֲבָל נְטִילַת יָדַיִם לְבֵית שַׁמַּאי תְּחִלָּה — לָא
סְבִירָא לְהוּ, מַאי טַעֲמָא? מִשּׁוּם פֵּרוּרִין. וּבֵית הִלֵּל אוֹמְרִים:
אִם שַׁמָּשׁ תַּלְמִיד חָכָם הוּא, נוֹטֵל פֵּרוּרִין שֶׁיֵּשׁ בָּהֶן כַּזַּיִת
וּמַנִּיחַ פֵּרוּרִין שֶׁאֵין בָּהֶן כַּזַּיִת. — מְסַיַּיע לֵיהּ לְרַבִּי יוֹחָנָן,
דְּאָמַר רַבִּי יוֹחָנָן: פֵּרוּרִין שֶׁאֵין בָּהֶם כַּזַּיִת — מֻתָּר לְאַבְּדָן
בַּיָּד. — בְּמַאי קָמִיפַלְּגֵי? בֵּית הִלֵּל סָבְרֵי: אָסוּר לְהִשְׁתַּמֵּשׁ
בְּשַׁמָּשׁ עַם הָאָרֶץ, וּבֵית שַׁמַּאי סָבְרֵי: מֻתָּר לְהִשְׁתַּמֵּשׁ
בְּשַׁמָּשׁ עַם הָאָרֶץ.

אָמַר רַבִּי יוֹסֵי בַּר חֲנִינָא אָמַר רַב הוּנָא: בְּכוּלֵּיהּ פִּרְקִין
הֲלָכָה כְּבֵית הִלֵּל, בַּר מֵהָא דַּהֲלָכָה כְּבֵית שַׁמַּאי; וְרַבִּי
אוֹשַׁעְיָא מַתְנֵי אִיפְּכָא, וּבְהָא נַמֵּי הֲלָכָה כְּבֵית הִלֵּל.

"בֵּית שַׁמַּאי אוֹמְרִים: נֵר וּמָזוֹן" וְכוּלֵּי. רַב הוּנָא בַּר יְהוּדָה
אִיקְּלַע לְבֵי רָבָא, חַזְיֵיהּ לְרָבָא דִּבְרִיךְ אַבְּשָׂמִים בְּרֵישָׁא,
אָמַר לֵיהּ: מִכְּדִי בֵּית שַׁמַּאי וּבֵית הִלֵּל אַמָּאוֹר לָא פְּלִיגֵי,
דְּתַנְיָא, בֵּית שַׁמַּאי אוֹמְרִים: נֵר וּמָזוֹן בְּשָׂמִים וְהַבְדָּלָה,
וּבֵית הִלֵּל אוֹמְרִים: נֵר וּבְשָׂמִים מָזוֹן וְהַבְדָּלָה! עֲנֵי רָבָא
בָּתְרֵיהּ: זוֹ דִּבְרֵי רַבִּי מֵאִיר, אֲבָל רַבִּי יְהוּדָה אוֹמֵר: לֹא
נֶחְלְקוּ בֵּית שַׁמַּאי וּבֵית הִלֵּל עַל הַמָּזוֹן שֶׁהוּא בַּתְּחִלָּה וְעַל
הַבְדָּלָה שֶׁהִיא בַּסּוֹף, עַל מָה נֶחְלְקוּ? עַל הַמָּאוֹר וְעַל
הַבְּשָׂמִים, שֶׁבֵּית שַׁמַּאי אוֹמְרִים: עַל הַמָּאוֹר וְאַחַר כָּךְ
בְּשָׂמִים, וּבֵית הִלֵּל אוֹמְרִים: בְּשָׂמִים וְאַחַר כָּךְ מָאוֹר; וְאָמַר
רַבִּי יוֹחָנָן: נָהֲגוּ הָעָם כְּבֵית הִלֵּל אַלִּיבָּא דְּרַבִּי יְהוּדָה.

"בֵּית שַׁמַּאי אוֹמְרִים: שֶׁבָּרָא" וְכוּלֵּי. אָמַר רָבָא: בְּ"בָרָא"

כּוּלֵּי עָלְמָא לָא פְּלִיגִי דְּבָרָא מַשְׁמַע, כִּי פְּלִיגִי — בְּ"בוֹרֵא",
בֵּית שַׁמַּאי סָבְרִי: "בּוֹרֵא" — דַּעֲתִיד לְמִבְרָא, וּבֵית הִלֵּל
סָבְרִי: "בּוֹרֵא" נַמֵּי דְּבָרָא מַשְׁמַע.

מְתִיב רַב יוֹסֵף: "יוֹצֵר אוֹר וּבוֹרֵא חֹשֶׁךְ", "יוֹצֵר הָרִים וּבֹרֵא
רוּחַ", "בּוֹרֵא הַשָּׁמַיִם וְנוֹטֵיהֶם"! אֶלָּא אָמַר רַב יוֹסֵף: בְּ"בָּרָא"
וּ"בוֹרֵא" כּוּלֵּי עָלְמָא לָא פְּלִיגִי דְּבָרָא מַשְׁמַע, כִּי פְּלִיגִי —
בְּ"מָאוֹר" וּ"מְאוֹרֵי", דְּבֵית שַׁמַּאי סָבְרִי: חֲדָא נְהוֹרָא אִיכָּא
בְּנוּרָא, וּבֵית הִלֵּל סָבְרִי: טוּבָא נְהוֹרֵי אִיכָּא בְּנוּרָא. תַּנְיָא
נַמֵּי הָכֵי, אָמְרוּ לָהֶם בֵּית הִלֵּל לְבֵית שַׁמַּאי: הַרְבֵּה מְאוֹרוֹת
יֵשׁ בָּאוּר.

"אֵין מְבָרְכִין" כּוּלֵּי. בִּשְׁלָמָא נֵר — מִשּׁוּם דְּלָא שָׁבַת, אֶלָּא
בְּשָׂמִים מַאי טַעֲמָא לָא? אָמַר רַב יְהוּדָה אָמַר רַב: הָכָא
בִּמְסִבַּת עוֹבְדֵי כּוֹכָבִים עָסְקִינַן, מִפְּנֵי שֶׁסְּתָם מְסִבַּת עוֹבְדֵי
כּוֹכָבִים לַעֲבוֹדָה זָרָה הִיא. הָא מִדְּקָתָנֵי סֵיפָא: אֵין מְבָרְכִין
לֹא עַל הַנֵּר וְלֹא עַל הַבְּשָׂמִים שֶׁל עֲבוֹדָה זָרָה, מִכְּלָל
דְּרֵישָׁא לָאו בַּעֲבוֹדָה זָרָה עָסְקִינַן! אָמַר רַב חֲנִינָא מְסוּרָא:
"מַה טַעַם" קָאָמַר, מַה טַעַם אֵין מְבָרְכִין לֹא עַל הַנֵּר וְלֹא עַל
הַבְּשָׂמִים שֶׁל עוֹבְדֵי כּוֹכָבִים וּמַזָּלוֹת? מִפְּנֵי שֶׁסְּתָם מְסִבַּת
עוֹבְדֵי כּוֹכָבִים לַעֲבוֹדָה זָרָה.

תָּנוּ רַבָּנָן: אוֹר שֶׁשָּׁבַת — מְבָרְכִין עָלָיו, וְשֶׁלֹּא שָׁבַת —
אֵין מְבָרְכִין עָלָיו. (מַאי שָׁבַת) וּמַאי לֹא שָׁבַת? אִי נֵימָא, לֹא
שָׁבַת מֵחֲמַת מְלָאכָה אֲפִלּוּ מִמְּלָאכָה דְּהֶיתֵּרָא, וְהָתַנְיָא:
אוֹר שֶׁל חַיָה וְשֶׁל חוֹלֶה — מְבָרְכִין עָלָיו! אָמַר רַב נַחְמָן
בַּר יִצְחָק: מַאי שָׁבַת? שֶׁשָּׁבַת מֵחֲמַת מְלֶאכֶת עֲבֵרָה. תַּנְיָא
נַמֵּי הָכֵי: עֲשָׂשִׁית שֶׁהָיְתָה דּוֹלֶקֶת וְהוֹלֶכֶת כָּל הַיּוֹם כֻּלּוֹ —
לְמוֹצָאֵי שַׁבָּת מְבָרְכִין עָלֶיהָ.

תָּנוּ רַבָּנָן: נָכְרִי שֶׁהִדְלִיק מִיִּשְׂרָאֵל וְיִשְׂרָאֵל שֶׁהִדְלִיק
מִנָּכְרִי — מְבָרְכִין עָלָיו, נָכְרִי מִנָּכְרִי — אֵין מְבָרְכִין עָלָיו.
מַאי שְׁנָא נָכְרִי מִנָּכְרִי דְּלָא — מִשּׁוּם דְּלָא שָׁבַת, אִי הָכֵי,
יִשְׂרָאֵל מִנָּכְרִי נַמֵּי הָא לָא שָׁבַת! וְכִי תֵּימָא, הָךְ אִיסּוּרָא

אֲזַל לֵיהּ וְהָא אַחֲרִינָא הוּא וּבִידָא דְיִשְׂרָאֵל קָא מִתְיַלְדָא,
אֶלָּא הָא דְתַנְיָא: הַמּוֹצִיא שַׁלְהֶבֶת לִרְשׁוּת הָרַבִּים — חַיָּב,
אַמַּאי חַיָּב? מַה שֶּׁעָקַר לֹא הִנִּיחַ וּמַה שֶּׁהִנִּיחַ לֹא עָקַר!
אֶלָּא, לְעוֹלָם דְּאִיסוּרָא נַמֵּי אִיתֵיהּ, וְכִי קָא מְבָרֵךְ —
אַתּוֹסֶפְתָּא דְהֶהֵיתָרָא קָא מְבָרֵךְ. אִי הָכִי, נָכְרִי מִנָּכְרִי נַמֵּי!
אִין הָכִי נַמֵּי, גְּזֵרָה מִשּׁוּם נָכְרִי רִאשׁוֹן וְעַמּוּד רִאשׁוֹן.
תָּנוּ רַבָּנָן: הָיָה מְהַלֵּךְ חוּץ לַכָּרָךְ וְרָאָה אוֹר, אִם רֹב
נָכְרִים — אֵינוֹ מְבָרֵךְ, אִם רֹב יִשְׂרָאֵל — מְבָרֵךְ. הָא גּוּפָא
קַשְׁיָא! אָמְרַתְּ: אִם רֹב נָכְרִים — אֵינוֹ מְבָרֵךְ, הָא מֶחֱצָה
עַל מֶחֱצָה — מְבָרֵךְ, וַהֲדַר תָּנֵי: אִם רֹב יִשְׂרָאֵל — מְבָרֵךְ,
הָא מֶחֱצָה עַל מֶחֱצָה — אֵינוֹ מְבָרֵךְ! בְּדִין הוּא דַּאֲפִלּוּ
מֶחֱצָה עַל מֶחֱצָה נַמֵּי מְבָרֵךְ, וְאַיְידֵי (דְּתָנָא) רֵישָׁא "רֹב
נָכְרִים", תָּנָא סֵיפָא "רֹב יִשְׂרָאֵל".
תָּנוּ רַבָּנָן: הָיָה מְהַלֵּךְ חוּץ לַכָּרָךְ וְרָאָה תִינוֹק וַאֲבוּקָה בְּיָדוֹ,
בּוֹדֵק אַחֲרָיו, אִם יִשְׂרָאֵל הוּא — מְבָרֵךְ, אִם נָכְרִי הוּא —
אֵינוֹ מְבָרֵךְ. מַאי אִירְיָא תִינוֹק, אֲפִלּוּ גָּדוֹל נַמֵּי! אָמַר רַב
יְהוּדָה אָמַר רַב: הָכָא בְּסָמוּךְ לִשְׁקִיעַת הַחַמָּה עָסְקִינָן,
גָּדוֹל — מוּכְחָא מִילְּתָא דְּוַדַּאי נָכְרִי הוּא, תִּינוֹק — אֵימַר
יִשְׂרָאֵל הוּא אִקְרִי וְנָקִיט.
תָּנוּ רַבָּנָן: הָיָה מְהַלֵּךְ חוּץ לַכָּרָךְ וְרָאָה אוֹר, אִם עָבֶה כְּפִי
הַכִּבְשָׁן — מְבָרֵךְ עָלָיו, וְאִם לָאו — אֵינוֹ מְבָרֵךְ עָלָיו. תָּנֵי
חֲדָא: אוֹר שֶׁל כִּבְשָׁן — מְבָרְכִין עָלָיו, וְתַנְיָא אִידָךְ: אֵין
מְבָרְכִין עָלָיו! לָא קַשְׁיָא: הָא בַּתְּחִלָּה, הָא לְבַסּוֹף. תָּנֵי
חֲדָא: אוֹר שֶׁל תַּנּוּר וְשֶׁל כִּירַיִם — מְבָרְכִין עָלָיו, וְתַנְיָא
אִידָךְ: אֵין מְבָרְכִין עָלָיו! לָא קַשְׁיָא: הָא בַּתְּחִלָּה, הָא
לְבַסּוֹף. תָּנֵי חֲדָא: אוֹר שֶׁל בֵּית הַכְּנֶסֶת וְשֶׁל בֵּית
הַמִּדְרָשׁ — מְבָרְכִין עָלָיו, וְתַנְיָא אִידָךְ: אֵין מְבָרְכִין עָלָיו!
לָא קַשְׁיָא: הָא דְּאִיכָּא אָדָם חָשׁוּב, הָא דְּלֵיכָּא אָדָם חָשׁוּב.
וְאִי בָעֵית אֵימָא: הָא וְהָא דְּאִיכָּא אָדָם חָשׁוּב, וְלָא קַשְׁיָא:
הָא דְּאִיכָּא חַזָּנָא, הָא דְּלֵיכָּא חַזָּנָא. וְאִי בָעֵית אֵימָא: הָא

וְהָא דְּאִיכָּא חַזָּנָא, וְלָא קַשְׁיָא: הָא דְּאִיכָּא סַהֲרָא, וְהָא דְּלֵיכָּא סַהֲרָא.

תְּנוּ רַבָּנָן: הָיוּ יוֹשְׁבִין בְּבֵית הַמִּדְרָשׁ וְהֵבִיאוּ אוֹר לִפְנֵיהֶם, בֵּית שַׁמַּאי אוֹמְרִים: כָּל אֶחָד וְאֶחָד מְבָרֵךְ לְעַצְמוֹ, וּבֵית הִלֵּל אוֹמְרִים: אֶחָד מְבָרֵךְ לְכֻלָּן, מִשּׁוּם שֶׁנֶּאֱמַר: "בְּרָב־עָם הַדְרַת־מֶלֶךְ". בִּשְׁלָמָא בֵּית הִלֵּל מְפָרְשֵׁי טַעֲמָא, אֶלָּא בֵּית שַׁמַּאי מַאי טַעֲמָא? קָסָבְרֵי: מִפְּנֵי בִּטּוּל בֵּית הַמִּדְרָשׁ. תַּנְיָא נַמִּי הָכֵי: שֶׁל בֵּית רַבָּן גַּמְלִיאֵל לֹא הָיוּ אוֹמְרִים "מַרְפֵּא" בְּבֵית הַמִּדְרָשׁ, מִפְּנֵי בִּטּוּל בֵּית הַמִּדְרָשׁ.

"אֵין מְבָרְכִין לֹא עַל הַנֵּר וְלֹא עַל הַבְּשָׂמִים שֶׁל מֵתִים". מַאי טַעֲמָא? נֵר — לִכְבוֹד הוּא דַּעֲבִידָא, בְּשָׂמִים — לְעַבּוּרֵי רֵיחָא הוּא דַּעֲבִידִי.

אָמַר רַב יְהוּדָה אָמַר רַב: כָּל שֶׁמּוֹצִיאָין לְפָנָיו בַּיּוֹם וּבַלַּיְלָה — אֵין מְבָרְכִין עָלָיו, וְכֹל שֶׁאֵין מוֹצִיאָין לְפָנָיו אֶלָּא בַּלַּיְלָה — מְבָרְכִין עָלָיו.

אָמַר רַב הוּנָא: בְּשָׂמִים שֶׁל בֵּית הַכִּסֵּא, וְשֶׁמֶן הֶעָשׂוּי לְהַעֲבִיר אֶת הַזֻּהֲמָא — אֵין מְבָרְכִין עָלָיו.

לְמֵימְרָא, דְּכָל הֵיכָא דְּלָאו לְרֵיחָא עֲבִידָא — לָא מְבָרְכִין עֲלֵוִיהּ, מוֹתִיבִי: הַנִּכְנָס לַחֲנוּתוֹ שֶׁל בַּשָּׂם וְהֵרִיחַ רֵיחַ, אֲפִלּוּ יָשַׁב שָׁם כָּל הַיּוֹם כֻּלּוֹ — אֵינוּ מְבָרֵךְ אֶלָּא פַּעַם אֶחָד, נִכְנַס וְיָצָא נִכְנַס וְיָצָא — מְבָרֵךְ עַל כָּל פַּעַם וָפַעַם, וְהָא הָכָא דְּלָאו לְרֵיחָא הוּא דַּעֲבִידָא וְקָמְבָרֵךְ! אִין, לְרֵיחָא נַמִּי הוּא דַּעֲבִידָא, כִּי הֵיכֵי דְּנוֹרְחוּ אֵינָשֵׁי וְנֵיתוּ וְנִזְבּוּן מִינֵּיהּ.

תְּנוּ רַבָּנָן: הָיָה מְהַלֵּךְ חוּץ לַכְּרַךְ וְהֵרִיחַ רֵיחַ, אִם רֹב עוֹבְדֵי כּוֹכָבִים — אֵינוּ מְבָרֵךְ, אִם רֹב יִשְׂרָאֵל — מְבָרֵךְ; רַבִּי יוֹסֵי אוֹמֵר: אֲפִלּוּ רֹב יִשְׂרָאֵל נַמִּי אֵינוּ מְבָרֵךְ, מִפְּנֵי שֶׁבְּנוֹת יִשְׂרָאֵל מְקַטְּרוֹת לִכְשָׁפִים. אַטּוּ כֻּלְּהוּ לִכְשָׁפִים מְקַטְּרָן?! הֲוָה לֵיהּ מִיעוּטָא לִכְשָׁפִים וּמִיעוּטָא נַמִּי לְגַמֵּר אֶת הַכֵּלִים, אִשְׁתְּכַח. רוּבָּא דְּלָאו לְרֵיחָא עֲבִיד, וְכָל רוּבָּא דְּלָאו לְרֵיחָא עֲבִיד — לָא מְבָרֵךְ.

אָמַר רַבִּי חִיָּא בַּר אַבָּא אָמַר רַבִּי יוֹחָנָן: הַמְהַלֵּךְ בְּעַרְבֵי

שַׁבָּתוֹת בִּטְבֶרְיָא וּבְמוֹצָאֵי שַׁבָּתוֹת בְּצִפּוֹרִי וְהֵרִיחַ רֵיחַ —
אֵינוּ מְבָרֵךְ, מִפְּנֵי שֶׁחֶזְקָתוֹ — אֵינוֹ עָשׂוּי אֶלָּא לְגַמֵּר בּוֹ אֶת
הַכֵּלִים.

תָּנוּ רַבָּנָן: הָיָה מְהַלֵּךְ בְּשׁוּק שֶׁל עוֹבְדֵי כּוֹכָבִים וּמַזָּלוֹת,
נִתְרַצָּה לְהָרִיחַ הֲרֵי זֶה חוֹטֵא.

"וְאֵין מְבָרְכִין עַל הַנֵּר עַד שֶׁיֵּאוֹתוּ". אָמַר רַב יְהוּדָה אָמַר
רַב: לֹא "יֵאוֹתוּ" יֵאוֹתוּ מַמָּשׁ, אֶלָּא כָּל שֶׁאִלּוּ עוֹמֵד בְּקָרוֹב
וּמִשְׁתַּמֵּשׁ לְאוֹרָהּ, וַאֲפִלּוּ בְּרָחוֹק מָקוֹם. וְכֵן אָמַר רַב אָשִׁי:
בְּרָחוֹק מָקוֹם שָׁנִינוּ.

מוֹתִיבֵי: הָיְתָה לוֹ נֵר טְמוּנָה בְּחֵיקוֹ אוֹ בְּפָנָס, אוֹ שֶׁרָאָה
שַׁלְהֶבֶת וְלֹא נִשְׁתַּמֵּשׁ לְאוֹרָהּ, אוֹ נִשְׁתַּמֵּשׁ לְאוֹרָהּ וְלֹא רָאָה
שַׁלְהֶבֶת — אֵינוֹ מְבָרֵךְ עַד שֶׁיִּרְאֶה שַׁלְהֶבֶת וְיִשְׁתַּמֵּשׁ
לְאוֹרָהּ: בִּשְׁלָמָא מִשְׁתַּמֵּשׁ לְאוֹרָהּ וְלֹא רָאָה שַׁלְהֶבֶת —
מַשְׁכַּחַת לָהּ דְּקָיְימָא בְּקֶרֶן זָוִית, אֶלָּא רָאָה שַׁלְהֶבֶת וְלֹא
נִשְׁתַּמֵּשׁ לְאוֹרָהּ הֵיכֵי מַשְׁכַּחַת לָהּ? לַאו דִּמְרַחֲקָא! לָא,
כְּגוֹן דְּעָמְיָא וְאָזְלָא.

תָּנוּ רַבָּנָן: גֶּחָלִים לוֹחֲשׁוֹת — מְבָרְכִין עֲלֵיהֶן, אוֹמְמוֹת —
אֵין מְבָרְכִין עֲלֵיהֶן. הֵיכֵי דָמֵי לוֹחֲשׁוֹת? אָמַר רַב חִסְדָּא: כָּל
שֶׁאִלּוּ מַכְנִיס לְתוֹכָן קֵיסָם וְדוֹלֶקֶת מֵאֵלֶיהָ.

אִיבַּעְיָא לְהוּ: אוֹמְמוֹת אוֹ עוֹמְמוֹת? תָּא שְׁמַע, דְּאָמַר רַב
חִסְדָּא בַּר אַבְדִּימֵי: "אֲרָזִים לֹא־עֲמָמֻהוּ בְּגַן־אֱלֹהִים".

וְרָבָא אָמַר: יֵאוֹתוּ מַמָּשׁ. וְכַמָּה? אָמַר עוּלָּא: כְּדֵי שֶׁיַּכִּיר בֵּין
אִיסָר לְפוּנְדְיוֹן, חִזְקִיָּה אָמַר: כְּדֵי שֶׁיַּכִּיר בֵּין מְלוֹזְמָא שֶׁל
טְבֶרְיָא לִמְלוֹזְמָא שֶׁל צִפּוֹרִי. רַב יְהוּדָה מְבָרֵךְ אַדְּבֵי אַדָּא
דַּיְילָא. רָבָא מְבָרֵךְ אַדְּבֵי גּוּרְיָא בַּר חָמָא. אַבַּיֵּי מְבָרֵךְ אַדְּבֵי
בַּר אֲבוּהַּ.

אָמַר רַב יְהוּדָה אָמַר רַב: אֵין מַחֲזִירִין עַל הָאוֹר כְּדֶרֶךְ
שֶׁמַּחֲזִירִין עַל הַמִּצְוֹת. אָמַר רַבִּי זֵירָא: מֵרִישׁ הֲוָה מְהַדַּרְנָא,
כֵּיוָן דִּשְׁמַעְנָא לְהָא דְּרַב יְהוּדָה אָמַר רַב, אֲנָא נַמֵּי לָא
מְהַדַּרְנָא, אֶלָּא אִי מִקְלַע לִי מִמֵּילָא — מְבָרֵיכְנָא.

"מִי שֶׁאָכַל" וְכוּלֵי. אָמַר רַב זְבִיד, וְאִיתֵּימָא רַב דִּימִי בַּר

אַבָּא: מַחֲלֹקֶת בְּשָׁכַח, אֲבָל בְּמֵזִיד – דִּבְרֵי הַכֹּל יַחֲזֹר לִמְקוֹמוֹ וִיבָרֵךְ. פְּשִׁיטָא, "וְשָׁכַח" תְּנַן! מַהוּ דְּתֵימָא הוּא הַדִּין אֲפִלּוּ בְּמֵזִיד, וְהַאי דְּקָתָנֵי "וְשָׁכַח" – לְהוֹדִיעֲךָ כֹּחָן דְּבֵית שַׁמַּאי, קָמַשְׁמַע לָן.

תַּנְיָא, אָמְרוּ לָהֶם בֵּית הִלֵּל לְבֵית שַׁמַּאי: לְדִבְרֵיכֶם, מִי שֶׁאָכַל בְּרֹאשׁ הַבִּירָה וְשָׁכַח וְיָרַד וְלֹא בֵרַךְ, יַחֲזֹר לְרֹאשׁ הַבִּירָה וִיבָרֵךְ? אָמְרוּ לָהֶן בֵּית שַׁמַּאי לְבֵית הִלֵּל: לְדִבְרֵיכֶם, מִי שֶׁשָּׁכַח אַרְנָקִי בְּרֹאשׁ הַבִּירָה, לֹא יַעֲלֶה וְיִטְּלֶנָה?! לִכְבוֹד עַצְמוֹ הוּא עוֹלֶה, לִכְבוֹד שָׁמַיִם לֹא כָּל שֶׁכֵּן.

הָנְהוּ תְּרֵי תַּלְמִידֵי, חַד עֲבִיד בְּשׁוֹגֵג כְּבֵית שַׁמַּאי וְאַשְׁכַּח אַרְנְקָא דְּדַהֲבָא, וְחַד עֲבִיד בְּמֵזִיד כְּבֵית הִלֵּל וְאַכְלֵיהּ אַרְיָא. רַבָּה בַּר בַּר חָנָה הֲוָה קָאָזֵל בְּשַׁיָּירָתָא, אָכַל וְאִשְׁתְּלִי וְלָא בָרֵיךְ. אָמַר, הֵיכִי אֶעֱבִיד? אִי אָמֵינָא לְהוּ "אַנְשַׁאי לְבָרֵךְ", אָמְרִי לִי: בָּרֵיךְ, כָּל הֵיכָא דִּמְבָרְכַתְּ לְרַחֲמָנָא מְבָרְכַתְּ: מוֹטָב דְּאָמֵינָא לְהוּ "אַנְשַׁאי יוֹנָה דְּדַהֲבָא". אָמַר לְהוּ: אַנְטְרוּ לִי, דְּאַנְשַׁאי יוֹנָה דְּדַהֲבָא, אַזִּיל וּבָרֵיךְ וְאַשְׁכַּח יוֹנָה דְּדַהֲבָא. וּמַאי שְׁנָא יוֹנָה? דִּמְתִילִי כְּנֶסֶת יִשְׂרָאֵל לְיוֹנָה, דִּכְתִיב: "כַּנְפֵי יוֹנָה נֶחְפָּה בַכֶּסֶף וְאֶבְרוֹתֶיהָ בִּירַקְרַק חָרוּץ", מַה־יוֹנָה אֵינָהּ נִצּוֹלֶת אֶלָּא בִּכְנָפֶיהָ, אַף יִשְׂרָאֵל אֵינָן נִצּוֹלִין אֶלָּא בְּמִצְוֹת.

"עַד אֵימָתַי הוּא" וְכוּלֵי. כַּמָּה שִׁעוּר עִכּוּל? אָמַר רַבִּי יוֹחָנָן: כָּל זְמַן שֶׁאֵינוֹ רָעֵב, וְרֵישׁ לָקִישׁ אָמַר: כָּל זְמַן שֶׁיִּצְמָא מֵחֲמַת אֲכִילָתוֹ. אָמַר לֵיהּ רַב יֵימַר בַּר שְׁלֶמְיָא לְמָר זוּטְרָא, וְאָמְרִי לָהּ רַב יֵימַר בַּר שִׁיזְבִי לְמָר זוּטְרָא: מִי אָמַר רֵישׁ לָקִישׁ הָכִי? וְהָאָמַר רַב אַמִּי אָמַר רֵישׁ לָקִישׁ: כַּמָּה שִׁעוּר עִכּוּל? כְּדֵי לְהַלֵּךְ אַרְבַּע מִילִין! לָא קַשְׁיָא: כָּאן בַּאֲכִילָה מְרֻבָּה, כָּאן בַּאֲכִילָה מְעַטֶת.

"בָּא לָהֶם יַיִן" וְכוּלֵי. לְמֵימְרָא, דְּיִשְׂרָאֵל אַף עַל גַּב דְּלֹא שָׁמַע כֻּלֵּהּ בְּרָכָה עוֹנֶה, וְכִי לֹא שָׁמַע הֵיכִי נָפֵיק? אָמַר חִיָּא

בַּר רַב: בְּשֶׁלֹּא אָכַל עִמָּהֶן. וְכֵן אָמַר רַב נַחְמָן אָמַר רַבָּה בַּר
אֲבוּהּ: בְּשֶׁלֹּא אָכַל עִמָּהֶן.

אֲמַר לֵיהּ רַב לְחִיָּא בְּרֵיהּ: בְּרִי, חֲטֹף וּבָרֵיךְ. וְכֵן אֲמַר רַב
הוּנָא לְרַבָּה בְּרֵיהּ: חֲטֹף וּבָרֵיךְ. לְמֵימְרָא, דִּמְבָרֵךְ עֲדִיף
מִמַּאן דְּעָנֵי "אָמֵן", וְהָתַנְיָא, רַבִּי יוֹסֵי אוֹמֵר: גָּדוֹל הָעוֹנֶה
"אָמֵן" יוֹתֵר מִן הַמְבָרֵךְ! אֲמַר לֵיהּ רַבִּי נְהוֹרַאי: הַשָּׁמַיִם! כֵּן
הוּא; תֵּדַע, שֶׁהֲרֵי גוּלְיָרִין יוֹרְדִין וּמִתְגָּרִין [בַּמִּלְחָמָה] וְגִבּוֹרִים
יוֹרְדִין וּמְנַצְּחִין. תַּנָּאֵי הִיא, דְּתַנְיָא: אֶחָד הַמְבָרֵךְ וְאֶחָד
הָעוֹנֶה "אָמֵן" בְּמַשְׁמַע, אֶלָּא שֶׁמְּמַהֲרִין לַמְבָרֵךְ יוֹתֵר מִן
הָעוֹנֶה "אָמֵן".

בָּעֵי מִינֵּיהּ שְׁמוּאֵל מֵרַב: מַהוּ לַעֲנוֹת "אָמֵן" אַחַר תִּינוֹקוֹת
שֶׁל בֵּית רַבָּן? אֲמַר לֵיהּ: אַחַר הַכֹּל עוֹנִין "אָמֵן" חוּץ
מִתִּינוֹקוֹת שֶׁל בֵּית רַבָּן, הוֹאִיל וּלְהִתְלַמֵּד עֲשׂוּיִין. וְהָנֵי מִילֵּי
בִּדְלָא עִידָּן מִפְטְרַיְיהוּ, אֲבָל בְּעִידָּן מִפְטְרַיְיהוּ — עוֹנִין.

תָּנוּ רַבָּנָן: שֶׁמֶן מְעַכֵּב אֶת הַבְּרָכָה, דִּבְרֵי רַבִּי זִילַאי; רַבִּי
זִיוַאי אוֹמֵר: אֵינוֹ מְעַכֵּב; רַבִּי אָחָא אוֹמֵר: שֶׁמֶן טוֹב מְעַכֵּב;
רַבִּי זֶהֱמַאי אוֹמֵר: כְּשֵׁם שֶׁמְּזֹהָם פָּסוּל לַעֲבוֹדָה, כָּךְ יָדַיִם
מְזֹהָמוֹת פְּסוּלוֹת לִבְרָכָה. אָמַר רַב נַחְמָן בַּר יִצְחָק: אֲנָא לָא
זִילַאי וְלָא זִיוַאי וְלָא זֶהֱמַאי יָדַעְנָא, אֶלָּא מַתְנִיתָא יָדַעְנָא;
דְּאָמַר רַב יְהוּדָה אָמַר רַב, וְאָמְרִי לָהּ בְּמַתְנִיתָא תְּנָא:
"וְהִתְקַדִּשְׁתֶּם" — אֵלוּ מַיִם רִאשׁוֹנִים, "וִהְיִיתֶם קְדֹשִׁים" —
אֵלוּ מַיִם אַחֲרוֹנִים, "כִּי קָדוֹשׁ" — זֶה שֶׁמֶן, "אֲנִי ה'
אֱלֹהֵיכֶם" — זוֹ בְּרָכָה.

Bibliographical Supplement: "Go Study"

Two sorts of further study may be undertaken. First, you may wish to examine other specimens of Talmudic literature. Second, you certainly will want to consider how the Talmud and related rabbinic collections have been used for the study of the history of Judaism and of the Jewish people in late antiquity. The answer is found in the systematic scholarly reconstructions, based upon Talmudic sources, of that history. I shall first of all propose some next steps in the study, in English, of Mishnah and Talmud, then provide an introductory bibliography through which the reader may find counsel for further studies.

Pre-1973

Further Texts

Certainly, the next Talmudic text should be *Avot* (The Fathers), in the translation and commentary of Judah Goldin, *The Living Talmud* (N.Y., 1957: Mentor, New American Library). Along with *Avot* should go its *Gemara*, *The Fathers According to Rabbi Nathan* (New Haven, 1955: Yale University Press), translated by Judah Goldin. These two texts do not exhibit the sort of closely reasoned argument we have examined. But they do provide a comprehensive account of the religious and intellectual ideals of the Talmudic rabbis, in Goldin's masterly translation of the Talmudic language and idiom.

Further tractates of Mishnah to be studied in English might well include the whole of *Berakhot* (Blessings), Chapter One of *Peah* (Gleanings), all of *Bikkurim* (First Fruits), Chapter Ten of *Pesahim* (Passover), Chapter Eight of *Yoma* (The Day of Atonement), Chapter Nine of *Sotah* (The Suspected Adulteress), Chapter Six of *Gittin* (Divorces), Chapter One of *Bava Qamma* (The First Gate; civil damages), Chapter Ten of *Sanhedrin* (on those who have a portion in the world to come), Chapter Three of *Avodah Zarah* (Idolatry), all of *Tamid* (The Daily Whole-Offering), Chapter Twenty-four of *Kelim* (Vessels Susceptible of Receiving Uncleanness), Chapter Two, paragraphs 2–7, of *Tohorot* (Cleannesses), Chapter Four of *Yadaim* (Unclean Hands). These chapters illustrate both the varieties of legal topics and themes, and some of the types of literary forms used for the formulation of Mishnaic law. The best translation of the Mishnah is in the Soncino Talmud (cited below), because the notes are copious and helpful.

A felicitous translation of a complete, and not too difficult, tractate is Henry Malter, *The Treatise Ta'anit of the Babylonian Talmud* (Philadelphia, 1928: Jewish Publication Society). The reader who wishes to study an entire tractate on his or her own, in English, may start here.

Jewish History and Religion in Talmudic Times

The place to begin is with Judah Goldin, "The Talmudic Period," in Louis Finkelstein, ed., *The Jews: Their History, Culture, and Religion* (Philadelphia, 1960: Jewish Publication Society); and Gerson D. Cohen, "The Talmudic Age," in Leo Schwarz, ed., *Great Ages and Ideas of the Jewish People* (N.Y., 1956: Random House). The essays by Menahem Stern, "The Hasmonean Revolt and Its Place in the History of Jewish Society and Religion," E. E. Urbach, "The Talmudic Sage—Character and Authority," and S. Safrai, "Elementary Education, Its Religious and Social Significance in the Talmudic Period," in *Journal of World History* XI, 1–2, 1968: *Social Life and Social Values of the Jewish People*, are concise and informative.

For an introductory account of the religious history of Babylonian Jewry in Talmudic times, my *There We Sat Down. Talmudic Judaism in the Making* (Nashville, 1972: Abingdon) is available. An analysis of the sources on pre-70 Pharisaic Judaism and an effort to construct a critical account are in my *From Politics to Piety: The Emergence of Pharisaic Judaism* (Englewood Cliffs, 1973: Prentice-Hall). My Haskell Lectures for 1972–1973 closely relate to the legal materials reviewed in this book. They are published as *The Idea of Purity in Ancient Judaism* (Leiden, 1973: E.J. Brill).

After reading the suggested essays and introductions, you will have formed your own inquiries. To find out how to pursue them, you will want to consult bibliographical guides, the best of which is Judah Goldin, "Judaism," in Charles J. Adams, ed., *A Reader's Guide to the Great Religions* (N.Y., 1965: The Free Press), pp. 191–228. Goldin gives a careful and responsible account of the scholarly literature before 1960. He surveys the state of knowledge up to 1960.

The Study of Judaism. Bibliographical Essays (N.Y., 1972: Ktav for Anti-Defamation League of B'nai B'rith) contains two papers of importance for our topic, Richard Bavier, "Judaism in New Testament Times," and John T. Townsend, "Rabbinic Sources." The former is a guide, by a student, for beginners in the study of ancient Judaism. The latter is an extraordinary account of the manuscripts, printed editions, translations, concordances, and major studies of ancient Jewish literature, translations of the Scriptures into Aramaic (Targumim), the Mishnah, Tosefta, Palestinian and Babylonian Talmuds, extracanonical tractates, and the like. Townsend's bibliography is, for its subject, without peer.

Moses Mielziner, *Introduction to the Talmud*, with a new bibliography, 1925–1967, by Alexander Guttmann (N.Y., 1968: Bloch Publishing Co.), contains helpful lists of books arranged according to various topics.

The Mishnah in English

Herbert Danby, *The Mishnah. Translated from the Hebrew with Introduction and Brief Explanatory Notes* (London, 1933: Oxford University Press) is a painstaking and, on the whole, accurate version. The notes do not offer much help to the beginner. Danby's translation of *The Code of Maimonides. Book Ten. The Book of Cleanness* (New Haven, 1954: Yale University Press. Yale Judaica Series, Vol. VIII) also should be mentioned. Maimonides presents the Talmudic purity laws with unparalleled thoroughness and clarity. The task of translation was challenging because of the complexity of the laws; it occupied Danby for more than five years.

Somewhat fuller notes and a good translation of the Mishnah, along with the Hebrew text, are provided by Philip Blackman, *Mishnayoth* (N.Y., 1965, Third Edition: The Judaica Press, Inc., Vols. I–VI). Knowledge of Hebrew is advantageous in using this translation, all the more so the commentary.

Yale University Press is publishing my translation of the Mishnah in 1984.

Studies on scholarship on the Mishnah, as well as on the exegetical collections called *midrash*, and on the *siddur* (Jewish Prayerbook), the Palestinian Talmud, and the Babylonian Talmud, are in *The Study of Ancient Judaism* (New York, 1981: Ktav Publishing House). See also *I. Mishnah, Midrash, Siddur. II. The Palestinian and Babylonian Talmuds*, edited by me, with essays by Gary G. Porton, Richard

S. Sarason, Baruch M. Bokser, and David Goodblatt. These essays review the bulk of modern and contemporary scholarship on the main components of the canon of Judaism.

The Talmud in English

As of 1973 the Palestinian Talmud had never been translated into English. A French translation, Moise Schwab, *Le Talmud de Je'rusalem* (Paris, 1871–1889, reprinted 1960: Editions G.-P. Maisonneuve), is in no way satisfactory. (My translation is now appearing at the University of Chicago Press, in thirty-five volumes.)

A complete and reliable English translation of the Babylonian Talmud was executed in Britain under the general editorship of Isidore Epstein and published by the Soncino Press, London, between 1935 and 1948 in thirty-five volumes. An eighteen-volume edition was issued in 1961. The translation is accompanied by brief and helpful notes. Some volumes of a bilingual edition have appeared. I wonder whether a person not already familiar with Hebrew and Aramaic and without a Talmudic text will fully follow the excellent work of the Soncino translators, for, being close to the original, it also is somewhat concise and preserves the Talmud's exceptional terseness. Often, too, the thrust of argument will not be wholly clear. But one may make considerable progress with the Soncino Talmud, a work of painstaking care and admirable intelligence.

An English translation, with extensive commentary, of selected chapters of the Talmud under the general editorship of A. Ehrman is being issued in fascicles by El-Am-Hoza as Leor Israel (Jerusalem and Tel Aviv, beginning in 1965) and the National Academy for Adult Jewish Studies of the United Synagogue of America (N.Y.). The commentary includes three parts. First come "realia," explanations, frequently not very scholarly, of the practical laws. These explanations are written in a pseudocritical spirit and exhibit a strong homiletical interest. Second, biographical notes are supplied, consisting of compilations of Talmudic allusions to various authorities mentioned in the text. The main commentary, third, is a wordy and prolix paraphrase and expansion of the translation of the Mishnah and *Gemara*. At some other points a commentary on the practical law is supplied.

A sixteen-page fascicle may cover a single folio-page of the Talmud; so far, there are twenty-five fascicles for tractate Blessings (*Berakhot*), reaching folio 17b; twenty fascicles of tractate on Betrothals (*Qiddushin*), for twenty-eight folios; and twenty fascicles for two chapters on the Middle Gate, civil law (*Bava Mesi'a'*), covering folios 33b through 57b. I think the English reader will find it difficult to use this "popu-

lar" translation, because anyone will need a score card to dope out the
four English sections on a given page. The actual Talmud on a page
is brief and truncated. One has to keep in balance a whole mass of
information—the translation of the Talmud, various notes strung out
along the sides; an extended, not particularly illuminating commentary, which is full of Hebrew words and therefore not entirely helpful
to the English reader. And each section of a page will continue on the
next, without regard to where the other columns of type have left off,
so one may end up reading three or four pages at once, going back and
forth. In the balance, the Soncino Talmud is much preferable.

B. Elizur-Epstein, *A Chapter of the Talmud* (Jerusalem, 1963)
translates the ninth chapter of *Bava Mesi'a'* with brief explanatory
comments. The work seems competent, especially helpful for those
who already know some Aramaic and Hebrew.

Anthologies

Three anthologies of Talmudic materials arranged according to
topics such as the law, divine mercy, hope and faith, and the like, may
be mentioned. The best is C. G. Montefiore and H. Loewe, *A Rabbinic
Anthology* (Cleveland and New York, 1963: Meridian Books. World
Publishing Co.; and Philadelphia: Jewish Publication Society of
America). This indeed is the finest anthology of materials pertinent to
the study of Judaism of any period. Montefiore and Loewe do not
merely collect and arrange interesting passages; they comment on
them, cross-reference and rework them. The reader has a pair of
reliable, urbane guides through thoughtfully selected and lucidly
presented materials.

The other anthologies are A. Cohen, *Everyman's Talmud* (N.Y.,
1949: E. P. Dutton & Co.), and Louis I. Newman with Samuel Spitz,
*The Talmudic Anthology. Tales and Teachings of the Rabbis. A
Collection of Parables, Folk-Tales, Fables, Aphorisms, Epigrams,
Sayings, Anecdotes, Proverbs, and Exegetical Interpretations* (N.Y.,
1945: Behrman House). Cohen strings together allusions to Talmudic
and related texts; but the texts are not fully translated. Newman's
compendium of "tales and teachings" is arranged to serve preachers
looking for stunning sayings. It will not meet any other purpose.

Talmudic Lore

A magnificent compilation of Talmudic and later legends, both
Jewish and Christian, about biblical history and biography is presented by Louis Ginzberg, *The Legends of the Jews* (Philadelphia,
1947: Jewish Publication Society, Vols. I–VII). Ginzberg paraphrases

the stories and arranges them according to the order of the biblical narrative. The stories are not distinguished as to their approximate time of origin, who told them, the texts in which they occur, and the like, so the collection as a whole is of limited historical utility. But the notes, in Vols. V–VI, are thorough and contain numerous important points. A one-volume summary is Louis Ginzberg, *Legends of the Bible* (Philadelphia, 1956: Jewish Publication Society) with a brilliant introduction by Shalom Spiegel, the master of Jewish lore. Spiegel's introduction constitutes an illuminating explanation for Jewish folklore and legend. A still better specimen of Talmudic and later folklore is Shalom Spiegel, *The Last Trial. On the Legends and Lore of the Command to Abraham to Offer Isaac As a Sacrifice: The Akedah. Translated from the Hebrew with an Introduction by Judah Goldin* (N.Y., 1967: Pantheon Books). Spiegel carries the biblical story through Talmudic and medieval times in a wide-ranging and highly literate account.

Talmudic Methodology

Little is available in English to delineate the method of Talmudic logic and the traits of the Talmud as literature. In general, Talmudists tend to neglect systematic presentation of such matters as the structure of Talmudic discussions and the formulation of arguments. An essay in these questions, admittedly not a complete guide but an important beginning, is Louis Jacobs, *Studies in Talmudic Logic and Methodology* (London, 1961: Vallentine, Mitchell). It is a sophisticated account of four logical and six literary questions, a model for further research. The papers by Bokser and Goodblatt cited above are comprehensive and complete.

Midrash

Midrash, from the root *darash*, "to seek," comprises the Talmudic interpretation of biblical literature. Midrashic literature dating from Talmudic and medieval times has been translated in the following works (among others): *Mekilta de Rabbi Ishmael*, by J. Z. Lauterbach (Philadelphia, 1933: Jewish Publication Society, Vols. I–III); *Midrash Sifre' on Numbers*, by P. P. Levertoff (London and N.Y., 1926: Macmillan); *Midrash Rabbah, translated into English with Notes, Glossary, and Indices*, under the editorship of H. Freedman and Maurice Simon (London, 1939: The Soncino Press, Vols. I–X); *The Song at the Sea, being a Commentary on a Commentary in Two Parts*, by Judah Goldin (New Haven, 1971: Yale University Press), covering tractate Shirta of Mekhilta; *The Midrash on Psalms*, by W. G.

Braude (New Haven, 1959: Yale University Press, Vols. I–II); *Pesikta Rabbati. Discourses for Feasts, Fasts, and Special Sabbaths*, by W. G. Braude (New Haven, 1968: Yale University Press, Vols. I–II); and the same translator's *Pesikta de Rav Kahana* is in print.

For the spirit of Midrashic inquiry, the best introduction is Maurice Samuel, *Certain People of the Book* (N.Y., 1955: Knopf). For the history of Midrashic traditions, the seminal work is Geza Vermes, *Scripture and Tradition in Judaism* (Leiden, 1961: E. J. Brill).

History

E. Schürer, *History of the Jewish People in the Time of Jesus Christ* (Edinburgh, 1886–1890: T. & T. Clark), is now in a revised and updated edition by Geza Vermes and Fergus Millar. It remains the standard account of Palestinian Jewry down to 70. We have in English no satisfactory history of that community from 70 to the end of its corporate existence in 425. For the Jews in the Roman Empire, the definitive account is Jean Juster, *Les juifs dans l'empire romain* (Paris, 1914; Vols. I–II). There is nothing like it in English. For Babylonian Jewry, one may find helpful this writer's *History of the Jews in Babylonia* (Leiden: E. J. Brill): *I. The Parthian Period* (1970, Second Edition); *II. The Early Sasanian Period* (1966); *III. From Shapur I to Shapur II* (1968); *IV. The Age of Shapur II* (1969); and *V. Later Sasanian Times* (1970). A supplementary study is *Aphrahat and Judaism. The Christian-Jewish Argument in Fourth-Century Iran* (Leiden, 1971: E. J. Brill).

On the Pharisees before 70, you may consult this writer's *The Rabbinic Traditions about the Pharisees before 70* (Leiden, 1971: E. J. Brill): *I. The Masters; II. The Houses; III. Conclusions;* this work is summarized in *From Politics to Piety*.

Talmudic Religion

Morton Smith, the great historian of religions in late antiquity, writes, "A gift for systematic theology . . . is a great handicap in the study of rabbinic literature." The reason is that systematic theology requires the imposition of an artificial construct, such as "the rabbis" or "the rabbinic mind," upon sayings and stories which derive from a great many discrete and unsystematic authorities, living in various countries, over a period of seven centuries and more. Consequently, it is misleading to systematize what to begin with derives from authorities whose sayings never were meant to be systematized. Still, we have valuable accounts of rabbinic theology, and, while subject to further refining and improvement, these works are illuminating. Foremost among them are the following: S. Schechter, *Some Aspects of Rabbinic Theology* (N.Y., 1936: Behrman House); George Foot Moore, *Judaism in the First Centuries of the Christian Era. The Age of the Tannaim* (Cambridge, 1954: Harvard University Press, Vols. I–III); Max Kadushin, *Worship and Ethics. A Study in Rabbinic Judaism* (Evanston, 1964: Northwestern University Press); Jacob Z. Lauterbach, *Rabbinic Essays* (Cincinnati, 1951: Hebrew Union College Press); and Louis Ginzberg, *On Jewish Law and Lore* (Philadelphia, 1955: Jewish Publication Society). The last-named work contains classic essays introducing the Palestinian Talmud (pp. 3–60) and on the allegorical interpretation of Scripture (pp. 127–152), among others.

Jewish mysticism, with roots in Talmudic Judaism, is masterfully laid forth in Gershom G. Scholem, *Major Trends in Jewish Mysticism* (N.Y., 1954: Schocken), one of the most important works in the study of the history of Judaism.

For the bearing of archaeological discoveries on the study of ancient Judaism, I recommend Erwin R. Goodenough, *Jewish Symbols in the Greco-Roman Period* (N.Y., 1953 et seq.: Bollingen Foundation, Vols. I–XIII).

By the Same Author

In addition to *History and Pharisees*, this writer's studies of Talmudic Judaism include the following: *A Life of Yohanan ben Zakkai* (Leiden, 1970, Second Edition, Completely Revised: E. J. Brill); *Development of a Legend. Studies on the Traditions Concerning Yohanan ben Zakkai* (Leiden, 1970: E. J. Brill); *Eliezer ben Hyrcanus. The Tradition and the Man* (Leiden, 1973: E. J. Brill, Vols. I–II); and *The Idea of Purity in Ancient Judaism* (The Haskell Lectures for 1973) (Leiden, 1973: E. J. Brill). In connection with the study of Talmudic literature and history, he has edited *The Formation of the Babylonian Talmud. Studies in the Achievements of Late Nineteenth and Twentieth Century Historical and Literary-Critical Research* (Leiden, 1970: E. J. Brill); and *The Modern Study of the Mishnah* (Leiden, 1973: E. J. Brill); as well as *A Soviet View of Talmudic Judaism. The Work of Yu. A. Solodukho* (Leiden, 1973: E. J. Brill).

For beginners, the following textbooks may prove helpful: *Way of Torah: An Introduction to Judaism* (Encino, 1974: Dickenson Publishing Co.), with its accompanying reader, *The Life of Torah* (Encino, 1974: Dickenson Publishing Co.); for an anthology of Jewish theology, *Theology of Judaism: Classical Issues and Modern Perspectives* (N.Y., 1973: Ktav Publishing House), and *Understanding Rabbinic Judaism* (N.Y., 1974: Ktav Publishing House); and, for rabbinic

Judaism in modern times, *American Judaism: Adventure in Modernity*
(Englewood Cliffs, 1972: Prentice-Hall).

Post-1973

To supplement the foregoing account, I call attention to two works
of fundamental importance in the study of the history and religion of
the Jews of Talmudic times. In history, the second volume of the
updating of Schürer's history appeared: Emil Schürer, *The History of
the Jewish People in the Age of Jesus Christ. Volume II*, Revised and
edited by Geza Vermes, Fergus Millar, and Matthew Black; Literary
Editor: Pamela Vermes (Edinburgh, 1979: T. & T. Clark).

In Jewish religion, an English translation of a work in 1973 avail-
able only in Hebrew appeared in 1975: Ephraim E. Urbach, *The Sages.
Their Concepts and Beliefs* (Jerusalem: The Magnes Press of the
Hebrew University).

The Palestinian Talmud has now come into English, in my translation: *The Talmud of the Land of Israel* (Chicago: University of
Chicago Press, beginning in 1982, Vols. I–XXXV). As of the end of
1984, Vols. XXIII–XXXV are in print. The remaining volumes will
appear at the rate of from three to five a year, and the entire set will be
in print by 1990.

By the Same Author

When I wrote the first edition of this book, I was just coming to
recognize the central problems in the historical description, analysis,
and interpretation of the canon of Judaism, of which the Talmud
forms the principal component. I revised this book just after complet-
ing my own reworking of the main parts of that entire canon of
religious literature and reconstructing the whole in a trilogy, *Foundations of Judaism: Method, Teleology, Doctrine: I. Midrash in Context.
Exegesis in Formative Judaism; II. Messiah in Context. Israel's History and Destiny in Formative Judaism;* and *III. Torah: From Scroll
to Symbol in Formative Judaism* (Philadelphia, 1983, 1984, and 1985,
respectively: Fortress Press). These complementary studies represent
the results of describing and interpreting Judaism in the methods I
framed and fully spelled out, through a commentary and history of
the law of the Mishnah and Tosefta, and through my translation and
studies of the Palestinian Talmud, between 1973 and 1983.

In order to acquaint the reader with the work of that intervening
decade, I next present an essay, with extensive notes, specifying the
problems, how they were solved, and the steps taken in their solution,
as well as the books that contain the exercises in research and
argumentation.

Current Events in the Study of Rabbinic Sources

To spell out for you[1] what has happened in the study of the ancient rabbinic texts, I have to introduce the texts and their problems. For without knowing the questions, of what use to you are the answers? And yet my task is to speak of texts which few have actually studied or even read in translation. Introducing work in a field essentially unknown to my readers requires a special effort. What I must ask is that you undertake a mental experiment. You must use your imagination to build a bridge from the known to the unknown.

What I wish to do is to lead you to a picture of what would be our problem in studying early Christianity, if the sources of early Christianity had reached us in the way, and in the condition, in which those of early rabbinic Judaism come down to us. That is to say, what should we know, and how should we know it, if the records of early Christianity were like the rabbinic literature of late antiquity?

So let us begin.

(1) What could we know, if all the literature of early Christianity had reached us in a fully homogenized and intellectually seamless form? Not only the New Testament, but all the works of the church fathers, from Justin to Augustine, now would be represented as expressions of one communal mind, dismembered and built into a single harmonious logical structure on various themes. True, they would be shown constantly to disagree with one another. But the range of permissible disagreement would define a vast area of consensus on all basic matters, so that a superficial contentiousness would convey something quite different: one mind on most things, beginning to end. The names of the fathers would be attached to some of their utterances. But all would have gone through a second medium of tradents and redactors—the editors of the compendium (the Patristic Talmud, so to speak)—and these editors picked and chose what they wanted of Justin, and what of Origen, what of Tertullian, and what

of Augustine, in line with what the editors themselves found interesting. In the end, the picture of the first six centuries of early Christianity
would be the creation of people of the sixth century, out of the sherds
and remnants of people of the first five. Our work then would be to
uncover what happened before the end through studying a document
which portrays a timeless world.

Not only would the document be so framed as implicitly to deny
historical development of ideas, but the framers also would gloss over
diverse and contradictory sources of thought. I do not mean only that
Justin, Irenaeus, and Tertullian would be presented as individual
authors in a single, timeless continuum. I mean that all Gnostic and
Catholic sources would be broken up into sense-units and their frag-
ments rearranged in a structure presented as representative of a single
Christianity, with a single, unitary theology. This synthesized ecu-
menical body of Christian thought would be constructed so as to set
out judgments on the principal theological topics of the day, and
these judgments would have been accepted as normative from that day
to this. So the first thing you must try to imagine is a Christianity
which reaches us fully harmonized and whole—a Christianity of Nicea
and Chalcedon, but not of Arians, Nestorians, monophysites and the
rest, so there is no distinctive Justin nor Augustine, no Irenaeus and
no Gnostics, and surely no Nag Hammadi, but all are one "in Christ
Jesus," so to speak.

(2) Let me emphasize that this would be not merely a matter of
early Christian literature's reaching us without the names of the
authors of its individual documents. The thing you must try to
imagine is that there would be no individual documents at all. Everything would have gone through a process of formation and redaction
which obliterated the marks of individuality. Just as the theology
would be one, so would the form and style of the documents which
preserved it. Indeed, what would be striking about this picture of
Christianity would be not that the tractate of Mark lacks the name of
Mark, but that all of the tractates of the Gospels would be written in
precisely the same style and resort to exactly the same rhetorical and
redactional devices. Stylistic unity so pervasive as to eliminate all
traces of individual authorship, even of most preserved sayings, would
now characterize the writings of the first Christians. The sarcasm of
Irenaeus, the majesty of Augustine, the exegetical ingenuity of Origen,
and the lucid historicism of Aphrahat—all are homogenized. Everyone
talks in the same way about the same things.

(3) And now to come to a principal task of the study of early Christianity: what should we know about Jesus, and how should we know

it, if sayings assigned to Jesus in one book were given to Paul in a second, to John in a third, and to "They said," or, "He said to them," in a fourth. Can you imagine trying to discover the historical Jesus on this turf? If even the provenance of a saying could not be established on the basis of all those to whom it is attributed, if, often, even a single *Vorlage* and *Urtext* could not be postulated? Then what sort of work on the biography and thought of any of the early figures of Christianity would be credible?

(4) This brings me to the most difficult act of imagination which I must ask you to perform: a supererogatory work of social imagination. Can you imagine a corner of the modern world in which this state of interpretation—of total confusion, of harmonies, homologies, homogenies, is not found confusing but reassuring? Can you mentally conjure up a social setting for learning in which differentiation is avoided and credulity rewarded? in which analysis is heresy, dismissed as worthless or attacked as "full of mistakes"? Can you conceive of a world in which repetition, in one's own words, of what the sources say is labelled scholarship, and anthologizing is labelled learning?[2] In New Testament scholarship, you must imagine, the principal task now is to write harmonies of the Gospels, and, in Patristic studies, to align the Catholic with the Gnostic, the second century with the fifth, the Arian and the Athanasian, monophysite and Nestorian. In a word, we speak of a world in which the Diatesseron is the last word in scholarship, and in which contentiousness about trivial things masks a firm and iron consensus. In this imagined world, scholars further hold that all the sources are historical, and merely alluding to them suffices to establish facts of history. If you can envision such a state of affairs, then you have entered the world of sources and scholarly orthodoxies confronted by us who study the ancient Judaism emergent from the rabbinic literature.

(1) I can spell out matters now very simply and very rapidly.

First, as to the axioms of scholarship, all the rabbinic sources are treated as representatives of a single, seamless world view and as expressions of a single, essentially united group, either the Jews as a whole, or, among the enlightened, *the* rabbis as a group. While some more critical souls concede there may have been distinctions between the first century rabbis' thought and that of the fourth, the distinctions make no material difference in accounts of "the rabbis" and their thought. Whether in anthologies or anthological essays (Moore, Montefiore and Loewe, Bonsirven, Urbach), *the* rabbis are represented in their views on God, world, and redemption, as though all rabbis for seven hundred years had the same thing to say as all others.

Now this representation of the rabbis is subject to an important, commonplace qualification. Everyone knows that the Talmuds abound in the recognition of differences between the teachings of different rabbis in different periods on different points in discussions of which traditions or source was followed by the proponent of this or that opinion. But the recorded differences are about particular, trivial points. The Talmudic discussion, moreover, is directed normally toward reconciling them. What is particularly lacking in available accounts of "the rabbinic mind" is, first, recognition and delineation of different general positions or basic attitudes, of the characteristics, make-up, and backgrounds of different schools; second, what is lacking is anything like adequate reporting of the change of teachings in the course of time and in relation to historical changes. Obviously, there is plenty of speculation on how an individual or a group reacted to a particular historical situation or event. But these random speculations are unsystematic and appear to be made up for the occasion. So these apparent exceptions to what I say have to be recognized—because they prove the accuracy of my description of the prevailing consensus.

(2) Second, as to the sources, the documents of earlier Rabbinic Judaism exhibit an internally uniform quality of style. So the scholars who represent a seamless world accurately replicate the literary traits of the sources of the portrait. It is exceedingly difficult to differentiate on formal or stylistic grounds among the layers of the Mishnah, which is the document of Rabbinic Judaism first brought to redaction. The two Talmuds then so lay matters out as to represent themselves as the logical continuity from the Mishnah. They do so by breaking up the Mishnah into minute units and then commenting on those discrete units of thought. Consequently, the Mishnah as a document, a document which presents its own world view and its own social system, is not preserved and confronted. Nor do the Talmuds present themselves as successive layers, built upon, but essentially distinct from the Mishnah. Rather, the Talmuds aim at completely harmonizing their own materials both with the Mishnah and among themselves, despite the self-evidently contradictory character of the materials. Once more we observe, there are limits to disagreement. The continuing contentiousness of the documents, their preservation of diverse viewpoints on single issues, underline the rigidly protected limits of permissible disagreement. Intense disagreement about trivialities powerfully reinforces basic unities and harmonies. The fact that, out there, were Jews who decorated synagogues in ways the Talmuds cannot have led us to anticipate, is mentioned only in passing, as if it is of no weight or concern. What matters to this literature is not how the Jews lived, nor

even how they worshiped, but only the discussions of the rabbinical schools and courts. What the documents say is what we are supposed to think, within the range of allowed difference. Consequently, the intellectually unitary character of the sources is powerfully reinforced by the total success of the framers and redactors of the sources in securing stylistic unity within documents and in some measure even among them.

(3) These facts have not prevented scholars, myself included, from writing about history, biography, and theology, upon the basis of the unanalyzed and unchallenged allegations of the rabbinic sources. Just as people had arguments about what Jesus really said and did before the rise of form-criticism, so the rage and secure contentiousness of scholars in this field mask the uncertainty of their entire structure. It is as if, as in the Talmuds themselves, by arguing on essentially minor points, the colleagues may avoid paying attention to the epistemolog-ical abyss beneath them all. So there are agreed-upon solutions to the problems of diverse authorities behind the same saying and amplifica-tion and variation of details in a single story. These commonly lead to very felicitous conclusions. If the same saying is in three mouths, it is because they agreed to say it. True, "we cannot be sure that they were not talking simultaneously in different places (thanks to the holy spirit)." Or, if there are three versions of essentially the same story, like the Sermon on the Mount and the Sermon on the Plain, it is because, in the wonderful ways of Providence, it happened two times. Every time the text says, "One time," that was, indeed, one event.

(4) Finally, as I have already hinted, these serendipitous facts, these happy agreements, these assured and unquestioned results of a hundred years of critical scholarship following upon fifteen hundred years of uncritical scholarship which produced the same results, enjoy the powerful support of the three great communities which read the rabbinical literature at all. I mean, Orthodox Jews in yeshivas, scholarly Jews in rabbinical seminaries and Israeli universities, and the generality of Christian scholars of the New Testament. To the Orthodox, the rabbinic sources are part of the whole Torah of Moses "our rabbi," the revealed word of God. For them, "our holy rabbis" cannot deceive. To the scholars in rabbinical schools and Israeli uni-versities, the critical program of scholarship on early Christianity is perceived from a distance. In their books and articles they settle com-plex questions of literary analysis and historical epistemology with an array of two assumptions, three logical arguments, and four "probative" examples.[3] They do not perceive the immense, detailed work which stands, for example, behind debates on Q and the Synoptic

problem. Indeed, the work of analysis of sources bores them. Whether work is original or dull, the bulk of it simply dismisses as settled, questions that would be deemed urgent in biblical and patristic literature and in the history of early Christiantiy. As to the New Testament scholars, their view is that things go better when we read rabbinical literature as a set of facts which speak for themselves, rather than complex problems requiring solutions. For them, the rabbinic literature as it stands, unanalyzed and uncriticized, tells us all about Jerusalem and Galilee in the time of Jesus. Billerbeck is a dictionary of facts, and the beginning of sound exegesis. Or, to put matters in a more theological way, in Gospels' research, salvation is of the Jews.

Now that I have described the state of the evidence in terms accessible to outsiders, I wish to outline some of the solutions to some of the problems, as I have seen them and worked them out.

Among the many problems of analysis and description left to me by the kindness of earlier scholars, two first attracted my attention. One I solved, one I did not solve, in the first critical work of the lot, which was *Development of a Legend: Studies on the Traditions Concerning Yohanan ben Zakkai*.[4] The first was how to deal with diverse versions of a story, the second, the analysis of the blatantly formalized character of much of the rabbinic literature. There is a reason for both the success and the failure. The choice of Yohanan ben Zakkai for the first break with the established way of doing things was dictated by the simple fact that eight years earlier I had written a biography in the accepted manner, organizing all the stories about, and sayings attributed to, the man in the order and categories indicated by their content. I further had assembled pretty much everything everyone else had said, in the same believing spirit, about the same stories. So now, having been asked whether or not I was doing history too soon and asking the wrong questions,[5] I thought it best to begin again from my own beginning. Since I had written Yohanan's life without analyzing the sources but, essentially, by merely alluding to or just citing them,[6] I realized that the new beginning had to start with the specification, translation, and analysis of all relevant materials. Laying all the cards on the table seemed the right way. Even now my students and I are criticized for spreading things out in front of the reader.[7] But this is an act of scholarly honesty and responsibility, and I do not mind being criticized for it. These are not sources which people know, and those who claim to know them have not analyzed them and made explicit what they believe they understand about them. So the paramount trait of the new school[8] was going to be a massive labor of new translation, and, of more importance, totally fresh exegesis.

But back to the main point. When confronting the same story running through Mishnah, Tosefta, the Talmuds, and the Tannaitic and other Midrashic compilations, I decided to see whether there were fixed relationships as the story moved from one document to another, and, if so, how I might account for them. What made matters difficult is that there is some doubt about the relative priority of the various documents. What I found, to sidestep that difficulty, was that relationships tend to be fixed, no matter the priority or posteriority of the documents. The general result is that the simplest version would be Mishnah's, then, details omitted would be given by Tosefta, usually further enriched by the Palestinian Talmud, and, at the end, by the Babylonian one. Since I was able to show that details added in a given version dealt with questions left open, or even generated, by another version, I showed that what we have are not several incidents, each of which happened on yet another occasion, but a single story, passing from one document to another and gaining or losing weight in its peregrinations. So we bid adieu to rabbinical equivalent of the Sermon on the Mount and the Sermon on the Plain. A second point which struck me then was that it was possible to make sense of the sorts of materials occurring in one document and not in some other. But the work on that question in *Development* is speculative and does not follow a uniform method.

That leads me to *Development*'s other, and closely related, problem, the whole issue of forms. I specifically wanted to know whether there really were fixed literary forms and rhetorical devices in the rabbinic literature. What I found was that while there clearly are highly formalized traits attached to sayings and stories of Yohanan ben Zakkai, they form no coherent unit associated distinctively with his name. And the literary traits seemed to be defined by the document in which they occurred.

At this point I had already reached what I would come to understand as the pivot of all further work, but I did not see it as such. I had stumbled across the simple fact that all analytical and critical work in rabbinical literature must begin in the study of specific documents, their formal traits, redactional preferences, and substantive interests. Now before I expand on that simple and obvious proposition, I have to say it did not even impress or occur to me for two more, sizable projects, *The Rabbinic Traditions about the Pharisees before 70*[9] and *Eliezer ben Hyrcanus: The Tradition and the Man.*[10] Both of these lengthy projects continued to ask essentially historical questions. That is to say, they continued to treat topics which carried me through the far reaches of diverse collections.

What I wanted to know in *Pharisees* was what the later rabbis had to tell us about the Pharisees, how they tell it to us, and whether it is so. What I found out—as distinct from what I wanted to know—was a great deal about the use of form-criticism as a rather sharp tool for literary analysis, about the mnemonic traits of important strata of the rabbinic literature, about the overall shape of the rabbinic traditions about the Pharisees, and about the difficulty of interpreting materials assigned to a given name or set of names when approached totally outside of the documents—that is to say, the systems—in which they occur. What I wanted to know about Eliezer ben Hyrcanus was what in fact we can say about the man. What I found out was a great deal about the history of a tradition associated with a given name. Not all of that history called into question the possibility of speaking of the man, as distinct from the tradition about him. The one striking fact was the discovery of a fairly disciplined approach to the spinning out of sayings. When I had isolated the layers of the tradition about Eliezer and recorded what I conceived to be their history, I found no tendency promiscuously and without warrant to place into Eliezer's mouth just about anything anyone wanted to. On the contrary, there is solid warrant in not only themes but specific principles assigned to Eliezer early in the formation of his tradition for nearly all of what appears in his name in later rabbinic documents. Not only so, but I found a solid tendency to consistency of theme and even principle in pretty much everything attributed to him. So if we cannot say much about the historical Eliezer, we can, at least, claim that what people did say in the name of Eliezer is internally consistent and tends to spin out diverse ideas expressive of uniform principles.

Three problems in my procedures to this point irritated me.

First, I found that I covered a wide range of topics, but each one superficially. The inner logic of a given ruling and its place in the unfolding frame of the chapter of law in which it found its place never fully revealed themselves. Consequently I could not find entire satisfaction in my results.

Second, I could not even in theory explain how to deal with sayings lacking attributions.[11] So the state of a law at a given point in time could not be ascertained.

Third, I recognized that, when all was said and done, I relied for my periodization of materials on attributions of sayings to specific figures and on that alone. What I saw in *Eliezer* was that while I did not take for granted everything in the name of Eliezer really was said by him, I did tend to assume that everything said about Eliezer in the name of some later authority really was said by that later authority. So it was a case of postponing the act of gullibility, not abandoning it.

Thus, a growing, unsolved dilemma no longer could be avoided.[12] I found myself on that same slippery turf which I had many times thought to have abandoned, because the only ground I had for assigning a saying to a given man or period was that the sources said he had said so. I had not moved far from the world in which the traditionalists would say that our sages would not lie,[13] and the modernists would say that they would not have assigned a saying to a given man if they did not have a reason (which is precisely what the old-timers were telling us in their quaint way). When I was at work on the history of the Jews in Babylonia, Brevard Childs had told me that I might be asking the historical question too soon. He certainly was right. But I now realized, not only was it a premature historical question, it also was a question meant to precipitate the writing of the wrong kind of history to begin with.

These several irritants goaded me to attempt something other than, and preparatory to, social and religious history, namely, a fresh look at a single document and its history. I had no difficulty choosing which one. It had to be the first in the rabbinic canon, so it was the Mishnah. The work on Mishnah has several facets, of which four are of widest general interest: exegesis, form, the use of attributions, and the issue of anonymous materials. Each may be briefly stated.[14]

(1) Exegesis: I found that all earlier exegetes took as their problem the placing of Mishnah's laws into relationship with all other laws, of all documents and all periods, so forming a single, urgent construct: *the* law, *the halakhah*. An account of what Mishnah means when seen by itself and in its own context could not be expected under such conditions. This I have provided.[15] I return to this matter in a moment.

(2) Forms: To determine the Mishnah's meaning to its original authors, I decided to ask whether Mishnah's language provided guidance.[16] What I learned is that the Mishnah provides its own first and best commentary through its highly formalized rhetoric and syntax. Analysis of the large-scale formal traits shows, moreover, that forms as we have them are mostly imposed within the processes of redaction. There is little formulation anterior to redaction of the Mishnah itself, and redaction proves in the end to constitute an act—the governing and commanding act—of formulation. It follows that Mishnah's highly distinctive forms themselves reveal little or no history. Form-history, strictly speaking, is not possible. The thesis of New Testament form-history may be sound, but it cannot find any

support whatsoever in the earliest document of Judaism. Since form-historians have commonly invoked Jewish procedures of oral formulation and oral transmission, I have to give them the sad news that these procedures, so far as they are indicated in the Mishnah, do not go back much before A.D. 200.[17]

(3) Of what good are attributions? To state matters simply, what we cannot show we do not know.[18] It follows that we have to find out what we can demonstrate so as to define what we can also falsify. Let me define with some precision the problem of attributions. There are in fact two separate questions. One is the question of the reliability of the exact quotation—*ipsissima verba*. I know no way to show that any rabbinic attribution contains *ipsissima verba* of the rabbi to whom the words are assigned. In fact it is easy to show that most of what is attributed takes the formal traits and adheres to the redactional requirements of the document in which the attribution appears. So it is uncommon to have anything like *ipsissima verba*. The second question, which is much more important, is that of the reliability of an attribution of the essential content of a statement. If we could show that the gist, if not the exact wording, of what is attributed to Hillel actually was said by him, then we should have information on how one person, either in the age in which Hillel lived or afterward, summed up what Hillel had said and we should be able to relate what that person thought he had said to what others of roughly the same time and place may have had on their minds. This is the important matter, not the wording of what is assigned. And here there has been some progress, if not enough. I am able to show whether a fair number of statements belong in the periods in which the men to whom these statements are attributed flourished. Let me now explain.

We can ask whether there are correlations among groups of sayings given in the names of authorities generally supposed to have lived in successive periods, intersecting sayings, dealing with a single topic. What I mean is this: If a saying is in the name of an earlier authority, is its principle or conception prior in logic, more primitive in principle or conception, than an intersecting saying given in the name of a later authority? If there is a correlation between temporal attribution and traits of logic or conception, so that what is claimed in the attribution to be early is shown in the character of what is attributed to be relatively primitive, then that saying may be shown to be prior to another—because a saying may also be shown to be posterior.[19]

(4) This matter of testing the value of attributions for the study of history, biography, law, and theology brings us to the much vexed matter of what is not attributed at all.[20] In the case of Mishnah, I was

startled to be unable to find the problem. The reason is in two parts. First, you have to know that Mishnah-tractate usually is not merely a collection of information but a careful essay about a set of problems concerning a given topic. A ruling lacking an attribution nonetheless finds its place within the intellectual framework of the tractate which contains it. There are very few which are so totally out of context as to be insusceptible to location or situation within an established framework. Second, when we work with the known, the pericope which can be located and reliably situated, we normally are able to relate the unknown to the known. It follows that an anonymous ruling containing an idea otherwise first attested in named materials, let us say, after A.D. 140, is not apt to go back to a period a hundred or two hundred years earlier.

In fact, the really interesting thing is not what the tractates of the Mishnah contain but what they assume. We now are in a position to describe the ideas held by people ultimately represented in the Mishnah at various stages in the Mishnah's history.[21] Since a history of Mishnah's law now is complete (though not fully printed as yet), we can proceed to give an account of two things. First, we can say with a measure of accuracy what ideas come relatively early in the history of Mishnaic law, even in the period before A.D. 70. Second and more compelling, we also are able to provide a catalogue of ideas taken for granted before Mishnah got underway. We know what the framers of Mishnah take for granted and treat as settled facts of life and law. This opens a second route toward the description of one part of the world of Judaism before 70, even though we must use a document which came to closure about a century and a half later. We may even engage in controlled speculation on the origins of some ideas and facts which lie deep in the Mishnah's substructure, and which do not appear in Scripture. This controlled speculation I call my method of hypothetical-exegetical reconstruction through a series of contrastive or analogical processes.[22] But that is another story, which need not be told here.

Rather, I wish now to specify the single most interesting thing contributed in my history of Mishnaic law. That is to remove Mishnah from the context of a whole transtemporal legal system and to insist that the document be read as a statement of a single system, a single world view, produced at a given moment by a group of people who addressed a distinct and distinctive set of problems. In this I have corrected what I believe to be the principal error in earlier work, which has been to treat all sayings and all stories, wherever they occur, as part of a single "rabbinic" corpus of materials, of pretty much identical origin and provenance, all to be handled atomistically and out of documentary context. Let me explain this point. When Mishnah is read in a larger framework than Mishnah, we are prevented from seeing Mishnah's materials as a coherent corpus on their own. This latter approach to Mishnah is absolutely opposite to our purpose. For I propose to state and historically to account for the unfolding of the law of Mishnah *in particular*. If we assume that Mishnah constitutes a single document—and the internal harmonious formal and intellectual traits of Mishnah require that we make that assumption— then we have no choice but to honor the limits of the document when attempting to describe and interpret it.

My work has differed from that of all earlier exegetes. Others read and interpret Mishnah in a different context, as part of a large, unitary corpus of law, *the halakhah*. It is the purpose of nearly all exegetes to relate each of the parts to the transcendent whole, and to force the whole to encompass all of the parts. It is not, as I originally thought, the ahistorical (or, anti-historical) and harmonistic purpose of the earlier exegetes which made their Mishnah-commentaries so intellectually prolix, indeed, indifferent and irrelevant to the text under discussion. That is a misunderstanding which it has taken me many years to recognize. It is, rather, that the earlier exegetes presuppose something much more profound, much less susceptible to articulation. This is the construct, "Jewish law," or "*halakhah*." To them Mishnah constitutes an important component of this construct. In their mind the correct approach to Mishnah's interpretation is to relate its *halakhah* to other *halakhah*, that is, to "*the* law." This harmonistic, atomistic and yet encompassing approach is natural for people who keep the law and who take for granted their audience wants to know *the* law, even though not all of the law of a given document is practical and practiced. But the point of interest is clear, and it explains to them what is relevant and what is not. Since social context and intellectual framework define what is relevant, their essays—to us, total chaos—to them are orderly and reliable. But the fact remains that in a different world, their language of exegesis is puzzling, just as is ours to them.

So, in all, what I hope to contribute in my history of Mishnaic law is to state clearly what Mishnah wishes to say, in *its* own setting, within the limits of *its* own redactional framework, upon the subjects chosen by *it*, and for purposes defined within the mind of those specific people, its authors, who flourished in one concrete social setting. Reading the document by itself, in its historical context and therefore outside of its atemporal, *halakhic* context, requires a different approach. That approach is represented, I firmly believe, in the pages of my books.

We have come a long way from that mental experiment I asked you to perform at the outset, to imagine what we should know about the first Christians, and how we should know it, if New Testament and Patristic literature, indeed all of the literary remains of the first five or six Christian centuries, reached us in the form of the Talmudic and Midrashic literature. So let me turn toward my conclusion by referring once more to the state of the field.

(1) No longer is it possible to treat the diverse corpus of rabbinical literature as a uniform whole. Once one document, a principal one, is shown to bear its distinctive formal and intellectual characteristics as I have shown in the case of the Mishnah, then all others must be subjected to appropriate analysis, to determine the characteristics of each.[23]

(2) No longer are the anonymity and the collective character of documents to be allowed to prevent differentiation and discrimination within a document and between documents. The work of harmonization is in ruins. The work of history may begin.

(3) No longer are we left to cope with all sayings, whatever document contains them, and to treat each as of equivalent weight to all others. Diverse attributions of a given saying in different documents are to be examined in the context of the preferences and tendencies of the several documents themselves. True, biography of the principal authorities of the Mishnah is not going to yield a rich account of someone's life and thought. The historical Meir is not going to be fully delineated.[24] But the place of an authority such as Meir in the unfolding of the law most assuredly is to be delineated.[25]

(4) To be sure, the institutional supports for what I regard as a credulous and gullible reading and use of the sources remain somewhat more than negligible. There never will be progress in the yeshivas; the rabbinical seminaries are not fertile ground for historical scholarship anyhow;[26] and the Christian believers will to believe. But what should be heartening to the enlightened is not the darkness but the light. Most of the work of history, biography, and the law and theology which has been published in this country, Canada, Britain, Germany, and Holland in recent years has taken full and ample account of the program I have outlined. So I think on the whole there has been truly amazing progress even in the institutions and politics of scholarship, a diffusion of new viewpoints far more rapid and complete than anyone could have dreamed ten years ago.

To conclude, I revert, for one last time, to the point of departure.

At the outset I emphasized the importance of trying to allow the literary and historical situation of early Christianity to serve as a metaphor for the problem of nascent Rabbinic Judaism. At the end I must construct the opposite of a simile, for at the foundations, the two are essentially opposite to one another. The work of studying early Christianity requires us to put together distinct individuals, systems of thought, institutions, and to find out how these diverse expressions of Christian experience form something coherent and say something cogent. In a word, the work of Nicea and Chalcedon also defines the labor of learning. The task of studying nascent Rabbinic Judaism is the opposite. In the Talmuds and midrashic compilations we have the result of centuries of harmonization and cogent construction. But understanding these documents and the world which they portray requires us to unpack them and see how they function. It is as if, from the Nicene Creed, we had to find our way back into the intellectual and theological issues of the earlier generations of Christians.

For in the end, knowing what people thought, without understanding the world about which they reflected, does not help us either to understand the people who did the thinking or to interpret the result of their reflection. While, without such understanding, we may take the results of their thinking—their theology, their exegesis of Scripture, and their law—and we may build on it for one purpose or another, we essentially know nothing of the inner structure of that building which we ourselves propose to construct. Not knowing the points of stress and places of tension in the building, not knowing the main lines of the foundation of the structure, not knowing the places at which the builder put the strongest joints and beams, we add to the building in total ignorance. It is not building. It is destruction—making things up as we go along.

To state matters more generally, in front of us is a labor of description and interpretation, establishing context and providing exegesis.[27] We have a sizable corpus of texts which clearly express a world view and propose to create a society and a way of life for a distinctive group of people. In order to describe that world view and to understand the society and way of life shaped by the ancient rabbis, we have to interpret texts. In order to interpret those texts, we have to establish context and setting. We have to describe the world in which the texts took shape and to offer a theory of questions which seemed urgent and compelling to the people who made the texts as they are and not in some other way. So the work of exegesis depends upon establishing the appropriate context of exegesis. At the same time, to describe the context we have to read the texts.

Just as there is no exegesis out of context, so there is no description of setting without appeal to the evidence of the texts. And yet, beyond text and context, lies yet another fact, which is the inner cogency and continuity of the texts, beyond their original context. For Judaism as we know it emerges from the documents under study, and its claim from ancient times to the present is to constitute the logically necessary spinning out of the principles contained in the ancient Torah of Moses "our rabbi" and of the rabbis of olden times. That inner logic which precipitates and governs the unfolding of the theology and law of the rabbis has itself to be discerned.[28]

There is then this threefold task, a triple cord not to be separated: text, context, inner logic. When we have discerned the threads of the cord and shown how they are interwoven, we shall perceive what holds together and imparts meaning to an ancient world which yet is with us.

If we ask ourselves why people should want to know about these things, we need not fall back upon the bankrupt claim that they merely are intrinsically interesting.[29] Nor do we have to offer historical salvation to scholars of early Christianity and say they cannot understand their subject without also knowing this one.[30] The formation of Judaism by itself is a compelling social and intellectual phenomenon, for among other such phenomena, it teaches us how to describe and interpret the interplay between the historical situation of a distinct society, on the one side, and the world view brought into being to explain and shape that historical situation, on the other. When we can relate the religious world view and way of life of the ancient Talmudic rabbis to the society whose vision they chose to shape and whose conduct and institutions they wished to govern, we can report much about what it is that religion, as a mode of constructing reality and explaining the world, is and what religion does.

Here, before our eyes, is the literature made by a particular group of men, in a particular time, for a particular society. That literature of antiquity defined what would happen for all time. In unpacking the end product, in taking it apart to see how it works, we can tell our own times more than a few things about this remarkable *thing*. For this was a world view and way of life capable of bringing order to the chaotic world of ancient times, and it remains capable of preserving a stable and enduring world from antiquity to the present. Given the world's potentialities for disorder and the difficulty of holding together any group of people subject to those ongoing disruptive forces affecting any continuing historical society, we should find more than merely interesting the story of Judaism's formative centuries. In a world of disintegration and an age of disorder, we should find urgent that story, indeed any story, of restraint, order, balance, and continuity—all in the name of the sacred.

What we have done in ten years is not what we shall do in twenty or fifty. The work has only begun on one document. There is an immense corpus of other documents awaiting attention. I am inclined to believe that my students' students will be able to frame questions and undertake a scholarly program of a precision and philosophical solidity of which we now can scarcely dream. To borrow a phrase from a great writer, we by no means are on the threshold of the beginning of the end. But we are well, well past the end of the beginning.

NOTES

1. This paper was presented as a plenary lecture at the Society of Biblical Literature meeting in New York City on November 16, 1979.

2. For the most recent example of anthology masquerading as scholarship, see Ephraim Urbach, *The Sages* (Jerusalem, 1975). The other phenomena noted here are exquisitely exemplified in Shmuel Safrai's dreadful *Compendia*, of which the generality of reviews has been remarkably unappreciative. But some of the essays admitted by Safrai as editor are by no means of the general standard of ignorance established in his own, predominant contributions to those volumes.

3. When my students and I first read the corpus of canonical scholarship on literary and historical questions of Mishnaic and Talmudic studies, we were amazed at the shoddy arguments and the slovenly research we encountered. The present characterization of scholarship effected through announcing a "brilliant" thesis and adducing a few examples which might illustrate it is no exaggeration. Compare the studies edited by me in *Formation of the Babylonian Talmud: Studies in the Achievements of Late Nineteenth and Twentieth Century Historical and Literary-Critical Research* and *The Modern Study of the Mishnah* (Leiden, 1973: E. J. Brill). See also Richard S. Sarason, "On the Use of Method in the Modern Study of Jewish Liturgy," in William S. Green, ed., *Approaches to Ancient Judaism: Theory and Practice* (Missoula, 1978: Scholars Press for Brown Judaic Studies), pp. 97–172; and the extended state-of-scholarship studies by Gary G. Porton, "Midrash: Palestinian Jews and the Hebrew Bible in the Greco-Roman Period," Baruch M. Bokser, "An Annotated Bibliographical Guide to the Study of the Palestinian Talmud," and David Goodblatt, "The Babylonian Talmud," in W. Haase, ed., *Aufstieg und Niedergang der ro¨mischen Welt*, II. *Principat.* 19.2 (Berlin and New York, 1979), pp. 103–138, 139–256, and 257–336), respectively. It is a pity that these important studies of the state of the question for Midrash, the Palestinian Talmud, and the Babylonian Talmud have been buried in such an overblown and expensive encyclopedia. Among the studies listed here one will find a guide to what has been done on the major documents of earlier Rabbinic Judaism.

4. Leiden, 1970: E. J. Brill.
5. This question came from Brevard S. Childs, Yale University, my teacher and friend for many years, in his reading of my *History of the Jews in Babylonia* (Leiden, 1965-1970: E. J. Brill) I-V. The prefaces of the later parts of that work will indicate I was concerned with the question and tried so to shape my studies as to take account of problems as yet unsolved. The matter recurs below.
6. *A Life of Yohanan ben Zakkai* (Leiden, 1962: E. J. Brill. Second Edition, Completely Revised, 1970). This book won a prize.
7. Reuben Kimelman, writing in the *Association for Jewish Studies Newsletter* of April, 1979, (of all places!) announces that he does not see why someone has to publish the sources and analyze them at all. These analyses he conceives to be mere notes to be kept in the study. What we are supposed to publish, in his view, is only the results. Granted the work is tedious, it seems to our group also to be necessary to lay it all out before the reader. Translation and exegesis are acts of scholarly responsibility. In the same unfortunate review, Kimelman announces that he does not think books of this kind should be published at all. And in the same place he pleads for tolerance of diverse methods.
8. It was a long time before I was willing to see myself as the founder of a school and those associated with me or using "my" methods as members of a school. But the persistent hostility of other scholars, particularly in rabbinical schools and Israeli Talmud departments, has persuaded me of the facts, which I have now accepted.
9. Leiden, 1971: E. J. Brill. I-III.
10. Leiden, 1973: E. J. Brill. I-II.
11. Anthony J. Saldarini was particularly persistent in pressing this question on me, and I owe much to his criticism.
12. This question is not ignored in *Eliezer*. It is raised and answered. But the answer is rather Talmudic and certainly not systematic. I did my best within my conceptual limitations of that period.
13. I am not making this up. See the concluding unit of my "The Talmud as History," in *Method and Meaning in Ancient Judaism* (Missoula, 1979: Scholars Press for Brown Judaic Studies). There I cite an actual correspondence between an Israeli pietist and an American modernist, in which the former states explicitly and in so many words his view that "our ancient rabbis would not lie." This argument is phrased in a more sophisticated way as well: "If you have no proof that a story is not true, you have to believe it, and it is history." My reply is, "If you cannot show it, you do not know it." I am inclined to think the entire argument is sterile, because it formulates issues in a hopeless way. It leads to no important insight and produces only episodic and not systematic exercises.
14. Summarized here are the main results of my *History of the Mishnaic Law of Purities* (Leiden, 1974-1977: E. J. Brill) I-XXII; *A History of the Mishnaic Law of Holy Things* (Leiden, 1979-1980: E. J. Brill) I-VI; *A History of the Mishnaic Law of Women* (Leiden, 1980: E. J. Brill) I-V; *A History of the Mishnaic Law of Appointed Times* (Leiden, 1981: E. J. Brill) I-V; and *A History of the Mishnaic Law of Damages* (Leiden, 1981-1982: E. J. Brill) I-V. The first of my students' commentaries on

Zeraim appears as Richard S. Sarason, *A History of the Mishnaic Law of Agriculture. Section Three. A Study of Tractate Demai. Part One* (Leiden, 1979: E. J. Brill). Other tractates presently underway are as follows: *Berakhot,* Tzvee Zahavy; *Peah,* Charles Primus; *Kilaim,* Irving Mandelbaum; *Shebiit,* Leonard Gordon; *Terumot,* Alan Peck; *Maaserot,* Martin Jaffee; *Maaser Sheni,* Peter Haas. *Hallah, Orlah,* and *Bikkurim* will soon be assigned. A byproduct of this work is a complete translation into English of Tosefta, published in six volumes as *Tosefta in English* by Ktav Publishing House. An important shift in the exegetical program took place between *Purities* and *Holy Things,* on the one side, and the other three divisions, on the other. I determined to make the commentary into a sustained exercise in the testing of the single proposition that Mishnah provides its own best commentary through the way in which its language is framed and its ideas are formed into formalized patterns. This use of form-criticism for essentially literary-critical and exegetical purposes led me to see the principal flaw in the established exegetical tradition on Mishnah (exclusive of Maimonides), which was its intention to discuss the content of Mishnah in the context of the law in general. That plan is wholly correct for lawyers and judges. But it does not help to enter into the original, historical meaning of the document. Since in places in which the Talmud is studied at all, the Talmudic text is used as an excuse for excurses on the Talmud's later commentaries, it will be clear that an entirely fresh approach to the exegesis of both Talmuds is called for; modern philological advances are not the only reason. In this regard the monumental and brilliant work of David Weiss Halivni, *Meqorot ummesorot* (Tel Aviv, 1968; Jerusalem, 1975, respectively) is to be cited. Halivni has completely revolutionized exegesis of the Talmud, because he has given the matter a whole new life.

15. I do not mean to suggest I believe I have completed the modern exegesis. I have hoped only to reopen the exegetical question entirely and to rephrase it in more fruitful terms than before. There are interesting problems of text, philology, and law to be taken up within the canons of contemporary criticism and hermeneutics.

16. Redaction-criticism is turned into an instrument of exegesis of forms and into a means of historical study in *Purities XXI.*

17. A more general critique of how New Testament scholarship has ignored its *own* critical methods when it approaches the rabbinic sources, and how the rabbinic scholars have happily encouraged this abdication of criticism, is in my "Use of the Later Rabbinic Evidence for the Study of First-Century Pharisaism," in Green, *op. cit.,* pp. 215–228. That paper began as a lecture at the University of Tübingen on the occasion of the 500th jubilee celebration. So even though there have been some modest problems of a political character, the critical program outlined in this paper has been accepted rapidly and enthusiastically in Judaic and New Testament scholarship in Germany, Holland, Britain, and France, as well as in the USA and Canada. This point becomes important later in my argument. Some younger American scholars working in the state of Israel have introduced the critical agendum even into the bastions of obscurantism there. The publications of Shamma Friedman, JTSA-Jerusalem, in Talmudic exegetical problems

are just as fresh, in their way, as David Halivni's. I call attention to the first-class analytical paper by Lee Levine, Hebrew University, "R. Simeon b. Yohai and the Purification of Tiberias: History and Tradition," *Hebrew Union College Annual* 49, 1978, pp. 143–186. I already have cited the major studies by David Goodblatt, Haifa University. It should also be pointed out that Israeli scholarship in other areas of ancient Judaism, particularly in archaeology, is not characterized by uncritical faith in everything the literary sources say, on the one side, or by slovenly and unsystematic use of what one likes and neglect of what one does not like. Clearly, intervening between scholarship and the practitioners thereof are obstacles of a theological or social character. What these are, and how we may explain the absence of an understanding of the critical agendum, are questions I cannot answer here. Nor do I know why in the state of Israel it is prohibited to make use of, or even cite my books, even where they have treated problems under discussion.

18. At this point I regret I have to part company with my teacher, Morton Smith. Compare the opening chapters of his *Jesus the Magician* (New York, 1978: Harper & Row), pp. 1–67, with his discourse on magic, pp. 68–139. The former discussion is tendentious; Smith sets out not to analyze a possibility but to prove a proposition. The shift in the tone of the book and in the character of the discussion when Smith turns to an academic account of magic in antiquity is stunning. This other part of the book is a model of academic clarity and deep learning, while the discussion on "the historical Jesus" is a morass of "proofs" of proposition.

19. The work of showing the interplay between logic and chronology established through attributions is complete for *Purities, Holy Things, Women, Appointed Times,* and *Damages.* For *Purities* it is accomplished tractate by tractate, and for the other divisions it is done in section two of the systematic volumes, respectively: *Holy Things VI, Women V, Appointed Times V,* and *Damages V.* It is on this basis that the history of the law is worked out. Alan J. Avery-Peck presently works on the equivalent problem for the division of Agriculture; his results are expected in about two years. At that point we shall have a complete picture, in full detail, of which attributions seem more reliable, which ones less so, and of how we may describe the unfolding of the tractates of the Mishnah and of the law contained in them, by the several periods into which the various authorities are naturally divided: before 70, 70 to 130, 140 to 170, and 170 to 200, respectively. I wish to stress that under discussion is not a proposal of an extensive exercise which should be done, but of work which is *now* complete and in print or in press.

20. The aforementioned exercises also take up, item by item, each unattributed saying or pericope, and, in context, show which ones say the same thing, in principle or in detail, as do the attributed sayings or pericopes, and which ones stand essentially outside of the framework of assigned units. If one has to generalize, I should say that unassigned pericopes either deal with trivial details or state in eloquent terms the most fundamental conceptions of a unit of thought—one extreme or the other. But that is only a generalization.

21. This is of special importance to the interests of New Testament scholarship,

since we now have a fairly sound basis for stating which rules and conceptions of Mishnah preserve conceptions which are prior to the generation of
70–120 and which, therefore, are apt to go back to the period before 70. I
plan now to present an account of Mishnah's testimony on the age of the
Second Temple as part of my history of the birth of Rabbinic Judaism, to
the end of the second century.

22. This is spelled out and illustrated in my "From Scripture to Mishnah: The
Exegetical Origins of Maddaf," Fiftieth Anniversary Festschrift of the
American Academy for Jewish Research, published as the *Proceedings of
the American Academy for Jewish Research*, 1979, pp. 99–111. It is crucial
to distinguish between formal *midrash*, assigned to Aqiba and Ishmael,
and contrastive-analogical exegesis, which we may reconstruct in a series
of logical steps, moving from Scripture to the facts taken for granted by
Mishnah. Essentially, my theory of the process posits that things are either
like each other, and therefore follow exactly the same rule, or not like each
other, and therefore follow the opposite rule from one another. On that
basis we can reconstruct thought-processes behind conclusions important,
e.g., in the primitive layers of Mishnah's tractate of *Zabim* and *Erubin*, to
name two obvious examples. The latter is spelled out in *Appointed Times
II. Erubin, Pesahim* (Leiden, 1981: E. J. Brill), "Introduction to *Erubin*."

23. I of course do not mean to suggest that the same results will emerge. But
each document must be seen whole and its concerns must be spelled out.
This I did for Sifra in *Purities VI. Negaim. Sifra* (Leiden, 1976: E. J. Brill).

24. The definitive statement of the problem of biography from the perspectives
outlined in this paper is William S. Green, "What's in a Name? The
Problematic of Rabbinic 'Biography,'" in Green, ed., *Approaches to
Ancient Judaism*, pp. 77–96. An account of the traditions associated with
the names of most rabbinic authorities through A.D. 120, except for Aqiba,
is pretty well complete. All the figures of the period before 70 are in my
Rabbinic Traditions about the Pharisees before 70. Those of the period of
70 to 120 are as follows: this writer's *Development of a Legend: Studies on
the Traditions Concerning Yohanan ben Zakkai; Eliezer ben Hyrcanus:
The Tradition and the Man;* William S. Green, *Joshua ben Hananiah*
(Leiden, 1980: E. J. Brill); Tzvee Zahavy, *The Traditions of Eleazar ben
Azariah* (Missoula, 1977: Scholars Press for Brown Judaic Studies); Shamai
Kanter, *Gamaliel of Yavneh* (Missoula, 1980: Scholars Press for Brown
Judaic Studies); Gary G. Porton, *The Traditions of Rabbi Ishmael. I. The
Non-Exegetical Materials. II. Exegetical Comments in Tannaitic Collec-
tions. III. The Exegetical Materials in Amoraic Collections* (Leiden, 1976,
1977, 1979, respectively: E. J. Brill), with a fourth volume under way; Joel
Gereboff, *The Traditions of Rabbi Tarfon* (Missoula, 1979: Scholars Press
for Brown Judaic Studies); minor figures, all in William S. Green, ed.,
Persons and Institutions in Early Rabbinic Judaism (Missoula, 1977:
Scholars Press for Brown Judaic Studies) as follows: Robert Goldenberg,
"The Deposition of Rabban Gamaliel II: An Examination of the Sources,"
pp. 9–48; Jack Nathan Lightstone, "Sadoq the Yavnean," pp. 49–148;
Diane Levine, "Eleazar Hisma," pp. 149–206; David Goodblatt, "The
Beruriah Traditions," pp. 207–236; and Ira Jeffrey Schiffer, "The Men of

the Great Assembly," pp. 237–276; and Jack N. Lightstone, *Yose' the Galilean* (Leiden, 1979: E. J. Brill) I (with two more volumes in preparation). It should be clear that a considerable exercise in the study of traditions associated with names of earlier authorities is now completed. Mention should once more be made of Lee Levine's analysis of the traditions of Simeon b. Yohai as well. But very little has been done on authorities of the period of 140–170. See the next note.

25. There are two such studies, Robert Goldenberg, *The Sabbath-Law of Rabbi Meir* (Missoula, 1978: Scholars Press for Brown Judaic Studies), and Charles Primus, *Aqiba's Contribution to the Law of Zeraim* (Leiden, 1977: E. J. Brill). In the historical parts of my studies of the tractates of the division of Purities I analyzed the role of all of the various named authorities in the unfolding of the law of the twelve tractates of that division. What I found was that, in general, the principal problems of the tractates do not emerge from the thought of an individual authority, on the one side, or from the *opposite* of a proposition maintained by an individual authority, on the other. The way in which a single master's thought does generate the problems to be discussed in connection with the analysis of a given topic (that is, the "generative problematic" of a tractate) is beautifully clear in Mishnah-tractate *Makhshirin*. That tractate is possible only within the principles given in the name of Joshua and Aqiba, since most of the problems defined and worked out in the tractate rest upon those principles. Had the position of Tarfon prevailed, there would be no such tractate as we know it. (I have often suggested that the same is so of *Terumot*. Had the view of Eliezer prevailed, the center of the tractate would not have been possible. But I have not succeeded in persuading any of my co-workers of that view.) I think considerably more work on the role of named authorities in the formation of the several Mishnah-tractates is to be done for Holy Things, Women, Appointed Times, Damages, and Agriculture.

26. This view has to be qualified. Even though such historical work on ancient Judaism as has come from the Reform and Conservative seminaries has been unsystematic or childish and uncritical (or both), recent appointments promise a better future. But the fact still remains that the graduates of the Reform and Conservative seminaries have yet to confront the historical challenges laid down in the work outlined in this paper. There is no postponing their either refuting or adopting the main propositions presented here. The reason is that the theologies of Reform and Conservative Judaism give a prominent place to the alleged critical-historical approach to the history and definition of Judaism upon which the reforms of Reform and Conservative Judaism are to be vindicated. Consequently a great many allegedly historical facts are adduced in the (historicistic) theological and *halakhic* discourse of the two reforming movements. It should be clear from what has been said here that most of those facts are based on an uncritical and therefore pseudo-historical reading of the sources of Talmudic law and theology.

27. This phase of the work is spelled out, and its theological implications articulated, in my *Method and Meaning in Ancient Judaism* (Missoula, 1979: Scholars Press for Brown Judaic Studies). It is in the exploitation of

the results of the historical work now drawing to a conclusion that the next phase in the study of the history of Judaism as we know it can get underway.

28. This matter of the inner logic of a tractate is explained in my "History and Structure," in *Method and Meaning*. The point is that a given topic, analyzed with a defined set of questions in mind, is going to yield only a limited number of possibilities for inquiry. Furthermore, within the limits of the facts of Scripture and the problematic of a tractate as Mishnah lays it out, there is a narrowly limited range of logical positions one is able to take. Stated simply: the law has its own inner logic, and it unfolds along the lines dictated by that logic. The motive-force which creates a tractate's secondary and tertiary layers of inquiry, its exercises in the application of the established principles to difficult cases in which two or more principles create problems of harmonization of diverse rules, and its inquiry into the gray areas of the law—these are what define the inner logic of the tractate. Factors external to the law's own logic play little or no role in the formation of the later layers of a tractate which unfolds over a fairly long period of time. We can account for the thought of the second-century authorities by reference to the positions taken by their predecessors in the first century and to the limited logical possibilities laid open by these positions. To put matters briefly: the law is inexorably generated within its own exegesis. The historical study of the law is in large measure the study of the logic, not the history, of ideas, certainly not of the interplay between law and society or law and historical events. On the centrality of exegesis in the history of religions, see Jonathan Z. Smith, "Sacred Persistence: Towards a Redescription of Canon," in Green, ed., *Approaches*, pp. 11–28. I must caution that fully grasping these things requires concrete study of particular tractates in context.

29. There must be better answers.

30. This has been the paramount apologetic, emerging from both pre-Hitler German and mid-century American Jewish scholarship. Its political and sociological importance is not to be ignored. But apologetics is not a scholarly enterprise and distorts the processes of learning, as I argue in "Use of the Later Rabbinic Evidence for the Study of First-Century Pharisaism," Green, *Approaches*, pp. 215–228.

List of Hebrew and
Aramaic Abbreviations

If you want . . . : אב"א – אי בעית אימא

If so . . . : א"ה – אי הכי

Says: או', אומ' – אומר

Afterwards: אח"כ – אחר כך

He said to him: א"ל – אמר לו

Even though: אע"פ – אף על פי

Even . . . : אפי' – אפילו

The House of Hillel: ב"ה – בית הלל

The House of Hillel says: בה"א – בית הלל אומרים

B. Hanna, a name: ב"ח – ב. חנא

The son of Rabbi . . . : ב"ר – בן רבי

The House of Shammai: ב"ש – בית שמאי

The House of Shammai says: בש"א – בית שמאי אומרים

Gemara: גמ' – גמרא

Another matter: ד"א – דבר אחר

The words of everyone, i.e., all agree . . . : ד"ה – דברי הכל

Lit. "The Name," a euphemism for God: ה' – השם

That is the rule . . . : ה"ה – הוא הדין

Here also: ה"נ – הכי נמי

He said thus: ה"ק – הכי קאמר

The Holy One, blessed be He: הקב"ה – הקדוש ברוך הוא

Etc.: וגו' – וגומר

וכו' – וכוליה :Etc.

חיי' – חייא :Hiyya, a name

טוהורו' – טוהרות :Ritually clean, pure

יקנ"ה – יין, קדוש, נר, הבדלה :Wine, Sanctification, light spices

ירמי' – ירמיה :Jeremiah, a name

כ"ע – כל עלמא :All the people

כו' – וכו' *See*

לי' – ליתא : . . . There is no

ל"ק – לא קשיא :It is no problem

מ"ט – מאי טעמא, מה טעם :What is the reason

מ"ש – מאי שנא, מה שנה : . . . What is the difference

נט"י – נטילת ידים :Washing the hands

ס"ד – סלקא דעתך :(Enter your mind (e.g., an idea

ע"ז – עבודה זרה :Idolatry

ע"ה – עם הארץ :An unlearned Jew, a common person

ע"י – על ידי :Because

עכו"ם

– עבודת כוכבים ומזלות :Idol worshipers and star worshipers

קודמ' – קודמאי :First

קמ"ל – קא משמע לן : . . . Thus we have been taught

ר' – רבי :Rabbi

ר"ה – רשות הרבים :Public path

ר"מ – רבי מאיר :Rabbi Meir

ת"ר – תנו רבנן :Our Rabbis taught

תנ"ה – תניא נמי הכי : . . . It is taught also here

Index of Biblical and Talmudic Passages

Index of Names and Subjects